T0180809

Communications in Computer and Information Science 2118

Rationale

The CCIS series is devoted to the publication of proceedings of computer science conferences. Its aim is to efficiently disseminate original research results in informatics in printed and electronic form. While the focus is on publication of peer-reviewed full papers presenting mature work, inclusion of reviewed short papers reporting on work in progress is welcome, too. Besides globally relevant meetings with internationally representative program committees guaranteeing a strict peer-reviewing and paper selection process, conferences run by societies or of high regional or national relevance are also considered for publication.

Topics

The topical scope of CCIS spans the entire spectrum of informatics ranging from foundational topics in the theory of computing to information and communications science and technology and a broad variety of interdisciplinary application fields.

Information for Volume Editors and Authors

Publication in CCIS is free of charge. No royalties are paid, however, we offer registered conference participants temporary free access to the online version of the conference proceedings on SpringerLink (http://link.springer.com) by means of an http referrer from the conference website and/or a number of complimentary printed copies, as specified in the official acceptance email of the event.

CCIS proceedings can be published in time for distribution at conferences or as post-proceedings, and delivered in the form of printed books and/or electronically as USBs and/or e-content licenses for accessing proceedings at SpringerLink. Furthermore, CCIS proceedings are included in the CCIS electronic book series hosted in the SpringerLink digital library at http://link.springer.com/bookseries/7899. Conferences publishing in CCIS are allowed to use Online Conference Service (OCS) for managing the whole proceedings lifecycle (from submission and reviewing to preparing for publication) free of charge.

Publication process

The language of publication is exclusively English. Authors publishing in CCIS have to sign the Springer CCIS copyright transfer form, however, they are free to use their material published in CCIS for substantially changed, more elaborate subsequent publications elsewhere. For the preparation of the camera-ready papers/files, authors have to strictly adhere to the Springer CCIS Authors' Instructions and are strongly encouraged to use the CCIS LaTeX style files or templates.

Abstracting/Indexing

CCIS is abstracted/indexed in DBLP, Google Scholar, EI-Compendex, Mathematical Reviews, SCImago, Scopus. CCIS volumes are also submitted for the inclusion in ISI Proceedings.

How to start

To start the evaluation of your proposal for inclusion in the CCIS series, please send an e-mail to ccis@springer.com.

Constantine Stephanidis · Margherita Antona ·
Stavroula Ntoa · Gavriel Salvendy
Editors

HCI International 2024 Posters

26th International Conference
on Human-Computer Interaction, HCII 2024
Washington, DC, USA, June 29 – July 4, 2024
Proceedings, Part V

 Springer

Editors
Constantine Stephanidis
University of Crete and Foundation for
Research and Technology - Hellas (FORTH)
Heraklion, Crete, Greece

Margherita Antona
Foundation for Research and Technology -
Hellas (FORTH)
Heraklion, Crete, Greece

Stavroula Ntoa
Foundation for Research
and Technology – Hellas (FORTH)
Heraklion, Crete, Greece

Gavriel Salvendy
University of Central Florida
Orlando, FL, USA

ISSN 1865-0929   ISSN 1865-0937 (electronic)
Communications in Computer and Information Science
ISBN 978-3-031-61962-5   ISBN 978-3-031-61963-2 (eBook)
https://doi.org/10.1007/978-3-031-61963-2

This Springer imprint is published by the registered company Springer Nature Switzerland AG
The registered company address is: Gewerbestrasse 11, 6330 Cham, Switzerland

If disposing of this product, please recycle the paper.

Foreword

This year we celebrate 40 years since the establishment of the HCI International (HCII) Conference, which has been a hub for presenting groundbreaking research and novel ideas and collaboration for people from all over the world.

The HCII conference was founded in 1984 by Prof. Gavriel Salvendy (Purdue University, USA, Tsinghua University, P.R. China, and University of Central Florida, USA) and the first event of the series, "1st USA-Japan Conference on Human-Computer Interaction", was held in Honolulu, Hawaii, USA, 18–20 August. Since then, HCI International is held jointly with several Thematic Areas and Affiliated Conferences, with each one under the auspices of a distinguished international Program Board and under one management and one registration. Twenty-six HCI International Conferences have been organized so far (every two years until 2013, and annually thereafter).

Over the years, this conference has served as a platform for scholars, researchers, industry experts and students to exchange ideas, connect, and address challenges in the ever-evolving HCI field. Throughout these 40 years, the conference has evolved itself, adapting to new technologies and emerging trends, while staying committed to its core mission of advancing knowledge and driving change.

As we celebrate this milestone anniversary, we reflect on the contributions of its founding members and appreciate the commitment of its current and past Affiliated Conference Program Board Chairs and members. We are also thankful to all past conference attendees who have shaped this community into what it is today.

The 26th International Conference on Human-Computer Interaction, HCI International 2024 (HCII 2024), was held as a 'hybrid' event at the Washington Hilton Hotel, Washington, DC, USA, during 29 June – 4 July 2024. It incorporated the 21 thematic areas and affiliated conferences listed below.

A total of 5108 individuals from academia, research institutes, industry, and government agencies from 85 countries submitted contributions, and 1271 papers and 309 posters were included in the volumes of the proceedings that were published just before the start of the conference, these are listed below. The contributions thoroughly cover the entire field of human-computer interaction, addressing major advances in knowledge and effective use of computers in a variety of application areas. These papers provide academics, researchers, engineers, scientists, practitioners and students with state-of-the-art information on the most recent advances in HCI.

The HCI International (HCII) conference also offers the option of presenting 'Late Breaking Work', and this applies both for papers and posters, with corresponding volumes of proceedings that will be published after the conference. Full papers will be included in the 'HCII 2024 - Late Breaking Papers' volumes of the proceedings to be published in the Springer LNCS series, while 'Poster Extended Abstracts' will be included as short research papers in the 'HCII 2024 - Late Breaking Posters' volumes to be published in the Springer CCIS series.

I would like to thank the Program Board Chairs and the members of the Program Boards of all thematic areas and affiliated conferences for their contribution towards the high scientific quality and overall success of the HCI International 2024 conference. Their manifold support in terms of paper reviewing (single-blind review process, with a minimum of two reviews per submission), session organization and their willingness to act as goodwill ambassadors for the conference is most highly appreciated.

This conference would not have been possible without the continuous and unwavering support and advice of Gavriel Salvendy, founder, General Chair Emeritus, and Scientific Advisor. For his outstanding efforts, I would like to express my sincere appreciation to Abbas Moallem, Communications Chair and Editor of HCI International News.

July 2024   Constantine Stephanidis

HCI International 2024 Thematic Areas and Affiliated Conferences

- HCI: Human-Computer Interaction Thematic Area
- HIMI: Human Interface and the Management of Information Thematic Area
- EPCE: 21st International Conference on Engineering Psychology and Cognitive Ergonomics
- AC: 18th International Conference on Augmented Cognition
- UAHCI: 18th International Conference on Universal Access in Human-Computer Interaction
- CCD: 16th International Conference on Cross-Cultural Design
- SCSM: 16th International Conference on Social Computing and Social Media
- VAMR: 16th International Conference on Virtual, Augmented and Mixed Reality
- DHM: 15th International Conference on Digital Human Modeling & Applications in Health, Safety, Ergonomics & Risk Management
- DUXU: 13th International Conference on Design, User Experience and Usability
- C&C: 12th International Conference on Culture and Computing
- DAPI: 12th International Conference on Distributed, Ambient and Pervasive Interactions
- HCIBGO: 11th International Conference on HCI in Business, Government and Organizations
- LCT: 11th International Conference on Learning and Collaboration Technologies
- ITAP: 10th International Conference on Human Aspects of IT for the Aged Population
- AIS: 6th International Conference on Adaptive Instructional Systems
- HCI-CPT: 6th International Conference on HCI for Cybersecurity, Privacy and Trust
- HCI-Games: 6th International Conference on HCI in Games
- MobiTAS: 6th International Conference on HCI in Mobility, Transport and Automotive Systems
- AI-HCI: 5th International Conference on Artificial Intelligence in HCI
- MOBILE: 5th International Conference on Human-Centered Design, Operation and Evaluation of Mobile Communications

List of Conference Proceedings Volumes Appearing Before the Conference

1. LNCS 14684, Human-Computer Interaction: Part I, edited by Masaaki Kurosu and Ayako Hashizume
2. LNCS 14685, Human-Computer Interaction: Part II, edited by Masaaki Kurosu and Ayako Hashizume
3. LNCS 14686, Human-Computer Interaction: Part III, edited by Masaaki Kurosu and Ayako Hashizume
4. LNCS 14687, Human-Computer Interaction: Part IV, edited by Masaaki Kurosu and Ayako Hashizume
5. LNCS 14688, Human-Computer Interaction: Part V, edited by Masaaki Kurosu and Ayako Hashizume
6. LNCS 14689, Human Interface and the Management of Information: Part I, edited by Hirohiko Mori and Yumi Asahi
7. LNCS 14690, Human Interface and the Management of Information: Part II, edited by Hirohiko Mori and Yumi Asahi
8. LNCS 14691, Human Interface and the Management of Information: Part III, edited by Hirohiko Mori and Yumi Asahi
9. LNAI 14692, Engineering Psychology and Cognitive Ergonomics: Part I, edited by Don Harris and Wen-Chin Li
10. LNAI 14693, Engineering Psychology and Cognitive Ergonomics: Part II, edited by Don Harris and Wen-Chin Li
11. LNAI 14694, Augmented Cognition, Part I, edited by Dylan D. Schmorrow and Cali M. Fidopiastis
12. LNAI 14695, Augmented Cognition, Part II, edited by Dylan D. Schmorrow and Cali M. Fidopiastis
13. LNCS 14696, Universal Access in Human-Computer Interaction: Part I, edited by Margherita Antona and Constantine Stephanidis
14. LNCS 14697, Universal Access in Human-Computer Interaction: Part II, edited by Margherita Antona and Constantine Stephanidis
15. LNCS 14698, Universal Access in Human-Computer Interaction: Part III, edited by Margherita Antona and Constantine Stephanidis
16. LNCS 14699, Cross-Cultural Design: Part I, edited by Pei-Luen Patrick Rau
17. LNCS 14700, Cross-Cultural Design: Part II, edited by Pei-Luen Patrick Rau
18. LNCS 14701, Cross-Cultural Design: Part III, edited by Pei-Luen Patrick Rau
19. LNCS 14702, Cross-Cultural Design: Part IV, edited by Pei-Luen Patrick Rau
20. LNCS 14703, Social Computing and Social Media: Part I, edited by Adela Coman and Simona Vasilache
21. LNCS 14704, Social Computing and Social Media: Part II, edited by Adela Coman and Simona Vasilache
22. LNCS 14705, Social Computing and Social Media: Part III, edited by Adela Coman and Simona Vasilache

47. LNCS 14730, HCI in Games: Part I, edited by Xiaowen Fang
48. LNCS 14731, HCI in Games: Part II, edited by Xiaowen Fang
49. LNCS 14732, HCI in Mobility, Transport and Automotive Systems: Part I, edited by Heidi Krömker
50. LNCS 14733, HCI in Mobility, Transport and Automotive Systems: Part II, edited by Heidi Krömker
51. LNAI 14734, Artificial Intelligence in HCI: Part I, edited by Helmut Degen and Stavroula Ntoa
52. LNAI 14735, Artificial Intelligence in HCI: Part II, edited by Helmut Degen and Stavroula Ntoa
53. LNAI 14736, Artificial Intelligence in HCI: Part III, edited by Helmut Degen and Stavroula Ntoa
54. LNCS 14737, Design, Operation and Evaluation of Mobile Communications: Part I, edited by June Wei and George Margetis
55. LNCS 14738, Design, Operation and Evaluation of Mobile Communications: Part II, edited by June Wei and George Margetis
56. CCIS 2114, HCI International 2024 Posters - Part I, edited by Constantine Stephanidis, Margherita Antona, Stavroula Ntoa and Gavriel Salvendy
57. CCIS 2115, HCI International 2024 Posters - Part II, edited by Constantine Stephanidis, Margherita Antona, Stavroula Ntoa and Gavriel Salvendy
58. CCIS 2116, HCI International 2024 Posters - Part III, edited by Constantine Stephanidis, Margherita Antona, Stavroula Ntoa and Gavriel Salvendy
59. CCIS 2117, HCI International 2024 Posters - Part IV, edited by Constantine Stephanidis, Margherita Antona, Stavroula Ntoa and Gavriel Salvendy
60. CCIS 2118, HCI International 2024 Posters - Part V, edited by Constantine Stephanidis, Margherita Antona, Stavroula Ntoa and Gavriel Salvendy
61. CCIS 2119, HCI International 2024 Posters - Part VI, edited by Constantine Stephanidis, Margherita Antona, Stavroula Ntoa and Gavriel Salvendy
62. CCIS 2120, HCI International 2024 Posters - Part VII, edited by Constantine Stephanidis, Margherita Antona, Stavroula Ntoa and Gavriel Salvendy

https://2024.hci.international/proceedings

Preface

Preliminary scientific results, professional news, or work in progress, described in the form of short research papers (4–11 pages long), constitute a popular submission type among the International Conference on Human-Computer Interaction (HCII) participants. Extended abstracts are particularly suited for reporting ongoing work, which can benefit from a visual presentation, and are presented during the conference in the form of posters. The latter allow a focus on novel ideas and are appropriate for presenting project results in a simple, concise, and visually appealing manner. At the same time, they are also suitable for attracting feedback from an international community of HCI academics, researchers, and practitioners. Poster submissions span the wide range of topics of all HCII thematic areas and affiliated conferences.

Seven volumes of the HCII 2024 proceedings are dedicated to this year's poster extended abstracts, in the form of short research papers, focusing on the following topics:

- Volume I: HCI Design Theories, Methods, Tools and Case Studies; User Experience Evaluation Methods and Case Studies; Emotions in HCI; Human Robot Interaction
- Volume II: Inclusive Designs and Applications; Aging and Technology
- Volume III: eXtended Reality and the Metaverse; Interacting with Cultural Heritage, Art and Creativity
- Volume IV: HCI in Learning and Education; HCI in Games
- Volume V: HCI in Business and Marketing; HCI in Mobility and Automated Driving; HCI in Psychotherapy and Mental Health
- Volume VI: Interacting with the Web, Social Media and Digital Services; Interaction in the Museum; HCI in Healthcare
- Volume VII: AI Algorithms and Tools in HCI; Interacting with Large Language Models and Generative AI; Interacting in Intelligent Environments; HCI in Complex Industrial Environments

Poster extended abstracts were accepted for publication in these volumes following a minimum of two single-blind reviews from the members of the HCII 2024 international Program Boards, i.e., the program committees of the constituent events. We would like to thank all of them for their invaluable contribution, support, and efforts.

July 2024

Constantine Stephanidis
Margherita Antona
Stavroula Ntoa
Gavriel Salvendy

26th International Conference on Human-Computer Interaction (HCII 2024)

The full list with the Program Board Chairs and the members of the Program Boards of all thematic areas and affiliated conferences of HCII 2024 is available online at:

http://www.hci.international/board-members-2024.php

HCI International 2025 Conference

The 27th International Conference on Human-Computer Interaction, HCI International 2025, will be held jointly with the affiliated conferences at the Swedish Exhibition & Congress Centre and Gothia Towers Hotel, Gothenburg, Sweden, June 22–27, 2025. It will cover a broad spectrum of themes related to Human-Computer Interaction, including theoretical issues, methods, tools, processes, and case studies in HCI design, as well as novel interaction techniques, interfaces, and applications. The proceedings will be published by Springer. More information will become available on the conference website: https://2025.hci.international/.

General Chair
Prof. Constantine Stephanidis
University of Crete and ICS-FORTH
Heraklion, Crete, Greece
Email: general_chair@2025.hci.international

https://2025.hci.international/

Contents – Part V

HCI in Mobility and Automated Driving

HCI in Psychotherapy and Mental Health

HCI in Business and Marketing

Towards Automated Creation of Adaptive Continuous Authentication Systems for Telework Scenarios

Adam Gałązkiewicz[(✉)] [iD] and Adam Wójtowicz[iD]

Department of Information Technology, Poznań University of Economics and Business,
Al. Niepodległości 10, 61-875 Poznań, Poland
galazkiewicz@kti.ue.poznan.pl

Abstract. Continuous authentication (CA) provides ongoing monitoring of user identity to mitigate the risk of unauthorized access to corporate assets. In this work, a new framework that automates building and maintaining adaptive CA systems intended for diverse teleworking environments is presented. In the proposed approach, a number of CA methods from four main categories are employed, namely: biometric-physiological, biometric-behavioral, interactive, and contextual. The proposed framework considers various decision factors, including user convenience, privacy, data and system security, authentication efficiency, infrastructure availability, and business requirements. It utilizes client requirements as well as empirical data derived from both laboratory experiments and log files of real-world CA systems in order to calculate the most efficient combinations of CA methods represented as sets of decision rules, that are customized for specific use case. The modular architecture and integration capabilities of this framework provide a robust foundation for ongoing research and development in the domain of telework security solutions.

Keywords: adaptive access control · behavior-based cybersecurity · behavioral biometrics · context-aware authentication and authorization · frictionless authentication · fusion of biometric modalities · privacy and security implications of biometric architectures · security and usability of combinations of authentication factors

1 Introduction

In post-pandemic economy where transition to remote work in many industries is observed, the concept of continuous authentication (CA) has emerged as a fundamental element in safeguarding data within corporate networks. The prevalence of telecommuting increases the vulnerability to security breaches, underscoring the importance of continuous monitoring of user identities in order to mitigate unauthorized access or usage of corporate assets. CA is an approach that enhances data security in remote work environments by employing various identity verification techniques to monitor users in real-time. The deployments of CA in telework applications allow not only to protect sensitive data but also to promptly respond to potential threats, thereby enhancing organization real-time defense capabilities against a wide range of telework-related risks.

CA refers to a persistent procedure that involves the verification of user identity through the use of authentication methods, which can be combined to enhance precision and fortify security measures. The effectiveness of CA systems relies on the inclusion of various authentication methods, preferably from various categories. The methods can be categorized into four primary classes: biometric-physiological, biometric-behavioral, interactive, and contextual. Biometric-physiological methods encompass the utilization of distinctive individual characteristics such as facial, voice or iris recognition and motion dynamics. Biometric-behavioral methods refer to the analysis of user behavior, such as the examination of keyboard typing dynamics, patterns of mouse movement or touchscreen gestures. The interactive methods employ patterns of user interaction with specific application, device or service. Ultimately, contextual methods may include variables such as the location of a user, the time at which system usage occurs, or even patterns in look of clothes worn during given period of time. The development of a formalized methodology for integrating diverse authentication methods has the potential to substantially augment security measures, thereby enabling organizations to more effectively mitigate the risks associated with telework breaches. The initial objective of the proposed work is to organize authentication methods in a coherent manner, facilitating the future development of sophisticated and integrated CA systems that are customized for specific teleworking business scenarios.

2   State of the Art

The CA field has gained significant scientific attention due to its various techniques and approaches. A comprehensive analysis on continuous and passive authentication technologies highlights critical aspects of multimodal biometric modalities for continuous user authentication, suggesting pathways for future advancements in secure internet services through the fusion of hard and soft biometric traits [1–3]. Other studies highlight the practical value of these technologies, such as enhancing system security through non-intrusive user identity verification using keystroke dynamics and gesture profiling, thereby offering a seamless security layer that does not impede user interaction [4, 5]. *DeepAuthen* is a framework that uses data from mobile sensors and employs machine learning techniques for user authentication [6]. Another framework, *DeepAuth* primarily focuses on the process of re-authenticating users within mobile applications. This is achieved by utilizing data obtained from motion sensors and conducting analysis in the time-frequency domain [7]. An alternative method, specifically designed for the BYOD (Bring Your Own Device) context, suggests a collaborative learning strategy that utilizes multiple machine learning models [8]. *ContAuth* framework enhances the robustness of behavior-based authentication by adjusting to new data through incremental learning [9]. On the other hand, *Itus* framework enables the seamless integration of novel authentication methods for Android devices [10]. In turn, research conducted in the realm of payment systems examines the concept of secure and convenient payments made at retail points of sale. These studies specifically explore the use of biometric techniques, such as face recognition, for the purpose of background authorization [11]. The study of CA methods in the IoT ecosystem offers valuable insights into the possible uses of these technologies, specifically in scenarios involving user authentication [12].

RemoteDesk is a company developing remote work solutions, specifically in the field of CA. The company has adopted a CA method that surpasses the conventional utilization of login information. RemoteDesk employs a blend of biometric calculations, continuous webcam monitoring, and keystroke mapping to authenticate users effectively during their remote work sessions [13]. The growing significance of security, privacy, and usability in CA systems indicates the development of this technology from theoretical frameworks to real-world applications, effectively addressing the evolving demands of remote work settings [14].

CA solutions in telework scenarios have become increasingly popular in recent years. *AuthCODE* system is an instance of a solution that utilizes a sophisticated and ongoing authentication system across multiple devices. The system places focus on safeguarding user privacy and provides a notable enhancement in efficiency when compared to conventional single-device systems [15]. The significance of ongoing user identity management in maintaining secure and consistent user-system interactions has been also emphasized in the field of distance learning [16] or financial transaction authorization [17].

Although there has been progress made in the CA field, there are still certain areas that necessitate further development. One challenge that persists is the integration of various devices and environments into a cohesive authentication system. Another important concern is how well these solutions can grow and adjust to quickly evolving technology environments, in order to maintain their effectiveness and relevance in the future.

3 Proposed Framework

The goal of the proposed framework is to automate creation and maintance of adaptive CA systems using various authentication methods in order to achieve an optimal balance between a number of factors. These factors include: user convenience, user productivity, user privacy, data security, system security, authentication efficiency, infrastructure availability and business requirements. The examination of various permutations of CA methods, such as biometric-physiological, biometric-behavioral, interactive, and contextual methods, is a core design element of the approach within the varied context of teleworking scenarios. Achieving a harmonious equilibrium between above mentioned factors is crucial in order to mitigate potential limitations on employee performance, while simultaneously upholding robust safeguards for data protection. The proposed framework aims to automate this process, allowing organizations to quickly and effectively adapt their CA systems in accordance with evolving security and business requirements. This framework is designed to extract input data from two main sources: formally defined requirement specification and empirical data obtained from both laboratory experiments and real-world CA systems. The requirement specification provides comprehensive information regarding the use case, including details on the devices that are available and the user parameters that are allowed. The provision of this information is the responsibility of the client-side business system designer. In turn, CA training data provides insights into the mutual dependencies among various authentication methods and their level of mutual compatibility. Based on provided data, the adaptive CA engine generates rule sets, which represent the most effective combinations of authentication methods. Figure 1 illustrates the flow of data starting from the formalized requirements specification and CA training data, passing through the adaptive authentication engine (AAE), and ultimately resulting in the creation of CA rule sets (CARS) dedicated to a specific system.

The AAE utilizes optimization algorithms to evaluate various aggregation matchings for authentication methods. The efficacy of this selection process relies on the examination of correlations among different factors and the assessment of their potential to enhance system security. The AAE analyzes the input data in order to identify the most effective combinations of methods that are customized to meet the specific demands of a given use case. The designer is offered a range of alternative CARS, each engineered to achieve comparable levels of security. This allows for the selection of the solution that best matches preferences and operational circumstances. The adaptive CA framework illustrated in Fig. 1 centralizes around a service provider (SP). SP operates an AAE, which is essentially the core of the system. It utilizes optimization algorithms to synthesize CA training data with client-specific requirements to formulate CARS. The training data is a collection of empirical data that reflects past authentication attempts, user behaviors, and system interactions, which is critical for the engine to adapt and refine its methods. At the client end, the deployment of the system uses CARS to perform real-time authentication, tailored to the unique specifications of the client environment. These specifications define the parameters of the authentication process, balancing factors such as user convenience, privacy, and security.

The authentication data sources are diverse, ranging from biometric to behavioral inputs like facial recognition, voice analysis, and keystroke dynamics. The accessibility and reliability of these inputs can vary between users and even sessions, introducing a dynamic component to the system operation. This dynamic nature is further exemplified in how the system handles each use case. It starts with a requirements specification that influences the interpretation of training data, subsequently guiding the generation of CARS. CARS are responsive to the availability of authentication factors at any given moment, ensuring decisions are made in the context of current data and the correlations between factors.

The framework is designed to be highly adaptable, providing individualized CARS for different employees and sessions. It intelligently assesses which factors are currently available and makes decisions in real-time, with each authentication instance meeting a certain security threshold. The system clusters various authentication methods into rule sets, combining them based on their interdependencies and individual security strengths. This results in a cohesive and secure authentication process that is tailored to the needs of each user and session, thereby providing a robust foundation for teleworking security that is both adaptable and user-centric.

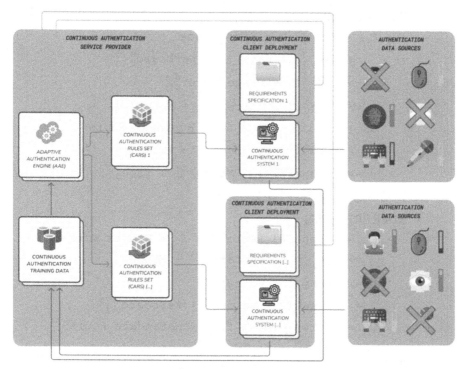

Fig. 1. Framework for automated creation and maintnance of adaptive CA systems

An example of CARS tailored to the requirements of sensitive data based on the context of access, such as the user location and the specific time of day, is presented below. It demonstrates how a mix of biometric and behavioral authentication factors—ranging from eye and face recognition to keyboard and mouse dynamics—is adeptly combined to protect various types of data under different circumstances. For instance, in securing access to Personally Identifiable Information (PII) within an open space, the presented scheme highlights the deployment of eye and face recognition alongside keyboard dynamics. This configuration is specifically designed to mitigate the increased risks of unauthorized access in less secure environments, showcasing the system's ability to adjust its security protocols dynamically and provide a security solution that is both effective and unobtrusive to the user's experience.

RULE SET 1 (RS1)

C_{DS} = PII & C_L = Open_Space

$\Rightarrow$ $Eye_{0.25}^{0.4}$ + $Face_{0.4}^{0.55}$ + $Keyboard_{0.35}^{0.25}$

$\Rightarrow$ $Eye_{0.6}^{0.65}$ + $Fingerprint_{0.4}^{0.8}$

$\Rightarrow$ $Face_{0.65}^{0.45}$ + $Voice_{0.2}^{0.25}$ + $Mouse_{0.15}^{0.45}$

C_{DS} = Health_Data & C_T = Business_Hours

$\Rightarrow$ $Face_{0.5}^{0.45}$ + $Voice_{0.25}^{0.8}$ + $Mouse_{0.25}^{0.5}$

$\Rightarrow$ $Keyboard_{0.35}^{0.35}$ + $Mouse_{0.35}^{0.25}$ + $Face_{0.3}^{0.7}$

$\Rightarrow$ $Eye_{0.8}^{0.7}$ + $Keyboard_{0.2}^{0.6}$

RULE SET 2 (RS2)

C_{DS} = Financial_Records & C_L = Remote_Work

$\Rightarrow$ $Eye_{0.8}^{0.55}$ + $Keyboard_{0.1}^{0.35}$ + $Mouse_{0.1}^{0.25}$

$\Rightarrow$ $Face_{0.8}^{0.75}$ + $Voice_{0.2}^{0.85}$

$\Rightarrow$ $Mouse_{0.6}^{0.25}$ + $Voice_{0.2}^{0.55}$ + $Keyboard_{0.2}^{0.25}$

C_{DS} = Source_Code & C_T = Nonstandard_Hours

$\Rightarrow$ $Face_{0.4}^{0.8}$ + $Keyboard_{0.6}^{0.7}$

$\Rightarrow$ $Voice_{0.65}^{0.45}$ + $Eye_{0.15}^{0.25}$ + $Mouse_{0.2}^{0.4}$

$\Rightarrow$ $Mouse_{0.35}^{0.95}$ + $Keyboard_{0.65}^{0.95}$

C_{DS} (Condition: Data Security): refers to conditions requiring sensitive information to be protected from unauthorized access and breaches. It dictates the security level required based on the data type, such as PII or corporate secrets.

C_T (Condition: Time): considers the specific time or period when access attempts are made, influencing the authentication process by adjusting requirements based on whether access is attempted during business hours, off-hours, or specific time-sensitive events.

C_L (Condition: Location): involves the geographical or physical context from which an access request originates, using location data to adjust authentication strength and methods based on perceived security risks of different locations.

AF_w^t (Authentication Factor): a security measure used to confirm the identity of a user. The threshold (t) is the minimum score that the authentication attempt must reach to be considered successful, and the weight (w) represents the share of the factor in the overall authentication process.

The practicality of the proposed adaptive CA framework can be best understood through specific use cases. Two hypothetical scenarios are presented, denoted C1 and C2, that demonstrate the framework's versatility and responsiveness to different tele-working requirements. Scenario C1 is situated within a high-security setting, characteristic to government contractors, where stringent security measures are paramount. The emphasis here is on deploying comprehensive authentication strategies, including sophisticated biometric verification and continuous user activity monitoring, to protect highly sensitive data from unauthorized access. This scenario demands a security-first approach, with the system dynamically adjusting to meet rigorous security standards and protocols. In contrast, scenario C2 unfolds within the context of a dynamic startup environment, where the operational ethos prioritizes flexibility and innovation. The challenge here is to integrate an authentication system that aligns with a fast-paced, collaborative work culture without being obtrusive. The solution leverages less invasive authentication methods, such as behavioral biometrics, that adapt to the user's interaction patterns, ensuring security measures do not impede productivity. This scenario demonstrates the framework's capacity to provide effective security while maintaining the agility essential to startup ecosystems, underlining its versatility across varying telework settings.

In the enhanced security scenario of C1, the authentication system employs a dynamic and session-specific approach to rule set verification, tailored to the current access capabilities of the individual worker. At the beginning of each session, the system conducts a real-time inventory of the pre-approved authentication tools at the employee's disposal. This could range from biometric devices to secure tokens, each with a predefined security value based on empirical evidence collected across multiple sessions. For example, if an employee attempts to log in without the usual biometric scanner available, the system might compensate by requiring a combination of mandatory factors and secondary measures from the list of allowed authorization factors—such as a smart card and a one-time password (OTP) generated by a secure application. The elevated weighting and thresholds for biometric factors such as "Eye" and "Face" in open spaces, as demonstrated in RS1, represent system's capacity to dynamically adjust authentication requirements, safeguarding sensitive data against unauthorized access in high-security contexts. This combination is evaluated against historical data to ensure its security value matches that of the primary biometric measure, allowing for uninterrupted yet secure access. The system's machine learning modules are continuously updated with data from each session, which enables it to discern patterns and correlations between different authentication factor pairs. It may discover, for instance, that the combination of a secure physical token and a behavioral biometric, like the rhythm of keyboard typing, consistently presents a security assurance level on par with a facial recognition check. This learning process is vital, particularly when employees are working in variable infrastructure conditions where not all authentication methods are always available.

In the less restrictive scenario of C2, the adaptive framework demonstrates a similar level of detail in its operation. The authentication strategies in RS2, which utilize a diverse mix of factors like "Mouse" and "Keyboard" for remote work, reflect the startup need for flexibility and non-intrusiveness, showcasing the framework's ability to integrate security measures that align with an innovative work culture. The system's detailed logs and observations are key to its adaptability. It identifies which authentication factor combinations are consistently reliable. Over time, it might note that certain pairs or groups of factors, such as typing pattern, the time taken to execute certain commands, and the regularity of application usage, can collectively match the security level provided by a biometric voice verification.

In both C1 and C2 cases, the system's advanced algorithms are fine-tuned to understand the depth of data security required. They are capable of recognizing when different factors, even those not traditionally considered as secure as biometrics, can, in fact, provide equivalent security. This granular understanding allows the system to construct a complex, multi-factor authentication strategy that can dynamically adjust to the availability of authentication tools, the context of access, and the unique behavioral patterns of each employee, thereby ensuring a secure, efficient, and user-centric authentication process for every session. Importantly, the approaches proposed in C1 and C2 are not mutually exclusive—they can be synergistically applied across subsequent scenarios through the implementation of specific requirements and rules. This integrated approach enables a seamless and flexible adaptation of the authentication framework, catering to a wide spectrum of security needs and operational contexts.

4 Conclusions

The primary advantage of the proposed framework resides in its ability to automatically generate CARS, thereby optimizing the trade-off between convenience, privacy, data and system security, authentication efficiency, infrastructure availability, and business requirements. Through comprehensive examination of various aggregation sets of authentication methods, this framework facilitates the development of effective solutions that are customized to meet the specific requirements of remote work business scenarios. Nevertheless, it has its limitations. The quality of the CARS produced may be influenced by the degree of expertise quality and skill set of an individual responsible for formulation of the requirement specification. The integration of other authentication systems can significantly expand the framework's range of potential applications.

The adaptive CA framework provides optimized rule sets for different business scenarios and incorporates a self-learning system. The framework can refine its CARS by analyzing empirical data from a specific company's CA systems in an iterative manner. This feature guarantees that the system adapts to the evolving security landscape and the operational requirements of a company. As a result, the security posture consistently improves, effectively addressing the specific challenges of teleworking environments.

However, an inherent limitation at the outset is the low quality and small volume of the learning datasets available, known as the "cold start" problem. This can impede the system's initial effectiveness in accurately adapting to security requirements. To mitigate this issue, the framework can be initially deployed in a controlled test environment. This approach allows for collection and incorporation of high-quality empirical data, enriching the learning datasets and enabling the system to overcome the cold start problem more effectively.

The proposed framework has the potential to serve as a foundation for the advancement of continuous authentication systems that are capable of adapting to changing conditions, business requirements and security threats. The modular characteristics and strong integration capabilities provide a robust base for future research and advancements in the field of teleworking security.

References

1. Jeong, J.J., Zolotavkin, Y., Doss, R.: Examining the current status and emerging trends in continuous authentication technologies through citation network analysis. ACM Comput. Surv. **55**(6), 122 (2022). https://doi.org/10.1145/3533705
2. Velásquez, I., Caro, A., Rodríguez, A.: Authentication schemes and methods: a systematic literature review. Inf. Softw. Technol. **94**, 30–37 (2018)
3. Dasgupta, D., Roy, A., Nag, A.: Toward the design of adaptive selection strategies for multi-factor authentication. Comput. Secur. 63 (2016). https://doi.org/10.1016/j.cose.2016.09.004
4. AlHusain, R., Alkhalifah, A.: Evaluating fallback authentication research: a systematic literature review. Comput. Secur. **111**, 102487 (2021). https://doi.org/10.1016/j.cose.2021.102487
5. Bailey, K., Okolica, J., Peterson, G.: User identification and authentication using multi-modal behavioral biometrics. Comput. Secur. 43 (2014). https://doi.org/10.1016/j.cose.2014.03.005
6. Mekruksavanich, S., Jitpattanakul, A.: Deep learning approaches for continuous authentication based on activity patterns using mobile sensing. Sensors **21**(22), 7519 (2021). https://doi.org/10.3390/s21227519
7. Amini, S., Noroozi, V., Pande, A., Gupte, S., Yu, P., Kanich, C.: DeepAuth: a framework for continuous user re-authentication in mobile apps. In: Proceedings of the 27th ACM International Conference on Information and Knowledge Management, pp. 2027–2035 (2018). https://doi.org/10.1145/3269206.3272034
8. de-Marcos, L., Cilleruelo, C., Junquera-Sánchez, J., Martínez-Herráiz, J.J.: A framework for BYOD continuous authentication: case study with soft-keyboard metrics for healthcare environment. In: Florez, H., Misra, S. (eds.) Applied Informatics, ICAI 2020. Communications in Computer and Information Science, vol 1277, Springer, Cham (2020). https://doi.org/10.1007/978-3-030-61702-8_24
9. Jagmohan, C., Kwon, Y.D., Hui, P., Mascolo, C.: ContAuth: continual learning framework for behavioral-based user authentication. In: Proceedings of the ACM on Interactive, Mobile, Wearable and Ubiquitous Technologies, vol. 4, pp. 1–23 (2020).https://doi.org/10.1145/3432203
10. Khan, H., Atwater, A., Hengartner, U.: Itus: an implicit authentication framework for android. In: Proceedings of the Annual International Conference on Mobile Computing and Networking, MOBICOM (2014). https://doi.org/10.1145/2639108.2639141
11. Wójtowicz, A., Chmielewski, J.: Technical feasibility of context-aware passive payment authorization for physical points of sale. Pers. Ubiquit. Comput. **21**, 1113–1125 (2017). https://doi.org/10.1007/s00779-017-1035-z
12. Al-Naji, F.H., Zagrouba, R.: A survey on continuous authentication methods in Internet of Things environment. Comput. Commun. **163**, 109–133 (2020). https://doi.org/10.1016/j.comcom.2020.09.006
13. RemoteDesk: Why Embrace Continuous Authentication in 2023? Unlocking Enhanced Security and Efficiency in Remote Work. https://www.remotedesk.com/why-embrace-continuous-authentication-in-2023/. Accessed 08 Mar 2024
14. Baig, A.F., Eskeland, S.: Security, privacy, and usability in continuous authentication: a survey. Sensors **21**, 5967 (2021). https://doi.org/10.3390/s21175967
15. Sciurba, F., Di Martino, B.: AuthCODE: a privacy-preserving and multi-device continuous authentication architecture based on machine and deep learning. Comput. Secur. **105**, 102204 (2021). https://doi.org/10.48550/arXiv.2004.07877

16. Portugal, D., Faria, J.N., Belk, M., et al.: Continuous user identification in distance learning: a recent technology perspective. Smart Learn. Environ. **10**, 38 (2023). https://doi.org/10.1186/s40561-023-00255-9
17. Wilusz, D., Wójtowicz, A.: Security analysis of transaction authorization methods for next generation electronic payment services. In: Moallem, A. (ed.) HCI for Cybersecurity, Privacy and Trust: Third International Conference, HCI-CPT 2021, Held as Part of the 23rd HCI International Conference, HCII 2021, Virtual Event, July 24–29, 2021, Proceedings, pp. 103–119. Springer International Publishing, Cham (2021). https://doi.org/10.1007/978-3-030-77392-2_8

Research on Consumers' Preference for Sustainable Fashion Labels

Bailu Guo[✉], Yunde Li, and Boyuan Wang

Art and Design Academy, Beijing City University, Beijing, China
13521505946@163.com

Abstract. Under the background of serious pollution in fashion industry, it is particularly important to provide sustainable commodity information to guide people's sustainable consumption. Labeling is regarded as a favorable tool to provide sustainable information by providing more information and knowledge about sustainable development and triggering consumers' cognitive response. At present, the research on sustainable fashion labels is mostly to provide consumers with a novel label to choose from, but under different shopping methods (physical stores and online shopping) and different shopping purposes (with and without clear purchasing goals), consumers' preferences for different labels have not been taken into account. The effective sample of this paper is 200. Firstly, it tests consumers' attitude towards sustainable fashion. Through data analysis, we found that although about half of the testers are vague about the concept of sustainable fashion, nearly 80% of the testers have a positive attitude towards sustainable fashion, and hope that enterprises or businesses can inform them of the sustainable attributes of goods. Secondly, we provide six different labeling methods for testers to inform the sustainability information of products and measure their preference for sustainable fashion labels. Finally, we provide two different shopping methods, online and offline, and two purposes with and without clear purchasing goals to test people's preferences for sustainable fashion brands under different shopping methods and purposes again. We found that, under the premise of not specifying the way of shopping (physical store and online shopping) and the purpose of buying (with and without a clear purchase goal), testers have obvious preference for QR code labels. Similarly, when shopping in online stores, testers still prefer QR code labels regardless of whether there is a clear purchase goal. However, in the form of online shopping, most testers prefer color labels regardless of whether they have a clear purchase target or not, while the popular QR code labels are not popular. In the future, in the process of purchasing fashion goods in physical stores, the application of QR code labels should become a field worthy of in-depth study.

Keyword: Sustainable fashion labels · Sustainable fashion · Sustainable consumption

C. Stephanidis et al. (Eds.): HCII 2024, CCIS 2118, pp. 13–19, 2024.
https://doi.org/10.1007/978-3-031-61963-2_2

1 Introduction

Abnormal global climate change, depletion of land and water resources, environmental pollution and reduction of biodiversity all tell that the sustainability of human society is facing great challenges. The pollution of fashion industry is seriously affecting the global sustainable development. According to the prediction of the United Nations, by 2050, the fashion industry will produce a quarter of the global carbon emissions every year, and by 2030, the global middle class population will increase from 3 billion in 2015 to 5.4 billion. If consumption continues to grow at the current rate, by 2050, the required natural resources will be three times that of the natural energy intake in 20001. It is particularly important to provide sustainable commodity information in fashion consumption to guide people's sustainable consumption. Labeling is regarded as a favorable tool to provide sustainable information by providing more information and knowledge about sustainable development and triggering consumers' cognitive response. At present, the research on sustainable fashion labels is mostly to provide consumers with a novel label to choose from, but under different shopping methods (physical stores and online shopping) and different shopping purposes (with and without clear purchasing goals), consumers' preferences for different labels have not been taken into account. In different situations, it is the purpose of this paper to study consumers' preference for not using labels.

2 Sustainable Fashion

The concept of "sustainable fashion" can be traced back to the book Silent Spring by American biologist Rachel Carson in 1962. In her book, she exposed the serious and extensive pollution caused by the abuse of agricultural chemicals. Although this book does not directly involve the concept of "sustainable fashion", its emphasis on environmental protection and sustainable development provides enlightenment for people to realize the necessity of sustainable fashion2. In 1987, Ms. Gro Harlem Brundtland officially used the concept of sustainable development for the first time in the report "Our Shared Future" of the World Commission on Environment and Development (WCED), and defined it as "development that can meet the needs of contemporary people without threatening the ability of future generations to meet their needs"3, which also laid the foundation for the development of sustainable fashion concept later. Sustainable fashion can reduce the damage to nature by reducing the carbon emissions of fashion industry, and now it involves not only fashion products, but also the production and consumption patterns of the whole fashion industry.

3 Label Testing

Studies have shown that there are at least two broad ways to make sustainability knowledge have an impact on consumption decisions. The first is to stimulate consumers' cognitive response by providing more information and knowledge about sustainable development. The second is that emotional attraction can trigger the emotional component of sustainable behavior4. This paper focuses on the first method, in which labels are regarded as a favorable tool to provide sustainable information. We have selected six kinds of labels, including text labels, sustainability labels, color labels, two-dimensional code traceability labels, sustainability certificates and material labels, as shown in Table 1.

Table 1. 6 label forms provided to testers.

Label format	Example
Text labels	Use text to indicate that the raw materials for this product are environmentally friendly
Sustainable signage	The product itself is printed with a small icon representing environmental protection
Color labels	There are color labels hanging around the product, such as light green labels representing general environmental protection, dark green labels representing very environmental protection, etc
QR code label	Generally, it has traceability function, and scanning the code can search for information about raw materials such as images, texts, videos, etc
Sustainable certificate	After purchasing the product, you can obtain an officially certified sustainability certificate
Material labels	Sample materials used to display the product

The valid sample in this paper is 200. First of all, we learned about the attitude of testers towards sustainable fashion. As shown in Fig. 1, although about half of the consumers in our survey are very vague about the concept of sustainable fashion, more than 80% of the testers hope to be told by enterprises whether this product has environmental protection and sustainability attributes when purchasing fashion products. This shows that testers pay more attention to the sustainable property of goods.

As shown in Fig. 2, 62% of the testers think that having sustainable and environmentally friendly labels on fashion products will increase consumers' sense of security just like having organic labels on food, but only 33% of them will check the labels before buying. This also shows that attractive label design is a field worthy of study.

After that, we provide testers with the above six kinds of labels to inform the sustainability information of products and measure their preference for sustainable fashion labels. Each tester can cast three votes. Through data analysis, it can be known that two-dimensional code labels, material labels and sustainable signs are favored by testers, as shown in Fig. 3. There are also many testers who think that the method of issuing the sustainability certificate is novel, but because the certificate is issued after purchasing the goods, many testers think that they will not choose this one when they want to know the sustainability attribute of the goods initially.

Finally, it provides two different shopping methods, online and offline, and has a clear purchase goal, such as the tester only wants a coat of a certain brand at this time and has no clear purchase goal, such as wandering around the mall, and randomly looking at a certain product, so as to test people's preference for sustainable fashion

▶ The tester's level of understanding of sustainable fashion

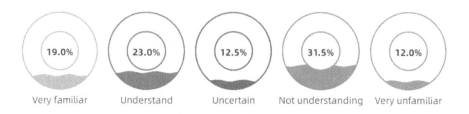

▶ Testers wish to be informed of the sustainability level of the product

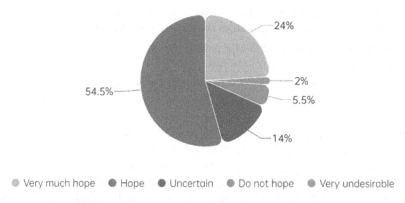

Fig. 1. The tester's attitude towards sustainable fashion

brands under different shopping methods and purposes again. As shown in Fig. 4, when shopping online, whether the tester has a clear purchase goal or not, the sustainable label prompt that the tester wants at this time is the QR code label. However, when shopping online, whether there is a clear purchase goal or not, testers hope to judge the sustainability attribute through color labels, as shown in Fig. 5. There are two reasons why there are obvious differences between online and offline shopping preferences for labels. First. In China, most consumers make online shopping through their mobile phones, so it is extremely inconvenient to scan the code. Secondly, most merchants will display their products in pictures, videos and other forms on the online shopping page, which also includes major product sustainability testing reports, etc. Testers think that it is not necessary to scan the code again in most cases. They prefer to see the sign of sustainability directly and clearly to determine the sustainability of goods.

▶ Testers believe that fashion products with sustainable labels will increase the sense of security

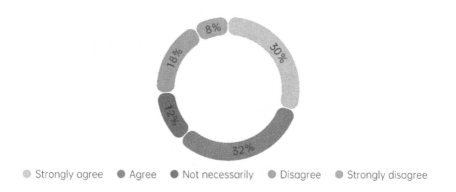

▶ The extent to which testers will look at labels when buying fashion goods

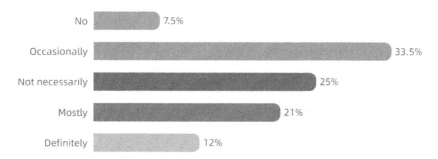

Fig. 2. Attitude of testers towards sustainable product labels

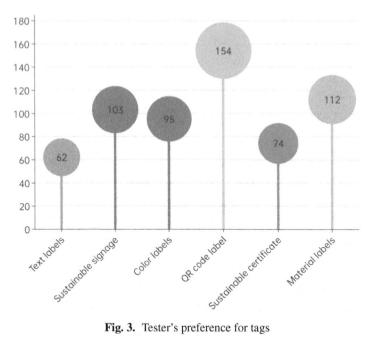

Fig. 3. Tester's preference for tags

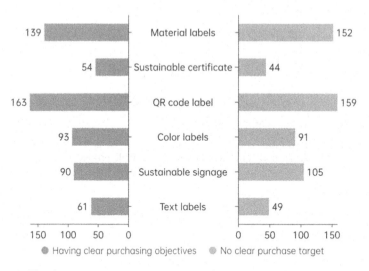

Fig. 4. Testers' preference for tags during physical store shopping

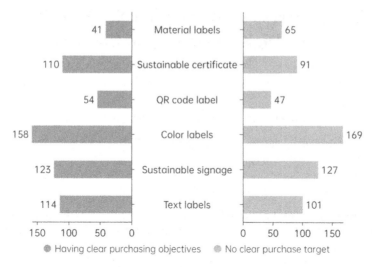

Fig. 5. Testers' preference for tags during online shopping

4 Conclusion

Although about half of the testers are vague about the concept of sustainable fashion, nearly 80% of the testers have a positive attitude towards sustainable fashion and hope that enterprises or businesses can inform them of the sustainable attributes of goods. Under the premise of not specifying the shopping mode (physical store and online shopping) and the purpose of buying (with or without a clear purchase goal), testers have obvious preference for QR code labels. Similarly, when shopping in online stores, testers still prefer QR code labels with or without a clear purchase goal, but in the form of online shopping, most testers prefer color labels with or without a clear purchase goal, while the popular QR code labels are not popular.

In the process of buying fashion goods in physical stores, the application of QR code tags has become a field worthy of in-depth study. In the future, we will focus on the research of sustainable QR code labels, and strive to design a QR code label that is popular with consumers.

References

1. Lee, L., Inglis, P.: Sustainable Revolution in the fashion industry and environmental protection. Fashion Beijing (04), 197–2011 (2019)
2. Carson, R., Ruilan, L., Changsheng, L.: Silent Spring. Jilin People's Publishing House (1997)
3. Jian, W., Juan, W.: Initiation of the concept of "sustainable development" and its significance-review of "Our Common Future." J. Tongren Univ. **16**(6), 4 (2014)
4. Turunen, L., Halme, M.: Communicating actionable sustainability information to consumers: the Shades of Green instrument for fashion. J. Clean. Prod. **297**(14), 126605 (2021)

Xian Metaverse - Extended Reality Technology Enabling Digital Economy in Commercial Neighborhoods

Jing Liang, Xiaofeng Ni[✉], and Fan Chen

Tongji University, No.1239 Siping Road, Shanghai 200092, China
alkovski0415@gmail.com

Abstract. Augmented reality is being applied in various fields. By combining digital content with the real world, information and data are instantly available, improving users' efficiency. However, since currently most augmented reality researches focus mostly on small indoor spaces (e.g., museums, classrooms), discussing the application of augmented reality as a technology in urban management such as digital economy, cultural heritage seems to be a research gap. In this paper, we will explore the design challenges of augmented reality application for cities and its contribution to the urban environment, digital economy and cultural heritage of cities by presenting Xian Yuan Universe, an augmented reality design project for a commercial street.

Keywords: Extended Reality · Urban Environment · Digital Economy

1 Introduction

With the release of Apple's spatial computing device, Vision Pro, a variety of spatial computing and reality augmentation technologies have returned to the public eye. Extended Reality (XR) is a three-dimensional immersive environment supplemented with multi-sensory information and feedback. XR solutions are categorized according to the range of digital content, from reality (extended reality) to virtual reality, and mixed reality in between [6]. Over the past decade, XR technologies have complemented human reality, greatly expanding the limits of the evolving human-computer interface. XR is becoming useful in everyday life as highly sophisticated XR technologies become more powerful, efficient, economical and refined [15].

XR technology opens new avenues for creating virtual content in urban environments and has the potential to fundamentally change the way we create and experience urban environments [44]. However, there is a research gap on how XR technology can be utilized to create immersive urban experiences that allow users to better explore the cultural heritage and enjoy the convenient features of the city.

This paper aims to fill this research gap by exploring the potential of Extended Reality technology in urban spaces. The article first reviews the literature related to the application of XR technology in the field of urban design and presents a vision of the

C. Stephanidis et al. (Eds.): HCII 2024, CCIS 2118, pp. 20–29, 2024.
https://doi.org/10.1007/978-3-031-61963-2_3

future XR city. Subsequently, the paper adopts a research by design (RtD) approach to introduce an extended reality neighborhood project implemented by our team in Taizhou, China, in the aspects of R&D process and application functions. Finally, the paper discusses the opportunities and limitations faced by XR technology in urban design, providing suggestions for further research in this area.

2 Literature Review

For a long time, theories of urban spatial cognition mainly focus on the field of urban geography, and people pay more attention to the morphology, structure and layout of the city, such as Ernest Burgess's concentric zone model [47] and Walter Christaller's central place theory [39]. In 1960, Kevin Lynch published his book The Image of City, in which he studied urban residents' perception of the urban environment through questionnaires and other research methods. He concluded that people who experience cities have a set of corresponding mental images in their minds, which he categorized as Paths, Edges, Districts, Nodes and Landmarks [48]. However, this emotional perception may change with the development of multimedia technologies. Manovich proposed the concept of augmented space for this purpose, arguing that technological applications such as surveillance, cellular space, and electronic displays have turned physical space into data space, and that spatial and informational layers play equally important roles in the level of human cognition [49]. It can be envisioned that for future city dwellers, the overall image of the city will be heavily influenced by multimedia (electronic screens, expanded reality) information and experiences.

In the field of urban design, there are already a number of researchers assisting civic decision-making and urban crisis response through immersive means such as mixed reality. For example, Weronika Szatkowska et al. create a safe simulation environment for designing and testing new decisions through immersive and serious games that allow participants to learn and understand the workings of a complex system, the city, through hands-on experience [7]. Yavo-Ayalon et al. combine a virtual reality system with a bus tour, where participants sit in a bus wearing a headset to show the impacts of flooding on the island [9].

There is still a gap in the research on how extended reality technology can change the urban environment and thus the experience and perception of urban residents. How can the virtual space layer be more closely integrated with the real space to create a better city experience for people and even enhance regional development? This paper adopts a research by design (RtD) approach to realize the research results through a extended reality application project.

3 Development

Located in Huangyan District, Taizhou City, Zhejiang Province, China, Guanhe Water Street is a commercial street along the river created by the local government, with the purpose of inheriting the culture of the Song Dynasty and enhancing the local tourism industry. The project uses a combination of extended reality art and digital video to create a digital street "Xian Yuan Universe" with local cultural styles, aiming to inherit and promote the local culture of the Song Dynasty while stimulating the economic development of the neighborhood.

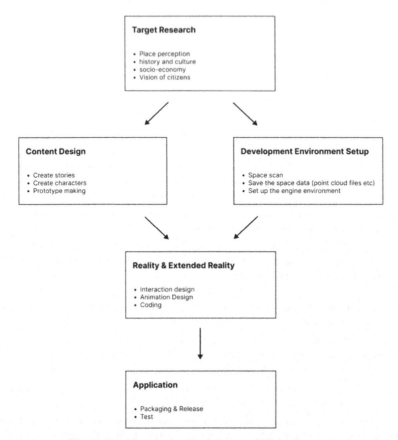

Fig. 1. Workflow in the development of Xian Metaverse

Figure 1 depicts the workflow in the development of the Xian Metaverse project. The project started with target research. According to Muratovski's theory [46], the research began with both desktop research and field research. The team first surveyed the neighborhood to create a preliminary spatial awareness of the neighborhood. Then, in order to better understand the local culture, the team members read the local documentaries as well as folk stories, visited museums, conducted interviews with locals, and finally confirmed the four cultural keywords. The designers used them as references for content design, which includes story creation, character creation, and prototype producing.

The development environment was set up in parallel with the content design. Engineers used devices such as drones and cell phones to scan the neighborhood spatially and collect point cloud files. These point cloud files were later uploaded to Huawei's cloud server, and converted into 3D models for subsequent creation and development processes (see Fig. 2).

Fig. 2. Point cloud files

The integration and development of the application is done in the Unity engine (see Fig. 3). In this step, art resources, particle effects, and interactive content are integrated into the unity scene according to a pre-completed content plan. The dynamic material effects of the resources are written in HLSL and the interactive content is written in C#. After the scene is built, the engineers package it in the form of unitypackage and publish it to the server for testing and debugging.

Fig. 3. Creation in Unity Engine

During the testing session, team members were equipped with cell phones that had pre-installed the software to walk around the block. They would see if the virtual resources were positioned accurately and without errors. Software compatibility with different devices was also an important consideration, as it was necessary to ensure that the software was available to most people.

4   Functions

Xian Metaverse provides users with three main experiences: AR performances, digital street scene and interactive activities.

4.1 AR Performances

In addition to the XR tech, the street also contains performances that combine multi-media forms such as 3D mapping, water projections, naked-eye 3D screens, and light shows. The performance is based on the narration between four characters, showing the local history, customs, celebrities, and technological development. Users can also watch this performance in their cell phones using the XR application, through which characters and scenes are no longer confined to a two-dimensional screen, but interact with the user up close and personal (Fig. 4).

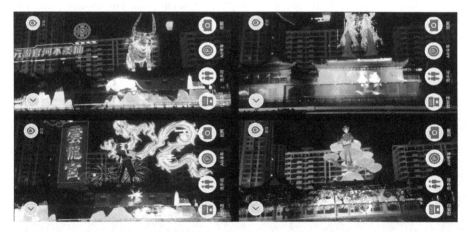

Fig. 4. AR performances

4.2 Digital Street Scene

Each store in the street is decorated with virtual signboards or advertisements. Users can click on the signboards in the virtual scene to inquire about the store's products, profiles, and other related information. Indoor and outdoor extended reality content is also articulable. Our team designed one of the coffee shops in the virtual world so that a virtual character greets and interacts with the user at the entrance of the store and allows the user to order by clicking on the menu, food models in the scene (Fig. 5).

4.3 Interactive Activities

The application provides users with interactive content such as the Interactive Wall and the Red Packets. The interactive wall is a virtual interactive space where users can write and post comments, which will be reviewed and posted as virtual pop-ups on the virtual wall visible to all users. The Red Packets, on the other hand, is refreshed at any time at any location in the neighborhood, and by clicking on the red packets in the virtual scene, users can get coupons for neighborhood stores.

Fig. 5. Indoor XR decorations

In addition, Xian Metaverse also accesses users' information with their privacy authorization and personalizes virtual scenes based on users' information. For example, as the user consumes more and more in the street, the virtual scene will become more abundant. Users of different ages and genders will also gain different virtual effects.

5   Discussion

In this project, we designed a digital XR application to explore the new potential of XR technology for residents to experience the urban environments. In previous research on extended reality applications, urban design has often been overlooked due to the high complexity of the multiple systems involved. At the end of the design project, we discuss the significance of the project's concept, the optimization of the development workflow, and the limitations of the existing technology.

5.1   XR Applications for Offline Consumption

Mixed reality applications often overlap with game design research due to their entertainment properties. Therefore, the consumption behavior of users in games can also be analogized to that in XR applications. Video games often provide users with a more refined gaming experience through consumption such as in-game purchases or DLC packages. In XR applications, virtual retailing can be considered in conjunction with offline retailing to promote the economy. Initial attempts have been made in Xian Metaverse. Electronic menus or hidden products are placed in the virtual scene for users to explore. As the user consumes more, the content of the virtual scene will be enriched.

5.2   New Interdisciplinary Teamwork Methodology

The development of Xian Metaverse involves a variety of fields, including urban design, spatial design, graphic design, software engineering, etc. However, the skills, tools, and even the way of thinking required by the creators are completely beyond the traditional education system. This is because in the process of project creation, the creators have to take into account both the real space and the virtual space, and also need to cooperate across disciplines to ensure the implementability of the project. This poses a new challenge to the teamwork approach of mixed reality application creation: project managers need to have more comprehensive and integrated interdisciplinary knowledge and capabilities to effectively assess the team's workflow and work efficiency; while creators need to balance realistic thinking and virtual eyesight, and possess the ability to accomplish interdisciplinary collaboration. During the design and development process, creators need to integrate and explore dynamic and diverse knowledge from multiple domains in order to create innovative and valuable systems [43].

5.3 Limitations

During the UX process, we identified many user experience low points. We believe these low points are due to limitations of the current software or hardware. The Xian Yuan Universe application is deployed on cell phones for reasons of availability to most users. Devices such as cell phones suffer from a smaller field of view, higher battery energy consumption, and poor portability in the actual touring experience. Powerful functionality, portability products like XR glasses may come out in the future. However, current hardware technology is difficult to drive the development and popularization of such products. In addition, problems such as low stability of point cloud recognition and loss of pose detection during fast movement are also easily triggered in the actual usage. These problems require the updating of computer vision recognition algorithms.

6   Conclusion

Using a research through design(RtD) approach, this paper presents an XR digital street project in Taizhou, China. The project demonstrates the possibilities of extended reality technology to enhance the urban environment and improve the experience of the urban residents. The project showcases the local history, culture, and technological development through a combination of AR performances, digital street scene, and interactive activities, providing a customized experience for the users based on their basic information, consumption data etc. Such extended reality applications based on urban environments also pose new challenges to creators during deployment and development. For creators, more interdisciplinary knowledge and more integrated capabilities are required to embrace new collaborative workflows when creating XR applications. Research has shown that extended reality applications can not only enhance urban environments and integrate urban culture into the civic experience, but also promote offline economy through, for example, integration with offline retail.

References

1. Herbert, G., Chen, X.: A comparison of usefulness of 2D and 3D representations of urban planning. Cartogr. Geogr. Inf. Sci. **42**, 22–32 (2015). https://doi.org/10.1080/15230406.2014.987694
2. LaLone, N., A. Alharthi, S., Toups, Z.O.: A vision of augmented reality for urban search and rescue. In: Proceedings of the Halfway to the Future Symposium 2019. pp. 1–4. Association for Computing Machinery, New York, NY, USA (2019). https://doi.org/10.1145/3363384.3363466

3. Symeonidis, S., et al.: An extended reality system for situation awareness in flood management and media production planning. Electronics **12**, 2569 (2023). https://doi.org/10.3390/electr onics12122569

4. Lin, J., Cao, L., Li, N.: Assessing the influence of repeated exposures and mental stress on human wayfinding performance in indoor environments using virtual reality technology. Adv. Eng. Inform. **39**, 53–61 (2019). https://doi.org/10.1016/j.aei.2018.11.007

5. Suzuki, R., Karim, A., Xia, T., Hedayati, H., Marquardt, N.: Augmented reality and robotics: a survey and taxonomy for AR-enhanced human-robot interaction and robotic interfaces (2022)

6. Milgram, P., Takemura, H., Utsumi, A., Kishino, F.: Augmented reality: a class of displays on the reality-virtuality continuum. In: Telemanipulator and Telepresence Technologies, pp. 282–292. SPIE (1995). https://doi.org/10.1117/12.197321

7. Szatkowska, W., Wardaszko, M.: Between urban resilience and serious gaming: applying games for policy implementation. In: Dhar, U., Dubey, J., Dumblekar, V., Meijer, S., Lukosch, H. (eds.) Gaming, Simulation and Innovations: Challenges and Opportunities, pp. 223–238. Springer International Publishing, Cham (2022). https://doi.org/10.1007/978-3-031-09959-5_19

8. BIM Based Virtual Environment for Fire Emergency Evacuation. https://www.hindawi.com/journals/tswj/2014/589016/. Accessed 03 Nov 2023

9. Yavo-Ayalon, S., Joshi, S., Zhang, Y., Han, R., Mahyar, N., Ju, W.: Building community resiliency through immersive communal extended reality (CXR). Multimodal Technol. Interact. 7, (2023). https://doi.org/10.3390/mti7050043

10. Meerow, S., Newell, J.P., Stults, M.: Defining urban resilience: a review. Landsc. Urban Plan. **147**, 38–49 (2016). https://doi.org/10.1016/j.landurbplan.2015.11.011

11. Park, S., et al.: Design and implementation of a smart IoT based building and town disaster management system in smart city infrastructure. Appl. Sci. **8**, 2239 (2018). https://doi.org/10.3390/app8112239

12. Ye, X., et al.: Developing human-centered urban digital twins for community infrastructure resilience: a research agenda. J. Plan. Lit. **38**, 187–199 (2023). https://doi.org/10.1177/088 54122221137861

13. Aina, Y.A., Abubakar, I.R., Almulhim, A.I., Dano, U.L., Maghsoodi Tilaki, M.J., Dawood, S.R.S.: Digitalization and smartification of urban services to enhance urban resilience in the post-pandemic era: the case of the Pilgrimage City of Makkah. Smart Cities. 6, 1973–1995 (2023). https://doi.org/10.3390/smartcities6040092

14. Rokhsaritalemi, S., Sadeghi-Niaraki, A., Choi, S.-M.: Exploring emotion analysis using artificial intelligence, geospatial information systems, and extended reality for urban services. IEEE Access. **11**, 92478–92495 (2023). https://doi.org/10.1109/ACCESS.2023.3307639

15. Levy, J., Liu, D.: Extended Reality (XR) environments for flood risk management with 3D GIS and open source 3D graphics cross-platform game engines: advances in immersive sea level rise planning technologies for student learning and community engagement. In: Arya, K.V., Tripathi, V.K., Rodriguez, C., Yusuf, E. (eds.) Proceedings of 7th ASRES International Conference on Intelligent Technologies, pp. 271–285. Springer Nature, Singapore (2023). https://doi.org/10.1007/978-981-99-1912-3_25

16. Sermet, Y., Demir, I.: Flood Action VR: a virtual reality framework for disaster awareness and emergency response training. Presented at the August 1 (2018). https://doi.org/10.1145/3306214.3338550

17. Kamel Boulos, M.N., Lu, Z., Guerrero, P., Jennett, C., Steed, A.: From urban planning and emergency training to Pokémon Go: applications of virtual reality GIS (VRGIS) and augmented reality GIS (ARGIS) in personal, public and environmental health. Int. J. Health Geogr. **16**, 7 (2017). https://doi.org/10.1186/s12942-017-0081-0

18. Frontiers | Immersive virtual reality field trips facilitate learning about climate change. https://www.frontiersin.org/articles/10.3389/fpsyg.2018.02364/full. Accessed 02 Nov 2023

19. Frontiers | Improving climate-change literacy and science communication through smart device apps. https://www.frontiersin.org/articles/10.3389/feduc.2019.00138/full. Accessed 04 Nov 2023

20. Fox, N., Campbell-Arvai, V., Lindquist, M., Van Berkel, D., Serrano-Vergel, R.: Gamifying decision support systems to promote inclusive and engaged urban resilience planning. Urban Planning. 7 (2022). https://doi.org/10.17645/up.v7i2.4987

21. Qiu, D., Lv, B., Chan, C.M.L.: How digital platforms enhance urban resilience. Sustainability 14, 1285 (2022). https://doi.org/10.3390/su14031285

22. Thaeppunkulngam, A., Jamieson, I., Tontisirin, N., Suebsuk, N.: Investigation of extended reality technologies as architectural and urban design tools for water-related disaster planning and mitigation investigation of extended reality technologies as architectural and urban design tools for water-related disaster planning and mitigation. Presented at the June 25 (2020)

23. Rydvanskiy, R.: Mixed reality interfaces in flood risk management. https://summit.sfu.ca/item/20829. Accessed 24 Oct 2023

24. Haynes, P., Hehl-Lange, S., Lange, E.: Mobile augmented reality for flood visualisation. Environ Model Softw. 109, 380–389 (2018). https://doi.org/10.1016/j.envsoft.2018.05.012

25. Corbisiero, F., Monaco, S.: Post-pandemic tourism resilience: changes in Italians' travel behavior and the possible responses of tourist cities. Worldwide Hospitality and Tourism Themes 13, 401–417 (2021). https://doi.org/10.1108/WHATT-01-2021-0011

26. Quagliarini, E., Currà, E., Fatiguso, F., Mochi, G., Salvalai, G.: Resilient and user-centered solutions for a safer built environment against sudden and slow onset disasters: the BE S2ECURe project. In: Littlewood, J., Howlett, R.J., Jain, L.C. (eds.) Sustainability in Energy and Buildings 2020, pp. 309–319. Springer, Singapore (2021). https://doi.org/10.1007/978-981-15-8783-2_26

27. Shih, N.-J., Qiu, Y.-H.: Resolving the urban dilemma of two adjacent rivers through a dialogue between GIS and augmented reality (AR) of fabrics. Remote Sens. 14, 4330 (2022). https://doi.org/10.3390/rs14174330

28. Neppalli, V.K., Caragea, C., Squicciarini, A., Tapia, A., Stehle, S.: Sentiment analysis during hurricane sandy in emergency response. Int. J. Disaster Risk Reduction. 21, 213–222 (2017). https://doi.org/10.1016/j.ijdrr.2016.12.011

29. Chittaro, L., Sioni, R.: Serious games for emergency preparedness: evaluation of an interactive vs. a non-interactive simulation of a terror attack. Comput. Hum. Behav. 50, 508–519 (2015). https://doi.org/10.1016/j.chb.2015.03.074

30. Oh, D., Phillips, F.Y., Mohan, A.V.: Smart City 2.0: strategies and innovations for city development. World Scientific (2023)

31. Blascovich, J., Loomis, J., Beall, A.C., Swinth, K.R., Hoyt, C.L., Bailenson, J.N.: TARGET ARTICLE: immersive virtual environment technology as a methodological tool for social psychology. Psychol. Inq. 13, 103–124 (2002). https://doi.org/10.1207/S15327965PLI1302_01

32. Elkins, D.N.: The human elements of psychotherapy: a nonmedical model of emotional healing. Am. Psychol. Assoc. Washington, DC, US (2016). https://doi.org/10.1037/14751-000

33. Peres, E., du Plessis, C., Landman, K.: Unpacking a sustainable and resilient future for Tshwane. Procedia Engineering. 198, 690–698 (2017). https://doi.org/10.1016/j.proeng.2017.07.120

34. Rzeszewski, M., Orylski, M.: Usability of WebXR visualizations in urban planning. ISPRS Int. J. Geo-Inf. 10, 721 (2021). https://doi.org/10.3390/ijgi10110721

35. Zhu, Y., Li, N.: Virtual and augmented reality technologies for emergency management in the built environments: a state-of-the-art review. J. Safety Sci. Resilience 2, 1–10 (2021). https://doi.org/10.1016/j.jnlssr.2020.11.004

36. Stone, N., et al.: Virtual reality for hazard mitigation and community resilience: an interdisciplinary collaboration with community engagement to enhance risk awareness. AIS Trans. Hum.-Comput. Interact. **13**, 130–144 (2021). https://doi.org/10.17705/1thci.00145

37. Portalés, C., Lerma, J.L., Navarro, S.: Augmented reality and photogrammetry: a synergy to visualize physical and virtual city environments. ISPRS J. Photogramm. Remote Sens. **65**, 134–142 (2010). https://doi.org/10.1016/j.isprsjprs.2009.10.001

38. Krauß, V., Boden, A., Oppermann, L., Reiners, R.: Current practices, challenges, and design implications for collaborative AR/VR application development. In: Proceedings of the 2021 CHI Conference on Human Factors in Computing Systems, pp. 1–15. Association for Computing Machinery, New York, NY, USA (2021). https://doi.org/10.1145/3411764.344 5335

39. Barnes, T.J.: "Desk Killers": Walter Christaller, Central Place Theory, and the Nazis. In: Meusburger, P., Gregory, D., Suarsana, L. (eds.) Geographies of Knowledge and Power, pp. 187–201. Springer Netherlands, Dordrecht (2015). https://doi.org/10.1007/978-94-017-9960-7_9

40. Makris, D., Moira, M.: Enhancing places' identities with augmented reality and novels. 5 (2018)

41. Marji, N., Thibault, M., Hamari, J.: Fantastical reality: designing virtual urban space through extended reality. Presented at the April 12 (2023)

42. Duarte, F., Firmino, R.J.: Infiltrated city, augmented space: information and communication technologies, and representations of contemporary spatialities. J. Archit. **14**, 545–565 (2009). https://doi.org/10.1080/13602360903187493

43. Sonnenwald, D.H.: Knowledge exploration in design: boundary spanning roles and strategies. Proc. ASIS Ann. Meeting **32**, 200–207 (1995)

44. Liao, T., Humphreys, L.: Layar-ed places: using mobile augmented reality to tactically reengage, reproduce, and reappropriate public space. New Media Soc. **17**, 1418–1435 (2015). https://doi.org/10.1177/1461444814527734

45. Rzeszewski, M., Naji, J.: Literary placemaking and narrative immersion in extended reality virtual geographic environments. Int. J. Digital Earth. **15**, 853–867 (2022). https://doi.org/10.1080/17538947.2022.2061619

46. Muratovski, G.: Research for designers: a guide to methods and practice, 1–100 (2021)

47. Burgess, E.W.: "The Growth of the City: An Introduction to a Research Project": from Robert Park et al., The City (1925). In: The Urban Geography Reader. Routledge (2005)

48. Lynch, K.: The Image of the City. MIT Press (1964)

49. Manovich, L.: The poetics of augmented space. In: Kronhagel, C. (ed.) Mediatecture: The Design of Medially Augmented Spaces, pp. 304–318. Springer, Vienna (2010). https://doi.org/10.1007/978-3-7091-0300-5_26

50. Zimmerman, J., Forlizzi, J.: Research through design in HCI. In: Olson, J.S., Kellogg, W.A. (eds.) Ways of Knowing in HCI, pp. 167–189. Springer New York, New York, NY (2014). https://doi.org/10.1007/978-1-4939-0378-8_8

Cultural Differences in Landing Page Informational Design of Business and Leisure Hotel Between Taiwan and Netherlands

Chih-Yen Lin[(⊠)] [iD] and Tseng-Ping Chiu [iD]

National Cheng Kung University, No.1, University Road, Tainan City 701, Taiwan
{p36121049,mattchiu}@gs.ncku.edu.tw

Abstract. In the digital age, with the Internet being central to our lives, this research shifts focus from luxury hotels to business and leisure hotels, catering to the Y and Z generations. We aim to explore the preferences of customers from diverse cultural backgrounds when accessing landing pages of these hotels. Two experiments will be conducted: one from an operator's perspective, examining landing page compositions across different countries, and the other from the customer's viewpoint, exploring visual preferences. Through these experiments, we seek to understand how cultural factors influence information preferences on landing pages, providing targeted recommendations to operators to better meet the needs of diverse consumers and enhance conversion rates.

Keywords: User Experience · Landing Page Performance · Cultural Variations · Cultural Cognition · Consumer Behavior · Hospitality Industry

1 Introduction

In the 21st century, the Internet is vital for hotels, serving as a global bridge. Before its widespread adoption, customers relied on traditional methods like calls or travel agencies, limiting their reach. With the Internet's rise in the mid-1990s, hotels swiftly established websites, expanding their reach globally [1–3].

First impressions, significantly impact conversion rates, particularly when customers are unfamiliar with a business [4]. The Landing Page of a hotel's website serves as a crucial strategic element in such scenarios. A well-designed Landing Page is the initial screen visitors encounter after clicking from online sources like ads or social media. It aims to attract visitors, deepen their impression, and encourage actions like reservations or contacting customer service [5]. In essence, a Landing Page is a goal-oriented guide that drives desired actions from visitors.

The study found that economy hotels are increasingly popular in both Eastern (see Fig. 1) [6] and Western countries (see Fig. 2) [7]. This trend, influenced by factors like inflation and employment challenges, is driven by younger generations (Gen Y and Gen Z) prioritizing budget and cost-effectiveness in accommodation choices, making economy hotels a significant lodging option in the market.

C. Stephanidis et al. (Eds.): HCII 2024, CCIS 2118, pp. 30–40, 2024.
https://doi.org/10.1007/978-3-031-61963-2_4

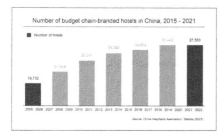

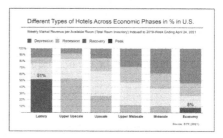

Fig. 1. The growth rate of economy hotels in China. [6] Image redrawn from this study.

Fig. 2. The economic downturn of economy hotels in the United States from 2019 to 2021. [7] Image redrawn from this study.

This study explores the evolving accommodation needs by focusing on business and leisure hotels favored by young professionals and leisure travelers. It examines how cultural constraints in Eastern and Western cultures affect the design of hotel websites and their appeal to international travelers, aiming to offer recommendations for improved design and consumer satisfaction.

2 Literature Review

2.1 Website Function and Quality

The Core Position and Evolution of Website Functionality. Website functionality evolves based on [8] web application development framework, which considers diverse website content in design [9]. In hotels, functionality is assessed by user needs during bookings, covering facility details, reservations, contact info, local insights, and management [10]. Transitioning from static Web 1.0 to interactive Web 2.0, hotels focus on user-generated content (UGC) for authentic information and entertainment [11]. They integrate features like online concierge services and social media for enhanced user interaction and shareable experiences, reflecting current digital trends [12, 13].

Effect of Website Quality on Consumer Online Intentions for Business and Leisure Hotels. The Internet is vital for business and leisure hotels, offering a cost-effective marketing platform that maintains competitiveness. Understanding consumer usage intentions is key to establishing an excellent website platform. Website quality, as highlighted by [14], involves four dimensions: intuitive interfaces, optimized speed, easy information location, aesthetics, interactive fun, completeness, integration with social media, membership programs, and image consistency [15, 16]. Leveraging these dimensions enhances user experience, leading to high satisfaction and engagement.

Evaluating Landing Page Elements. The Landing Page is crucial for website success and optimizing it for better conversion rates involves several key elements. The company logo should be strategically placed to build trust. Textual content should be powerful, conveying information quickly and evoking emotions. The Unique Value Proposition (UVP) should highlight key features concisely to communicate benefits effectively. In the Hero Shot, clear presentation of product features reduces uncertainty, while storytelling creates emotional engagement. Trust is built through certification badges and recognizable faces. Pricing and promotions attract customers. Lastly, the Call-to-Action (CTA) design should be clear, guiding users to the next step and boosting conversion rates [17].

2.2 Cross-Cultural Research

East-West Culture: Self-Concept Differences. Eastern and Western cultures differ significantly in self-perception due to their respective philosophies and religions [18]. In Eastern cultures influenced by Confucianism, Taoism, and Buddhism, individuals emphasize interdependence and collective responsibility. Conversely, Western cultures prioritize individual rights and freedoms, as seen in "The Social Contract" [19]. These cultural disparities influence how people view themselves and their relationships, with Eastern cultures emphasizing collective interests, relationships, and harmony. In contrast, Western cultures valuing individual rights, freedom, and achievements.

East-West Culture: Thinking Style. Eastern and Western cultures exhibit different cognitive styles, analytical and holistic, linked to their natural and social environments. Analytical thinking focuses on individual objects, associated with an independent self, while holistic thinking considers context and relationships, associated with an interdependent self [20].

Cultural Differences in Consumer Behavior and Information Preferences. Culture significantly influences consumer behavior, with individualistic cultures driven by personal preferences and collectivist cultures emphasizing social influences [21]. In the East and West, advertisers employ differing strategies; American advertisers focus on direct brand communication to aid individual decision-making, while Japanese advertisers prioritize emotional appeals akin to friendships, using methods like stories and aesthetics [22]. Overall, cultural influences, especially in individualistic and collectivist cultures, predict behavioral differences in hotel choices. Individualistic cultures prefer personalized services and unique experiences, while collectivist cultures prioritize social factors and shared experiences, shaping hotel selection tendencies.

Indulgence versus Restraint: Hedonism and Utilitarianism. Geert Hofstede's cultural dimensions model, especially the Indulgence versus Restraint (IVR) dimension, is relevant to this study's investigation of how Landing Page visuals affect customer behavior. IVR reflects a society's tolerance for indulgent behaviors, with indulgent societies allowing more freedom for pleasure pursuits and restrained societies emphasizing self-control [23].

Data from Hofstede Insights shows that Eastern countries like Japan and Taiwan tend to have lower IVR values (42 and 49 points), preferring self-restraint and value for money. In contrast, Western countries like the United States or the Netherlands tend to have higher IVR values (both have 68 points), favoring indulgence and personal enjoyment [24].

2.3 Hotel Information Preferences of Travelers

Strategies for Hotel Landing Page Design for East and West Travelers. In cultural studies, proposed five dimensions of travel-related information: utilitarianism, risk avoidance, indulgence, sensation seeking, and sociability, categorized into functional cognition and experiential pursuit [25]. Utilitarian information provides factual descriptions, used for daily life risk management [26]. Conversely, travelers seek experiential information for new destinations, with indulgence enhancing trip expectations [27]. This aligns with (Hofstede, 2011) and the Indulgence dimension, suggesting countries prioritize utilitarian information for lower indulgence and experiential for higher tendencies [24]. Hotels can use this to design landing pages for diverse cultural needs.

3 Hypotheses

Three hypotheses are proposed in this study. Firstly, due to lower hedonic desires and a focus on cost-effectiveness among Eastern audiences, it is expected that Eastern landing pages lean more towards utilitarian aspects compared to Western counterparts (H1). Secondly, individualistic audiences are expected to prefer hedonic images and narratives compared to collectivistic audiences (H2a). In contrast, collectivistic audiences are expected to prefer utilitarian images and narratives compared to individualistic audiences (H2b).

4 Study 1

In the first study, we'll analyze Landing Pages of economy-class hotels in Taiwan and the Netherlands, with similar GDP per capita but different cultures. We aim to explore their content and design differences, considering the impact of Eastern and Western cultures. We expect (a) Dutch hotel pages to prioritize visual entertainment, while (b) Taiwanese pages will focus more on comprehensive information, reflecting a stronger emphasis on utilitarian aspects.

4.1 Method

This study analyzes Moxy Hotel's Landing Page, a three-star business and leisure hotel under Marriott International, collecting data from two hotels in Taiwan and four in the Netherlands. We examined elements like the Hero image, Main Headline, subhead, CTA, Navigation buttons, and Logo, aiming to understand their relative distribution and assess user experience across Eastern and Western regions.

4.2 Results

The first study found that Moxy Hotels in the Netherlands heavily emphasize the hero image, accounting for an overwhelming 99.4%. The remaining portion is allocated to the operational experience through Navigation buttons, constituting 0.6% (see Table 1).

In Taiwan, the hero image still dominates but to a lesser extent (M = 71.03%), with additional textual content (Main Headline M = 2.33%, The supporting subhead M = 5.97%), CTA (M = 1.51%), and Navigation buttons (M = 0.26%). This provides evidence that in the Taiwan region, business and leisure hotels offer a more diverse range of content elements on their Landing Page, not limited solely to visual presentation but emphasizing detailed information and user experience. This supports our hypothesis 1 that websites in the Eastern region may tend to emphasize utilitarianism.

Table 1. The proportion of elements on the landing page of Dutch Moxy Hotels.

Landing Page	Hero Shot	Navigation buttons
Amsterdam Houthavens Page	99.44%	0.56%
Amsterdam Airport Page	99.44%	0.56%
Hague Page	99.44%	0.56%
Utrecht Page	99.44%	0.56%

Table 2. The proportion of elements on the landing page of Taiwan Moxy Hotels.

Landing Page	Hero Shot	Main headline	Supporting subhead
Taichung Page	65.61%	2.01%	3.37%
Hsinchu Page	79.16%	2.80%	9.87%

Call to Action	Navigation buttons	Logo
2.30%	0.30%	0%
0.33%	0.21%	1.34%

5   Study 2

In Study 1, we examined how the landing page format of business leisure hotels affects businesses. Transitioning to Study 2, we focused on consumer perspectives to understand preferences for visual and informational elements on landing pages. Our aim is to explore cross-cultural differences in consumer perceptions and behaviors regarding landing page displays. We anticipate that (a) individualistic consumers will prefer visually engaging elements highlighting entertainment and personal experiences, while (b) collectivistic consumers will prioritize specific and practical information fostering a group atmosphere (see Table 2).

5.1   Method

Material. This study used Two-Way Between-Subjects ANOVA for statistical analysis, considering two main factors: (a) Indulgence degree and (b) Self Cognition, each with two levels; for (a), the levels were Hedonic and Utilitarian, and for (b), the levels were Independent and Interdependent. Visual elements like hero shots depicted hedonic and utilitarian aspects (e.g., contra. Sting entertainment facilities with room configurations), while textual elements conveyed narratives of independent and interdependent self-cognition (e.g., personal enjoyment versus family and friends' gathering) (see Fig. 4). Logos or brand certifications were excluded to avoid influencing the results (see Fig. 3).

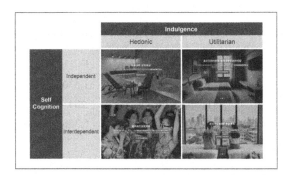

Fig. 3. The example of Two-Way Between-Subjects ANOVA of Study 2.

Participants. This study recruited 137 participants from Generation Y and Z, aged between 18 and. 40 (M_{age} = 27.05, 32.85% male, 67.15% female).

Procedure. Participants will complete a two-part questionnaire. Firstly, they will undergo a Two-Way Between-Subjects ANOVA based on birthdates, viewing images and responding to ten questions assessing psychological processes post-visual stimuli on the Landing Page, focusing on Attention and Interest. Questions are designed based on the AIDMA scale [28], with the first six addressing Attention and Interest and the next four serving as a Manipulation Check. Responses are on a five-point Likert scale. Secondly, participants will fill out the Psychological Collectivism scale to evaluate individualism and collectivism tendencies on a seven-point Likert scale, providing insights into their psychological characteristics.

5.2 Results

Attention. Through Two-Way Between-Subjects ANOVA, we analyzed the impact of indulgence and self-cognition on different facets of Attention, including visual page caught attention (see Table 3), text Content caught Attention (see Table 4), and visual page caught the eye (see Table 5). Results revealed that, for visual page caught attention, the main effects of indulgence (F (1,136) = 1.530, p = .218) and self-cognition (F (1,136) = .204, p = .652, partial η2 = .002) were not significant. However, a significant interaction effect was observed between indulgence and self-cognition (F (1,136) = 6.380, p = .013). In terms of text content caught attention, the main effects of indulgence (F (1,136) = .316, p = .575) and self-cognition (F (1,136) = .012, p = .913) were not significant. Nevertheless, a significant interaction effect was noted (F (1,136) =

4.611, p = .013). For visual page caught the eye, the main effects of indulgence (F (1,136) = .234, p = .629) and self-cognition (F (1,136) = .388, p = .534) were not significant. However, a significant interaction effect was observed (F (1,136) = 3.892, p = .051). The data suggest that indulgence and self-cognition do not independently influence these dependent variables. Nevertheless, a significant interaction effect exists, suggesting that under specific conditions, the impact of indulgence and self-cognition collectively influences these dependent variables.

Table 3. Dependent Variable: Visual page caught attention of Study 2.

Source	df	Mean Square	F	p	partial η2
Indulgence	1	.751	1.530	.218	.011
Self-Cognition	1	.100	.204	.652	.002
Indulgence * Self-Cognition	1	3.133	6.380	.013	.046

Note: * means p < 0.05

Table 4. Dependent Variable: Text content caught attention of Study 2.

Source	df	Mean Square	F	p	partial η2
Indulgence	1	.222	.316	.575	.002
Self-Cognition	1	.008	.012	.913	.000
Indulgence * Self-Cognition	1	3.234	4.611	.034	.034

Note: * means p < 0.05

Table 5. Dependent Variable: Visual page caught the eye of Study 2.

Source	df	Mean Square	F	p	partial η2
Indulgence	1	.139	.234	.629	.002
Self-Cognition	1	.230	.388	.534	.003
Indulgence * Self-Cognition	1	2.310	3.892	.051	.028

Note: * means p < 0.05

Based on the post-hoc test results, when self-cognition is interdependent, and indulgence is hedonic, visual page caught attention significantly outperforms utilitarian scenarios (p = .009). Conversely, in situations with self-cognition as independent and indulgence as hedonic, visual page caught attention is lower than utilitarian scenarios, though not significantly (p = .364) (see Fig. 5). Similar trends are observed for text content caught attention in interdependent, hedonic (p = .057) versus independent, hedonic (p = .265) scenarios (see Fig. 6), and visual page caught the eye in interdependent, hedonic (p = .054) versus independent, hedonic (p = .295) scenarios (see Fig. 7). These findings highlight the nuanced influence of self-cognition and indulgence on attention.

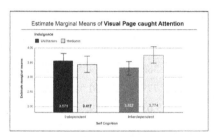
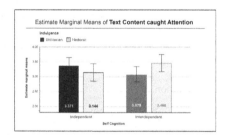

Fig. 4. Estimate Marginal Means of Visual Page caught Attention of Study 2.

Fig. 5. Estimate Marginal Means of Text Content caught Attention of Study 2.

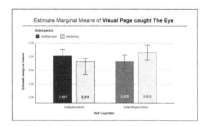

Fig. 6. Estimate Marginal Means of Visual Page caught The Eye of Study 2.

Interest. Through Two-Way Between-Subjects ANOVA, we analyzed the impact of indulgence and self-cognition on different facets of Interest, including curious (see Table 6), and impression (see Table 7). Results revealed that, for curious, the main effects of indulgence (F (1,136) = .950, p = .331) and self-cognition (F (1,136) = .110, p = .740) were not significant. Nevertheless, a significant interaction effect was noted (F (1,136) = 4.168, p = .043). For impression, the main effects of indulgence (F (1,136) = .380, p = .539) and self-cognition (F (1,136) = .777, p = .380) were not significant. However, a significant interaction effect was observed (F (1,136) = 5.630, p = .019). The data indicate that indulgence and self-cognition do not exert independent effects on curious and impression—these dependent variables. However, a notable interaction effect emerges, signifying that, under specific conditions, the combined influence of indulgence and self-cognition for curious and impression collectively impacts these dependent variables.

Table 6. Dependent Variable: Curious of Study 2.

Source	df	Mean Square	F	p	partial η2
Indulgence	1	.694	.950	.331	.007
Self-Cognition	1	.081	.110	.740	.001
Indulgence * Self-Cognition	1	3.046	4.168	.043	.030

Note: * means p < 0.05

Table 7. Dependent Variable: Impression of Study 2.

Source	df	Mean Square	F	p	partial η2
Indulgence	1	.254	.380	.539	.003
Self-Cognition	1	.519	.777	.380	.006
Indulgence * Self-Cognition	1	3.766	5.630	.019	.041

Note: * means p < 0.05

Based on the post-hoc test results, when self-cognition is interdependent, and Indulgence is hedonic, curious significantly outperforms utilitarian scenarios (p = .035). Conversely, in situations with self-cognition as Independent and indulgence as hedonic, curious is lower than utilitarian scenarios, though not significantly (p = .364) (see Fig. 8).

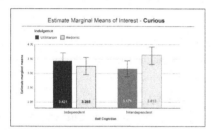 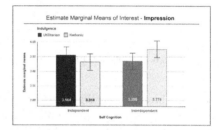

Fig. 7. Estimate Marginal Means of Curious of Study 2.

Fig. 8. Estimate Marginal Means of Impression of Study 2

6   Conclusion and Discussion

Based on the first case study of Landing Pages for business and leisure hotels in the Netherlands and Taiwan, notable conclusions were drawn. The Dutch Landing Page emphasizes visual presentation, primarily focusing on the hero image, while the Taiwanese Landing Page incorporates more content, including text, calls to action, and navigation buttons, offering a richer experience. This suggests that the Eastern region prioritizes detailed information and user experience over mere visual appeal. Further analysis supports Hypothesis 1, indicating that Eastern Landing Pages emphasize utility due to lower sensory pleasure demands and a focus on cost-effectiveness. This reflects a cultural preference in the East for practicality and information completeness, distinguishing it from Western cultures emphasizing sensory experiences.

The second study initially expected individualistic viewers to prefer hedonistic visuals and narratives, while collectivistic viewers would prioritize utilitarian aspects. However, the results showed that both indulgence and self-construal did not independently impact attention and interest. Instead, an interaction effect between indulgence and self-construal was observed, suggesting a shared influence on visual page engagement.

Specifically, participants with interdependence tendencies and a preference for hedonism were more attracted to visual pages. Conversely, those with independent self-construal and a leaning towards utilitarianism showed better performance in capturing attention and interest. In summary, contrary to the initial hypothesis, viewers with a collectivistic inclination, characterized by interdependence, are more attracted to the entertainment and emotional appeal of visual pages, while individualistic viewers prioritize specific hotel information, considering sensory and entertainment elements less important.

Overall, these two studies provide valuable insights into understanding the preferences of people for Landing Pages of business and leisure hotels in different cultures and individual traits. This has practical implications for hotel businesses designing web pages and advertisements that cater to the diverse needs and preferences of global audiences.

References

1. Bonn, M.A., Furr, H.L., Susskind, A.M.: Using the internet as a pleasure travel planning tool: an examination of the sociodemographic and behavioral characteristics among internet users and nonusers. J. Hosp. Tourism Res. **22**(3), 303–317 (1998)
2. Walle, A.: Tourism and the internet: opportunities for direct marketing. J. Travel Res. **35**(1), 72–77 (1996)
3. Weber, K., Roehl, W.S.: Profiling people searching for and purchasing travel products on the world wide web. J. Travel Res. **37**(3), 291–298 (1999)
4. Potts, K.: Web Design and Marketing Solutions for Business Websites. Apress (2007)
5. Harwood, M., Harwood, M.: Landing Page Optimization for Dummies. John Wiley & Sons, Hoboken (2009)
6. China Hospitality Association, & Website (sgpjbg.com). (June 21, 2022). Number of budget chain-branded hotels in China from 2015 to 2021 [Graph]. In: Statista. Retrieved February 28 (2024). https://www.statista.com/statistics/1131191/china-number-of-budget-hotels/
7. STR. U.S. Market Recovery Monitor (2021). https://www.hospitalitynet.org/news/4104191.html
8. Lu, M.T., Yeung, W.I.: A framework for effective commercial web application development. Internet Res. **8**(2), 166–173 (1998)
9. Gretzel, U., Yuan, Y.-L., Fesenmaier, D.R.: Preparing for the new economy: advertising strategies and change in destination marketing organizations. J. Travel Res. **39**(2), 146–156 (2000)
10. Chung, T., Law, R.: Developing a performance indicator for hotel websites. Int. J. Hosp. Manage. **22**(1), 119–125 (2003)
11. Krumm, J., Davies, N., Narayanaswami, C.: User-generated content. IEEE Pervasive Comput. **7**(4), 10–11 (2008)
12. Perdue, R.R.: Internet site evaluations: the influence of behavioral experience, existing images, and selected website characteristics. J. Travel Tour. Mark. **11**(2–3), 21–38 (2002)
13. Bender Stringam, B., Gerdes, J., Jr.: Are pictures worth a thousand room nights? Success factors for hotel web site design. J. Hosp. Tour. Technol. **1**(1), 30–49 (2010)
14. Li, L., Peng, M., Jiang, N., Law, R.: An empirical study on the influence of economy hotel website quality on online booking intentions. Int. J. Hosp. Manage. **63**, 1–10 (2017)
15. Aziz, N.S., Kamaludin, A.: Assessing website usability attributes using partial least squares. Int. J. Inf. Electron. Eng. **4**(2), 137 (2014)
16. Loiacono, E.T., Watson, R.T., Goodhue, D.L.: WebQual: a measure of website quality. Mark. Theory Appl. **13**(3), 432–438 (2002)

17. Hubert, T.: 11 Landingpage Elemente im Bewertungsraster (2010). http://www.konversionsk raft.de/landing-pageoptimierung/11-landingpage-elemente-imbewertungsraster.html
18. Dov Cohen, S.K.: Handbook of Cultural Psychology (2019)
19. Rousseau, J.-J.: Basic political writings (2011)
20. Nisbett, R.E., Peng, K., Choi, I., Norenzayan, A.: Culture and systems of thought: holistic versus analytic cognition. Psychol. Rev. **108**(2), 291 (2001)
21. Markus, H.R., Kitayama, S.: Culture and the self: implications for cognition, emotion, and motivation. In: College Student Development and Academic Life, pp. 264–293. Routledge (2014)
22. Miracle, G.E.: Feel-do-learn: an alternative sequence underlying Japanese consumer response to television commercials. In: The proceedings of the 1987 Conference of the American Academy of Advertising, pp. R73−R78 (1987)
23. Hofstede, G.: Dimensionalizing cultures: the Hofstede model in context. Online Read. Psychol. Cult. **2**(1), 8 (2011)
24. Hofstede, G.: Country comparison tool (2023). https://www.hofstede-insights.com/country-comparison-tool
25. Cho, M.-H., Jang, S.: Information value structure for vacation travel. J. Travel Res. **47**(1), 72–83 (2008)
26. Holbrook, M.B.: Beyond attitude structure: toward the informational determinants of attitude. J. Mark. Res. **15**(4), 545–556 (1978)
27. Vogt, C.A., Fesenmaier, D.R.: Expanding the functional information search model. Ann. Tour. Res. **25**(3), 551–578 (1998)
28. Wei, P.-S., Lu, H.-P.: An examination of the celebrity endorsements and online customer reviews influence female consumers' shopping behavior. Comput. Hum. Behav. **29**(1), 193–201 (2013)

Designing 3D Avatar Influencer for Live Streaming Interactions

Alvaro Lourenço(✉) ⓘ, Everton Aleixo, Matheus Nogueira ⓘ,
Raphael Moraes ⓘ, Beatriz Dutra, Gabriele Penalber, and Mauro Teófilo

Sidia, Manaus, Brazil
{alvaro.lourenco,everton.aleixo,matheus.nogueira,raphael.moraes,
beatriz.dutra,gabriele.penalber,mauro.teofilo}@sidia.com

Abstract. Presents topics on the conception of overall style and behavior, along with technical and publishing factors impacting the craft of a humanly credible 3D avatar for the context of the digital influencer industry. The use of motion capture and mobile apps as controllers for the 3D avatar are discussed, engendering questions on the fit of those technologies with the processes of the marketing industry, specially amidst the theme of style consistency. Live natural interactions between humans and human-controlled avatars were practiced during Samsung Live Commerce, a special news series aired from 5 countries across Latin America, reporting some unstructured results on the avatar performance. The course of building/using the technology for commercial purposes is finally discussed along with literature to understand the most important futures for SAM-Live sequels.

Keywords: Avatar · Digital influencer · Live streaming · Motion capture

1 Introduction

That girl in the Fig. 1 is SAM. She was devised by training teams of Samsung's SEDA and LAO units back in 2020. The avatar was publicized within Samsung's marketing endeavors for Latin America, starting from Black Friday 2021. SIDIA hereby reports on SAM-Live: the building of real-time technologies onto this particular avatar, using AI but not scoping it as in recent discussions of these particular tools [1]. The specific significance of SAM-Live is the experience of a real interaction exercise with virtual humans [2] in a commercial setting of live events, which happened in January 2023.

Fig. 1. SAM: Samsung digital influencer.

Work supported by Sidia, R&D founded by Samsung.

The original version of the chapter 5 has been revised. Address of the Institutional affiliations of the Authors has been corrected. A correction to this chapter can be found at https://doi.org/10.1007/978-3-031-61963-2_45

The work is not particularly relevant for using a credible human digital avatar in the context of the digital influencer industry -a number of evident characters/branding already made that [3]- but mainly for the creation of live mediated instances of interaction between humans and humanized avatars within a controlled setting. "SAM-Live" technology gave a prosaic appearance for SAM during human mediated live streams, interpreting "life as usual" behaviors of an young girl created to appeal for the generation Z, publicized as environmentally aware, engaged with fashions and innovations, being multi-athletic and technology enthusiast, highly opinionated in e-sports, and of course a sponsored fan of Samsung products [4].

A number of authors stated the efficiency of using influencers [3,5] and avatars [6–8] in marketing campaigns along the past two decades, but a tenable theory for this field is still reported as absent these days [3,8]. Even fewer empirical studies are on the topic of "live" natural interactions between humans and avatars. And within the setting limitations of the live special news events (Samsung Unpacked 2023), the findings gleaned useful parallels between the available science and concerns found along the craft of SAM's technology. An attempt to achieve science's presumable gains, while avoiding some known investment pitfalls [3].

This work discusses the conception of overall style [8], including specifics of artistic processes and their performance in runtime software; particular controls for a real human avatar; and overall range of applicability of attained results [9], with some measurements. It describes a case study of building a technology that allowed live, natural and human level conversations between humans and humanly operated virtual avatars, underscoring the craft of style and manifestation of the character rather than discussing ways of building artificial personality to it. A deterministic neural network was indeed applied for specific features like lip syncing, but AI was entire and intentionally eschewed for building conversations, mainly because they followed strict and shifting marketing guidelines.

2   The Drivers for Appearance and Personality

SAM-Live builds into SAM the abilities support the work of digital influencers: a marketing strategy proven to raise levels of trust, loyalty, perceived authenticity and interactions between consumers and brands [5]. However, studies on the novel influencer trend often lack the live-streaming part of the job, maybe due to the recency of its popularization, and arguably the meager extent of this activity within the role. That would possibly justify the scarcity of foundational theory addressing the effects of live-streaming on user participation, perception, identity and behavior building.

This is just the opposite for digital avatars: in which effects on human interactions and shopping behavior are fairly studied. Discussions are generally split between concerns of appearance and personality, and the implications of these in users behaviors/responses. Appearance was found to be typically driven by visual approach, realism, attractiveness and cuteness, whereas personality is laid upon character's narrative, its content approach, authority, and behavior. Effects ranges widely from specific emotions to complex social identity dynamics.

For appearance, avatars might not be necessarily graphic [10], but anthropo-morphism is stated to impact interlocutory judgements favorably, even given the human inclination to assign human traits to non-human entities. Even without consensus over form [3], "form realism" does raise expectations to interact [8], frequency of interaction overtime [10], eventually triggering affective responses [11]. Among shoppers, attractive characters are persuasive at intermediate levels of involvement, and expert characters persuade better in higher levels of involve-ment [6]. The term "beauty" is often skipped as an indicator of avatar appearance, but the discernment between "cute" and "strange" relates respectively to higher or lower intensity of interactions with users [12].

Personality mixes concerns over content niches and backstories, picturing a dependence between character traits and interaction effects. The authority (savviness) of avatars reaches superior persuasion levels after some time building involvement. The backstory [3] and the social nature of contents [8] accelerate the user interactions. Models are proposed to identify/pivot between influencer profiles and strategy according to their maturity, market context and desired results, usually contrasting key attributes: authoritative vs exploratory (domain breadth), intimate vs impersonal (social presence), entertaining vs informative (content approach) [13]. Decisions on story, social availability, content approach and domain, beget distinct personalities that implicates in different relationships with the audience. Authors generally converge in a factor of "behavior realism" [8], arguably much more important than "form realism" itself.

The effects of behavior realism (BR) are always non trivial. Alone BR ensures higher level of responses to character stories [8]. It outperforms "form realism" (FR) responses, sometimes even "fixing" substandard FR [14]. BR also has knack to bridge "uncanny valleys", raising interactions regardless of the involved FR. So often BR is reported as a core decision of making avatars that humane control is considered consequent to its communication performance [2,8,10]. It drives audience's reactions, judgements, attributions, beliefs, and attitudes, to a point that some caution is indeed prescribed when replacing avatar's operators [10].

As avatar's "behavior realism" drives users interactions, an investigation of perceptions, attitude, etc., within the game industry revealed profound influence on behavior as well. Relationships between avatars and virtual objects [7] affect the social interaction dynamics, and adjacently, the use of avatars for merchan-dising impacts shopping behavior as well [6]. Avatars reach advanced levels of social influence by eliciting the "Proteus effect" [12]: a phenomena in which peo-ple conform to the mental model of particular avatar, with observable impacts on their self-expression and social relatedness to others in a group [15]. Not enough, avatars can cause intense emotional attachment [5], eventually reaching actual infatuation episodes [11].

These last findings comes from specific industries, but convenient intercon-nections between general reports can still be explored. Object-attachment and social self-identification effects, change on shopping behaviors, emotional reac-tions, or the ability to transfer expectations [15] and behaviors [11] to real life. Avatars are definitely laid out along with favorable prospects for SAM to explore in its live marketing venture.

Driver group	Driver topic as found in literature review	Mkt led	Audience reaction					Driver score
			favourable judgements ★★★★	higher interactivity ★★★★★★★	higher persuasion ★★★	higher Influence ★★★	better communication ★★★★★	
Other	human control		✓	✓		✓	✓	17
Appearance	form realism		✓	✓				9
Appearance	cuteness			✓				5
Personality	behavior realism			✓				5
Other	virtual objects					✓		3
Appearance	attractiveness				✓			2
Personality	anthropomorphism	✓	✓	✓				9
Personality	story / narrative	✓		✓				5
Personality	social content	✓		✓				5
Appearance	visual approach	✓	✓					4
Other	time building involvement	✓			✓			2
Personality	authority	✓			✓			2

Fig. 2. Rationale used to spot the concerns of SAM's appearance and behavior.

Findings on prior literature were plotted, ranked and analyzed to spot responsibilities for SAM-Live project (Fig. 2), which is part of a broader marketing endeavor. "Drivers" for SAM-Live (within the black outline) were appraised by "audience reactions" (relevance expressed between 1 to 5 stars), following project objectives. The final "driver score" ranked the main topics of attention of our avatar, originating the final selection with the minimum score of 5 (above the red line). The lesser ones were saved for a 2nd iteration of SAM-Live.

3   The Course to Define a Real-Time Approach

Prior science leaned project to use human operation as a "gold strategy" to maximize behavior realism, and trigger a range of responses between audiences and SAM. In form realism, team should not deviate from SAM's visual style, which was taken as a comfortable limit: not entirely but just sufficiently realistic in order to build levels of realistic behavior. Initially, there was the expectation to successfully enable a complete live operation of SAM, through a motion capture solution available in company: the Rokoko's "Full Performance Suit II" [16]. Several unsuccessful iterations of implementing it however culminated in the adoption of a mixed approach: motion captured and animated.

The motion capture (mocap) solution [16] revealed a big number of imperfections, making it impracticable to completely rely on the tool in order to build real-time controls. Tracking for the face worked; the motion data for head, neck, spine, and pelvis were usable *after* post capturing work; but shoulders, elbows, legs, hands and fingers were remarkably inconsistent with the captured movement (example in Fig. 3). In the lesser part in which these were usable, they still presented some (seemly human) spring-like bounces at the end of movements, which was considered artistically detrimental to the stylized appearance of SAM, stressing it towards the "uncanny valley" for being "excessively real". All given, team ultimately found ways to work with the "assistance" of the mocap tool, instead of using it as a direct solution to control all avatar behavior.

The unreliable mocap solution [16] for live real-time control connects to the art pipeline with a plugin - Rokoko Studio- that is not extensible enough to allow debugging of configuration issues, eventually patching a way to fix the solution. It is closed-source and supplier did not have enough information about causes for the problem. The complexity of such algorithms and errors outreached the project team's expertise,

Fig. 3. Motion capture inconsistency in the avatar, before and after applied fixes.

but some authors indeed reported success building simpler and reliable markerless solutions from few sensors and/or low dimensional control signals [17]. It *could not* be rocket science, but the available plugin only transposed the captured information to the avatar, including the errors baked into animated keyframes, so no workarounds were made.

The mixed approach to mocaps inevitably required a prebuilt animation library of every avatar reaction. The approach would involve manual work, but was surprisingly on top of the opinions of the most leaders, not for its simplicity or superiority over the mocap solutions, but mainly for the behoof of style consistency. This opinion appeared when co-designing and testing prototypes with the marketing team, with the worry that the mocap would handle just too much of SAM's personality to a multi-country set of operators, thus leading to inconsistent body language for SAM across countries. A strategy was set to centralize all motion capturing in a single person, assuming the actor dependency as a natural finding of SAM-Live project. One that went unpredicted by project plan and prior literature review.

The available mocap solution [16] was not entirely dropped, having its provided behaviors cherry picked by the animators to perform a mixed approach: part motion captured, part artist and computer animated. This bundled the qualities of the reliable part of mocaps, with another portion of revised/rebuilt mocap animation to cover the unreliable parts. Figure 4 summarizes the approach taken to maximize behavior realism, given such context and resources.

Group	Mocap data	Quality	Approach
A	facial expressions	reliable	use as is, excluding group B
B	mouth, gaze, blinks	reliable	replace with procedural animations
C	head, neck, spine, pelvis	partly reliable	improve mocap result, use as guide for group D
D	shoulders, elbows, legs, hands, fingers	unreliable	replace with keyframe animation

Fig. 4. Summary of behavior decisions based on mocap quality.

The separation of behaviors in groups considered that gestures from group D drive avatar communication, whilst identity is generally ruled by how SAM moved its torso (group C). This discernment allowed, for instance, the identification of a masculine or feminine actor using SAM. So as the group C went only partially used, it played an important assistance role when timing and framing the animations created in the group D. Behaviors from the group A -sourced from Apple's extensive set of face anchors [18], were transferred without issues onto the avatar, excluding those used in SAM's procedural parts (group B).

The team explored some behavior independence in ways to ease decision-making complexity [9] and allow operators to orchestrate reactions with concurrent animations. To lower SAM proficiency requirements the group B automated most of the independent animations: blinks played randomly within restricted time intervals; gaze followed the camera with the option to be "unlocked" and defaulted to mocap data [19] -by user choice and automatically- after a certain threshold of head rotation (to avoid awkward "side staring" poses). Head was centered by default, with options to look sideways.

Lips were special and required a deterministic neural network built from tagging four phonemic classes (o, a, th, f) atop of mocap's blendshapes [19]. After training these tags against their respective audio source the model became able to determine mouth blendshape values for any audio wave, delivering sufficient realism even in the absence of additional phonemic classes (b, e, i, m, p).

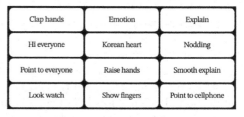

Fig. 5. Actions available for SAM.

These approaches to the challenge of behavior independence allowed for sufficient behavior realism, and counterbalanced the need to train the operators. Idle movements were set to a random and non-repeatable set of animations concurrent with all specific communication actions of group D (Fig. 5). And with a great deal of animations being automatic, "Actions" became almost the sole concern of SAM operators, thus lowering their learning curve.

4   The Technical Quirks and Its Consequences

The implementation nudged project decisions as findings appeared. Mocap limitations entailed the creation of animations groups (Fig. 4), those groups defined the animation scope (Fig. 5), the production pipeline, and all required technology assistance. Likewise, game engine definition came after comparing visuals and simulation of Unity and Unreal, with clearly advantages of the latter: hair, cloth, lighting and shading (Fig. 6). With every technology assessed, the overall software architecture was put as the available in Fig. 7.

These progressive decisions narrowed the avatar's applicability [9] -i.e.: Many times SAM is harshly animated in order to attain frontal appearance goals, generating untreated glitches in the backside cannot be seen within current usage settings. This limited SAM-Live, as a prosaic guise for an avatar otherwise portrayed as an active globetrotter and k-pop dancer. The weight of prior decisions will certainly impact over the addition of new behaviors, and next versions would need to revisit decisions, perhaps from as early as the mocap phase.

This progression also implied on unplanned changes in the expected workflow of the team, with some deserved mentions on the issues of having to isolate behaviors out of mocap data, clean and ease of its animation curves; and dealing with scarce documentation of Unreal's visual programming tool. The unforeseen tasks were managed as risks along the project.

Fig. 6. Decision to use Unreal over Unity, after hair and appearance benchmark.

5   An Avatar Controller for a Fragmented User Base

Section 3 presents the mobile controller as a strategy for style consistency, but as SAM was utilized by Samsung groups across Latin America, the crafting of the controller also needed to make them use. The culture entangled in such operation, however, hopped several actors onto SAM production. Executive, scripting, voiceover, acting, post-production, all influence SAM at some point, often not in a predictable fashion. So

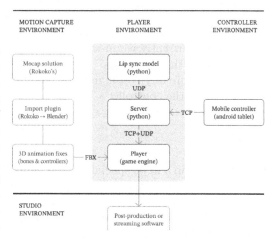

Fig. 7. Software architecture for SAM-Live.

project ultimately witnessed SAM-Live capabilities being appropriated in many ways, and some not always for complete live purposes.

The controller approach purposefully constrained the avatar's manners and behaviors, in order to allow different countries to use the voiceover artist already selected for their specific campaigns, typically paired with the work of a copywriter. This implied however on a variety of pre-production schemes: ideas for a speech raised by executives was sometimes handled to the voiceover artist, leaving SAM operators with no copywrite input to assist on the selection of SAM's actions; other times even with copywriters work, specific instructions for SAM's actions went entirely amiss, leaving operators no options other than to perform SAM "free style"; sometimes the screen feed would come directly from SAM's player to the broadcast, but sometimes it would go through post-production beforehand; at times SAM's live speeches were not only pre-recorded but also pre-interpreted, leaving the team guessing how much of this production profile would come from existent dynamics of TV studios, or from eventual interaction issues when using the proposed controller (Fig. 8).

For that, users of the controller were listened in the pursuit of improvement opportunities. The most frequent requirement were surprisingly for clothing (constrained to 6 distinct looks). The second and last major requirement was about controlling the Actions, with half mentions approving the controller, and other half splitting between: 1) improved controls to switch actions, and 2) direct operation of the hands, which currently is animated along with the actions.

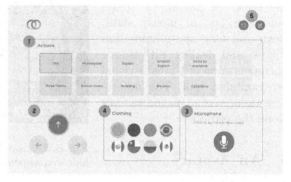

Fig. 8. SAM Live controller UI where the user: 1) Tap+holds to perform actions; 2) Tap+holds to look sideways; 3) Taps to toggle lip-sync.

1 and 2 relate directly to the mocap limitations faced (Sect. 3), with 1 targeting at least partly the controller's UI.

6   Results

SAM went live in 5 news special events held by Samsung in Brazil, Mexico, Chile, Peru and Paraguay, aired aside Samsung's Unpacked event in February 2023 [20]. Shows were typically broadcast in social platforms, moderated by a presenter, in which SAM figured as a remote participant from other "virtual" studio, sometimes even from world's iconic places (e.g.: Fig. 9). SAM generally commented the announcements and the special offers defined by country commerce teams, bantering along with humans.

Fig. 9. SAM's live broadcast streamed from many locations, including at King Sejong's statue (inventor of Korean alphabet), at Gwanghwamun Square boulevard in Seoul.

As a commerce tool, SAM-Live did not organized country units in one arching study about its performance, generally eliciting comments and measurements sparsely from Samsung teams and tools. The appearance of SAM in Live Commerce online streams was measured, and reports showed a persistent increase in positive comments along the shows, with undisclosed positive repercussions on sales. These findings allude exclusively to internal data, which was not obtained in a structured study, so they serve only as an evidence of results yielded from SAM-Live project.

7   Discussion

SAM Live stands as a case report on building avatars from premises of common software teams. Demonstrates how caveats were worked as the team amassed experience on simpler grade of motion capture technologies, and its limitations. Presents how the individualization of avatar behaviors emerged as a group strategy upfront framed to orient production and operationalize behaviors of the avatar. And within that work, how motion capture in general should be considered as a managed risk for projects within analogue settings.

Reviewed literature in topics of avatars in influencer/marketing, its animation concerns, the social/emotional implications of its interactions with humans- was indeed able to anticipate some cruxes of the work: the pivotal role of behavior realism in triggering higher levels of interactions; form realism as marginal and even dependent of its behavior counterpart; the contrasting abundance of material concerning avatar building and use, with the scarce info on live-influencer marketing with avatars. The early studies unfortunately missed apparent relationships between the avatar craft and specifics of animation processes, specially when using motion capture technologies.

Project continuation revealed further discussions of building technical and operational strategies to uphold style consistency when scaling the avatar operations globally. The subject involves implications between art direction and level of expected form realism, revealing incidental incompatibility with certain motion capture processes, particularly when encountering the predicament of "too much realism" (Sect. 3). Team digressed over the existence of a technology to "filter" the excessively human movements into more cartoonish variants, which was not encountered in a brief contextual search.

SAM-Live also demonstrated that -for sakes of economy or style consistency- there are alternatives for commercial avatars outside the full-natural control through mocap body data, bringing forth varied levels of technology complexity. Examples of it in the big number of simple animations used, the simpler "look-at" automations made for head and eye, and the more advanced neural networks trained to manage the mouth. That attempts to simplify may pose a viable strategy to reduce the complexity of controllers, even when considering supervening hindrances when adding more independent behaviors. That the challenge of applicability diversification [9] can relate to the coverage offered through case-by-case adjustments of the solution, which often delineate specific contexts of use, rather than a multi-purpose use of the technology.

There were minor discoveries on undesired restrictions of introducing SAM to new 3D objects and environments, due to prior project setup and decisions. The pressing need to relate the avatar with devices and utilities has been molding discussions about new phases for the project. This has already encompassed the addition of phones, watches and buds animations to SAM, but as those animations become more complex, it shall be beneficial to inspect deeper references on the influence of avatars when working identity through virtual objects, which had lesser appearance in this study [7].

8   Next Steps

The main concern of SAM Live still around issues of style consistency and actor dependency/replacement, which involves challenges on unifying personality of voice and movement. A voice cloning algorithm is being assessed to allow consistent voice timbre, so that any voiceover media can sound just alike regardless of voiceover actor. Regarding movement, the endeavors are to select one professional performer/actor to elevate SAM Live appearances to a non-prosaic level, more compatible with the idol figure SAM became [21].

Second topic is enriching SAM's attitude regarding other objects and scenes. This allows deeper engagement with audiences, and tentatively in non mediated communication through live streams. Some improvements on the mocap technology and current solution architecture will eventually be necessary.

Third topic is enhancing SAM's controls while preserving the fruitful automation strategy. The team is testing natural interactions to allow face controls to

SAM in real-time, right from mocap equipment. The bet is that this might amplify behavior realism dramatically, as it directly enriches the performance of the face. In parallel, there is a number of experiments to feed audio with spoken sentences through AI, in order to automatically trigger SAM's behaviors (actions and face expressions).

References

1. Nah, F.F.-H., Zheng, R., Cai, J., Siau, K., Chen, L.: Generative ai and chat-gpt: applications, challenges, and ai-human collaboration. J. Inform. Technol. Case Appli. Res. **25**, 277–304 (2023)
2. Badler, N.I.: Real-time virtual humans. pages 4–13. IEEE Comput. Soc (1997)
3. Moustakas, E., Ranganathan, C., Lamba, N., Mahmoud, D.: Perspectives of experts on marketing effectiveness of virtual influencers, Blurring lines between fiction and reality (2020)
4. Sarfraz, H.: Meet sam - samsung's enthralling virtual influencer (June 2023)
5. Jun, S., Yi, J.: What makes followers loyal? the role of influencer interactivity in building influencer brand equity. J. Product Brand Manag. **29**, 803–814 (2020)
6. Holzwarth, M., Janiszewski, C., Neumann, M.M.: The influence of avatars on online consumer shopping behavior. J. Market. **70**, 19–36 (2006)
7. Nagy, P., Koles, B.: My avatar and her beloved possession: characteristics of attachment to virtual objects. Psychol. Market. **31**, 1122–1135 (2014)
8. Miao, F., Kozlenkova, I.V., Wang, H., Xie, T., Palmatier, R.W.: An emerging theory of avatar marketing. J. Market. **86**, 67–90 (2022)
9. Badler, N.I., Palmer, M.S., Bindiganavale, R.: Animation control for real-time virtual humans (1999)
10. Nowak, K.L., Fox, J.: Avatars and computer-mediated communication: a review of the definitions, uses, and effects of digital representations on communication. Rev. Commun. Res. **6**, 30–53 (2018)
11. Bopp, J.A., Müller, L.J., Aeschbach, L.F., Opwis, K., Mekler, E.D.: Exploring emotional attachment to game characters. pp. 313–324. Association for Computing Machinery, Inc, (Oct 2019)
12. Freeman, G., Maloney, D.: Body, avatar, and me: the presentation and perception of self in social virtual reality. Proc. ACM Hum.-Comput. Interact. **4**, 1 (2021)
13. Gross, J., Wangenheim, F.V.: The big four of influencer marketing. a typology of influencers (April 2018)
14. Seymour, M., Riemer, K., Kay, J.: Interactive realistic digital avatars-revisiting the uncanny valley. In: Proceedings of the 50th Hawaii International Conference on System Sciences (2017)
15. Messinger, P.R., Smirnov, K., Bone, M.: Virtual worlds research: Consumer behavior in virtual worlds on the relationship between my avatar and myself (2008)
16. Rokoko ROW. Full performance capture (2023)
17. Chai, J., Hodgins, J.K.: Performance animation from low-dimensional control signal (2005)
18. Rokoko ROW. Rokoko's face captur (2024)
19. Apple Inc. Apple arface blend shapes (2024)
20. Samsung Brasil. Samsung | galaxy live shop (July 2023)
21. Cheil. Sam - flip your way (official music video) (2023)

Research on IP Image Design of New Tea Drinks Brands Based on Kansei Engineering

Xinyuan Ma, Lishan Rao, and Zhijuan Zhu[✉]

School of Mechanical Science and Engineering, Huazhong University of Science and Technology, Wuhan, People's Republic of China
zhuzhijuan@hust.edu.cn

Abstract. With the increasing homogenization of products in the new tea drinks industry and the change of consumers' emotion driven consumption, IP based brands has become an inevitable trend for the upgrading of new tea drinks brands, and IP image design is an important part of it. However, designers lack design guidelines with few theoretical studies on IP image design for new tea drinks brands when practicing.

Therefore, based on Kansei Engeering (KE), the mapping relationship between consumer preferences and IP image of new tea drinks brands is established through quantitative data; the corresponding design basis and evaluation indexes are given; the key design elements for IP image design of new tea drinks brands are provided; new possibilities of IP image design of new tea drinks brands are explored.

Keywords: IP Image Design · Kansei Engineering · new tea drinks brands · Semantic Differential evaluation

1 Introduction

1.1 Background

In recent years, product homogenization in the new tea drinks industry has become more and more intense, while consumer groups increasingly prioritize emotional purchase experience. Therefore, many new tea drinks brands have begun actively exploring IP (IP, Intellectual Property) based brands [1] to upgrade their brands and achieve differentiation.

New tea drinks are composed of premium whole leaf tea (mainly black tea and oolong tea) as its core ingredient, supplemented with milk, fruits, cream, crushed nuts, and other additional materials. Compared with traditional tea drinks, they have a comprehensive upgrade in marketing promotion, brand development and other aspects. With the help of the Internet and new media tools, they employ a mindset geared towards creating viral products, principles of communication, and modern corporate management strategies for refined management and branding operations [2].

C. Stephanidis et al. (Eds.): HCII 2024, CCIS 2118, pp. 52–60, 2024.
https://doi.org/10.1007/978-3-031-61963-2_6

Consumer perception of brand IP during product purchases is inherently subjective. To quantify it and establish an evaluation model, the application of Kansei Engeering (KE) proves indispensable. KE is a tool to convert customer perceptions into tangible product parameters, and provide support for future product design [3].

1.2 Research Overview

Since 2015, China has entered the first year of IP based brands marketing, witnessing the rapid emergence of the marketing value associated with brand IP. However, there remains a dearth of theoretical research concerning IP based brands of new tea drinks brands both domestically and internationally. Only a handful of literature pieces regarding IP based brands are available for reference.

In "Development Strategies of Cross-Border Marketing for Brand IP", Li, W. (2017) [4] emphasizes that to evoke cultural satisfaction and spiritual resonance among consumers, brands must adopt a content-oriented, emotional approach, which is essentially IP based brands. In "IP Based Brands", Li, Z. (2018) [5] argues that not all brands are inherently IP, but they have the potential to evolve into one, and IP represents the advanced stage of brand evolution. Ning, Y. (2019) [6] analyses the visual design characteristics of brand IP and summaries them as follows: personalized cartoon characters, narrative and interactive elements, and brand extensibility.

Currently, research on KE in the field of brand IP image design is exceedingly rare, and its research methodology is not widely employed in this domain.

Xu, X. (2008) [7] summarized the core content of various network image design concepts and extracted the KE factors in each concept, but did not involve the study of brand IP image design. Zhu, Z. (2018) [8] analyzed the principles of brand logo design and studied the impact of the three dimensions on brand logo design, namely, "attention & memory", "industry matching" and "visual preference". Then they constructed a model of brand logo design and evaluation based on KE. The evaluation system was examined in multiple directions, which is clear, rigorous and scientific, and has reference value for the IP image design of new tea drinks brands. Pan, W. (2021) [9] used the semantic differential method to study the mapping relationship between perceptual imagery adjectives and each sample, and determined the CMF design elements of Bluetooth speakers based on the experimentally derived mapping relationship. Finally, she verifies the feasibility of this method and process through the speaker appearance design project of Sanji Audio Technology Co., Ltd. We believe that the research process and design practice process are worth learning.

In conclusion, this paper initially explored the research of KE in the IP image design of new tea drinks brands, which has certain research significance.

1.3 Content and Framework

The research content and framework of this paper is as follows (see Fig. 1. Research Framework).

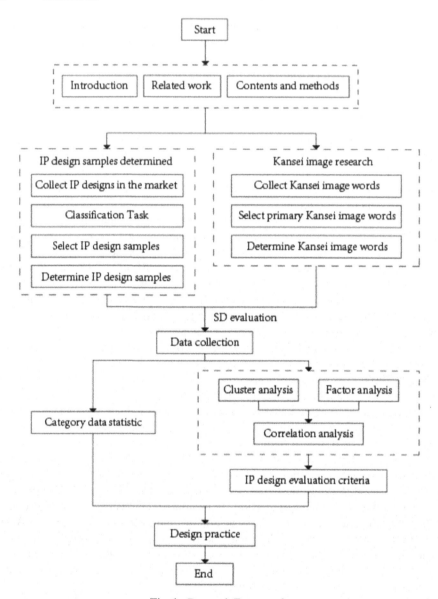

Fig. 1. Research Framework

2 Research Process and Interpretation

Through the collection, collation and comparison of a large amount of data, 8 representative samples were identified from the existing IP images of 34 new tea drinks brands in the Chinese market (Table 1), and 10 representatives pairwise Kansei words were identified from 61 pairwise Kansei words (Table 2).

Table 1. Determined representative samples of IP design

Representative samples of IP design Sn (Total: 8)

S1	S2	S3
S4	S5	S6
S7	S8	

Table 2. The 10 pairwise Kansei image words

	Pairwise Kansei words		Pairwise Kansei words
A1	Restrained-vivid	A6	Colorless-colorful
A2	Chilly-lovely	A7	Complex-simple
A3	Hard-soft	A8	Traditional-fashionable
A4	Changeable-unified	A9	Hard to recall-easy to recall
A5	Single-varied	A10	Dislike-like

The representative samples and Kansei words constitute the Semantic Differential Scale (Table 3), and the quantitative data of participants' subjective feelings towards the representative samples are obtained (Fig. 2. Line chart of the mean of the image scores for 8 samples). A total of 130 participants aged 18–25 years participated in the questionnaire survey.

Table 3. Example of the SD scale questionnaire

	-2	-1	0	1	2	
Restrained	O	O	O	O	O	Vivid

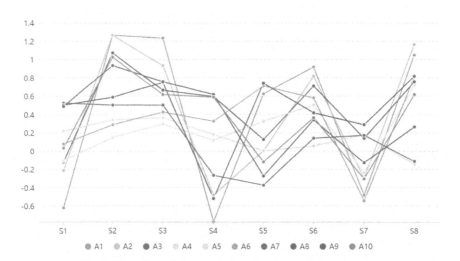

Fig. 2. Line chart of the mean of the image scores for 8 samples

3 Results and Discussion

SPSS statistical software was used to analyze the survey results. Firstly, the relationship between these 9 variables is explored by cluster analysis method. Then, the factor analysis is used to find common factors to achieve dimensionality reduction. Finally, the correlation analysis is used to determine whether there is a correlation between these common factors and IP preferences.

Taking 9 pairwise Kansei image words as variables of cluster analysis, the results are shown in Fig. 3. Cluster result of 9 pairwise Kansei words, indicating that 9 pairwise Kansei image words can be divided into 3 groups: ① A1, A2, A3, A5, A6; ② A8; ③ A4, A7, A9.

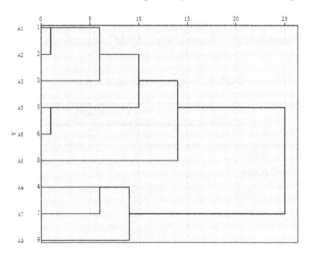

Fig. 3. Cluster result of 9 pairwise Kansei words

According to "variance contribution rate/cumulative contribution rate", the weights of the first three factors are 0.50395, 0.33753 and 0.15853 in turn (Table 4).

Table 4. Example of the SD scale questionnaire

Component	Initial eigenvalues			Rotation sums of squared loadings		
	Total	% of variance	Cumulative %	Total	% of variance	Cumulative %
1	4.178	46.419	46.419	2.853	31.704	31.704
2	2.798	31.09	77.509	2.802	31.138	62.842
3	1.314	14.602	92.111	2.634	29.268	92.111
4	0.403	4.474	96.585			
5	0.247	2.739	99.324			
6	0.047	0.527	99.851			
7	0.013	0.149	100			
8	−7.53E-17	−8.37E-16	100			
9	−2.68E-16	−2.98E-15	100			

Note: Extraction method: Principal Component Analysis

As shown in Table 5, among the three common factors, the words with high scores are as follows:

1. Changeable-unified (A4), Complex-simple (A7);
2. Hard-soft (A3);
3. Traditional-fashionable (A8).

According to the meaning of word pairs, the first, second and three common factors are renamed as "Complexity", "Texture" and "Style" respectively.

Table 5. Rotated component matrix

	Component		
	1	2	3
A4	0.906		
A7	0.891		
A5	-0.694	0.522	
A6	-0.670		
A3		0.930	
A9	0.540	0.784	
A8			0.985
A1		0.544	0.791
A2		0.659	0.729

Notes: Extraction method: Principal Component Analysis

The comprehensive scores of common factors F and A10 of 8 samples were analyzed for correlation. Pearson correlation coefficient r is 0.628, indicating a strong correlation. Therefore, it can be seen that the higher the F is, the higher the A10 (Dislike-like) is.

Obtain the design key elements and evaluation criteria. As shown in Table 6, the three factors of "complexity", "texture" and "style" should be paid attention to in the design and evaluation of IP image. For designers, the evaluation criteria and the weights proposed in this result will help them design IP or modify existing IP. When enterprise managers choose IP design schemes, they can also select schemes based on these three factors. An IP with a higher composite factor score will be associated with more visual preferences, so it is easy to choose an IP scheme by calculating a weighted score of the three factors.

Table 6. Factors that affect preferences

Factor	Weight	Pairwise Kansei words
Complexity	0.50395	Changeable-unified; Complex-simple
Texture	0.33753	Hard-soft
Style	0.15853	Traditional-fashionable

4 Design Practice

Design practice -- Take Chinese tea brands "A Little" as an example. A Little takes quality, service and affordable price as the basis, and creates competitive advantages with personalized product lines.

1. **Basis.** The brand insists on using high-quality raw materials provided by well-known manufacturers, with unified standards and processes. Starting from customer demand, it takes consumption purpose as the principle of categorization, which facilitates customers' choice. In addition, it always maintains a relatively moderate price point.

2. **Advantages.** Customers can not only choose the existing milk tea, but also can match themselves to get personalized drinks [10].

The brand's classic drink is Boba Milk Tea (see Fig. 4. Boba Milk Tea (https://www.alittle-tea.com/)), attributed to the lovely round shape of the Boba pearl in this drink. The brand's logo is shown in Fig. 5. A Little Logo (https://www.alittle-tea.com/).

Fig. 4. Boba Milk Tea (https://www.alittle-tea.com/)

Fig. 5. A Little Logo (https://www.alittle-tea.com/)

The perceptual elements of the IP image of new tea drinks brands were counted, analyzed and summarized in the previous section. The three keywords we got from it are complexity, texture and style, which also guided the subsequent IP image design.

1. Complexity: Consider the complexity of the overall form of IP. Visually, it needs to be unified, vivid and clean.

2. Texture: Consider the overall material tendency of IP. It can express personality; such as soft texture will tend to bring a friendly feeling. The material should be tender and soft, so that people can feel the affinity and vitality of the brand.
3. Style: Consider the image characteristics of IP. On the basis of "A Little" brand style, the uniqueness of IP image should be grasped to attract consumers' attention.

Figure 6 IP image display and role introduction shows the IP design.

Fig. 6. IP image display and role introduction

References

1. Xu, H.: "YOYO" IP Image Design Based on Emotional Design Theory. University of South China (2020)
2. Jiang, M.: Development status and future prospects of new tea industry. Agric. Archaeol. **41**(2), 221–227 (2021)
3. Simon, T.W.S., Eklund, J., Axelsson, J.R.C., et al.: Concepts, methods and tools in Kansei engineering. Theor. Issues Ergon. Science **5**(3), 214–231 (2004)
4. Li, W.: Development strategies of cross-border marketing for brand IP. Res. Transm. Competence **1**(10), 246 (2017)
5. Li, Z.: IP Based Brands. China Fashion **12**(12), 72–73 (2018)
6. Ning, Y.: Research on brand visual identity design in the context of IP based brands. Shanghai Normal University (2019)
7. Xu, X.: The research for idea of web image design based on Kansei engineering. Shandong University (2008)
8. Zhu, Z.: Research on brand logo design and evaluation model based on Kansei engineering. Huazhong Unversity of Science and Technology (2018)
9. Pan, W.: Research and practice of CMF design method for bluetooth speaker based on perceptual image. Huazhong Unversity of Science and Technology (2021)
10. Wang, Y.: Exploration on innovative marketing model of traditional catering industry in internet age——successful marketing case based on a little milk tea. Foreign Econ. Relat. Trade **26**(9), 106–108 (2019)

Design Embedded in SME's Organizational Culture Model

Yichen Meng[(⊠)] and Su Guo

College of Design and Innovation, Tongji University, Shanghai, People's Republic of China
miya_mengyc@163.com

Abstract. In the context of rapid development and fierce market competition, organization problems are mostly "wicked problems" that cannot be clearly defined. To tackle these problems, we need new technological innovations, new cognitive attitudes, and new operating rules. Embedding design into an organization's culture can help it better adapt to external changes and challenges, stimulate innovative thinking, and promote the integration and development of internal values, enabling the organization to maintain a competitive edge in contemporary society. This article reexamines the value of design within the specific organizational context of small and medium-sized enterprises (SMEs), offering a new definition of its role and a specific framework for its function.

Keywords: Organizational culture · Design thinking · Design roles · SMEs

1 Introduction

In recent years, the role of design within organizations has continually expanded and ascended, with an increasing recognition that the stage for design practice is not merely business but organizations at large [1]. No organization is static: as open systems, they inevitably evolve with changes in the external environment and internal relationships. Thus, the core issues encountered in organizational operations often feature uncertainty, non-linearity, and ambiguity, areas where design discipline has unique advantages. Numerous cases from commercial enterprises detail the effectiveness of design at different levels of the organization and attempt to cultivate design as an organizational capability and a prominent method of achieving business goals. The 2015 DMI assessment of the market value of publicly traded companies in the United States showed that companies driven by design have maintained a significant stock market advantage over the past decade [2], a finding also confirmed by McKinsey's Design Index survey [3]. Of course, the impact of design goes far beyond that, with design thinking gaining popularity across the globe, more and more SMEs are paying attention to design and want to try to use it as a core strategy to drive business innovation and development.

Compared with large companies, SMEs face more significant pressure in market competition. They usually need more brand awareness and business richness [4] to obtain advantages through differentiated positioning and services with limited resources and financial support. On the other hand, many SMEs lack precise goal-setting and effective

C. Stephanidis et al. (Eds.): HCII 2024, CCIS 2118, pp. 61–68, 2024.
https://doi.org/10.1007/978-3-031-61963-2_7

collaboration mechanisms [5], and they continue to employ outdated management styles when faced with rapidly changing external environments, which significantly hampers their strategic development. Especially in the face of large-scale emergencies, such as the outbreak of COVID-19 in 2019, they often find themselves passively enduring crises, unable to innovate or transform proactively.

A review of design-related literature among SMEs shows that many researchers and practitioners in the design field have shifted their attention to this aspect. However, they tend to emphasize concepts such as design teams, design projects, and designers while ignoring more multidimensional organizational roles, such as collaborative models with internal and external designers [6–8]. Another line of study, while considering and describing the stepped forces of design, lacks a unique and detailed elaboration, like design is regarded as the core competence to promote multi-level innovation in enterprises [9–12]. Therefore, this study aims to introduce a new perspective based on organizational culture, emphasizing a holistic embedding approach closer to SMEs.

The research will unfold in the following processes. Firstly, through literature analysis, the development of organizational culture and the crossover with design are sorted out to confirm the study's feasibility and necessity. Secondly, the Denison Model of organizational culture in management is introduced as the basis for questionnaire surveys and semi-structured interviews. Finally, the interview content is coded step by step, and four roles of design in SMEs' organizational culture model are summarized, and each role is positioned and explained in detail.

2   Design and Organizational Culture

When we regard organizational culture as the core of a business, it means that it is not just one aspect or characteristic but a driving force that shapes the organization's identity, guides employee behavior, influences decision-making processes, and ultimately determines the overall operation and development of the organization.

The development of organizational culture has always been in the condition of multi-disciplines interaction, especially in sociology, psychology, anthropology, and management, which constantly put forward the understanding and definition of organizational culture from their perspectives, enriching our multi-dimensional cognition of this concept. The introduction of culture into the organizational context is credited to Elliott Jaques's 1951 publication, "The Changing Culture of a Factory", which considered people's collective work, desires, and visions within an organization as a form of culture. In 1979, Andrew Pettigrew, professor of Strategy and Organization at Oxford University, formally proposed the term—organizational culture. Drawing from his sociological background, he believed that culture is a fusion of symbols, ideologies, languages, rituals, and myths generated within an organization [13], through which its members transmit and maintain their values, beliefs, and norms. Later studies have further described this transmission process: members accept and internalize the shared history formed in dealing with the organization's internal and external challenges and subconsciously interpret their future behavior and decisions [14, 15]. It is not difficult to see that organizational culture is dynamic and complex, which requires a more exploratory and creative way of thinking to understand. Integrating design into the structure and culture of an organization to gain a competitive advantage is receiving increasing attention from managers.

The issues addressed by design are often described as ill-defined and structurally improper "wicked problems" [16] that cannot be solved using conventional methods. In tackling such problems, design showcases its unique advantage through the "reflective practice" process [17]. It allows designers to maintain openness, thereby finding and defining problems in seemingly chaotic situations. Through this flexible and creative approach, the design responds to the symptoms of the problem and delves deeper into the real root causes, enabling the solution to impact a more comprehensive and sustainable level. Tim Brown, President of IDEO, a design and innovation consulting firm, mentioned in his book "Change by Design" that innovation perspectives centered purely on technology are now more unsustainable than ever, and management philosophies based solely on existing strategic options are likely to be overwhelmed by new developments both domestically and internationally. Design thinking offers a new choice, relying on our ability to intuit, recognize patterns, construct ideas with emotional and functional significance, and transform these ideas into tangible actions. This method increases the likelihood of successful innovation and promotes a more flexible and adaptable work culture within organizations. Jeanne Liedtka also emphasizes that the focus of design is on the process, understanding it as a verb, with the expectation of iterating through multiple experiments to test various solutions, actively addressing the tension between possibilities and constraints, especially suitable for decision-making scenarios filled with uncertainty and ambiguity [18].

Another significant feature of organizational culture is the focus on the human element: the behaviors, values, beliefs, and interactions of employees within a business broadly define the essence and direction of its culture. During the 1980s, Japanese businesses, which had been previously underestimated, demonstrated significant economic effectiveness, prompting analyses of how different cultural models impact business development. The well-known Theory Z emphasizes long-term employment, collective decision-making, strong interpersonal relationships, and caring management, fostering a work culture based on trust, participation, and mutual respect. Thomas Peters and Robert Waterman explained in "In Search of Excellence" that effective management practice delegates decision-making power, reduces hierarchical structure, and empowers employees with greater autonomy and initiative. Managing people well and creating a fear-free work environment where everyone can perform their best is far more meaningful than buying a new machine to increase production [19]. These views regard people as valuable resources within the organization, highlighting the central position of human-centered approaches in shaping organizational culture and revealing the natural compatibility between design thinking and organizational culture.

Although much evidence shows a close relationship between design and organizational culture, the actions through which design impacts organizational culture, especially in the context of SMEs, urgently need to be verified. Through in-depth research on the specific role and mechanism of design in shaping and improving the organizational culture of SMEs, more precise guidance and practical strategies can be provided for SMEs to cope with future market changes.

3 Methods and Approaches

This research is based on the organizational culture model from the famous professor Denison of IMD in Switzerland due to a comprehensive index from inside to outside open system perspective. This model not only focuses on the organization's internal characteristics but also emphasizes the organization's external environment and regards the organization as a dynamic changing organism, which meets the needs of the research background.

The researcher invited 10 SMEs with high design relevance in selecting research objects. Using a questionnaire survey and semi-structured interviews, we investigate their organizational culture structure and how interventions are designed. Due to the limitation of the sample size of this survey and the different understanding of the scoring standards, this study does not carry out cross-organizational comparison but only discusses the role of cultural characteristics and design actions of organizations based on different assessment dimensions within a single organization.

In the questionnaire survey, we asked organizations to rate themselves based on the 12 dimensions of the Denison model. To ensure the accuracy and comprehensiveness of the content, we selected key leaders in the organization as research subjects. According to the scoring results, a cultural model corresponding to each organization was drawn to show the structural cultures of different organizations from four quadrants: Involvement, Consistency, Adaptability, and Mission (Fig. 1). The specific dimensions in the figure can be compared with Denison's organizational culture model.

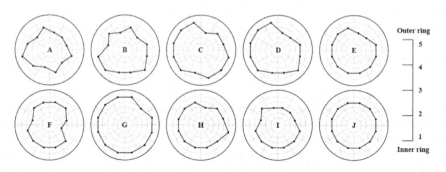

Fig. 1. Cultural model map of 10 organizations

To further explore the relationship between these characteristics of cultural expression and design actions, we conducted a 2-h semi-structured interview with each interviewee. Based on their morphological differences in each quadrant, interviewees were asked to describe the basis for scoring, including their practice and daily observation. The content of the interview is analyzed using the grounded theory. The valuable concepts are extracted from the bottom by coding the text data layer by layer. Then, the categories and core concepts are summarized by connecting the concepts in a series. There are three levels of coding: the initial open coding, the focused coding, and the final concept generation. The researchers finally constructed four design role concepts through the processes of inspection, comparison, conceptualization, and generalization. The following is an example of the coding process using "consistency" (Fig. 2).

Datas	Initial Codings	Focused Codings	Final Concept
"Our team is a mix of people from various backgrounds; it's great, but due to different professional learning, everyone brings their requirements. The design balances these demands, always trying to find common points or a better direction." (Jason)	Identify each individual's core perspectives and insights, facilitating consensus-building among them.	Improve the decision-making process.	Design as Coordinator
"They might be trying to express similar ideas using different terminologies. As a leader with a design background, I always keep quiet at first, carefully understand each person's intentions, and help convey and summarize more understandably." (Ben)	Communication barriers stem from different knowledge systems, and understanding others' real intentions can help us build bridges for dialogue.	Promote communication and cooperation.	
"In small companies, the hierarchy can be relatively chaotic, and job roles aren't always clear. We often find ourselves doing tasks that go beyond our call of duty, with communication and coordination taking up a large part of our work." (Michelle)	There is a high degree of reliance on communication skills due to the blurring of roles due to incomplete organizational structures.	Design of working mode.	
"Compared to other departments, design workers advocate for a more open, collaborative, and innovative work environment, aiming to create more opportunities for cross-departmental communication, rather than just working in isolation."(Ellen)	The combination of knowledge from different fields is more conducive to innovation.	Coordinate multiple resources.	
"I often find myself consciously or unconsciously connecting some resources, thinking of more creative solutions, even though these methods might seem a bit outlandish at times."(Linda)	Long-term innovation thinking training can be more systematic in looking at the problem.	Sense of personal achievement.	

Fig. 2. The coding process using "consistency" as an example

4   Design-Driven Organizational Culture Innovation Framework in SMEs

Based on the above analysis of these organizational cultures, this paper proposes a new role of design for SMEs and its specific impact in playing this role. The matrix maintains the internal and external dimensions of the Denison model's vertical axis. However, this horizontal dimension is removed because flexibility and stability can no longer be used to divide organizational problems into design goals. The design referred to here is no longer limited to the process involving designers but regards design as a way to promote innovative thinking and mean to drive organizational development. Below are the four core concepts that have been constructed – the four roles of design and a detailed description of each role (Fig. 3).

4.1   Design as Motivator

As a motivator, design needs to deal with a series of human-related issues from individuals to teams. The Human-centered concept enables the design to fully consider the needs of people when applying design methods and knowledge. When dealing with all individuals in the organization, we do not abstract them into mechanical elements for management but make the organization more humane and give more humanistic care.

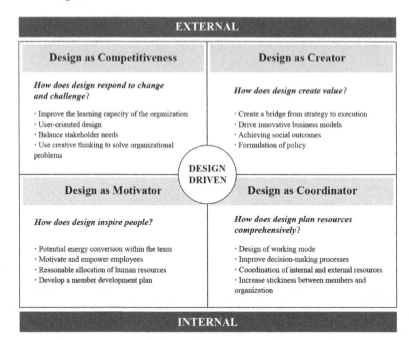

Fig. 3. Design-driven Organizational Innovation Framework in SMEs

- When the internal energy between different individuals is unbalanced, let members drive each other through the transfer of knowledge or emotional mobilization;
- Design various incentive programs to mobilize employees' enthusiasm tools and methods;
- Master the characteristics and abilities of each employee and make reasonable work arrangements;
- Design long-term growth plans and training programs that meet the development needs of employees.

4.2 Design as Coordinator

Coordination is a dynamic process in which various dispersed resources, even those with opposite performances are sorted out according to the principle of integrity and orderly coordination to achieve the optimal effect. This is a design in itself. The role of design as an integrator has been reflected as early as in the product development process and then developed to close the gap between the enterprise and upstream through the integration of the supply chain. However, as people continue to practice design, the scope of this ability has been far more than that. The design method with service design as the core helps various types of enterprises and organizations improve their sustainability and better serve their users.

- Design a reasonable operation structure and work mode by combining the organizational strategy and organizational resources;
- Design the decision-making process and mechanism suitable for the current organizational form;
- Personnel deployment of core members and external members in continuous projects and short-term projects;
- Strengthen members' sense of identity and belonging to the organization.

4.3 Design as Competitiveness

It has been recognized that design can enhance the competitiveness or differentiation of enterprises. The existence of design departments in many companies also enhances the brand's premium ability by creating products, services, and experiences comprehensively.

- Take design culture as an organizational culture, adapt to changes, and keep learning;
- Introduce a human perspective, user-oriented design into all steps of the problem-solving process;
- Coordinate the demands of multiple stakeholders to maximize the overall interests;
- In the face of new challenges, use new techniques to break through organizational work problems.

4.4 Design as Creator

How to use design to help enterprises succeed concerns global enterprises and entrepreneurs. When the traditional model is not competent for the current situation, design thinking provides the most attractive hope: creation.

- When the design is deeply embedded into an organization, it provides a new perspective to solve the difficulties encountered by the "top-down" and "bottom-up" practice paths and creates logical links in the transition of each connection point;
- On the organizational mission, it provides a way to achieve economic and social results in practice, not only as a source of increased sales and better profits but also to stimulate corporate social responsibility;
- Policy formulation is understood as a design problem and design activity.

5 Conclusion

This paper provides four directions for design-driven organizational innovation of SMEs. These four directions can be seen as a comprehensive framework, providing a reference path for design to enter SMEs and also complementing the emerging trend of design in organizations.

References

1. Boztepe S, Dilnot C, Heskett J.: Design and the creation of value. J. Des. Creation Value, 1–248 (2017).
2. Rae, J.: Design value index exemplars outperform the S&P 500 index (again) and a new crop of design leaders emerge. J. Des. Manag. Rev. **27**, 4–11 (2016). https://doi.org/10.1111/drev.12040
3. Sheppard, B., Yeon, H., London, S.: Tapping into the business value of design. J. McKinsey Q. (2018)
4. Öztamur, D., Karakadılar, I.S.: Exploring the role of social media for SMEs: as a new marketing strategy tool for the firm performance perspective. J. Procedia-Soc. Behave. sci. **150**, 511–520 (2014). https://doi.org/10.1016/j.sbspro.2014.09.067
5. Berends, H., Reymen, I., Stultiëns, R.G.L., et al.: External designers in product design processes of small manufacturing firms. J. Des. Stud. **32**, 86–108 (2011). https://doi.org/10.1016/j.destud.2010.06.001
6. Bruce, M., Morris, B.: Managing external design professionals in the product development process. J. Technovation. **14**, 585–599 (1994). https://doi.org/10.1016/0166-4972(94)90041-8
7. Czarnitzki, D., Thorwarth, S.: The contribution of in-house and external design activities to product market performance. J. J. Prod. Innovation Manage. **29**, 878–895 (2012). https://doi.org/10.1111/j.1540-5885.2012.00935.x
8. Gulari, M.N., Fairburn, S., Malins, J.: Assessing the effectiveness of design-led innovation support for SMEs. J. (2013)
9. Gerlitz, L.: Design management as a domain of smart and sustainable enterprise: business modelling for innovation and smart growth in Industry 4.0. Entrepreneurship Sustain. Issues **3**(3), 244–268 (2016). https://doi.org/10.9770/jesi.2016.3.3(3)
10. Kramoliš, J., Staňková, P.: Design and its impact on the financial results of enterprises based on managers opinions. J. J. Competitiveness (2017). https://doi.org/10.7441/joc.2017.02.05
11. Wormald, P.W., Evans, M.A.: The integration of industrial design capability within UK SMEs: the challenges, opportunities and benefits. J. Int. J prod. Dev. **9**, 343–356 (2009). https://doi.org/10.1504/IJPD.2009.027469
12. Borja de Mozota, B.: The four powers of design: a value model in design management. J. (2006)
13. Pettigrew, A.M.: On studying organizational culture. J. Adm. Sci. Q. **24**, 570–581 (1979). https://doi.org/10.2307/2392363
14. Schein, E.H.: Organizational culture and leadership (2010)
15. Martin, J., Siehl, C.: Organizational culture and counterculture: an uneasy symbiosis. Organ. Dyn. **12**(2), 52–64 (1983). https://doi.org/10.1016/0090-2616(83)90033-5
16. Buchanan, R.: Wicked problems in design thinking. Des. Issues **8**(2), 5 (1992). https://doi.org/10.2307/1511637
17. Visser, W.: Schön: design as a reflective practice. J. Collect. **2**, 21–25 (2010)
18. Liedtka, J.: Why design thinking works. J. Harvard Bus. Rev. **96**, 72–79 (2018)
19. Deming, W.E.: Improvement of quality and productivity through action by management. J. National prod. Rev. **1**, 12–22 (1981). https://doi.org/10.1002/npr.4040010105

Machine Learning for Forecasting Entrepreneurial Opportunities – A Literature Review

Daniel Szafarski$^{(\boxtimes)}$ (iD) and Mahsa Fischer (iD)

Heilbronn University of Applied Sciences, Heilbronn, Germany
{daniel.szafarski,mahsa.fischer}@hs-heilbronn.de

Abstract. Business opportunity is one of the key pillars of entrepreneurship research. So far, there is little research on the combination of artificial intelligence and entrepreneurship. This article makes a twofold contribution to this through a systematic literature analysis. On the one hand, the existing approaches for generating or identifying the business opportunity are compiled from 25 publications and presented in a concept matrix. On the other hand, promising approaches and current research focuses, such as the analysis of patents with the help of text mining methods and Latent Dirichlet Allocation (LDA), are extracted, which provides further research incentives.

Keywords: Machine Learning · Business Opportunities · Innovation · Entrepreneurship · Success Prediction · Text Mining · Literature Review

1 Introduction

The current economic situation is characterized by rapid change, dynamic innovation and uncertainty. True innovation and long-term market success often lies in the creation or identification of new means that haven't been recognized by market participants previously [4,10,24]. Therefore, the discovery and development of opportunities has been a central component of entrepreneurship research for many years but is now more relevant than ever before [43,49]. Current studies show that numerous publications have already looked at it from a variety of perspectives [14,31,43]. The technological possibilities offer new opportunities in the application of existing concepts as well as the need for new theories in this context [35]. Extracting relevant information at the right time can have a major impact on business success. It seems obvious to use machine learning (ML) for these tasks, as it has already demonstrated its enormous potential in numerous use cases e.g. innovation management [46]. For this reason, Giuggioli and Pellegrini [12] also describe a need for further research in the area of entrepreneurial opportunity. This demand can also be supported by the publication by Obschonka and Audretsch [36], according to which the influence of

C. Stephanidis et al. (Eds.): HCII 2024, CCIS 2118, pp. 69–78, 2024.
https://doi.org/10.1007/978-3-031-61963-2_8

artificial intelligence in the research field of entrepreneurship has hardly been scientifically investigated so far. This motivates the following article to take a closer look at the following research question: "How are ML methods currently used to identify entrepreneurial opportunities in science?".

2   Theoretical Background

2.1   Entrepreneurship

As mentioned in the introduction, the field of entrepreneurship is viewed from different perspectives and is an extremely popular and diverse field of research. For this reason, there is as yet no clear, generally accepted definition of the term [4,45]. Newer definitions in particular view entrepreneurship as a multi-stage process in which individuals identify and evaluate an entrepreneurial opportunity and then exploit it in the form of a business start-up or innovation [8,42,48]. New innovative entrepreneurship means observing the market closely, thinking in a networked and lateral way, questioning existing products and developing new solutions that satisfy customer needs and thus create new value [2,3].

2.2   Entrepreneurial Opportunity

An opportunity itself can refer to the creation and introduction of an innovative product or the founding of a new company [3,8]. According to Shane and Venkataraman [42], an entrepreneurial opportunity exists if a product can be sold on the market at a higher price than its resources and processing costs. At the same time, a business idea itself as well as its further development and modification [5,7] and the arise from technological possibilities [41] can be understood as an entrepreneurial opportunity. While an idea is a creative result, only its examination and development leads to a corresponding opportunity [7,15]. Research associates the term primarily with the areas of creation, discovery and recognition of further processes and concepts [43]. There are two basic perspectives [1]. One view is based on the discovery of an existing opportunity in the market, whereas the other is based on the systematic creation of new opportunities through a creative process [2]. The search is usually understood as an active process that is stimulated by previous experience, market and customer knowledge and access to relevant information, among other things [2,3].

2.3   Machine Learning

Depending on the method used, the terms *deep learning, machine learning* or *artificial intelligence* (AI) are used. AI can be understood as a term for advanced, intelligent computer systems. This term has become a buzzword in science and practice, which has led to the synonymous use of AI and ML [11,13]. ML is a mathematical algorithm that has the ability to recognize and independently learn complex patterns in large data sets and therefore solve different problems and situations. Depending on the data used, the task can be specified more precisely. Traditionally, supervised and unsupervised learning are differentiated, although there are now also more advanced forms such as *reinforcement learning* and hybrid forms such as *self-supervised learning* [16,34]. One of the key success factors is the development of *artificial neural networks* (ANN) based on the *Multilayer Perceptron* towards deeper ANNs, which have improved learning capabilities and are summarized under the term deep learning [16,25,34].

3   Methodology

This work is based on the research design according to Webster and Watson [52] as well as Fettke et al. [9] in order to present the current state of the art. Public availability and the German or English language were used as selection criteria and conducted using a search string. For this purpose, the six literature databases *ACM Digital Library, AIS Electronic Library, IEEE Xplore Digital Library, SpringerLink, Google Scholar* and *Science Direct* were examined. In total, 420 potentially relevant publications were identified. Based on their abstracts, a forward and backward search for further relevant publications and the removal of duplicates, a final corpus of 25 publications remained for this analysis. The publications were then analyzed further using qualitative content analysis according to Mayring [32]. In order to answer the research question the dimensions shown in table 1 were applied according to a previously created coding guide.

4   Results

4.1   Types and Causes of Entrepreneurial Opportunities

In 64% of the publications examined, the opportunity is considered in connection with the further development and modification of an existing product portfolio in established companies. The existing product range and corresponding patents and property rights are used as a starting point for the conceptualization of new ideas. Examples span various industries, including chinese elderly care [30], mobile payments [37], and the turkish textile industry [6], with specific cases like *Thermo Fisher Scientific* [33] and the *Samsung Galaxy Note 5* [18]. Only three studies focus on entrepreneurship, all related to further development. Additionally, 44% of studies explore opportunities in new technologies, with a few considering their application in established firms.

Different concepts are recognizable in the publications with regard to the cause of an entrepreneurial opportunity. In close to half publications (40%), the opportunity or idea is gained on the basis of new technological progress. This is followed by the generation of new ideas through the identification of gaps and the combination of two concepts in 28% of cases. The combination of two concepts with technological progress can be identified three times, which demonstrates the adaptation of existing, successful trends to other use cases. Market dynamics and

Table 1. Concept matrix for mapping the current state of the art

Column headers (author references):
[5] Dereli & Durmuşoğlu · [14] Jeong et al. · [15] Jeong et al. · [16] Jeong et al. · [17] Jin et al. · [18] Kim et al. · [19] Kim & Choi · [20] Kim et al. · [23] Lee & Lee · [24] Lee et al. · [25] Lee & Lee · [26] Lee et al. · [27] Li · [30] Mun et al. · [35] Park & Geum · [36] Pournemat & Weiss · [38] Russo et al. · [39] Seo et al. · [43] Song et al. · [46] Talbot & Talbot · [49] Wang & Chen · [50] Wang et al. · [52] Yoon & Magee · [53] Yoon et al. · [54] Zhang et al.

Category	Concept	[5]	[14]	[15]	[16]	[17]	[18]	[19]	[20]	[23]	[24]	[25]	[26]	[27]	[30]	[35]	[36]	[38]	[39]	[43]	[46]	[49]	[50]	[52]	[53]	[54]	Σ
Opportunity type	Technological	X					X			X	X	X				X		X		X		X	X	X			11
	Entrepreneurship		X												X		X										3
	Further development and modification		X	X	X	X		X			X	X	X	X	X	X	X		X		X				X	X	16
Origin of the opportunity	Utilization of technological progress	X			X	X		X	X							X						X	X	X	X		10
	Market dynamics	X						X							X	X	X		X								6
	Internal (corporate) capabilities									X	X				X				X		X						5
	Identification of new customer needs		X																								1
	Combination of two concepts						X			X	X					X		X		X						X	7
	Gap identification			X									X				X				X	X	X	X			7
	Adaptation of existing patterns	X													X				X							X	4
Data foundation	Patents	X			X	X	X		X	X	X	X			X	X		X	X	X		X	X	X	X		17
	Trademarks	X		X											X												3
	Scientific publications																								X		1
	Design property rights			X																							1
	Mergers and Acquisition (M&A) Use Cases															X											1
	External Data Platforms (e.g. Bloomberg)								X							X											2
	News														X												1
	Social Media		X													X										X	3
	Company and product information	X			X		X												X		X				X		6
	Advertisement					X																					1
	Policy data													X													1
	Project data													X					X								2
ML algorithms	K-means Clustering	X				X																					2
	ORCLUS																						X				1
	(General) Text Mining						X	X	X	X		X	X						X	X		X	X	X	X		12
	Vector Space Model							X	X													X	X	X			5
	Latent Dirichlet Allocation (LDA)			X	X				X					X			X								X	X	7
	Rapid Automatic Keywords Extraction (RAKE)															X											1
	SAO Semantic Information Identification																	X									1
	Syntactic Parser																	X									1
	Sentiment Analyse			X																							1
	Link-prediction		X		X		X					X											X				5
	Apriori Algorithmus							X																			1
	Support Vector Machine (SVM)															X							X				2
	Semantic Similarity						X			X		X				X					X		X	X		X	8
	Similarity Measurements	X		X							X				X				X								5
	Association Rule Mining									X	X							X									3
	Graph Convolution Network (GCN)															X											1
	Collaborative filtering								X			X															2
	Structural Hole Theory								X																		1
	Generative Topographic Mapping			X																				X			2
	Fuzzy Logic	X																									1
	Logistic Regression														X				X								2
	Random Forest					X									X												2
	Naïve Bayes									X																	1
	Gradient Boosting														X												1
	Angle-based Outlier Detection								X														X	X			3
	Local Outlier Factor (LOF)								X																		1
	Fuzzy Grade-of-Membership Model																			X							1
	Conditional Probability Method																X									X	2
Support degree	Preparation	X	X		X	X		X		X	X	X	X			X			X		X	X		X	X	X	16
	Proposal		X		X		X	X							X	X		X	X			X					9
Challenges	Research		X	X		X		X		X	X				X				X	X	X		X		X	X	13
	Domain	X		X						X	X				X				X						X		7
	Concept/Procedure			X		X		X		X		X			X	X		X	X	X			X		X	X	13
	Data basis	X	X		X					X	X	X			X	X			X	X			X		X	X	13
	Technological (ML)		X		X					X					X				X		X		X		X	X	8
	Operationalization			X	X	X		X				X			X			X	X	X			X		X		11
	Evaluation		X			X	X			X	X				X				X		X		X		X		9
																										Σ	25

internal capabilities account for 24% and 20% of opportunities, respectively, with 16% adapting existing patterns to new situations. Remarkably, only one study focuses on identifying new customer needs for idea generation.

4.2 Data Basis and Support by ML

Patents are by far the most important (64%) basis for generating new ideas. However, different aspects of patents are used depending on the publication. In the sample, company or product-specific information was explicitly used six times (24%). Social media data and trademarks were used in three cases each. Project data was used twice. In addition, six other publications use data sources that are only used in this one case. These include data on design property rights and scientific publications, which are semitically similar to patents, as well as advertising, news and external platforms such as Bloomberg.

Regarding the degree of support, 64% of the studies focus on preparation, while 36% are aimed at proposal, indicating most don't offer explicit recommendations. Instead, they process the identified data sources to aid end users in spotting entrepreneurial opportunities, either by classifying patents based on relevance and novelty or through visual graphics.

4.3 ML Methods for Identifying Opportunities

A total of 28 different methods were differentiated as part of the analysis. At the same time, almost half (48%) refer to *Text Mining* and five contributions (20%) use link prediction as a supercategory, which can be realized on the basis of several concrete methods. Specifically, 28% of the publications use *Latent Dirichlet Allocation* (LDA), a method for modeling topics that makes it possible to identify the distribution and affiliation of words to topic clusters from a text corpus. Some publications apply LDA for topic and keyword identification, grouping related patents [19,23,54]. The *Vector Space Model* (VSM), *semantic similarity* and similarity measurement are applied five times (32%). For the reverse use case of identifying data points that do not fit into an existing graph, the *Angle-based Outlier Detection*, the *Local Outlier Factor* (LOF) method and the *Structural Hole Theory* are used in three cases. *Support Vector Machine* (SVM), *logistic regression* and *Random Forest* are each used twice, with Park and Geum [37] comparing their effectiveness. Additional methods from diverse application contexts were noted but not detailed due to the reason of scope.

4.4 Evaluation and Performance of the ML-Techniques

A general comparison of performance between the publications examined is not possible due to their individuality, e.g. because of different data sources. The majority (64%) develop a method that is applied to a specific use case. Here, the functionality is usually checked by the plausibility of the concrete results in the specific application case which, however, does not allow any statement to be made about the general quality. In turn, 9 publications (36%) explicitly measure and evaluate performance. For this purpose, widely used quantitative metrics in the field of ML such as *Accuracy, Error Rate, Precision* and *Recall* are used. As an example, Jin et al. [20], compared with a manual approach, and achieved an accuracy of 80.64%, although a low recall value of 48.65%. This indicates that the approach is only poorly able to identify all connections of the manual process. However, the high precision score of 62.07% is also worth mentioning, which suggests that the approach is well able to identify connections that remained undetected by the experts. Further authors compare their performance with other methods in order to compare the performance of the new approach.

4.5   Challenges of the Publications and the ML Methods

Six main key challenges were identified. Out of the 25 publications examined, 20 address several challenges, while the remaining 5 do not mention any and will not be discussed further. On average, one publication addresses challenges in more than half of the identified areas (3.6). In 13 publications, the main challenges lie in the focus area *Research*. These include, above all, the weaknesses of research with regard to validity and generalizability, most of which are listed as limitations. Challenges with the *concept* are revealed equally frequently. Here, the authors reveal concept gaps and weaknesses in both usability and results. Challenges with the *data basis* are also pointed out 13 times. These publications address various topics, including data quality, domain-specific factors, and thresholds for narrowing down relevant data points. Additionally, the text discusses the time delay between discovery and patent granting. The hindered usability and generalization of these tools pose a difficulty for their intended usage. Eleven citations point to problems with *operationalization*, since, for example, many cases require initial input by experts as well as the fact that not all connections are found by ML or possible to scale. Eight publications also describe challenges in connection with the *technical implementation of ML methods* while Seven see further challenges in the area of the *domain*.

5   Conclusion

In summary, the systematic analysis of 25 publications made it possible to identify the state of the art in the identification of entrepreneurial opportunities with the help of ML. The main focus of current research is on the analysis of patents in the context of identifying technological opportunities. At the same time, entrepreneurial opportunities in the context of entrepreneurship are rarely explicitly promoted. A closer look at the data basis revealed a focus on natural language texts, and their processing using NLP methods. Reference is often made to the general methods of text mining, whereby the methods of LDA and semantic similarity are widely used in current research. For further identification of entrepreneurial opportunity, relevant entities are extracted from the data sources and linked in a graph structure. With the help of advanced, diverse network analysis algorithms, opportunities are extracted on this basis, primarily on the basis of technological progress. Challenges with a focus on data sources, concept and operationalization have been identified, which question the holistic nature and generalizability of the approaches. Nevertheless, the isolated performance metrics of the publications show the effectiveness of the approaches, which legitimizes further interest and hope. However, the findings presented have limitations, include incomplete coverage and variability in methodological detail, complicating direct comparisons. Future research should validate these findings, explore universal models or novel approaches like Large Language Models (LLM) or generative AI, and address the operational challenges identified.

References

1. Alvarez, S.A., Barney, J.B.: Discovery and creation: alternative theories of entrepreneurial action. Strategic Entrepreneurship J, **1**(1-2), 11–26 (2007)
2. Ardichvili, A., Cardozo, R., Ray, S.: A theory of entrepreneurial opportunity identification and development. J. Bus. Ventur. **18**(1), 105–123 (2003)
3. Baron, R.A.: Opportunity recognition as pattern recognition: how entrepreneurs "connect the dots" to identify new business opportunities. Acad. Manag. Perspectives **20**(1), 104–119 (2006)
4. Baumol, W.J.: Formal entrepreneurship theory in economics: existence and bounds. J. Bus. Ventur. **8**(3), 197–210 (1993)
5. Davidsson, P.: Entrepreneurial opportunities and the entrepreneurship nexus: a re-conceptualization. J. Bus. Ventur. **30**(5), 674–695 (2015)
6. Dereli, T., Durmuşoğlu, A.: Classifying technology patents to identify trends: applying a fuzzy-based clustering approach in the Turkish textile industry. Technol. Soc. **31**(3), 263–272 (2009)
7. Dimov, D.: Beyond the single-person, single-insight attribution in understanding entrepreneurial opportunities. Entrepreneurship Theory Pract. **31**(5), 713–731 (2007)
8. Eckhardt, J.T., Shane, S.A.: Opportunities and entrepreneurship. J. Manag. **29**(3), 333–349 (2003)
9. Fettke, P.: State-of-the-art des state-of-the-art: Eine untersuchung der Forschungsmethode "review" innerhalb der Wirtschaftsinformatik. Wirtschaftsinformatik **4**(48), 257–266 (2006)
10. Gaglio, C.M., Katz, J.A.: The psychological basis of opportunity identification: entrepreneurial alertness. Mall Bus. Econ. **16**, 95–111 (2001)
11. Gbadegeshin, S.A., et al.: What is an artificial intelligence (ai): a simple buzzword or a worthwhile inevitability? In: ICERI2021 Proceedings vol. 1, pp. 468–479 (2021)
12. Giuggioli, G., Pellegrini, M.M.: Artificial intelligence as an enabler for entrepreneurs: a systematic literature review and an agenda for future research. Inter. J. Entrepreneurial Behav. Res. (2022)
13. Grewal, D.S.: A critical conceptual analysis of definitions of artificial intelligence as applicable to computer engineering. IOSR J. Comput. Eng. **16**(2), 09–13 (2014)
14. Hansen, D.J., Monllor, J., Shrader, R.C.: Identifying the elements of entrepreneurial opportunity constructs: recognizing what scholars are really examining. Inter. J. Entrepreneurship Innovat. **17**(4), 240–255 (2016)

15. Hsieh, C., Nickerson, J.A., Zenger, T.R.: Opportunity discovery, problem solving and a theory of the entrepreneurial firm. J. Manage. Stud. **44**(7), 1255–1277 (2007)
16. Janiesch, C., Zschech, P., Heinrich, K.: Machine learning and deep learning. Electr. Markets **31**(3), 685–695 (2021)
17. Jeong, B., Ko, N., Son, C., Yoon, J.: Trademark-based framework to uncover business diversification opportunities: application of deep link prediction and competitive intelligence analysis. Comput. Ind. **124**, 103356 (2021)
18. Jeong, B., Yoon, J., Lee, J.M.: Social media mining for product planning: a product opportunity mining approach based on topic modeling and sentiment analysis. Inter. J. Inform. Mana. **48**(2017), 280–290 (2019)
19. Jeong, Y., Park, I., Yoon, B.: Identifying emerging research and business development (r&bd) areas based on topic modeling and visualization with intellectual property right data. Technol. Forecasting Soc. Change **146**(2018), 655–672 (2019)
20. Jin, G., Jeong, Y., Yoon, B.: Technology-driven roadmaps for identifying new product/market opportunities: use of text mining and quality function deployment. Adv. Eng. Inform. **29**(1), 126–138 (2015)
21. Kim, B., Gazzola, G., Lee, J.M., Kim, D., Kim, K., Jeong, M.K.: Inter-cluster connectivity analysis for technology opportunity discovery. Scientometrics **98**(3), 1811–1825 (2014)
22. Kim, J.E., Choi, Y.J.: A Methodology of Predicting Market Convergence Opportunity Using Machine Learning for Small and Mid-Size Enterprises **142**(Dta), 146–149 (2016)
23. Kim, M., Park, Y., Yoon, J.: Generating patent development maps for technology monitoring using semantic patent-topic analysis. Comput. Ind. Eng. **98**, 289–299 (2016)
24. Kirzner, I.M.: Entrepreneurial discovery and the competitive market process: an austrian approach. J. Econ. Literat. **35**(1), 60–85 (1997)
25. Lecun, Y., Bengio, Y., Hinton, G.: Deep learning. Nature **521**(7553), 436–444 (2015)
26. Lee, C., Lee, G.: Technology opportunity analysis based on recombinant search: patent landscape analysis for idea generation. Scientometrics **121**(2), 603–632 (2019)
27. Lee, J., Ko, N., Yoon, J., Son, C.: An approach for discovering firm-specific technology opportunities: Application of link prediction to F-term networks. Technol. Forecasting Soc. Change **168**(2020), 120746 (2021)
28. Lee, M., Lee, S.: Identifying new business opportunities from competitor intelligence: an integrated use of patent and trademark databases. Technol. Forecast. Soc. Chang. **119**, 170–183 (2017)
29. Lee, O.J., Park, S.Y., Kim, J.T.: IdeaNet: potential opportunity discovery for business innovation. CEUR Workshop Proc. **2794**, 5–8 (2020)
30. Li, C.: Market opportunity and policy support for Chinese old aging industry: an application of text mining. SHS Web Conf. **39**, 01015 (2017)
31. Mary George, N., Parida, V., Lahti, T., Wincent, J.: A systematic literature review of entrepreneurial opportunity recognition: insights on influencing factors. Inter. Entrepreneurship Manag. J. **12**(2), 309–350 (2016)
32. Mayring, P., Fenzl, T.: Qualitative inhaltsanalyse. In: Baur, N., Blasius, J.H. (eds.) Handbuch Methoden der empirischen Sozialforschung, pp. 543–556. Springer, Wiesbaden (2014)
33. Mun, C., et al.: Discovering business diversification opportunities using patent information and open innovation cases. Technol. Forecasting Soc. Change **139**(2018), 144–154 (2019)

34. Murphy, K.P.: Machine learning: a probabilistic perspective. MIT press (2012)
35. Nambisan, S.: Digital entrepreneurship: toward a digital technology perspective of entrepreneurship. Entrepreneurship: Theory Pract. **41**(6), 1029–1055 (2017)
36. Obschonka, M., Audretsch, D.B.: Artificial intelligence and big data in entrepreneurship. Small Bus. Econ. **55**(3), 529–539 (2020)
37. Park, M., Geum, Y.: Two-stage technology opportunity discovery for firm-level decision making: GCN-based link-prediction approach. Technol. Forecast. Soc. Chang. **183**(July), 121934 (2022)
38. Pournemat, M., Weiss, M.: Identifying business opportunities using topic modeling and chance discovery. In: The ISPIM Innovation Conference - Innovating Our Common Future (June 2021)
39. Russo, D., Spreafico, M., Precorvi, A.: Discovering new business opportunities with dependent semantic parsers. Comput. Ind. **123**, 103330 (2020)
40. Seo, W., Yoon, J., Park, H., youl Coh, B., Lee, J.M., Kwon, O.J.: Product opportunity identification based on internal capabilities using text mining and association rule mining. Technol. Forecasting Soc. Change **105**, 94–104 (2016)
41. Shane, S.: Technological opportunities and new firm creation. Manage. Sci. **47**(2), 205–220 (2001)
42. Shane, S., Venkataraman, S.: The Promise of Entrepreneurship as a field of reseanc. Acad. ol Manag. fleview **25**(1), 217–226 (2000)
43. Short, J.C., Ketchen, D.J., Shook, C.L., Ireland, R.D.: The concept of "Opportunity" in entrepreneurship research: past accomplishments and future challenges. J. Manag. **36**(1), 40–65 (2010)
44. Song, K., Kim, K.S., Lee, S.: Discovering new technology opportunities based on patents: text-mining and F-term analysis. Technovation **60–61**(January), 1–14 (2017)
45. Stevenson, H.H., Jarillo, J.C.: A paradigm of entrepreneurship: entrepreneurial management. Strategic Manag. J. **11**(Corporate Entrepreneurship (Summer, 1990)), 17–27 (1990)
46. Szafarski, D., Beckmann, H.: Einsatz von Machine Learning im Innovationsmanagement. Angewandte Forschung in der Wirtschaftsinformatik **2022**, 273–286 (2022)
47. Talbot, B.G., Talbot, L.M.: Business radar : opportunity analysis and metric estimation using a fuzzy grade-of-membership model. Technol. Rev. (2014), 87–112 (2003)
48. Timmons, J., Spinelli, S., Prescott, E.: New Venture Creation: Entrepreneurship for the 21st Century (2010)
49. Venkataraman, S.: The distinctive domain of entrepreneurship research. Adv. Entrepreneurship, Firm Emergence Growth **3** (1997)
50. Wang, J., Chen, Y.J.: A novelty detection patent mining approach for analyzing technological opportunities. Adv. Eng. Inform. **42**(June), 100941 (2019)
51. Wang, M.Y., Fang, S.C., Chang, Y.H.: Exploring technological opportunities by mining the gaps between science and technology: Microalgal biofuels. Technol. Forecast. Soc. Chang. **92**, 182–195 (2015)
52. Webster, J., Watson, R.T.: Analyzing the past to prepare for the future?: writing a literature review. MIS Q. **2**(26), 13–23 (2002)
53. Yoon, B., Magee, C.L.: Exploring technology opportunities by visualizing patent information based on generative topographic mapping and link prediction. Technol. Forecasting Soc. Change **132**(2017), 105–117 (2018)

54. Yoon, J., Seo, W., Coh, B.Y., Song, I., Lee, J.M.: Identifying product opportunities using collaborative filtering-based patent analysis. Comput. Ind. Eng. **107**, 376–387 (2017)
55. Zhang, C., Wang, H., Xu, F., Hu, X.: IdeaGraph plus: a topic-based algorithm for perceiving unnoticed events. In: Proceedings - IEEE 13th International Conference on Data Mining Workshops, ICDMW 2013, pp. 735–741 (2013)

Generative AI for Visionary Leadership - Desirability and Feasibility Assessments from an Expert Survey

Tero Villman$^{(\boxtimes)}$ ⓘ and Jari Kaivo-oja ⓘ

Finland Futures Research Centre, Turku School of Economics, University of Turku, Tampere, Finland

{tero.villman,jari.kaivo-oja}@utu.fi

Abstract. The integration of artificial intelligence (AI) into various areas of management has become a subject of growing interest. Various applications of generative AI potentially transform many types of business and managerial tasks in the future, possibly leading to deepened human–computer interactions and relationship between leadership and technology particularly with the combination of human and artificial intelligence.

A yet-to-be-explored application area for generative AI in management is visionary leadership and strategic decision-making. Modern organizations and society at large urgently require visions for the future addressing complex challenges, offering alternative pathways, inspiring commitment, and empowering action, while enabling flexibility and adaptability.

Recognizing the transformative potential of generative AI and the different aspects of visionary leadership, we explore the potential and application areas of generative AI for visionary leadership through a survey. We collected insights from 25 management, leadership, AI, and foresight experts to discover the potential and limitations of generative AI for the five domains of visionary leadership: (1) Vision Formulation, (2) Vision Communication, (3) Vision Integration, (4) Vision Realization, and (5) Vision Learning.

The results suggest that Vision Communication and Vision Learning are the domains with the highest and Vision Formulation with the lowest potential for generative AI applications according to desirability and feasibility analyses.

Previous studies of visionary leadership have not examined the role of technology, moreover the role of generative AI for visionary leadership. Thus, this pilot study can be viewed as an opening to this emerging research avenue, and an expansion to existing visionary leadership research.

Keywords: Generative artificial intelligence · visionary leadership · vision · strategic decision-making · vision formulation · vision communication · vision integration · vision realization · vision learning

1 Introduction

In today's rapidly evolving business and technological landscape, the integration of artificial intelligence (AI) into various areas of management has become a subject of growing interest. Especially since the recent surge of various applications of generative artificial

© The Author(s), under exclusive license to Springer Nature Switzerland AG 2024
C. Stephanidis et al. (Eds.): HCII 2024, CCIS 2118, pp. 79–91, 2024.
https://doi.org/10.1007/978-3-031-61963-2_9

intelligence – "a branch of AI that can create new content such as texts, images, or audio that increasingly often cannot be distinguished anymore from human craftsmanship" – many types of business and managerial tasks are potentially transformed in the future as the technology and its applications are anticipated to produce profound changes to the ways in which knowledge is created, processed, managed, maintained and shared in organizations [1]. This progression may further deepen human–computer interactions and, especially in the context of organizations and business, symbiotic relationship between leadership and technology through hybrid intelligence – the combination of human and artificial intelligence for achieving objectives and producing superior outcomes than each could have reached independently, and the associated continuous improvement via mutual learning [2].

A yet-to-be-explored application area for generative AI in the field of management is visionary leadership and strategic decision-making. Research indicates that visions can be principal antecedents of organizational performance and visionary leadership has been found to have a positive influence on organizational alignment, strategy execution, organizational growth, organizational learning, employee and customer satisfaction, organizational attractiveness, and long-term shareholder value [3–11]. However, visionary leadership is not without its challenges. For example, the misalignment between middle managers' and top management's visions can create confusion and uncertainty among team members and decrease the commitment of the team to the organization [12]. Generative AI may offer solutions to the challenges and enable entirely new avenues for the development of visionary leadership on, e.g., the premise of hybrid intelligence and when combined with other advanced technologies such as metaverse, virtual worlds, avatars, and digital twins in business, managerial and organizational contexts. A very broad and challenging question is whether AI-based expert systems can support visionary leadership and decision-making. A hypothesis is that generative AI can make visionary leadership more accessible due to the complementary nature of human and artificial intelligence: where one is lacking, the other is augmenting.

Recognizing the transformative potential of generative AI and the different aspects related to visionary leadership, this explorative study is the first of its kind to investigate the potential and applications areas of generative AI for visionary leadership. Through a survey, we collect data from a targeted diverse group of management, leadership, AI, and foresight experts to discover both the potential and limitations of generative AI for the five main domains of visionary leadership: (1) Vision Formulation, (2) Vision Communication, (3) Vision Integration, (4) Vision Realization, and (5) Vision Learning.

After describing the theoretical background, this short paper presents, analyzes, and discusses the initial results of the expert survey, especially the quantitative results on how desirable and feasible the application of generative AI for visionary leadership is, and how experts evaluate the feasibility and desirability of a special set of statements regarding the futures of generative AI for visionary leadership.

Previous studies of visionary leadership have not examined the role of technology, not to mention the role of generative AI for visionary leadership. This is the first empirical study linking fundamental theoretical hypotheses of visionary leadership to the uses and applications of generative AI in leadership functions, and thus addresses an existing research gap and contributes to further the academic discourse on the intersection of artificial intelligence and management. Some key hypotheses of visionary leadership and management are tested for the first time in this empirical study. Thus, while presented as a short paper, this pilot study can be viewed as an opening to this emerging research avenue and an expansion to existing visionary leadership research. Furthermore, it suggests more specific research issues and topics for future-oriented research, especially concerning the key question, how to benefit from generative AI in the context of visionary leadership.

2   Theoretical Background

As the study focuses on generative AI and visionary leadership, we will next discuss these two themes based on literature and provide definitions used in the study.

2.1   Generative Artificial Intelligence: Background and Current Challenges

The historical phases of artificial intelligence and its development phases can be studied with various sources [13–17]. AI applications have become an integral part of daily life, with technologies like virtual assistants, recommendation systems, and autonomous vehicles gaining widespread use. In current ongoing discussions the increasing integration of AI into various sectors has raised ethical concerns and led to considerations about responsible AI development. Governments and organizations are working on establishing regulations to address these challenges. Also, some AI experts assert that we are living in a simulation. [18]

Today, business leaders are struggling to understand how seriously they should take the latest phenomenon in the world of artificial intelligence; *generative AI* [19]. Generative artificial intelligence (generative AI, GenAI,[1] or GAI) is artificial intelligence capable of generating different types of content often in response to prompts. Generative AI models learn the patterns and structures of their input training data and then generate new data that has similar characteristics. The term "generative AI" refers to computational techniques that are capable of generating seemingly new, meaningful content such as text, images, or audio from training data. [1, 13, 14, 18, 19] More specifically, generative AI can be defined as "a branch of AI that can create new content such as texts, images, or audio that increasingly often cannot be distinguished anymore from human craftsmanship". The widespread diffusion of this technology with examples such as Dall-E 2, GPT-4, and Copilot is currently revolutionizing the way we work and communicate with each other. [1]. For the purposes of this study, we will use the aforementioned definition by Feuerriegel et al. [1] to describe generative artificial intelligence.

2.2   Visionary Leadership: Definitions and Five Key Domains

Modern organizations and society at large urgently require visions for the future that address complex challenges, offer alternative pathways, inspire commitment, and empower action, while enabling flexibility and adaptability. A vision depicting the expectations of an individual or a group on influencing the future [20] provides crucial assistance for navigation, especially in complex, uncertain, and challenging times [3]. However, as van der Helm [20] argues, we need to "understand what turns an expression or a claim about 'a future that could be' into the idealised future of a vision, how those claims are created, how they obtain their authority, and how they move from an ideational to an action-based level.''. We need to develop the ability to create and articulate a clear and inspiring vision that evokes an emotional response and forms a bridge between people as well as between idea and action, to communicate a vision in a way that inspires and energizes, to motivate the work towards achieving the vision, and to create a sense of shared purpose and commitment, and integrate the vision into the organization in ways that it is used as a guiding framework for decision-making and everyday behavior – in other words, we need visionary leadership [4, 21, 22].

Visionary leadership can be viewed as "verbal communication of an image of a future for a collective with the intention to persuade others to contribute to the realization of that future" [23], or more broadly as a specific leadership type that can vary significantly from leader to leader in terms of style, content, and context [21], to build visionary organizations [6, 24]. Summarizing previous discussions in literature and for the purposes of this study, we approach visionary leadership through what we call the five main domains of visionary leadership: (1) Vision Formulation, (2) Vision Communication, (3) Vision Integration, (4) Vision Realization, and (5) Vision Learning. *Vision Formulation* refers to the practices, capabilities, activities, tools, and frameworks associated with creating and developing the content of a vision. This may involve, for example, imagination, strategic and futures thinking, environmental and horizon scanning, alternative scenarios and images of the future, analysis and value assessments, and different kinds of visioning methods and techniques. Vision Formulation can be analyzed from both individual and group perspectives, as a more individual endeavor, a more collaborative co-creative process, or anything in between. *Vision Communication* refers to the practices, capabilities, activities, tools, and frameworks associated with expressing, transmitting, and interpreting the content of a vision. It can utilize various forms, such as written, spoken, visual, auditory, tactile, and kinesthetic, and channels, including personal, organizational, mass media, social media, virtual reality, and other emerging digital means. Vision Communication can be analyzed from both individual and group perspectives, particularly focusing on the dynamics of communication among individuals and within groups involving multidirectional flows of information and feedback loops. *Vision Integration* refers to the practices, capabilities, activities, tools, and frameworks associated with ensuring organizational alignment with a vision, making the vision relevant to all levels and roles in the organization, and using the vision as a guiding framework for decision-making and everyday behavior. *Vision Realization* refers to the practices, capabilities, activities, tools, and frameworks associated with pursuing the ambitions of the formed vision in practice in the short, medium, and long terms. *Vision Learning* refers to the practices, capabilities, activities, tools, and frameworks associated with monitoring and evaluating the implementation of the formed vision, and interpreting and informing of needs for adaptation, and refinement in response to new insights.

While there are many definitions used to define a vision [20], we refer to it as "a meaningful expression portraying the fundamental nature and characteristics of preferred futures to unite and empower the actions of those who want to create them" [25]. In addition, we incorporate the specific characteristics used in the business and organizational context, where vision can be perceived as a holistic "picture of the future company" integrating goals, strategies, and action plans based on analysis, imagination, intuition, and values [3], or an umbrella concept consisting of a guiding philosophy including the core values and beliefs and purpose of an organization, and a tangible image (of the future) involving a mission and a vivid description of the future state in which the mission is realized [24]. For the purposes of this study, we will use the presented definitions of vision and the five domains of visionary leadership.

3 Materials and Methods

Next, we will present the research design, data collection, and data analysis of the study.

3.1 Research Design

The research design outlined the overall structure and strategy of the investigation, guiding the collection and analysis of data. The research was focused on a key question: How does generative AI impact the five domains of visionary leadership? In addition, we were interested in if and how generative AI is facilitating visionary leadership now and in the future.

The rationale for the pilot expert study was linked to potential developments of generative AI and its impacts on the key domains of visionary leadership. The key research question is important, and the findings of this study are highly relevant and contribute to further research development. The research design of this pilot study was planned to produce reliable and valid results with an expert survey [26, 27] based on the theoretical background and utilizing the presented definitions to ensure that the study was well grounded in literature. The survey was developed iteratively involving feedback from experienced researchers to ensure both technical and scientific quality. This approach led to refinements with enhancements to the questions and overall survey structure. Quantitative approaches were focused on desirability and feasibility evaluations of applying generative AI in the field of visionary leadership, and qualitative approaches were focused on argumentation of experts concerning the use of generative AI.

To begin with, the survey included the definitions of generative AI, visions and visionary leadership as defined in the theoretical background. Then, the survey was comprised of background information, quantitative and qualitative questions. The respondents were asked to provide their background information as the only mandatory set of questions. This included age, country of residence, sector, current role or profession, years of professional experience, and description of professional expertise and experience. *Two quantitative questions* were designed to understand how desirable and feasible the application of generative AI for the five domains of visionary leadership is perceived, and how experts evaluate the feasibility and desirability of a special set of nine statements regarding the futures of generative AI for visionary leadership. The answers were given on a scale from zero to ten. Additionally, the experts were asked to provide brief supporting arguments based on their professional expertise, experiences, and expectations. *Five qualitative questions* inquired how the experts envision generative AI contributing to the different domains of visionary leadership, what the key limitations that should be considered are, where they see the most value in applying generative AI for visionary leadership in organizations, how generative AI can assist in developing the maturity of visionary leadership, and finally, what the likely pitfalls of generative AI applications for visionary leadership are.

3.2 Data Collection and Analysis

The survey was aimed at management, leadership, foresight, and AI experts. Participants were recruited through professional networks including universities, research organizations, businesses, and business development organizations, and through directly contacting known key experts. The data collection was conducted during February and March 2024. The size of the sample was 25 (n = 25). Based on the responses, we can interpret that the respondents were experienced, the majority with over ten years of work experience in their occupations, in their respective fields representing various sectors: Public Sector (4), Private Sector (3), Non-Profit Sector (1), Academia (12), Independent (4), and Other (1). 24 respondents were from Finland, and one from Peru. Three respondents were between 35–44, five between 45–54, ten between 55–64, and seven 65 years of age or above. Current professional roles included, e.g., professor, senior advisor, development director, founder, research director, rector, teacher, entrepreneur, foresight practitioner, consultant, commercial lead, editor in chief, futurist, and AI researcher. In terms of years of professional experience, there were six to 10 years (5), 11 to 20 years (5), and over 20 years(15). In addition, the respondents descriptions of their professional expertise and experience include, but are not limited to, AI specialist, board member in several organizations, teaching, research, writing, consulting, expert in management and leadership research, expert in knowledge and innovation management, research in organizational capabilities and innovation, managing design departments, design teams, groups and projects, business Development, ICT, technology foresight for business development, teaching and research in strategic foresight and futures studies, research and consultation in future studies, risk assessment and ethics of AI, executive consultant, serial entrepreneur, CEO and AI expert.

The data analysis in this short paper is based on the quantitative analyses of the expert assessments. The quantitative data was approached with basic statistical descriptive analyses, including minimum values, lower quartiles, medians, averages, upper quartiles, maximum values, and standard deviations. This enabled the understanding of the expert evaluations, and the observation of consensus and divergence in relation to desirability and feasibility assessments.

3.3 Ethical Considerations and Limitations

Artificial intelligence is a theme with significant ethical considerations. Considering the implementation of the study, it is important to follow principles of responsible research. The data collection complied with the international data protection law (EU General Data Protection Regulation) on ensuring data security, processing of personal data, and anonymization. Also, a detailed privacy note was included in the survey.

Since this is a short conference paper, we focus on presenting and analyzing the quantitative data. Qualitative data will be used to develop a full research paper. While the experts were asked to provide brief supporting arguments to their quantitative assessment, only a few were put in. In addition, we want to note that the survey data was collected in Finland and mostly represents views of Finnish experts.

4 Results: Generative AI and Visionary Leadership

Next, we will present the results of the expert survey. The results of two quantitative questions are presented as tables in which the values of each column are highlighted with different shades from white background specifying the lowest value of that column and darker shades of grey for higher values.

4.1 How Desirable and Feasible is the Application of Generative AI for Visionary Leadership?

According to the expert survey, based on median evaluation, Vision Communication (7,00) and Vision Learning (6,50) are seen as the most feasible domains of visionary leadership for the application of generative AI (see Table 1). Vision Formulation, Vision Integration, and Vision Realization were assessed as similarly feasible (5,00). All domains received high maximum values from some experts (9.00 or 10.00). The upper quartile of Vision Learning (8,75) was the highest, Vision Formulation and Vision Communication were the same (8,00), and Vision Realization and Vision Integration had the lowest upper quartiles. Regarding the lower quartile, all domains were relatively close to one another (between 3,00 and 4,00). Vision Communication and Vision Learning received the highest lower quartile evaluations (4.00), and Vision Formulation (3.00) the lowest. Some experts evaluated the feasibility of the application of generative AI for Vision Integration and Vision Learning as zero, while Vision Communication received the highest minimum value (2.00).

Based on the evaluations, we interpret that Vision Communication is the domain of visionary leadership with the highest feasibility for generative AI applications. The second promising domain is Vision Learning, although it received a minimum value of zero from one expert. The least feasible domains are harder to interpret due to the relatively similar evaluations and standard deviations, but Vision Integration seems as the least feasible especially based on the lowest upper quartile. This is a relevant finding for strategy and visionary leadership experts as this is a topical issue for businesses to consider.

Based on the medians, Vision Communication (7,00) and Vision Learning (7,00) are seen as the most desirable domains for applications of generative AI for visionary leadership, and Vision Formulation (4,00) as the least desirable domain (see Table 2). Similarly, Vision Communication and Vision Learning received the highest maximum value (10,00) from some experts, while Vision Realization received the lowest maximum value (8,00). The upper quartiles follow the median and maximum values as Vision Communication and Vision Learning were seen as the most desirable domains (8,00) and Vision Formulation as the least desirable (5,00). Based on the lower quartile, Vision

Table 1 How feasible is the application of generative AI for visionary leadership?

Domains of Visionary Leadership	Min. Value	Lower Quartile	Median	Average	Upper Quartile	Max. Value	Standard Deviation
1. Vision Formulation	1,00	3,00	5,00	5,24	8,00	9,00	2,47
2. Vision Communication	2,00	4,00	7,00	6,29	8,00	10,00	2,52
3. Vision Integration	0,00	3,75	5,00	5,10	6,25	10,00	2,36
4. Vision Realization	1,00	3,50	5,00	5,42	7,00	9,00	2,34
5. Vision Learning	0,00	4,00	6,50	6,28	8,75	10,00	2,76

Formulation got the lowest evaluations (3,00), and Vision Learning (5,25) the highest. It is worth noting that all but Vision Learning (2,00) got the minimum value of zero.

Based on the evaluations, we interpret that Vision Learning is the domain of visionary leadership with the highest desirability for generative AI applications. The second promising desirable domain is Vision Communication. The domain of least desirability for applications of generative AI is Vision Formulation with a significant margin. However, it is worth noting that Vision Realization has similarly low evaluations with the lowest standard deviation.

Table 2 How desirable is the application of generative AI for visionary leadership?

Domains of Visionary Leadership	Min. Value	Lower Quartile	Median	Average	Upper Quartile	Max. Value	Standard Deviation
1. Vision Formulation	0,00	3,00	4,00	4,81	5,00	9,00	2,52
2. Vision Communication	0,00	4,00	7,00	5,90	8,00	10,00	2,62
3. Vision Integration	0,00	4,75	5,50	5,15	7,00	9,00	2,39
4. Vision Realization	0,00	5,00	6,00	5,32	6,00	8,00	2,00
5. Vision Learning	2,00	5,25	7,00	6,39	8,00	10,00	2,35

When the desirability and feasibility assessments are compared, we can estimate the so-called Desirability-Feasibility Gap. A positive value indicates greater desirability than feasibility, a negative value greater feasibility than desirability, and zero a match between desirability and feasibility. The application of generative AI for Vision Formulation is less desirable than feasible, Vision Communication equally desirable and feasible, and Vision Integration, Vision Learning, and Vision Realization as more desirable than feasible (see Table 3).

Table 3 Desirability-Feasibility Gaps of Applications of Generative AI for Visionary Leadership (Desirability Assessment minus Feasibility Assessment)

Desirability-Feasibility Gap	1. Vision Formulation	2. Vision Communication	3. Vision Integration	4. Vision Realization	5. Vision Learning
Median	-1,00	0,00	0,50	1,00	0,50
Average	-0,43	-0,38	0,05	-0,11	0,11

4.2 How Would You Assess the Desirability and Feasibility of the Following Statements?

The detailed analysis of statements (see Table 4) reveals that the most feasible statements are statement "2. Generative AI can be used to effectively communicate a vision in a personalised way to each and every stakeholder", "5. Generative AI can monitor and evaluate the implementation of a vision", and "6. Organizations can use generative AI to learn from and reflect their vision". The analysis unveils that the least feasible statements are statement "8. Ethical considerations do not affect the use of generative AI for visionary leadership in organizations", thus implying that ethical questions have an affect. So-called middle of range statements were statement "1. Organizations can create and develop clear and compelling visions with generative AI", "7. Generative AI can interpret and inform of needs for refining a vision", and "9. Regulation limits the use of generative AI for visionary leadership in organizations". Other statements were consented a bit more strongly.

Table 4 How would you assess the feasibility of the following statements?

Statements	Min. Value	Lower Quartile	Median	Average	Upper Quartile	Max. Value	Standard Deviation
1. Organizations can create and develop clear and compelling visions with generative AI	0,00	3,00	5,00	4,78	6,50	10,00	2,30
2. Generative AI can be used to effectively communicate a vision in a personalised way to each and every stakeholder	0,00	5,00	7,00	6,04	8,00	10,00	2,70
3. Organizations can use generative AI to align decision-making and everyday behaviours with their vision	0,00	4,00	6,00	5,74	7,50	10,00	2,43
4. Generative AI can help implement visions	0,00	3,00	6,00	5,10	7,00	8,00	2,32
5. Generative AI can monitor and evaluate the implementation of a vision	3,00	6,00	7,00	6,90	8,00	9,00	1,81
6. Organizations can use generative AI to learn from and reflect their vision	2,00	5,00	7,00	6,64	8,75	10,00	2,30
7. Generative AI can interpret and inform of needs for refining a vision	3,00	5,00	5,00	5,87	7,50	9,00	1,94
8. Ethical considerations do not affect the use of generative AI for visionary leadership in organizations	0,00	1,00	2,00	2,48	5,00	6,00	2,06
9. Regulation limits the use of generative AI for visionary leadership in organizations	1,00	3,25	5,00	5,39	7,00	10,00	2,73

The detailed analysis of statements reveals that the most desirable statements are statements "2. Generative AI can be used to effectively communicate a vision in a personalised way to each and every stakeholder" and "6. Organizations can use generative AI to learn from and reflect their vision" (see Table 5). In addition, the analysis reveals statement "8. Ethical considerations do not affect the use of generative AI for visionary leadership in organizations" as the most undesirable one, suggesting ethical considerations as desirable. The other statements received middle-of-range assessments.

Statements "1. Organizations can create and develop clear and compelling visions with generative AI", "4. Generative AI can help implement visions", and "9. Regulation limits the use of generative AI for visionary leadership in organizations" were such middle-range statements. Experts may have had difficulties in fully accepting or rejecting these statements.

Table 5 How would you assess the desirability of the following statements?

Statements	Min. Value	Lower Quartile	Median	Average	Upper Quartile	Max. Value	Standard Deviation
1. Organizations can create and develop clear and compelling visions with generative AI	0,00	3,00	5,00	5,00	7,00	10,00	2,75
2. Generative AI can be used to effectively communicate a vision in a personalised way to each and every stakeholder	0,00	4,50	7,00	5,87	8,00	10,00	2,75
3. Organizations can use generative AI to align decision-making and everyday behaviours with their vision	0,00	4,50	6,00	5,83	7,50	10,00	2,50
4. Generative AI can help implement visions	0,00	3,00	5,00	4,76	6,00	9,00	2,41
5. Generative AI can monitor and evaluate the implementation of a vision	2,00	5,00	6,00	6,14	8,00	9,00	2,33
6. Organizations can use generative AI to learn from and reflect their vision	2,00	5,00	7,00	6,64	8,75	10,00	2,28
7. Generative AI can interpret and inform of needs for refining a vision	1,00	5,00	6,00	6,00	8,00	9,00	2,41
8. Ethical considerations do not affect the use of generative AI for visionary leadership in organizations	0,00	1,00	2,00	3,00	5,00	9,00	2,59
9. Regulation limits the use of generative AI for visionary leadership in organizations	0,00	5,00	5,50	5,94	8,00	10,00	2,67

Based on the Desirability-Feasibility Gap, statements "4. Generative AI can help implement visions" and "5. Generative AI can monitor and evaluate the implementation of a vision" are seen as more feasible than desirable, and statements "7. Generative AI can interpret and inform of needs for refining a vision" and "9. Regulation limits the use of generative AI for visionary leadership in organizations" more desirable than feasible (see Table 6). The other statements were assessed equally desirable and feasible.

Table 6 Desirability-Feasibility Gaps of Statements Regarding the Futures of Generative AI for Visionary Leadership (Desirability Assessment minus Feasibility Assessment)

Desirability - Feasibility Gap	1. Organizations can create and develop clear and compelling visions with generative AI	2. Generative AI can be used to effectively communicate a vision in a personalised way to each and every stakeholder	3. Organizations can use generative AI to align decision-making and everyday behaviors with their vision	4. Generative AI can help implement visions	5. Generative AI can monitor and evaluate the implementation of a vision	6. Organizations can use generative AI to learn from and reflect their vision	7. Generative AI can interpret and inform of needs for refining a vision	8. Ethical considerations do not affect the use of generative AI for visionary leadership in organizations	9. Regulation limits the use of generative AI for visionary leadership in organizations
Median	0,00	0,00	0,00	-1,00	-1,00	0,00	1,00	0,00	0,50
Average	0,22	-0,17	0,09	-0,33	-0,76	0,00	0,13	0,52	0,56

5 Conclusions

In this pilot study, we investigated the potential and applications areas of generative AI for visionary leadership. Through a survey, we collected data from a targeted diverse group of management, leadership, AI, and foresight experts to discover the potential and limitations of generative AI for the five main domains of visionary leadership: (1) Vision Formulation, (2) Vision Communication, (3) Vision Integration, (4) Vision Realization, and (5) Vision Learning.

By combining the feasibility and desirability evaluations of the application of generative AI for the five domains of visionary leadership and the set of nine statements regarding the futures of generative AI for visionary leadership, we interpret that Vision Communication is currently the domain with the highest potential for generative AI applications. This is supported also with statement "2. Generative AI can be used to effectively communicate a vision in a personalised way to each and every stakeholder" being evaluated amongst the most feasible and most desirable. Since the Desirability-Feasibility Gap of Vision Communication is zero (equally desirable and feasible), there can be a solid opportunity for applications of generative AI.

The domain with the second highest potential for generative AI applications is currently Vision Learning. This is supported with statement "6. Organizations can use generative AI to learn from and reflect their vision" being evaluated as the most feasible and desirable. Since the Desirability-Feasibility Gap of Vision Learning is positive (more desirable than feasible), the current potential may be a bit lower than with Vision Communication, but Vision Learning can be a domain with worthy objectives for developing more advanced generative AI applications to close the gap.

The domain with the lowest potential for generative AI applications according to desirability and feasibility analyses is currently Vision Formulation. Interestingly, the domain was seen as more feasible than desirable, which can signal, e.g., hesitance to make use of the current potential of generative AI applications for various reasons. Furthermore, possibly related to this, too, the results indicate the importance of ethical considerations in the context of generative AI for visionary leadership based on the contrary desirability and feasibility assessments to the statement "8. Ethical considerations do not affect the use of generative AI for visionary leadership in organizations".

We look forward to expanding this short paper using the qualitative survey data, which is likely to provide more depth to the presented results. We believe this pilot study can be viewed as an opening to the emerging research avenue to the role of technology, especially generative AI, for visionary leadership, an expansion to existing visionary leadership research, and practical value added to strategic decision-making.

Acknowledgements. We would like to thank each of the 25 respondents for their expert assessments. We thank EDIH Robocoast, Allied ICT Finland, the "Methods and tools for foresight and strategy work" Facebook group, the ProDigy project, and the Smart City Digital Twins project for their support.

Disclosure of Interests. The authors have no competing interests to declare that are relevant to the content of this short paper.

References

1. Feuerriegel, S., Hartmann, J., Janiesch, C., Zschech, P.: Generative AI. Bus. Inf. Syst. Eng. (2023). https://doi.org/10.1007/s12599-023-00834-7.
2. Dellermann, D., Ebel, P., Söllner, M., Leimeister, J.M.: Hybrid intelligence. Bus. Inf. Syst. Eng. **61**, 637–643 (2019). https://doi.org/10.1007/s12599-019-00595-2
3. Wilson, I.: Realizing the power of strategic vision. Long Range Plan. **25**, 18–28 (1992). https://doi.org/10.1016/0024-6301(92)90271-3
4. Taylor, C.M., Cornelius, C.J., Colvin, K.: Visionary leadership and its relationship to organizational effectiveness. Leaders. Organ. Dev. J. **35**, 566–583 (2014). https://doi.org/10.1108/LODJ-10-2012-0130
5. Baum, J.R., Locke, E., Kirkpatrick, S.: A longitudinal study of the relation of vision and vision communication to venture growth in entrepreneurial firms. J. Appl. Psychol. **83**, 43–54 (1998). https://doi.org/10.1037/0021-9010.83.1.43
6. Collins, J., Porras, J.I.: Built to Last: Successful Habits of Visionary Companies. Harper Business, New York (1994)
7. Cheema, S., Javed, F.: Employee Engagement and Visionary Leadership: Impact on Customer and Employee Satisfaction. Presented at the (2015)
8. Haque, M., TitiAmayah, A., Liu, L.: The role of vision in organizational readiness for change and growth. Leadersh. Organ. Dev. J. **37**, 983–999 (2016). https://doi.org/10.1108/LODJ-01-2015-0003
9. Kantabutra, S., Avery, G.: Proposed model for investigating relationships between vision components and business unit performance. J. Manage. Organ. **8**, 22–39 (2002). https://doi.org/10.5172/jmo.2002.8.2.22
10. McGivern, M.H., Tvorik, S.J.: Vision driven organizations: measurement techniques for group classification. Manage. Decis. **36**, 241–264 (1998). https://doi.org/10.1108/00251749810211045
11. Sltten, T., Mutonyi, B.R., Lien, G.: Does organizational vision really matter? An empirical examination of factors related to organizational vision integration among hospital employees. BMC Health Serv. Res. **21**, 483 (2021). https://doi.org/10.1186/s12913-021-06503-3
12. Ates, N.Y., Tarakci, M., Porck, J.P., van Knippenberg, D., Groenen, P.J.F.: The dark side of visionary leadership in strategy implementation: strategic alignment, strategic consensus, and commitment. J. Manage. **46**, 637–665 (2020). https://doi.org/10.1177/0149206318811567
13. Pickover, C.A.: Artificial intelligence: an illustrated history: from medieval robots to neural networks. Sterling (2019)
14. Toosi, A., Bottino, A.G., Saboury, B., Siegel, E., Rahmim, A.: A brief history of AI: how to prevent another winter a critical review. PET Clinics. **16**, 449–469 (2021). https://doi.org/10.1016/j.cpet.2021.07.001
15. Morar, F.-S.: Reinventing machines: the transmission history of the Leibniz calculator. British J. Hist. Sci. **48**, 123–146 (2015)
16. Nahin, P.J.: The Logician and the Engineer: How George Boole and Claude Shannon Created the Information Age. Princeton University Press (2012). https://doi.org/10.1515/9781400844654
17. Brannan, J.: The World's First Calculator – The Pascaline. https://juliabrannan.com/historical-articles/the-worlds-first-calculator-the-pascaline/. Accessed 13 Mar 2024
18. Kissinger, H.A., Schmidt, E., Huttenlocher, D.: The Age of AI and Our Human Future. John Murray, London (2021)
19. McAfee, A., Rock, D., Brynjolfsson, E.: How to Capitalize on Generative AI (2023). https://hbr.org/2023/11/how-to-capitalize-on-generative-ai

20. van der Helm, R.: The vision phenomenon: towards a theoretical underpinning of visions of the future and the process of envisioning. Futures **41**, 96–104 (2009). https://doi.org/10.1016/j.futures.2008.07.036

21. Westley, F., Mintzberg, H.: Visionary leadership and strategic management. Strateg. Manag. J. **10**, 17–32 (1989). https://doi.org/10.1002/smj.4250100704

22. Kohles, J.C., Bligh, M.C., Carsten, M.K.: The vision integration process: applying rogers' diffusion of innovations theory to leader–follower communications. Leadership **9**, 466–485 (2013). https://doi.org/10.1177/1742715012459784

23. van Knippenberg, D., Stam, D.: Visionary leadership. In: Day, D.V. (ed.) The Oxford Handbook of Leadership and Organizations. Oxford University Press, Oxford (2014). https://doi.org/10.1093/oxfordhb/9780199755615.013.013.

24. Collins, J.C., Porras, J.I.: Organizational vision and visionary organizations. California Manag. Rev. **34**, 30–52 (1991). https://doi.org/10.2307/41166682

25. Villman, T.: The preferred futures of a human-centric society: a case of developing a life-event-based visioning approach (2021)

26. Tobi, H., Kampen, J.K.: Research design: the methodology for interdisciplinary research framework. Qual. Quant. **52**, 1209–1225 (2018). https://doi.org/10.1007/s11135-017-0513-8

27. Blair, G., Coppock, A., Humphreys, M.: Research Design in the Social Sciences: Declaration, Diagnosis, and Redesign. Princeton University Press, Princeton (2023)

Research on the Design of Tourism Cultural and Creative Products in Ancient Cities in China from the Perspective of Experience

Zeyi Wang, Weishang Liu$^{(\boxtimes)}$, and Yali Si

Yanshan University, Hebei Qinhuangdao 066000, China
909998497@qq.com

Abstract. In order to meet the deep inner needs of travelers and awaken people's deep resonance for the tourism culture of ancient cities in China, so that tourists can have a better user experience, the quality theory is introduced into the design of cultural and creative products of ancient cities in China, and the design strategy of cultural and creative products of ancient cities in line with the user experience under the development of The Times is discussed. First of all, this paper sorts out the connotation and characteristics of "sensory substance", and creates three structural levels and five core levels of sensory substance theory. According to the fit degree of sensory experience level and Luanzhou Ancient City tourism cultural and creative products level, the user experience model of Luanzhou Ancient City cultural and creative products is constructed, the commonality of ancient city tourism culture in tourist user experience is sought, and the design method meeting user needs is explored. Combined with the five core layers of quality theory, this paper explores the symbolic representation strategies of cultural and creative products from the three layers of color representation, shape representation and material representation. Then from the sensory element mining, narrative situation building, individual emotional awakening to explore the sensory element extraction strategy. Finally, Luanzhou Ancient City is taken as the research object for design practice test.

Keywords: Quality experience · Ancient Chinese city · Tourism cultural and creative product design · Experience level

1 Characteristics of Quality Theory and Levels of Experience Creation

1.1 Characteristics of Quality Theory

"Quality" is an artistic term that first appeared in American philosophy. Both C.S. Peirce and C.I. Lewis have elaborated on "quality experience". They summarized the concept of sensory quality into four characteristics: First, when the word "sensory quality" is used in visual experience, it refers to the objective properties of the object presented to the experience, that is, the appearance of things; Second, sensory substance includes not only simple or complex sensory experience, but also non-sensory experience; Third, the direct experience of personal experience through personal behavior experience; Fourth, sensory quality is related to people's conscious experience, which is subjective and personal. The first, third, and fourth features were adopted by most people in the use of sensory quality theory and have been used ever since [1]. In the design products derived from cultural IP, the application of sensory quality theory pays more attention to emotional experience than other types of product design.

Lin Rongtai mentioned in 2014 that quality theory is mainly reflected in five core aspects of product design: Attractiveness, Beauty, Creativity, Delicacy and Engineering. Among them, attractiveness is the description of the attraction, inducement and story of the product. Attractiveness generally contains a rich cultural, emotional background and back story, which can attract consumers and provide users with a profound quality experience; At the level of beauty feeling, it is required to explore aesthetic feeling from external perspectives such as product shape, material, decoration and color. Through various external quality images, beautiful shape, suitable material, exquisite decoration and harmonious color are used to form aesthetic perception at the level of aesthetic feeling, so that experiencers can intuitively feel the aesthetic feeling of products through visual experience. Creativity refers to the description of the innovation, originality and individuation of the product, emphasizing that the product can provide a differentiated and unique feeling, criticizing the uniqueness and homogeneity of the current product, aiming at the needs and personality of the users, bringing consumers touch and pleasure through various ingenious ideas, and producing some kind of memory or empathy experience; Delicacy refers to the precision, delicacy, delicacy and other characteristics of the product, which has high requirements for the delicacy of the details of the product structure; Engineering mainly refers to the production process of products, sophisticated technology, strong functionality, can meet the needs of users. The designed products are easy to operate, easy to understand, ergonomic, safety, durability and full design can be guaranteed.

1.2 Level Creation of Quality Experience

Clarifying the level of sensory quality theory is a necessary way to design popular cultural and creative design products, meet the deep emotional needs of users, and understand users' sensory quality experience of cultural and creative products. Through the above description of the characteristics of quality by Peirce and other scholars, the characteristics of quality theory can be sorted into a multi-level structure. According to Peirce's description of the characteristics of sensory substance theory, we can see that the sensory substance theory has a multi-level structure. By summarizing the above characteristics, the quality theory can be roughly divided into three levels, which realize the step transformation from the physical level to the spiritual level and from the concrete level to the abstract level, so as to better realize the transformation of quality theory and cultural and creative product design [2], (see Fig. 1).

1. Surface structure: the transformation of visual quality through visual experience. According to Peirce's first statement on the characteristics of sensory quality, that is, "the objective properties of objects presented to the subject of experience", it can be seen that this level of characteristics of sensory quality theory is the embodiment of the external characteristics of objectively existing objects, and it is the first cognition of objects by experiencers that can transform these characteristics into observable objective existence attributes such as shapes, colors, materials and textures that we can see visually. The expression of visual characteristics of sensory quality is the basic level of sensory quality image, which is combined with the product image and gradually deepened on the basis of this level to generate the deep structure of sensory quality image.

2. Intermediate structure: The characteristic transformation of behavioral sensory substance is realized through behavioral experience. According to Peirce's third point on the characteristics of sensory quality: "Sensory quality is experienced by the behavior of the experience subject." It can be seen that sensory quality features need to carry out visual translation of situations through experiencers' behavioral experience, integrate objects and events with situations, enrich the narrative scenes of cultural and creative products, and make the background and stories endow cultural and creative products with vitality and stimulate users' sensory systems [3]. Through this level of transformation, cultural and creative products can be rich with a more unique sense of story and interaction, so that users have a stronger emotional experience.

3. Deep structure: Realizing the characteristic transformation of consciousness through conscious experience. The fourth point of Peirce's characterization of sensory quality is: "Sensory quality is related to the conscious experience of the experience subject, which is private and subjective." It can be seen that this level is mainly the inner level experience generated by the experiencer's conscious activities, and is the deep sensory quality experience stimulated by users according to their own personal experience, cultural accumulation and thinking mode. It can be seen that this level carries the cultural background, thought and emotion and humanistic feelings of things, and is the core layer of the sensory quality theory, and also the superposition of many factors such as taste, realm and experience of the experiencer.

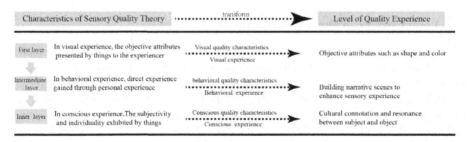

Fig. 1. Theoretical characteristics of sensory quality and transformation of quality experience level

2 Ancient City Tourism Cultural and Creative Products

2.1 Characteristics and Cases of Ancient City Tourism Cultural and Creative Products

Ancient city tourism cultural and creative products, as a branch of cultural and creative products, refer to the cultural content of ancient city or its cultural resources expressed through the creative expression of designers, and the unique cultural concepts of ancient city in the tourism category such as local conditions and people, architectural landscape, folk culture, allusions to legends, dialect culture, history and culture are designed. Transform cultural and creative products with market value and economic value. Let visitors feel the cultural connotation of the ancient city while buying local cultural and creative products. Ancient city tourism cultural and creative products are a summary of ancient city tourism culture. Their design and development can tap the national cultural traditions of various regions in China, and based on this design, the traditional culture of ancient city is combined with the modern popular aesthetic, which can meet the needs of tourists for ancient city tourism and enable the effective dissemination and promotion of ancient city tourism culture.

Three famous ancient cities in China are Lijiang in Yunnan Province, Pingyao in Shanxi Province and Langzhong in Sichuan Province. Their characteristics are different, with their own unique tourism cultural resources and historical connotation. With its excellent ancient city characteristics as its continuous design source, to create a variety of tourist cultural and creative products. Among them, the old town of Lijiang has designed many tourism cultural and creative products with myths and legends as the theme based on its widely spread allusions and myths. In the tourism cultural and creative design of Pingyao Ancient City, the design products based on the Pingyao County government and the buildings of Pingyao Ancient City are integrated into the modern products, and the scenic spot buildings, historical stories and traditional culture are integrated into the modern products to grasp the characteristics of "national tide wind" and design fashionable and connotation cultural and creative design products. The design of Langzhong ancient City's cultural and creative products mainly takes the unique regional culture of Sichuan as the design source, extracts the characteristic cultural IP elements, pays attention to the design strategy of "cultural and creative + food", creates the tourism cultural atmosphere through food marketing and punch card, accurately grasps the tourism needs of tourists and consumers, injects fresh blood into the traditional culture, and enables tourists to experience the ancient city culture more immersed [4].

2.2 Hierarchical Construction of Luanzhou Ancient City Tourism and Cultural Resources

Based on the tourism cultural resources of Luanzhou Ancient City and consumers' demand for tourism cultural and creative products of Luanzhou Ancient City, the tourism cultural resources of Luanzhou Ancient City are divided into three levels (as shown in Fig. 2). The first structure is the tourism cultural resources that can be visually expressed, such as the shapes of Luan river stone, Yanshan Mountain and Luan River in the natural landscape elements, and the derivation of celebrity culture can be used as the visual sensory layer for secondary creation [5]. Elements of industrial culture, such as the material of ceramics and the texture of steel, can also be classified as surface structures. The intermediate structure is a tourism cultural resource that can be expressed through interactive stories, and can be satisfied by tourists' personal experience. Such as allusion legend elements, folk culture and dialect culture elements. The inner structure is a tourism cultural resource that can reflect the cultural connotation and values, such as the historical and cultural factors and spiritual beliefs of Luanzhou Ancient City, which can inspire and inspire future generations through cultural and creative products [6].

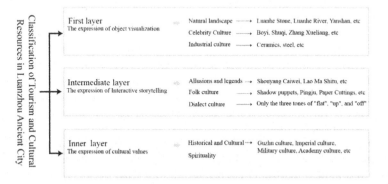

Fig. 2. A hierarchical analysis of Luanzhou Ancient City tourism cultural resources

2.3 Analysis of the Fit Degree Between Quality Experience Level and Luanzhou Ancient City Tourism Cultural Resources

After sorting and analyzing the survey data, it can be seen that the respondents' demand for Luanzhou Ancient City tourism cultural and creative products is generally divided into three aspects, which are consistent with the level of quality and experience. First, the physical and cultural aspect of tourism cultural and creative products is the appearance attribute of the product: respondents mentioned "creative shape" and "aesthetic color" as the main consumption needs, which is consistent with the surface structure with visual sensory quality characteristics in the quality theory; Second, the behavioral culture level is the narrative attribute of the product: respondents repeatedly mentioned the "sense of interaction with the product", "strong practicality" and "experience the cultural story", which is consistent with the middle structure with the characteristics of behavioral sensibility in the sensory quality theory; The third is the spiritual and cultural level, that is, the emotional attributes of the product: the interviewees mentioned "cultural identity", "satisfying cultural feelings", and "regional cultural inheritance", which are consistent with the deep structure with the characteristics of consciousness in the sensory quality theory, as shown in Fig. 3. It can be seen that in the design of Luanzhou Ancient City tourism cultural and creative products, consumers' demand for products has a strong fit with the level of sensory quality and experience, that is, capturing the product's shape and color elements, adding narrative interaction and enriching emotional attributes are important factors for designers to consider. Guided by the theory of sensory quality, the design of Luanzhou Ancient City tourism cultural and creative products is an effective way to meet the needs of consumers and realize the cultural inheritance of Luanzhou.

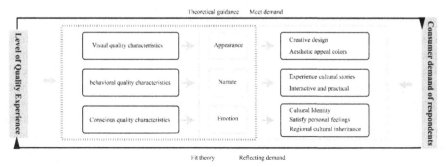

Fig. 3. Analysis of the fit degree of quality theory with the cultural and creative products of Luanzhou Ancient City of the interviewed group

3   Analysis of Design Strategies of Luanzhou Ancient City Tourism Cultural Creation from the Perspective of Experience

3.1   Design Model of Luanzhou Ancient City Tourism Cultural and Creative Products Under Quality Experience

The three levels of sensory quality theory can correspond to the first structure, intermediate structure and inner structure of Luanzhou Ancient City tourism culture and cultural and creative product design respectively. From the perspective of quality theory, the relationship and transformation between quality experience level and tourism cultural products are shown in Fig. 4. Among them, the tourism cultural elements of Luanzhou Ancient City are divided into three levels: physical culture, behavioral culture and spiritual culture. The three levels of culture are disassembled, combined and re-created to encode the tourism cultural elements, and combine them with the three levels of quality theory to generate the extraction strategy of Luanzhou Ancient City tourism cultural quality elements under sensory quality experience [7]. Then, five sensory core layers, such as charm, beauty, creativity, refinement and engineering, are used to represent cultural symbols and reproduce the modeling characteristics of cultural features, so as to generate the modeling representation extraction strategy of Luanzhou Ancient City tourism cultural and creative products under the quality theory [8]. Among the five core layers of quality theory, "charm" is embodied by fashion taste, cultural connotation and deep impression. This level is the overall evaluation of the final effect of cultural and creative products. The "beauty" layer is reflected by comfortable color, pleasing to the eye and attractive appearance; The first layer of "engineering" is reflected by excellent skills, strong operability and exquisite structure, which mainly evaluates the practicability of cultural and creative products; The " beauty" layer is expressed by strong and durable, smart material and delicate construction method; The " creativity" layer is expressed by a strong sense of story, a strong sense of design, and a sense of strangeness, mainly for the evaluation of the interactivity of cultural and creative products. The five core layers of sensory quality theory run through the whole design process of tourism cultural and creative products, and also exist in the extraction of sensory quality elements. In the symbolic representation extraction strategy of Luanzhou Ancient City tourism cultural and creative products under the sensory quality theory, the color representation is more focused on the level of "beauty", the form representation is more focused on "engineering" and "creativity", and the material representation is more focused on "refinement". In this way, cultural characteristics can be reproduced, so that tourists can interact with the products through the use and observation of the purchased cultural and creative products, realize the interpretation of the products, and realize the decoding of the cultural and creative products to the maximum extent according to the knowledge accumulation and cultural literacy of consumers, and realize the transmission of cultural content.

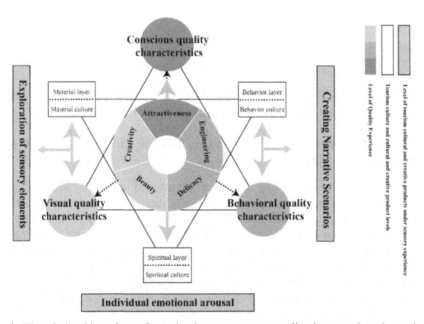

Fig. 4. The relationship and transformation between sensory quality theory and tourism cultural creative products

Based on the analysis and integration of Luanzhou Ancient City's tourism cultural resources and the analysis of the level of sensory quality experience characteristics, the design model of Luanzhou Ancient City's tourism cultural and creative products is established in combination with Luanzhou Ancient City's regional characteristic culture and the relationship between Luanzhou Ancient City's cultural and creative products and users. The design model of Luanzhou Ancient City's tourism cultural products incorporating sensory quality theory is mainly divided into three parts, which are as follows: Sensory symbols mining, narrative situation building, individual emotion awakening.

It is based on the integration and sorting of Luanzhou Ancient City cultural resources, the design of Luanzhou Ancient City cultural and creative products and the feedback of users' emotional cognition and experience.

3.2 Sensory Element Extraction Strategy of Luanzhou Ancient City Tourism Culture Under Sensory Theory

1. Semiotic Symbol Mining Based on First Structure

The sensory symbols of Luanzhou Ancient City cultural and creative products can be deeply explored from the natural culture and celebrity culture, and the sensory images of these objects can be integrated into the design of cultural and creative products. Through the visual experience analysis and processing of sensory quality theory, the dominant characteristics of tourism culture of Luanzhou Ancient City can be extracted, which will help form the presentation of tourism cultural and creative products containing regional cultural factors of Luanzhou Ancient City. Through the tangible material and cultural images, consumers and tourists can have an association with Luanzhou culture. Mining the representative cultural symbols of Luanzhou Ancient City is the basis for the design of Luanzhou Ancient City tourism cultural and creative products. Natural landscape elements such as Luanhe River, Yanshan Mountain, Luanhe stone, Yanshan Pagoda, Confucian Temple, Zijin Pagoda, lunar old Temple, etc., extract their shapes, patterns and so on around their own characteristics and regional characteristics to choose the appropriate design of sensory quality image; In celebrity culture, Boyi, Shuqi and Empress Dowager Xiao, who are particularly representative and unique in the historical development of Luanzhou, can be selected to design their derivative images, and elements can be extracted by combining the visual images left over from historical archives and the shapes performed in movies and dramas. It also includes the visual parts of folk culture, such as Luanzhou shadow play in the basic image of the horn, the Sant horn, the clear horn, the end horn, the clown horn, the beard horn, the big horn, the fairy demon and other characters, the first image of different characters, the classic character carving of paper cutting, etc. These representative Luanzhou cultural symbols can encourage consumers and tourists to associate with these tourism cultural symbols, so as to promote the spread of Luanzhou culture and the publicity of Luanzhou Ancient City scenic spot [9].

2. Narrative Context Based on the Middle Structure

The narrative context creation of Luanzhou Ancient City cultural and creative products is to construct specific scenes through symbols such as speech, hearing, behavior and context content, so as to reproduce the scene and trigger the sensory experience of tourists and users. The layer structure should not only be based on the image property of the product in the surface structure, but also take into account the emotional property of the product in the inner structure. The middle layer structure requires designers to fully understand and master the regional culture of Luanzhou Ancient City, and deeply understand the narrative elements of Luanzhou Ancient City, such as celebrity anecdotes, allusions and legends. Only when designers incorporate these narrative elements into cultural and creative products and create narrative scenes from cultural and creative products, can buyers or users of cultural and creative products experience the charm of Luanzhou culture. Through their sensory aesthetic activities, the core exposition of the narrative scene is realized. Such as Luanzhou ancient city "old horse", "Boyi Shuqi", "seeking ants for water" and "Lady Yang complain" and other allusion legends and celebrity anecdotes, so that consumers in the story created by the immersion experience of cultural and creative products [10]. Luanzhou folk culture is mainly in the form of performance, which is the advantage of making cultural and creative products experience. For example, "Luanzhou Shadow Play" is a dynamic form achieved through the interaction between people, people and objects, and people and scenery. It uses behavioral experience to arouse the users' desire for use and satisfy their sense of immersion in time and space, so that they can gain a deep understanding of intangible cultural heritage. Because of the special folk culture of Luanzhou Ancient City -- shadow play, Pingju and so on, it also needs the participation of auditory language. The scene can be rendered with the help of dialect culture to form interesting interaction with consumers, and consumers can have a more distinct sensory experience process through operation and interaction, so that tourists can reach a resonance from the body and even the spirit. Abstract objects are concretified, perceptual image elements more suitable for application are finally achieved through narrative context, which deeply integrates Luanzhou culture and products, promotes consumers' re-cognition of the cultural connotation of Luanzhou Ancient City, and arouses the cultural belonging of local people who come to Luanzhou Ancient City for rest and the sense of cultural experience and exploration of tourists from other places.

3. Individual Emotional Arousal Based on Deep Structure

The purpose of sensory experience is to awaken the deepest emotional level in the hearts of the audience and users, and it is a deep ideological structure built on the spiritual and psychological level of tourists. This layer structure is the core layer for the thorough integration of sensory quality theory into Luanzhou Ancient City tourism cultural and creative products, and is the deep cultural experience and emotional significance brought by Luanzhou Ancient City to tourists. For Luanzhou Ancient City, due to its unique regional culture, historical evolution, social development and other reasons, tourists should feel different from other ancient cities and towns. This emotion is exactly the tourists' different sensory experience of Luanzhou Ancient City, which requires designers to deeply understand this sensory quality, combine the unique regional culture, social environment, local people's cognition of Luanzhou Ancient City, the unique historical stories of Luanzhou Ancient City, and the life stories of Luanzhou celebrities, refine them into sensory quality elements and integrate them into the products, and strive to enable tourists to use the products. Across the limitations of space and time, through his own sensory quality awareness experience, he can play a resonance effect with the Luanzhou Ancient City culture, so that Luanzhou Ancient City cultural creation can play a delayed effect in the future life, so that tourists can still experience the pleasant mood and feelings when they visit Luanzhou Ancient City after leaving Luanzhou Ancient City, and can experience the deep culture of Luanzhou Ancient City. In the design of cultural and creative products, select the images that can most make tourists have deep emotional resonance, and show them through symbolic and metaphorical design, so as to meet the sensory quality needs of tourists with sufficient cultural value. For example, through the stories of "First Yang collecting Wei" and "Yi Qi letting the country", people feel the charm of losing their character and individual personality awakening, and achieve psychological and spiritual satisfaction.

4 Design Practice of Luanzhou Ancient City Tourism Cultural and Creative Products from the Perspective of Experience

4.1 Visual Translation of Sensory Symbols of Surface Structures

Firstly, for the folk culture represented by Luanzhou shadow puppets, the paper summarizes and extracts the characteristics of the patterns of Luanzhou shadow puppets' clothing and hair. By using the abstract and generalized design method mentioned above, it forms traditional patterns such as four leaf patterns, double happiness patterns and water patterns through standardization and translation, and generates two continuous patterns, and then gives it "HELLO! Luanzhou!" Standard colors for the series. Then, the first images of Luanzhou shadow puppets were listed and popularized, including Sheng, Deng, Jing, Mo, Chou, beard, etc., to highlight the facial carving features of shadow puppets. These patterns and initial images are applied to cultural and creative products, so that the characteristics of Luanzhou shadow play are incorporated into cultural and creative products such as calendars and bookmarks, as shown in Fig. 5.

Fig. 5. Luanzhou shadow play calendar, bookmarks -- "HELLO! Luanzhou!" Series of cultural and creative products display

Secondly, the characteristic buildings of Luanzhou Ancient City and the scenic spot buildings of Luanzhou Ancient City that tourists are interested in are investigated, and their morphological and color representations are copied, so as to carry out secondary creation. Based on the architectural image formed by this translation, the image is reprocessed, and then the sensory quality situation visual presentation of the middle structure is carried out, and the tourism cultural and creative products of Luanzhou Ancient City are designed.

4.2   Visual Presentation of the Narrative Situation of the Middle Structure

For the creation of middle-level narrative situation, the sensory symbols of the surface structure are added to the situation, making it a complete illustration with a sense of story and atmosphere. For the sensory quality image elements of Luanzhou Ancient city scenic spots mentioned on the surface, contextual image elements are added to extract, such as the representative situational image of Luanzhou Ancient City, such as Luanshui Longxiang, Yanshan tiger, Xiangyun surrounded by clouds, sunrise in the east and other atmospheric images. The combination of situational elements and architectural elements of scenic spots makes the single building more vivid, creates a scene picture full of artistic conception, and makes people associate with the beautiful scenery of Luanzhou Ancient City. The visual generation of narrative scenarios is shown in Fig. 6.

Fig. 6. Luanzhou ancient city architectural attractions illustration design

4.3   Integration and Expression of Individual Emotion in Deep Structure

In the expression of individual emotions, it is hoped that tourists can show deep communication through the interaction with cultural and creative products. When they see the purchased cultural and creative products, the happy scene of visiting Luanzhou Ancient City in the past can be vividly remembered, and they also hope to experience the metaphysical spiritual resonance through the materialized products and feel the charm of Luanzhou culture. "HELLO! Luanzhou!" The slogan of the theme cultural and creative brand "view the scenery of mountains and rivers, see the beauty of four times" is deeply planted in the cultural and creative products, and gives emotional blessings to various figurative items of Luanzhou Ancient City. The visual translation of sensory symbols in the surface structure and the visual presentation of narrative situations in the middle structure are re-endowed with meaning. The visual translation process from the surface sensory symbols to the middle narrative context and then to the deep individual emotion integration expression finally presents the design of Luanzhou Ancient City tourism cultural and creative products. See Fig. 7.

Fig. 7. "HELLO! Luanzhou!" Cultural and creative Products display

5   Conclusion

The design of cultural and creative products of ancient city tourism from the perspective of quality experience can make tourism cultural and creative products become the link between ancient city culture and tourists' inner resonance, increase the interaction with ancient city culture through in-depth consideration of tourist user experience, effectively strengthen tourists' cognition of ancient city culture with Chinese characteristics behind cultural and creative products, and arouse tourists' inner emotional experience and resonance. This study is expected to bring new vitality to the tourism of ancient cities with characteristics under the background of frequent international exchanges, promote the tourism quality and brand of ancient cities in China, encourage more travelers to correctly understand and understand the culture with Chinese characteristics, and bring new ideas for the construction and development of cultural and creative products of ancient cities.

References

1. Ling, L.I.U.: Origin of the concept of "perceptual quality." J. Dialect. Nat. **35**(3), 60–63 (2013)
2. Weishang, L., Ran, L., Anqi, W.: Packag. Eng. **43**(10), 335–342 (2012)
3. Zhirong, Z.: On the "Image" in the creation of aesthetic image. J. Yunnan Normal Univ. (Philos. Soc. Sci. Edn.) **52**(06), 86–94 (2019)
4. Wang, J.: Research on the design of Ancient City cultural and creative products under the background of Cultural and Tourism Integration. Qingdao University of Science and Technology, pp. 8–10, Shandong (2022)
5. Chen, K.: Research on Regional cultural Creative Product Design Based on the Perspective of Communication, pp. 38–41. Hunan University, Hunan (2018)
6. Zhao, J.: Research on the design of Daqing Cultural and Creative products based on Regional cultural Semiotics, pp. 21–24. Northeast Petroleum University, Heilongjiang (2021)
7. Ranlong, W.U., Wangqun, X.I.A.O.: Design strategies of cultural and creative products based on regional culture. J. Landsc. Res. **14**(05), 75–78 (2019)
8. Jun, Y., Yuan, W., Li, X.: Research on product design method based on sensory quality theory analysis. Packag. Eng. **37**(24), 28–33 (2016)

9. Tian, Y.: Research on the development of Luanzhou Ancient City cultural tourism products based on tourists' perception, pp. 15–16. Yanshan University, Hebei (2021)
10. Yang, T.: Research on Creative product design based on regional culture, 25p. China University of Mining and Technology, Jiangsu (2020)

A Machine Learning Approach to Predict Bin Defects in E-commerce Fulfillment Operations

Zachary Weaver and Rupesh Bharadwaj$^{(\boxtimes)}$

Supply Chain and Fulfillment Analytics, Chewy Inc., Wilkes Barre, PA, USA
rupeshbharadwaj@gmail.com

Abstract. Bin location is the smallest possible unit inside a fulfillment center building where a product is stored to pick customer orders. Inventory in each bin inside a modern fulfillment center is tracked by the warehouse management system. Inventory discrepancies between inventory records in the warehouse management system and on hand inventory in the bin are referred to as bin defects. Bin defects in e-commerce fulfillment centers pose significant challenges, impacting operational efficiency, customer satisfaction, legal compliance, and overall profitability. This paper presents a comprehensive predictive model leveraging machine learning techniques to anticipate bin defects within fulfillment centers. The study involves the analysis of historical data primarily encompassing item attributes, location attributes, and any actions that might change the current state of a bin. The proposed model in this paper has been trained, tested, and implemented in an enterprise environment, and it can be easily leveraged by any e-commerce fulfillment centers to optimize their inventory control strategies. Promising predictive capabilities demonstrated by the model substantiate the model's effectiveness in preemptively identifying defective bins that can severely impact order fulfillment process. A successful integration of this model into organization's broader inventory management strategy will enable fulfillment centers to proactively implement preventive measures, reducing the occurrence of defects, minimizing inventory losses, reducing labor costs, and optimizing operational workflows. Further implications of this research extend to streamlining quality control processes and fostering a proactive approach toward mitigating inventory defects in fulfillment centers.

Keywords: Inventory Control · Inventory Discrepancies · Inventory Management · Bin Defects · Cycle Counting · E-commerce · Fulfillment Operations · Machine Learning · Naïve Bayes · Warehouse Management System (WMS)

1 Introduction

E-commerce order fulfillment is the process in which online orders are picked from the shelves, packed into boxes, and shipped to the final customer [1]. The fulfillment operation has six basic components- receiving inventory, storing and ordering inventory, picking inventory items from shelves, packaging the picked items for shipment, shipping

© The Author(s), under exclusive license to Springer Nature Switzerland AG 2024
C. Stephanidis et al. (Eds.): HCII 2024, CCIS 2118, pp. 105–112, 2024.
https://doi.org/10.1007/978-3-031-61963-2_11

boxes to customers, and handling returns [1]. Availability of the right inventory at the right time is critical to the success of fulfillment operations [2]. Misalignment between physical and virtual inventories can cause a range of problems for retailers including but not limited to increasing operational costs, missing on-time delivery, and deteriorating customer experience. Suppose a product listing on a company's website shows items available to place an order, but physically there are no on-hand inventories to ship that order to the customer. The order will either be pushed to the backorder queue or cancelled after making the customer wait for a couple of days. The whole experience will lead to customer dissatisfaction and reflect poorly on the company's reputation. Ensuring inventory level is correctly captured in the company's warehouse management system (WMS) is also critical to SOX compliance and any non-compliance with the provisions of the SOX can lead to severe penalties [3, 4].

Implementing cycle counting strategy is the most effective way to track inventory level in a fulfillment center and prevent any misalignment between virtual inventory in the system and physical inventory on the shelves [5]. According to KPMG, one of the world's leading professional services firms, "Management of a company is required to establish procedures under which inventory is physically counted at least once a year" [6]. Cycle counting is considered more efficient as a small set of bins is picked periodically and counted instead of counting the whole physical inventory in a fulfillment center and halting the operations. Cycle counting is typically done on a monthly or quarterly basis, though some businesses may do small counts weekly or daily [5].

This paper proposes a machine learning based strategy that can effectively track if the bin locations are defective, i.e., inventory in WMS does not match with the inventory on the shelves. The strategy was developed and tested in an enterprise environment, and it consistently produced results either similar to or superior to the results produced by opportunity-based counts.

2   Current State of Cycle Counting and Proposed Improvement

Cycle counting is an inventory control process aimed to find and correct "defective" bins [5]. A defective bin is when a location within a fulfillment center (where product is stored) contains a mismatch of the number of units (or the item itself) between what is physically on the shelves and what the WMS estimates.

Some organizations perform random counts by counting a set number of unique locations generated by the WMS (warehouse management system) under the RANDOM count name. These are locations that are randomly selected from a pool of locations that have not been counted yet for auditing purposes as every location in the fulfillment center must be counted at least once throughout the year. The results of this count form the "random defect rate" that is the proportion of these randomly selected bins which are incorrect (contain a mismatch between the inventory available physically and the inventory shown in the system). The primary goal of inventory control is to get this rate as close to zero as possible. The higher this rate is, the more probable encountering an incorrect bin is during the picking process; if this bin depletes physically while the system still thinks inventory exists, the picker must report this and move on to their next pick while that location attempts to be replenished. This causes a delay in picking which can impact shipping times and, if the fulfillment center doesn't have enough inventory to replenish the item, can potentially cause that order to be cancelled, leading to customer dissatisfaction.

WMS also generates opportunity-based cycle counts called WMS-Induced counts which are based off set triggers and parameters within the fulfillment center [5]. These counts are highly effective and might capture defects as high as 40% in a fulfillment center setting. The problem, however, is that these counts are very reactive and are not generated frequently enough to make a noticeable impact on the random defect rate.

Our proposed solution to this problem is to introduce a completely general counting strategy which leverages data around the fulfillment center location and item within the location to estimate the likelihood of this location being defective; we could then use this list of most probable locations to check and adjust. If we have a high enough volume of these counts with a good enough defect rate, this could, in theory, reduce the overall random defect rate, improving the general inventory health of the building.

3   Modeling Methodology

3.1   Problem Statement

To estimate the likelihood of a location being defective, we'll need some type of probabilistic model to take in data related to the location itself and the item within the location and output a value between 0 (least likely) to 1 (most likely) that we can use to generate a list of locations for inventory control team members to count.

3.2   Model Goals

For this model, the bare minimum goal is achieving a defect rate of double the random defect rate, the probability that a randomly selected location is defective. It is found that the average random defect rate is 5% for the fulfillment centers that participated in this study, so the bare minimum goal can be set to 10%. The ideal goal is achieving a defect rate similar to opportunity-based count called WMS-Induced counts, these counts are triggered when a certain process or transaction is done within the fulfillment center such as insufficient inventory reported by an order picker.

3.3   Selection of Variables

There are three primary types of variables that can be considered when estimating if a bin is likely to be defective: item attributes, location attributes and activities. Item attributes relate to information about the item within the bin, location attributes relate to information about the bin itself and activities relate to information about any human interaction with a bin location such as how often it's counted, how many times it's being picked from, etc.

After some experimentation, below is the current list of variables being considered:

- Bin fill % – location attribute
- Item weight – item attribute

- Item volume – item attribute
- Location bay – location attribute
- Aisle sequence – location attribute
- # items in bin – location attribute
- Days since last count on bin – activity
- # picks since last count – activity

3.4 Model Statement and Assumptions

For this model, we decided to go with Naïve Bayes which is a natural choice for a probabilistic model and allows us to take distributional information from each of the independent variables, unlike an expectation estimator (such as logistic regression) which does not take any information related to the distributions of its independent variables [7].

The general mathematical statement of the model is as follows:

$$P(defective = 1|X_1, X_2, \ldots, X_n) = \frac{P(defective = 1)P(X_1, X_2, \ldots, X_n|defective = 1)}{P(defective = 1)P(X_1, X_2, \ldots, X_n|defective = 1) + P(defective = 0)P(X_1, X_2, \ldots, X_n|defective = 0)}$$

As the name implies, we naively assume that each variable, X_n, is independent of each other, making it easy to compute the joint probability $P(X_1, X_2, \ldots, X_n) = \prod_{i=1}^{n} P(X_i)$. Even though this doesn't represent the complicated reality, it is still usually a good estimate [8].

Another assumption is made on the distribution of each of the variables. For the continuous variables, essentially all of these follow an approximate exponential distribution, and all categorical variables are fit with a categorical distribution.

4   Model Development

4.1   Language Choice

The selection of C++ as the implementation language for our model stems from several strategic considerations. Primarily, the prevalent packages available in languages offering Naïve Bayes predominantly support Gaussian distributions, limiting the model's flexibility. Our requirement to accommodate arbitrary distributions for various variables, particularly in the context of potential future feature expansions, led us to opt for C++.

4.2   Code Architecture

In the data preprocessing phase, information is extracted from a raw CSV file to establish a set of data containers intended for both training and input data within the framework of our predictive model. Each data container encompasses an array of data columns along with associated distribution types, classifying underlying columns as real numbers, discrete numbers, or categories (strings). For the training data, two distinct data containers are allocated: one for the null distribution, representing locations without identified defects (labeled '0' in the dataset), and another for the alternative distribution, encompassing locations with detected defects (labeled '1' in the dataset). The input data is a pull of the current snapshot of the inventory at the time the model runs and lacks '0' or '1' labels as this is what's used to generate predictions on.

Subsequently, the constructed training and input data are fed into the model object. The model iterates through each column in the null distribution dataset, fitting the relevant parameters based on the specified distribution. Simultaneously, the alternative distribution dataset undergoes a similar iteration, with parameters being fitted for each distribution. This process yields two sets of distributions corresponding to the null and alternative scenarios, encapsulating conditional distributions conditioned on the presence or absence of defects in the bins.

Upon completion of the parameter fitting, the input data is introduced to the model's prediction method. This method iterates through each row of the input data, passing the row to both sets of distributions. Each column of the row is evaluated within the context of the respective distributions, providing estimates of the conditional distribution for both null and alternative scenarios. This process is repeated for all features (columns) in the given row. The estimated probabilities are then combined using the naïve Bayes formula, as detailed in Sect. 3.4, resulting in the formulation of the estimated probability for the given location.

Following the estimation for each location (row), minor post-processing steps are implemented, such as filtering out probabilities below 0.10. The probabilities are subsequently sorted in descending order, prioritizing the most likely locations. The final output is then constrained to a predetermined number of locations that the fulfillment center is willing to count, ranging from 150 to 1000 locations per day.

5 Results

Below is a collection of tables showing the count results over a month period from fulfillment centers participating in our experimental count strategy for the three various counts: RANDOM counts, WMS-Induced counts, and our proposed count strategy.

Count Type	Fulfillment Center	Defective Bins	Counted Bins	Defect %
RANDOM	X1	857	11,469	7%
RANDOM	X2	324	7,048	5%
RANDOM	X3	536	14,949	4%
RANDOM	X4	569	10,043	6%
RANDOM	X5	930	11,586	8%
RANDOM	X6	429	9,640	4%
RANDOM	ALL	3,645	64,735	6%

Count Type	Fulfillment Center	Defective Bins	Counted Bins	Defect %
WMS-Induced	X1	3,965	6,850	58%
WMS-Induced	X2	1,117	2,907	38%
WMS-Induced	X3	1,902	3,962	48%
WMS-Induced	X4	1,983	3,753	53%
WMS-Induced	X5	2,712	4,749	57%
WMS-Induced	X6	1,926	3,295	58%
WMS-Induced	ALL	13,605	25,516	53%

Count Type	Fulfillment Center	Defective Bins	Counted Bins	Defect %
MODEL	X1	230	444	52%
MODEL	X2	340	872	39%
MODEL	X3	70	147	48%
MODEL	X4	381	920	41%
MODEL	X5	287	510	56%
MODEL	X6	171	448	38%
MODEL	ALL	1,479	3,341	44%

Since our model is in an experimental stage, fulfillment centers are conservative in allocating labor hours and try to preserve their labor for other counting strategies, but we still have a large enough sample size to make inferences on the impact of the strategy across all of the fulfillment centers, we are almost consistently achieving a 40–50% defect rate, close to meeting our ideal goal as stated in Sect. 3.2.

The defect rates of WMS-Induced count strategy and our proposed strategy are both significantly better than the defect rate of randomly counting bins. Despite our proposed strategy having a smaller defect rate, it's important to note that WMS-Induced counts are purely reactive to specific events that happen within the fulfillment center and cannot be used generally. We cannot utilize WMS-Induced count to proactively look for issues within inventory. Our proposed strategy is a predictive counting strategy meant to fill in this gap - it's intended to be used proactively to search for issues in our current inventory and serves as a complementary count strategy to WMS-Induced count strategy. The overlap of locations generated by these two strategies is minimal and by using both together, we have a system of reactive and proactive strategies to improve overall inventory quality. The successful implementation of our predictive model can bring down defects recorded by WMS-Induced count (opportunity-based strategy) significantly as bins are adjusted for the right level of inventory even before WMS or order picker reports any anomalies.

6   Conclusions and Future State

The current state of the model has consistently sustained a defect rate comparable to that of opportunity-based WMS-Induced counts. These counts are reactive checks triggered by predetermined parameters within the fulfillment center. As shown in the previous section, our model demonstrated a defect rate of 44%, whereas the baseline random defect rate stood at just 6%. This represents an improvement of 7.33 times over randomly counting bins, effectively achieving one hour of results from a random count strategy in just over 8 min.

While the defect rates in WMS-Induced counts exceed those of our model, it should be noted that our model produces exclusively proactive counts, in contrast to WMS-Induced strategy, which triggers counts only upon meeting predetermined fulfillment center conditions. Relying solely on reactive counts presents limitations, as the ability to scale count volume is constrained by the number of opportunities generated by WMS. In contrast, our proactive count system mitigates this limitation, allowing for flexible allocation of inventory control labor to identify and rectify defective bins proactively. The integration of both count types establishes a comprehensive system of effective counting strategies that encompasses both reactive and proactive approaches, thereby enhancing overall inventory management.

Our available fulfillment centers are presently operating with a limited set of bins, as our current counting strategy is in the experimental phase. The next crucial step involves scaling up the volume of counts to assess whether the observed defect rate remains consistent across a broader population of bins. Confirming the stability of the defect rate on a larger scale will empower us to consider phasing out less effective traditional counting methods currently in use. Furthermore, as part of our ongoing research, we intend to explore additional variables that can be integrated into the model to enhance its predictive accuracy.

Moreover, the model has undergone training and testing in fulfillment centers sharing similar layouts and inventory mixes. Alterations in fulfillment center layout or inventory mix may impact the model's results, an effect yet to be estimated. Upcoming steps will test the model in a variety of fulfillment center settings to understand the general efficacy of the proposed count strategy model.

Acknowledgements. The authors would like to thank Aakash Bhatt (Sr. Research Scientist), Charles Bryan (Sr. Data Scientist), and Marissa Stafford (Sr. Director) for their constructive criticism of the manuscript.

References

1. Michael Tarn, J., Razi, M.A., Joseph Wen, H., Perez, A.A.: E-fulfillment: the strategy and operational requirements. Logist. Inf. Manage. **16**(5), 350–362 (2003)
2. Singh, D.J.: Concepts of Inventory and related technical terminologies. IJRTI. **7**(8), 1–13 (2022)
3. Feng, M., Li, C., McVay, S.E., Skaife, H.: Does ineffective internal control over financial reporting affect a firm's operations? Account. Rev. **90**(2), 529–557 (2015)

4. Maximizing Efficiency: How to Optimize Your Sox Compliance Cycle Counting Process, oboloo (2023). https://oboloo.com/blog/maximizing-efficiency-how-to-optimize-your-sox-compliance-cycle-counting-process/. Accessed Nov 2023
5. Rossetti, M., Collins, T., Kurgund, R.: Inventory cycle counting–a review. In: The Proceedings of the 2001 Industrial Engineering Research Conference, vol. 1, pp. 457–463 (2001)
6. Accounting and Auditing Update - Issue No. 44/2020, KPMG (2020). https://assets.kpmg.com/content/dam/kpmg/in/pdf/2020/03/chapter-2-aau-covid-19-financial-reporting-inventory-impact-relaxations.pdf
7. Taheri, S., Mammadov, M.: Learning the Navie bayes classifier with optimization models. Int. J. Appl. Math. Comput. Sci. **23**(4), 787–795 (2013)
8. Lowd, D., Domingos, P.: Naive bayes models for probability estimation. In: Proceedings of the 22nd International Conference on Machine Learning (2005)

Teaching Practices and Reflections on AIGC in Brand Advertising Design

Dong Wei[1]([✉]) [iD], Lingxuan Li[1,2] [iD], and Zongyuan You[1] [iD]

[1] Advertising Institute, Communication University of China, Beijing 100024, China
weidong@cuc.edu.cn
[2] Celtic Studies and Social Sciences, The College of Arts, University College Cork, Cork T12 YN60, Ireland

Abstract. Generative Artificial Intelligence (AIGC) technology has been quickly evolving since 2022, with advertising becoming one of its most popular applications. This opens up new potential and difficulties for current and future brand advertising design education. This article investigates AIGC's design thinking transformation in brand advertising design using the course "AIGC: Machine-Assisted Innovative Design for Brand Advertising" offered at Communication University of China (CUC) during the summer semester of 2023. The goal is to help students comprehend AI art and machine learning, to break down the homogenization of AIGC-generated outcomes from an art and design standpoint, and to develop students' critical thinking skills so that they can reconsider the creative value of the human brain. The course is structured into two parts: the first part focuses on learning and experiencing AIGC technologies such as ChatGPT, Midjourney, Runway, and others, and applying them thoroughly in design practice. The second half of the course focuses on China Chic brand advertisements and uses hand-drawing, computer-aided design, and AICG to create a whole case design. The course findings demonstrate that AIGC tools have a high level of innovation in the creative process, but there are some issues such as uncontrollability and homogeneity that require humans to spend more time and energy adapting. Students agreed that generative AI can be an effective technique to inspire human creativity, and that when employing AIGC tools, designers should look for ways to collaborate with AI rather than viewing it as a total replacement for humans.

Keywords: AIGC · "Experience, Process and Reflection" · Teaching Practice

1 Introduction

Since 2022, generative artificial intelligence (AIGC) has been growing at a rapid pace. ChatGPT has over 180.5 million users as of January 2023, and Midjourney users will be reaching 20 million by March 2024. The advertising industry is the field where AIGC is most applied and has a broad prospect and potential. People use Midjourney to quickly prototype artistic concepts to exhibit to clients before beginning work on them [1]. ChatGPT can help increase creativity, optimize content production, strengthen market research, and more, so improving advertising effectiveness and brand value.

© The Author(s), under exclusive license to Springer Nature Switzerland AG 2024
C. Stephanidis et al. (Eds.): HCII 2024, CCIS 2118, pp. 113–124, 2024.
https://doi.org/10.1007/978-3-031-61963-2_12

Advertising creativity and design are among the industries that best show the creative value of the human brain. In the educational sector, more and more art colleges are introducing AIGC into classroom instruction, and the merging of art and technology has become inevitable. How to combine learning to use AIGC with advertising propositions in advertising teaching to create effective and actionable course content while also guiding students to develop critical thinking skills is a topic that advertising education must address and solve immediately.

Based on teaching practice, this course adopts "experience, process, reflection" as its teaching concept, uses China Chic brand design as its project work, collaborates with AIGC to improve people's ability in advertising creativity and design, objectively views people's change as the creative subject in design thinking and the specific design process, and serves as a teaching reference mode for related design majors.

2 Literature Review

AI-generated content (AIGC) is being explored as a new form of art [2, 3]. With the advancement of artificial intelligence, computers exhibit more and more artistic "creativity" in accordance with human will. The impact of computer-generated art (CG-art) on artistic creativity is being investigated, with a focus on defining what constitutes an AI-generated artwork and its potential for appreciation by human audiences [4]. Intelligent machines gradually get rid of human intervention in the content creation process, and gradually transform from imitating human thinking and behavior to equal or even surpass human creativity [5]. AIGC has also reshaped contemporary understanding of creativity and challenged the unique creative ability of human beings [4]. Although AIGC still has much room for development in details, accuracy, and extreme event handling, its initial performance is impressive, with some achievements comparable to those of experienced creators. Generative AI is undergoing rapid innovation and will become a new life form in the digital world with unlimited potential [6].

Despite all the benefits AIGC can provide to creatives, it has limitations. To begin with, machine-generated content has no meaning on its own, and machines cannot understand creativity as well as humans, necessitating human judgment to determine whether machine-generated content meets the purpose of the advertising creative and to participate in the generation process or specify and optimize the meaning of the results. Second, AI can simply generate a vast number of realistic photos and movies, resulting in lies and falsehoods and leading people to believe things that are not genuine. Finally, there are some hazards connected with depending too much on AICG for creative work. If designers or marketers rely too much on machine learning algorithms in search of simple solutions rather than original thinking, the usage of these algorithms may result in standardization of artistic expression [7]. Advertising creativity becomes a search process, and image production no longer represents a professional privilege but rather a democratized right.

There is a fear that machine-trained work will be an endless plagiarism of the artistic style of already existing work. Generative AI systems such as ChatGPT and Midjourney are trained on large, publicly available datasets that include copyrighted works. AI developers have argued that such training is protected under fair use, while copyright holders have argued that it infringes their rights [8].

Another contentious topic is whether AIGC-generated content is copyright-protected. The topic of whether the copyright of text and images generated by humans utilizing AIGC with natural language belongs to humans or computers has not been resolved. The US Copyright Office canceled its earlier copyright protection for Kris Kashtanova's drawing "Zarya of the Dawn" in March 2022, stating that only human-created works are eligible for protection [9]. On November 27, 2023, the Beijing Internet Court (BIC) ruled in an infringement lawsuit (Li v. Liu) that an AI-generated image is copyrightable and that a person who prompted the AI-generated image is entitled to the right of authorship under Chinese Copyright Law [10].

Which part of the AIGC-generated work is unique to the individual? Which component is generated by AIGC? These kinds of problems are a crucial basis for assessing the copyright of AIGC and consequently demand more extensive discussion and more particular case studies. The use of AIGC-generated text, images, and videos in this course is solely for educational purposes, which falls under the category of fair use, and it also provides more concrete practical examples for AIGC copyright issues.

Leveraging Artificial Intelligence, especially artificial intelligence-generated content (AIGC), presents both opportunities and challenges for innovative design education [11]. Recent research has found that including AIGC into design conceptualisation can dramatically boost educators' self-efficacy[1] [11]. Simultaneously, the dynamic spatial design[2] provided by AIGC technology creates potential for innovative design solutions and plays an important role in crisis response in design and education [12]. In the field of industrial design, AIGC has the potential to transform existing generative technologies and improve design processes [13]. As the subject of generative design pedagogy evolves, the mature application of AIGC technology will result in substantial breakthroughs in design education [14, 15].

The course instructor (i.e., the author of this paper) integrates AIGC into the traditional teaching of advertising creativity and design. ChatGPT can be used for research and analysis, as well as to generate copy and have it judged by a human. When employing image generators like Midjourney and Runway, students can include generative AI into their design concepts while avoiding copyright infringement [16]. The course encourages students to use AI technologies to spark creativity and design tools (such as Photoshop, Illustrator, and Premiere) to make changes to fulfill the design purpose. The students' work and design process were documented and subsequently assembled into a book, which will be published by Posts & Telecom Press in July 2024 as a concrete reference for related institutions' curricula.

---

[1] Self-efficacy refers to an individual's belief in his or her ability to complete a task.

[2] Dynamic spatial design is the process of adjusting and optimizing spatial layouts and designs in real-time environments using digital technologies and data-driven approaches.

3 Methodology

This study used a mixed-method approach to gather information and data from AIGC in the brand advertising design classroom, which included questionnaire survey, interview, classroom observation method, and practical research.

Information was collected using www.wjx.cn. The sample consisted of 32 undergraduate students in the course "AIGC: Machine-Assisted Innovative Design for Brand Advertising", taught by a faculty member of the Department of Communication Design, with two master's degree students serving as teaching assistants for the course. The questionnaire's goal was to understand and quantify students' impressions of how they used AIGC tools, how they changed before, during, and after the course, how they understood creativity, and how AIGC and humans collaborated during the creative process. The interviews asked open-ended questions to both teachers and students, allowing them to fully evaluate the course and AIGC from both a teaching and learning standpoint. The study's interview and questionnaire methodology combined qualitative and quantitative approaches. Furthermore, to protect the participants' rights and interests, the Academic Ethics Committee of Communication University of China approved the questionnaire and interviews for this study, and all participants completed an informed consent form.

The classroom observation approach is mirrored in the course data collecting questionnaire, as well as the "recording of the teaching process and student feedback". To understand changes in the students' attitudes at each stage, questionnaires were distributed to them one week before the course began, halfway through the course, and one week after the course ended. The course achieves the following objectives via several teaching modules: (1) to comprehend AI art and practice machine learning. (2) to learn and experience AIGC tools such as Chat-GPT, Midjourney, Artbreeder, Stable Diffusion, and Runway, and to be able to use the above A tools for branding and advertising design. (3) to re-examine human creativity in the design process and develop critical thinking skills. (4) to break the phenomenon of AI homogenization from the perspective of art design. At the same time, the course requires students to record their insights on a daily basis, to look at new technologies objectively, and to critically recognise and use AIGC tools based on their design practice.

The purpose of the practical study is the students' design experience utilizing AIGC in line with the course tasks. The workshop lasts two weeks, with the first week focused on learning and experiencing AIGC tools in a collaborative group setting, as well as comprehensively applying AI techniques in specific design practices. Content production for radio commercials, logo design (see Fig. 1), brand virtual spokespersons, Product concept design (see Fig. 2), video advertisements (see Fig. 3), and other projects.

In the second week, based on the strategy sheets provided by other groups, use AICG and combine hand-drawing and other computer design tools (Photoshop, Illustrator, etc.) to carry out brand design (see Fig. 4), which includes brand logo, product photography, poster design, shop design, and so on. It establishes the groundwork for future research into the use of AIGC in teaching brand advertising design.

Fig. 1. Logo Design, Chat-GPT & Midjourney, Authors: Jiao Jingtao, Chen Yitong, Bai Jie

Fig. 2. Product Concept Design, Chat-GPT & Midjourney, Authors: Sun Rui, Yin Meiqi, Wu Zifan, Li Dongrun

Fig. 3. Video Advertising, Runway, Author: Jiang Randi, Wang Yiran, Ji Yu and An Zhuohui

Fig. 4. China Chic Brand Design, Midjourney, Canva & Photoshop, Authors: Sun Rui, Yin Meiqi, Wu Zifan, Li Dongrun

4 Result

The questionnaire's objective was to evaluate the students' experiences with utilizing the AIGC tool in the process of designing brand advertising, including all course participants and an offline presentation mode. The questionnaire had a total of 32 participants, with 25% being second year students and 75% being third-year students. In terms of age, 65.63% of the participants were 21–23 years old, 28.13% were 24–26 years old, and 3.13% were under 18 and 27 years old or older, respectively. In terms of gender identity, there were 9 males and 23 female students. Majors included design (65.63%), advertising (28.13%), and media (6.25%).

4.1 Survey on AIGC Course

The course research was separated into three phases: before, during and after the course. Before the course, some students had used AIGC and had varied degrees of comfort with it, but the majority were positive about the AIGC technology and its applications. During the course, students stated that the AIGC technology was a creative enabler, but it could not realize all of the user's ideas and concepts. Following the session, students had a positive attitude toward AIGC. Furthermore, the clear majority of students stated that they wanted to continue utilizing AIGC technology in the future.

Before Course. This section of the survey focused on the students' use of AIGC tools and their perceptions. 71.88% of students reported having previously known or used AIGC technology, but 42.86% were not very comfortable with AIGC's involvement in design creation, while 35.71% were comfortable, 21.43% were completely comfortable, and no students were not at all comfortable with AIGC.

In terms of attitudes on AIGC technology, 46.88% were favorable, 37.5% were ordinary, and 15.63% were very favorable. Concerning the use of AIGC technology in brand advertising design (see Fig. 5), 46.88% of students were optimistic, 28.13% were neutral, 21.88% were very optimistic, and 3.13% were not very optimistic.

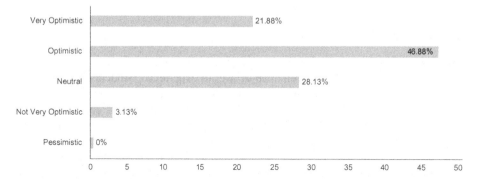

Fig. 5. Students' attitudes towards the use of AIGC technology in brand advertising design.

During Course. This section of the survey focused on the constraints of technology and the role AIGC plays in creation. 81.25% of students said they were constrained by AIGC's technology. In terms of the role of AIGC technology in creation (see Fig. 6), 46.43% of students said it helps to some extent but is not a major component. 28.57% of students said it helps to structure current ideas but not enough to spark innovation. A further 17.86% of students decided to significantly improve their ability to generate new ideas. The remaining 7.14% of students believed that AIGC had little influence on the choice of creative solutions.

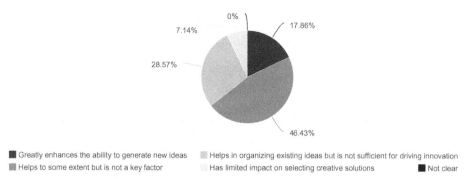

Fig. 6. The role that students see AIGC technology playing in the creative process.

After Course. This section of the poll addressed the shift in students' perceptions and their willingness to continue using AIGC in the future. 65.63% of the students retained a positive view with AIGC, 28.13% altered their attitude from negative to positive, and 6.25% remained negative. 93.75% of students stated they would continue to utilize AIGC technology to help them create brand advertising designs in the future.

4.2   Survey on AIGC Technology

This section of the questionnaire was designed to elicit students' feelings and thoughts on everything from specific performance to overall experience. Students believed that the diversity of generated results worked best, and that AIGC was superior at generating rich and abstract scenarios. However, AIGC has limited autonomous comprehension, and its primary function is to stimulate creativity and generate design sketches. In terms of relationships, around half of the students thought that tool synergy was average, while the majority thought that the human-computer interaction was both competitive and cooperative. In terms of social dangers, most students said that rigorous supervision and severe rules were required.

Specific Evaluation of Technical Performance. The survey first evaluates the raw AIGC's performance using four evaluation criteria: coherence, creativity, diversity, and technological realism, and then summarizes its excellence. Second, AIGC autonomous comprehension and stereotyping were studied. Diversity was the best performer among the four evaluation categories (see Fig. 7), with 53.13% of students rating the diversity of AIGC technology-generated content as good, 18.75% as average, 15.63% as excellent, and the remaining 12.5% as poor.

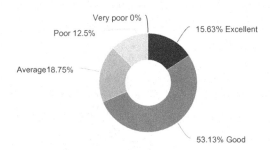

Fig. 7. Student evaluations of the diversity of AIGC technology-generated content.

On this basis, 78.13% of the students think that AIGC tools are better at enriching abstract scenarios than concrete and fine content. In terms of AIGC tools' ability to understand design logic and emotional needs autonomously, 31.25% of respondents believe their level is good and average, respectively. Those who selected not so good and not good accounted for 21.88% and 15.63%, respectively.

In reaction to the findings, 50% of the students thought they contained a lot of stereotypes, 25% thought the quantity of stereotypes was acceptable, 21.88% thought there were a lot of stereotypes, and 3.13% thought there were not many. Students' responses to open-ended questions generally classified stereotype explanations as "data bias," "training algorithm limitations," and "socio-cultural influences."

Comprehensive Experience of Technology Use. This section of the survey focuses on the social pitfalls of AIGC tools, the interaction between the tools and AIGC and human creators, and the impact of not being a native English speaker. Regarding AIGC social hazards 62.5% of students said that serious concern and severe regulation was required. 28.13% of students expressed worry about the need to strike a balance between technology and morality. 6.25% of students were indifferent, stating that ethical difficulties and social pitfalls are inevitable as technology advances. The remaining 3.13% of students were less concerned and thought its influence was limited.

Based on their experience utilizing several tools cooperatively, 40.63% of students rated AIGC coordination as average, 31.25% as good, 21.88% as not so good, and 3.13% as very good and not so good. In terms of the human-computer interaction, 56.25% of students believed it was both competitive and cooperative, with AIGC technology and creators inspiring one another to foster innovation. 31.25% of students believed it was a collaborative and symbiotic connection in which AIGC technology offered the producers with new creative tools and concepts. Another 12.5% of pupils believe AIGC technology will substitute and challenge traditional creators.

Since the language of instruction in this course was Chinese, whether the English prompt words could fully express the students' creativity was a matter of concern. Among them, 46.88% of the students said that they were mostly able to express it, while 43.75% of them found it difficult at times. The percentage of students who chose to be fully able to express, rarely able to express, and not able to express at all was 3.13% respectively.

4.3 Instructor Observation

When creating the teaching plan, the teacher considered the differences in students' knowledge of AIGC or their lack of experience designing brand advertisements, and guided students to understand and master the AIGC tool using a variety of methods, including classroom lectures, peer-to-peer exchanges, and self-study content.

During the process of using AIGC to create brand advertisements, the teacher provided specific solutions based on the various problems encountered by the students, guided the students to use AIGC rationally, balanced creativity between machine and human, and prevented the students from over-reliance on the AIGC tool and losing originality in brand advertisement design. Furthermore, according to input from teaching assistants, students focus primarily on the AIGC tool's parameter settings and functionality during the first 4–5 days. As the course continued, the focus switched to how to improve the AIGC technology's understanding of cultural context and cue words in order to develop better works. Thus, AIGC is a creative aid that can be mastered in the short term. In addition, at the end of each day's lesson, the teacher encouraged students to share their design ideas, processes, and difficulties, and promoted critical thinking by commenting on their works to improve their AIGC creation.

5 Conclusions

This study explores the learning experience of AIGC for a self-proposed brand advertisement design aim, emphasizing the design teaching process and critically examining the benefits and drawbacks of AIGC for design and creativity through student reflections. The role of AIGC in the design process is clearly proved, as is the human cultural background, design experience, and empathy that AI lacks.

Depending on the time of study and amount of difficulty, students generally found mastering the AIGC tool uncomplicated. However, ensuring that the created outputs properly fulfill the design requirements is a difficult process that necessitates ongoing debugging and refinement, and students were required to strike a compromise between their subjective preferences and the generated outcomes. The investigation of students' opinions on the AIGC technology indicated that students generally believed that the AIGC technology performed better in terms of diversity, but that it still needs to be improved in terms of coherence and creativity. However, pupils reported being impressed by AIGC's innovation. Students should perceive AIGC as an intelligent collaborator and imaginative creator, but never as a design leader, because there is no alternative for human creativity and leadership.

Because of the complexity of the Chinese style and cultural background, subjective will plays a more significant part in China Chic Design, and the tool selection is also more diverse, reflecting the relationship between humans, AIGC, and computer-aided design tools more comprehensively: AIGC serves as a source of creative inspiration, concept production, and rapid presentation throughout the design process, while human subjectivity, emotion, and empirical judgement serve as selection criteria, and other design tools are utilized to refine the work.

However, there are some flaws in the study. The design topics of the brand advertising were entirely imaginary propositions generated by the students among themselves, and incorporating examples of actual businesses would have increased the study's usefulness in terms of creative techniques, ethical discussions, and evaluation of the impacts used.

To summarize, this course provides insight into the future of teaching advertising design. Generative AI technologies are uncomplicated to learn, but in the context of brand advertising design, humans and machines must collaborate and co-create. With the rapid development of AIGC, the machine's creativity will increase, as will the demand for critical thinking and design. The future curriculum in creative design for brand advertising at AIGC will focus on increasing human creativity training and coordinating the collaborative relationship between humans and AIGC tools.

Acknowledgments. I'd like to thank Communication University of China and the Advertising Institute for their support and recognition of the "AIGC: Machine-Assisted Innovation in Brand Advertising Design" course, as well as co-authors Lingxuan Li and Zongyuan You for their contributions as teaching assistants in the course and thesis, and all of the students for their hard work and participation.

Disclosure of Interests.   The authors declare no conflict of interest.

References

1. Holz, D.: Founder of AI art generator Midjourney, on the future of imaging. http://www.the register.com/2022/08/01/david_holz_midjourney/. Accessed 18 Mar 2024
2. Wu, Z.-H., Fan, M., Tang, R.-T., Ji, D.-W., Mohammad, S.: The art of artificial intelligent generated content for mobile photography. In: Kurosu, M., Hashizume, A. (eds.) Human-Computer Interaction. HCII 2023. LNCS, vol. 14014, pp. 438–453. Springer, Cham (2023). https://doi.org/10.1007/978-3-031-35572-1_29
3. Negueruela del Castillo, D., Schaerf, L., Ballesteros, P., Neri, I., Bernasconi, V.: Newly Formed Cities: an AI Curation (2023)
4. Arriagada, L.: CG-art: an aesthetic discussion of the relationship between artistic creativity and computation. University of Groningen, Groningen (2023). https://doi.org/10.33612/diss. 693764937
5. Tao, W., Gao, S., Yuan, Y.-L.: Boundary crossing: an experimental study of individual perceptions toward AIGC. Front. Psychol. **14**, 1185880 (2023). https://doi.org/10.3389/fpsyg. 2023.1185880
6. Wu, J., Gan, W., Chen, Z., Wan, S., Lin, H.: AI-Generated Content (AIGC): A Survey (2023). https://doi.org/10.48550/arXiv.2304.06632
7. The Future of Creativity in an AIGC-Dominated World. https://quickcreator.io/articles2/fut ure-creativity-aigc-world. Accessed 18 Mar 2024
8. Zirpoli, C.: Generative Artificial Intelligence and Copyright Law. Copyright, Fair Use, Scholarly Communication, etc. (2023)
9. Chinese court declares AI-generated image protected by copyright, a first ruling of its kind. https://www.globaltimes.cn/page/202312/1304471.shtml. Accessed 20 Mar 2024
10. Beijing Internet Court Grants Copyright to AI-Generated Image for the First Time. https://copyrightblog.kluweriplaw.com/2024/02/02/beijing-internet-court-grants-cop yright-to-ai-generated-image-for-the-first-time/. Accessed 21 Mar 2024
11. Huang, K.-L., Liu, Y.-C., Dong, M.-Q.: Incorporating AIGC into design ideation: a study on self-efficacy and learning experience acceptance under higher-order thinking. Thinking Skills and Creativity (2024). https://doi.org/10.1016/j.tsc.2024.101508
12. Sedon, M.F., Birkök, M.C., Chen, Y.: ICEKIM 2023: Proceedings of the 4th International Conference on Education, Knowledge and Information Management. European Alliance for Innovation, Nanjing, China (2023)

13. Mostafa, M.: A framework for leveraging artificial intelligence to improve industrial design practices. Int. Des. J. **12**(6), 257–269 (2022). https://doi.org/10.21608/idj.2022.267388
14. What can AIGC Bring to Education: EDTK.US Announced to Launch AI-embedded Online Application Tools. https://www.jcnnewswire.com/pressrelease/81320/2/What-can-AIGC-Bring-to-Education:-EDTKUS-Announced-to-Launch-AI-embedded-Online-Application-Tools. Accessed 20 Mar 2024
15. Bozkurt, A., Junhong, X., Lambert, S., Pazurek, A., Crompton, H., et al.: Speculative futures on ChatGPT and generative artificial intelligence (AI). Asian J. Distance Educ. **18**(1), 53–130 (2023)
16. How WIRED Will Use Generative AI Tools I WIRED. https://web.archive.org/web/20231230055221/https://www.wired.com/about/generative-ai-policy/. Accessed 20 Mar 2024

Corporate Responsibility in Fashion: A Comparative Analysis of Sustainability Reporting Indicators

Duan Wu, Haoyue Lei[(✉)], Jin Ning, and Zixin Ren

Shanghai International College of Design and Innovation, Tongji University, Shanghai 200000, China
{wuduan,leihy,2233744,2233746}@tongji.edu.cn

Abstract. This paper analyzes sustainability reports (SRs) from fashion companies LVMH, KER, and ELC, emphasizing corporate responsibility (CR). This study aims to provide insights into SRs from these three leading companies, offering a glimpse into the information disclosure status in the fashion industry. Using the ESG (Environmental, Social, Governance) reporting framework and qualitative coding method, the SRs, and its indicator themes and items are examined. The findings of this paper reveal massive and fragmented SR data, hindering cross-company comparisons, and suggesting areas for SR improvement, notably in addressing social and governance CR. Moreover, LVMH and ELC prioritize quantitative CR integration, while KER focuses on qualitative CR descriptions. Despite diverse strategies, all SRs demonstrate a commitment to CR with varying data transparency levels.

Keywords: Cooperation responsibility · Fashion industry · Sustainable Report · ESG framework · disclosed indicators

1 Introduction

The global fashion industry is a significant economic force but faces criticism for its environmental and social unsustainability. Meanwhile, there is a growing consumer focus on sustainability in this industry, particularly regarding emissions and working conditions (Adrienne et al., 2022). Fashion companies have responded to this demand by increasingly promoting their cooperate responsibility (CR) and sustainability practices, by issuing sustainability reports (SR) with quantitive digits and qualitative descriptions (Chun et al., 2021). These SRs contribute to aligning mandatory business practices with voluntary social-benefit practices (Aras & Crowther, 2009), at least provoking the awareness of CR.

However, scholars often criticize SRs as potential marketing tools. SRs are accused as tools of greenwashing, particularly when they contain overwhelming information (Chun et al., 2021). Besides, since the reporting framework employment is voluntary, the disclosed indicative data in SRs vary, making it challenging to compare performance

C. Stephanidis et al. (Eds.): HCII 2024, CCIS 2118, pp. 125–148, 2024.
https://doi.org/10.1007/978-3-031-61963-2_13

across companies. Thus, this lack of standardization overwhelms consumers and fuels suspicion, requiring explanations of the relationship between SRs and business practices.

The top three companies, in this industry hold significant influence in the market, similarly in sustainable practices. These companies are Moët Hennessy Louis Vuitton (LVMH), Kering SA(KER), and The Estée Lauder Companies Inc. (ELC) (Deloitte, 2023). Their contributions to sustainability have gradually been noticed. Their enhanced data transparency scores, surpassing the industry average (Fashion Revolution, 2023), making them perfect samples for this study. Therefore, this paper examines the data disclosure status in the fashion industry by analyzing specific SRs from these leading companies using quantitative research methods. To this end, three research questions are posed: How do these companies disclose SRs data? What themes of sustainability do these SRs focus on the most? How are CR implied in SRs by these companies?

2   Methods

2.1   Theoretical Method: ESG Framework and 3CR Model

The ESG reporting framework serves as a widely adopted standard for reporting strategies, encompassing Environmental, Social, and Governance factors. Commonly, investors utilize this framework to evaluate non-financial performance and corporate responsibilities (Li et. al., 2021; Bose, 2020). Three chosen companies in this study also adopt the ESG framework alongside various reporting tools. Thus, in this study, this framework is used to analyze and compare the SRs.

The primary focus of these reports is on Corporate Responsibilities (CRs) and their associated benefits. The 3CR model, developed by Halme and Laurila (2009), categorizes CR into Philanthropy, CR Integration, and CR Innovation based on their relationship to the core business. This model illustrates the increasing integration of CR into the core business, along with the accumulation of potential benefits. In this study, the 3CR model is used to examine report indicators and texts, to uncover tangible benefits inherent in the data.

2.2   Quantitative Coding Method for Report Indicator

This study utilizes the research methodology proposed by Roca and Searcy (2012) to conduct a detailed analysis of SR data. Given the diverse narrative styles present in SRs, employing machine learning for comprehension and data collection is deemed impractical. Instead, the chosen methodology employs a manual coding system to analyze indicator items. Initially, the prefaces and indicator descriptions in the SRs are examined to identify narrative differences. Afterwards, indicators are then coded based on the ESG framework and 3CR types. Through this systematic approach, insights into the status of data disclosure are derived, offering valuable perspectives on sustainability reporting within the fashion industry.

The SR data in this paper are retrieved directly from the official websites of three companies, excluding ratings and indices data from third-party sources. However, it is noteworthy that these companies follow different auditing periods. ELC typically releases its SR in November of each year, reporting data for that specific year. In contrast, the other two often publish their SRs in the middle of the subsequent year. As a result, as of February 2024, the latest SRs of LVMH and KER are that of 2022. Thus, this study uses SR for the last three years: 2020, 2021, and 2022. It is important to highlight that the year referenced corresponds to the time of data collection rather than the publication date.

3   Analysis of SRs Characteristics

Three insights emerge from the analysis of report characteristics. Firstly, the data are distributed across a substantial volume of reports, totaling 36 over three years for the three companies (Fig. 1). While specific reports address social and environmental aspects, none focus on governance. Notably, KER surpasses others significantly by publishing the most SRs, with 10 in 2021, and all companies experience a shared peak in publication during the same year.

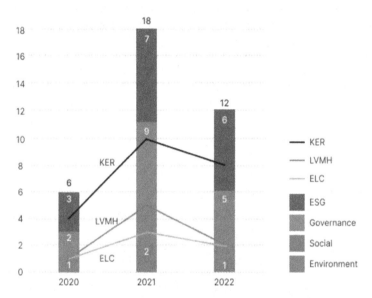

Fig. 1. The volume and theme of SRs of three companies: 2020–2022

Besides, the length of each report are significant. LVMH and ELC issue annual ESG reports, averaging 137 pages and 42,647 words, respectively. Conversely, KER divides its reports into one environmental report and one social-governance report each year, supplementing them with an editable ESG database in 2023. Furthermore, each company publishes several supplementary and relatively short reports, averaging 25.88 pages. Notably, KER published a total of 20 supplemental reports over the three years, primarily focusing on its environmental CR.

While conveying such amount of information, companies utilize various tools for report narration, encompassing nine different systems. Only the Carbon Disclosure

Project (CDP) is universally used across all reports. However, the sheer volume of reports and the use of tools do not directly indicate the positive contributions of companies. Nevertheless, they do impact the effectiveness of communication with the public and influence receptivity of readers to the data.

In conclusion, these insights quantitatively highlight the challenge of comparing SR data across companies. Consequently, comprehensive SRs from 2020 to 2022 from the three companies are selected for further examination, comprising three reports from LVMH, three from ELC, and one database from KER (Appendix 1).

4   Analysis of SRs Indicators

4.1   The Indicators Theme Based on ESG Framework

After coding all indicator items based on the ESG framework, a total of 226 indicators are collected (Appendix 2). Among these companies, KER leads in the number of indicator items. Figure 2 presents these indicators categorized by theme. Within each company, consistency in data disclosure is evident, alongside a growing tendency to provide more specific details to the public. For example, in 2020, the companies only provided a vague total greenhouse gas emissions number, whereas by 2022, specific figures were added for each scope and category. However, across the companies, only 12 of indicator were disclosed by all companies, and 150 of them were disclosed by only one company, making horizontal comparisons impossible.

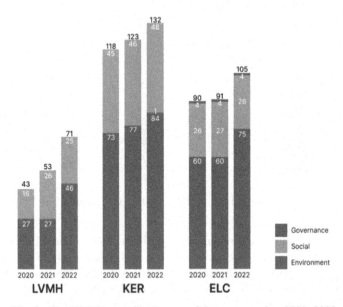

Fig. 2. The ESG theme of indicators of three companies: 2020–2022

Furthermore, the disclosure status of data is uneven. The environmental data is the most disclosed for all companies, constituting 66% of all items (Fig. 2). Remarkably, the above mentioned most disclosed 12 indicators are all related to environmental sustainability, focusing on energy, greenhouse gas emissions, and packaging issues. In contrast, governance sustainability is less accessible to the public, with only ELC disclosing four indicators about the board of directors over these years.

In conclusion, while the number and precision of indicators have increased over the years within the companies, the variation in indicator themes and items hinders cross-company comparisons in this industry. Moreover, the disclosure status of ESG data is uneven, with governance sustainability being the less revealed one.

4.2   The Indicator Item Based on the 3CR Model

CR emerges as the central theme across all SRs, with notable variations in its depiction among the companies. For example, LVMH employs the term "responsibility" a total of 440 times, while ELC mentions it 73 times, while KER does not include it in its database. CR integration emerges as the most emphasized aspect, with over 90% of indicators provided (refer to Fig. 3). These indicators notably highlight CR integration within the product portfolio, such as the disclosure of 11% of data points on sustainably certified raw resources used in the original production line.

In terms of Philanthropy, LVMH and ELC demonstrate their commitment through both qualitative and quantitative methods. For instance, LVMH illustrates its support for cultural institutions qualitatively (9% of total pages) and quantitatively (10% of indicators). Conversely, KER adopts a distinctive reporting strategy for CR, offering only qualitative descriptions for CR in its reports, focusing more on CR innovations.

In conclusion, CR are predominantly revealed through qualitative descriptions instead of quantitative indicators, with CR integration being the most extensively disclosed aspect. Meanwhile, CR Innovation relies on qualitative information.

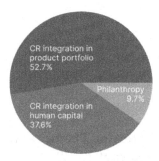

Fig. 3. The portion of indicators according to the 3CR model

5   Conclusion and Discussion

This analysis of SRs from LVMH, ELC, and KER sheds light on the CR within the fashion industry. Adopting the theoretical reporting framework and qualitative coding method, the characteristics, the indicator theme and items of SRs are discussed. Initially, the analysis of the SR characteristics proves the fragment and overwhelming data, hindering the horizontal comparison in the industry. Subsequently, report samples are selected and analyzed, revealing a difference in the accessibility of ESG data. While environmental factors receive the most attention across the companies, the lag of the other two indicates areas for improvement in future SRs. Moreover, for the CR disclosure, companies focus on qualitative descriptions, with CR integration is prioritized by the other two. In conclusion, these insights offer valuable guidance for the future of SRs in the industry, aiming to enhance communication efficiency, address the uneven disclosure status of ESG data, and incorporate quantitative indicators for demonstrating CRs. In the end, though having differences in reports, all three companies demonstrate a commitment to CR, showing noticeable degrees of data transparency.

Acknowledgements. The authors would like to thank the faculty team and peers in the Sustainability in Business lecture for inspiring this study with their insightful discussions and knowledge sharing. We also acknowledge that this paper did not receive any funding support.

Appendix 1.

Company	SR document	Year of publish	Year of the data	Page
LVMH	Social & Environmental Responsibility report	2021	2020	144
	Social & Environmental Responsibility report	2022	2021	148
	Social & Environmental Responsibility report	2023	2022	160
KER	ESG Databook	2023	2022	/
ELC	Citizenship & Sustainability Report	2020	2020	117
	Social Impact & Sustainability Report	2021	2021	127
	Social Impact & Sustainability Report	2022	2022	152

Appendix 2. Analysis of Indicator Themes and Items in Sustainability Reports of Three Companies: 2020–2022

ESG	Topic	Indicator Items	LVMH			KER			ELC			SUM
			2020	2021	2022	2020	2021	2022	2020	2021	2022	
Governance	Board of Directors	total Board count							1	1	1	3
		total Board count, by gender							1	1	1	3
		total Board count, by color							1	1	1	3
		total Board count, by age							1	1	1	3
Social	Workforce structure	Total employees				1	1	1	1	1	1	6
		Total employees with disabilities				1	1	1				3
		Total employees, by region				1	1	1	1	1	1	6
		Total employees, by age group				1	1	1	1	1	1	6
		Total employees, by gender				1	1	1	1	1	1	6
		Total corporate employees by job level, by gender				1	1	1	1	1	1	6
		Total employees by role type, by gender				1	1	1	1	1	1	6
		Total employees by role type, by race/ethnicity				1	1	1	1	1	1	6
		Regular employees by generation				1	1	1				3
		Regular employees, by region							1	1	1	3
		Temporary employees, by region				1	1	1	1	1	1	6

(continued)

(continued)

ESG	Topic	Indicator Items	LVMH			KER			ELC			SUM
			2020	2021	2022	2020	2021	2022	2020	2021	2022	
		Regular full-time employees, by gender							1	1	1	3
		Regular part-time employees, by gender							1	1	1	3
		Temporary full-time employees, by gender							1	1	1	3
		Temporary part-time employees, by gender							1	1	1	3
	Hiring and departure	Total number of new hires on permanent contracts				1	1	1				3
		Percentage of women hired				1	1	1				3
		Percentage of non-managers hired				1	1	1				3
		Percentage of permanent contracts				1	1	1				3
		Percentage of fixed-term contracts				1	1	1				3
		Total turnover rate				1	1	1		1	1	5
		Voluntary turnover rate				1	1	1		1	1	5
		Involuntary turnover rate				1	1	1		1	1	5
		Dismissal for economic reasons				1	1	1				3

(continued)

(continued)

ESG	Topic	Indicator Items	LVMH			KER			ELC			SUM
			2020	2021	2022	2020	2021	2022	2020	2021	2022	
		Leavings initiated by the employee				1	1	1				3
		Retirements				1	1	1				3
		Departure by mutual agreement				1	1	1				3
		Other departures				1	1	1				3
	Training of employees	Training on the importance of non-discrimination general	1	1	1	1	1	1				6
		structured training policy	1	1	1							3
		skill safeguard	1	1	1							3
		training in risk prevention and first aid		1	1	1	1	1				5
		Total number of hours of safety training				1	1	1				3
		Total number of employees trained on safety				1	1	1				3
		training for HRs			1		1					2
		training for recruiters/non-managers		1	1	1	1	1				5
		training for managers		1	1	1	1	1				5
		training for women				1	1	1				3

(continued)

(continued)

ESG	Topic	Indicator Items	LVMH			KER			ELC			SUM
			2020	2021	2022	2020	2021	2022	2020	2021	2022	
		training for men				1	1	1				3
		implemented initiatives for people from Seniors		1	1								2
		skill development initiatices		1	1								2
		an in-house school focusing on customer experience and sales		1	1								2
		their own internal crafts school		1	1								2
	Complaints	Total Number of complaints received				1	1	1				3
		Number of complaints received and closed				1	1	1				3
		Number of complaints received outstanding				1	1	1				3
		Number of complaints that led to an investigation				1	1	1				3
		Number of Code of Ethics breaches found among the complaints closed				1	1	1				3
		Behavior and management				1	1	1				3
		Alignement with internal policies				1	1	1				3

(continued)

(continued)

ESG	Topic	Indicator Items	LVMH			KER			ELC			SUM
			2020	2021	2022	2020	2021	2022	2020	2021	2022	
		Alignment with local regulations				1	1	1				3
		Management of COVID-related issues					1					1
	Safety and well-being of employees	Unadjusted gender pay gap						1				1
		Adjusted gender pay gap by band						1				1
		work-life balance adaptation	1									1
		flexible working hours	1	1	1							3
		safeguard mental health		1	1							2
		health and safety program		1	1							2
		analyze their health and safety performance once a year		1	1							2
		an annual day promoting health		1	1							2
		introduced key measures to ensure the health and safety of their most at-risk employees	1									1
		Employees with access to a doctor through work		1								1
		employees eligible for parental leave							1			1

(continued)

(continued)

ESG	Topic	Indicator Items	LVMH			KER			ELC			SUM
			2020	2021	2022	2020	2021	2022	2020	2021	2022	
		maternity/paternity/adoption leave	1						1			2
		Days Away, Restricted or Transfer Rate (DART)							1	1	1	3
		Overall lost time				1	1	1	1	1	1	6
		Severity rate of work-related accidents (Number of days lost per thousand hours worked)				1	1	1				3
		Total fatalities							1	1	1	3
		Total Recordable Incidents	1			1	1	1	1	1	1	7
		Total Recordable Incident Rate							1	1	1	3
		Employee Resource Groups							1	1		2
		Total number of overtime hours				1	1	1				3
		Average weekly working time for full-time employees				1	1	1				3
		Total number of working hours of industrial action				1	1	1				3
		Employees covered by a centralized whistle blowing system		1								1
	Social initiative	Social initiative for women	1	1	1							3

(continued)

(continued)

ESG	Topic	Indicator Items	LVMH 2020	LVMH 2021	LVMH 2022	KER 2020	KER 2021	KER 2022	ELC 2020	ELC 2021	ELC 2022	SUM
		Social initiative for people with disabilities	1	1	1							3
		social initiative for people from the LGBTI community	1	1	1							3
		Employees covered by an Alert Line			1							1
		Employees covered by the LVMH Heart Fund		1	1							2
		Percentage of employees covered by the European Work Council						1				1
		People helped		1	1							2
	Charity funding	Total charitable contributions		1	1				1	1	1	5
		Employee donations							1	1	1	3
		Amount matched by company							1	1	1	3
	Social partnership	Partnerships established	1	1	1							3
		Partnerships to empower job seekers	1									1
		Partnerships to empower women	1									1
		Partnerships to promote equal education	1									1

(continued)

(continued)

ESG	Topic	Indicator Items	LVMH			KER			ELC			SUM
			2020	2021	2022	2020	2021	2022	2020	2021	2022	
		Partnerships to support vulnerable people	1									1
	Employee volunteerism	volunteer involved		1	1				1	1	1	5
		volunteer hours			1				1	1	1	3
Environment	Energy	Energy consumption	1	1	1	1	1	1	1	1	1	9
		Change in energy consumption	1	1	1	1	1	1	1	1	1	9
		Energy consumption by Electricity	1	1	1	1	1	1	1	1	1	9
		Energy consumption by Non-renewable Electricity				1	1	1	1	1	1	6
		Energy consumption by Renewable Electricity				1	1	1	1	1	1	6
		Energy consumption by Natural gas	1	1	1	1	1	1				6
		Energy consumption by Fuel oil	1	1	1	1	1	1	1	1	1	9
		Energy consumption by Non-renewable Fuel oil							1	1	1	3
		Energy consumption by Renewable Fuel oil							1	1	1	3
		Energy consumption by Steam	1	1	1	1	1	1				6

(continued)

(continued)

ESG	Topic	Indicator Items	LVMH			KER			ELC			SUM
			2020	2021	2022	2020	2021	2022	2020	2021	2022	
		Energy consumption by Chilled water	1	1	1							3
		Energy consumption by Renewable energy	1	1	1	1	1	1	1	1	1	9
		Energy intensity (normalized to net sales)							1	1	1	3
		Estimated electricity for non-consolidated stores	1	1	1				1	1	1	6
	Water	water consumption for "process" purpose	1	1	1	1	1	1	1	1	1	9
		Industrial water of groundwater				1	1	1				3
		Industrial water from public network				1	1	1				3
		Domestic water				1	1	1				3
		Change in water consumption	1	1	1				1	1	1	6
		Withdrawal							1	1	1	3
		Discharge							1	1	1	3
		Water consumption from all areas with water stress							1	1	1	3

(continued)

(continued)

ESG	Topic	Indicator Items	LVMH 2020	LVMH 2021	LVMH 2022	KER 2020	KER 2021	KER 2022	ELC 2020	ELC 2021	ELC 2022	SUM
		Water withdrawn from all areas with water stress							1	1	1	3
		Water consumption intensity (thousand cubic meters normalized to net sales)							1	1	1	3
		Reduction in water withdrawal at manufacturing sites									1	1
		Percentage of water discharged				1	1	1				3
		Chemical oxygen demand after treatment	1	1	1		1	1				5
	Air	Scope 1&2 Change in GHG emissions	1	1	1	1	1	1	1	1	1	9
		Scope 1&2 direct GHG emissions	1	1	1	1	1	1				6
		Scope 1 Energies				1	1	1				3
		Scope 1 Natural gas				1	1	1				3
		Scope 1 Heating oil				1	1	1				3
		Scope 1 LPG				1	1	1				3
		Scope 1 Fuel for transportation and on-site handling				1	1	1				3
		Scope 1 Other energies					1	1				2
		Scope 1 Company cars				1	1	1				3

(continued)

(continued)

ESG	Topic	Indicator Items	LVMH 2020	LVMH 2021	LVMH 2022	KER 2020	KER 2021	KER 2022	ELC 2020	ELC 2021	ELC 2022	SUM
		Scope 1&2 indirect greenhouse gas emissions	1	1	1	1	1	1				6
		Scope 1 GHG emissions				1	1	1	1	1	1	6
		Scope 2 GHG emissions				1	1	1	1	1	1	6
		Scope 2 Market-based				1	1	1			1	4
		Scope 2 Market-based, by Electricity				1	1	1			1	4
		Scope 2 Market-based, by Thermal				1	1	1			1	4
		Scope 2 Location-based				1	1	1			1	4
		GHG intensity				1	1	1	1	1	1	6
		Carbon Neutral									1	1
		progress towards Net Zero							1	1	1	3
		Breakdown of direct and indirect emissions	1	1	1				1	1	1	6
		Scope 3 reduction per unit revenue									1	1
		Scope 3 GHG emissions	1	1	1	1	1	1	1	1	1	9
		Category 1: Purchased goods and services						1	1	1	1	4
		Category 2: Capital goods							1	1	1	3

(continued)

(continued)

ESG	Topic	Indicator Items	LVMH			KER			ELC			SUM
			2020	2021	2022	2020	2021	2022	2020	2021	2022	
		Category 3: Fuel and energy related activities2						1			1	2
		Category 4: Upstream transportation and distribution	1	1	1			1	1	1	1	7
		Category 5: Waste generated in operations									1	1
		Category 6: Business travel						1	1	1	1	4
		Category 7: Employee commuting									1	1
		Category 9: Downstream transportation and distribution	1	1	1			1			1	5
		Category 11: Use of sold products						1			1	2
		Category 12: End-of life treatment ofsold products						1			1	2
		Category 15: Investments						1			1	1
		VOCs - for the Group's tanneries					1	1				2
	Ttransportation	Upstream transportation	1	1	1	1	1	1				6
		Upstream Road				1	1	1				3
		Upstream Marine				1	1	1				3
		Upstream Air				1	1	1				3

(continued)

(continued)

ESG	Topic	Indicator Items	LVMH			KER			ELC			SUM
			2020	2021	2022	2020	2021	2022	2020	2021	2022	
		Upstream Rail				1	1	1				3
		Downstream transportation	1	1	1	1	1	1				6
		Downstream Road				1	1	1				3
		Downstream Air					1	1				2
		Business travel				1	1	1				3
		Business travel Air travel				1	1	1				3
	Package	total packaging quantity	1	1	1	1	1	1	1	1	1	9
		packaging non-renewable			1	1	1	1	1	1	1	7
		packaging renewable			1	1	1	1	1	1	1	7
		metal packaging			1	1	1	1				4
		plastic packaging			1	1	1	1				4
		Recycled plastic packaging				1	1	1				3
		Bio-based plastic packaging				1	1	1				3
		Other plastic packaging				1	1	1				3
		paper/card board packaging			1	1	1	1				4
		Recycled paper and cardboard packaging				1	1	1				3
		Certified paper and cardboard packaging				1	1	1				3
		Other paper and cardboard packaging				1	1	1				3

(continued)

(continued)

ESG	Topic	Indicator Items	LVMH			KER			ELC			SUM
			2020	2021	2022	2020	2021	2022	2020	2021	2022	
		Other packaging materials packaging			1	1	1	1				4
		Glass packaging			1	1	1	1				4
		Increase in the amount of post-consumer recycled (PCR) material in packaging							1	1	1	3
		Forest-based fiber cartons FSC certified							1	1	1	3
		Virgin petroleum content in plastic packaging									1	1
		Packaging made from post-consumer recycled content and/or renewable materials							1	1	1	3
		Packaging given to customers rate							1	1	1	3
		Packaging given to customers	1	1	1		1	1			1	6
	Waste	Waste production	1	1	1	1	1	1	1	1	1	9
		Change in waste produced	1	1	1	1	1	1	1	1	1	9
		Recycling waste				1	1	1	1	1	1	6
		Recovery, including energy recovery waste				1	1	1	1	1	1	6

(continued)

(continued)

ESG	Topic	Indicator Items	LVMH 2020	LVMH 2021	LVMH 2022	KER 2020	KER 2021	KER 2022	ELC 2020	ELC 2021	ELC 2022	SUM
		Landfill waste							1	1	1	3
		Incineration waste							1	1	1	3
		Other treatment method waste							1	1	1	3
		Change in hazardous waste produced	1	1	1	1	1	1	1	1	1	9
		Reuse				1	1	1	1	1	1	6
		Recycling				1	1	1	1	1	1	6
		Composting							1	1	1	3
		Recovery; including energy recovery							1	1	1	3
		Landfill							1	1	1	3
		Percentage of waste recovered	1	1	1							3
	Raw resources	Grapes – Sustainable wine growing certification			1							1
		LWG certification of tanneries for bovine and ovine leather			1	1	1	1				4
		LWG certification of tanneries for crocodile skin leather			1	1	1	1				4
		Certified cotton			1	1	1	1				4
		Certified organic cotton				1	1	1				3
		Certified recycled cotton				1	1	1				3

(continued)

(continued)

ESG	Topic	Indicator Items	LVMH			KER			ELC			SUM
			2020	2021	2022	2020	2021	2022	2020	2021	2022	
		Certified paper			1	1	1	1				4
		Certified fur			1	1	1	1				4
		Certified Cashmere				1	1	1				3
		Certified sheep wool			1	1	1	1				4
		Certified cellulosic fibers				1	1	1				3
		Certification for all crocodile farms supplying the Group's tannery			1							1
		Diamonds: RJC COP			1							1
		Gold: RJC COP certification			1	1	1	1				4
		Gold: RJC COC certification			1	1	1	1				4
		new suppliers screened using environmental and social criteria							1	1	1	3
		strategic suppliers screened using environmental and social criteria 29							1	1	1	3
		Number of third-party on-site supplier audits							1	1	1	3
		Total amount of palm oil sourced (thousand metric tons)							1	1	1	3

(continued)

(continued)

ESG	Topic	Indicator Items	LVMH			KER			ELC			SUM
			2020	2021	2022	2020	2021	2022	2020	2021	2022	
		Total palm oil certified by RSPO, by certification type			1				1	1	1	4
		Palm oil Identity Preserved							1	1	1	3
		Palm oil Segregated							1	1	1	3
		Palm oil Mass Balance							1	1	1	3
		Palm oil Book & Claim							1	1	1	3
		Total palm-based ingredients sourced through certified-sustainable physical supply chains							1	1		3

References

1. Mok, A., Hong, Y., Zihayat, M.: The trends of sustainability in the luxury fashion industry: A Triple Bottom Line analysis. J. Glob. Fash. Market. **13**(4), 360–379 (2022). https://doi.org/10.1080/20932685.2022.2085601
2. Aras, G., Crowther, D.: Corporate sustainability reporting: a study in disingenuity? J. Bus. Ethics **87**, 279–288 (2009)
3. Bose, S.: Evolution of ESG Reporting Frameworks. In: Esty, D.C., Cort, T. (eds.) Values at Work. Palgrave Macmillan, Cham (2020). https://doi.org/10.1007/978-3-030-55613-6_2
4. Chun, E., Joung, H., Lim, Y.J., Ko, E.: Business transparency and willingness to act environmentally conscious behavior: applying the sustainable fashion evaluation system "Higg Index." J. Glob. Scholars Market. Sci. **31**(3), 437–452 (2021)
5. Deloitte: Global powers of luxury goods (2023). https://www.deloitte.com/global/en/Industries/consumer/analysis/gx-cb-global-powers-of-luxury-goods.html. Accessed Nov 2023
6. Fashion Revolution: Transparency (2023). https//www.fashionrevolution.org/about/transparency/
7. Halme, M., Laurila, J.: Philanthropy, integration or innovation? Exploring the financial and societal outcomes of different types of corporate responsibility. J. Bus. Ethics **84**, 325–339 (2009). https://doi.org/10.1007/s10551-008-9712-5
8. Li, T.-T., Wang, K., Sueyoshi, T., Wang, D.D.: ESG: research progress and future prospects. Sustainability **13**(21), 11663 (2021). https://doi.org/10.3390/su132111663
9. McKinsey & Company (2024). https://www.mckinsey.com/industries/retail/our-insights/state-of-fashion
10. Roca, L.C., Searcy, C.: An analysis of indicators disclosed in corporate sustainability reports. J. Clean. Prod. **20**(1), 103–118 (2012)

Travel Service Smart Application Design for Travel Track Recording and Sharing

Chenghao Yang[✉] and Sixu Hong

Xiamen University, Xiamen 361000, People's Republic of China
2116913@students.uca.ac.uk

Abstract. Currently, all major travel service brands have smart applications for travel guide recommendations, but most of them are generalised travel route recommendations. Almost all of them suffer from insufficient personalised services, limited social interactions, and insufficient formal innovation. This paper aims to respond to the lack of an effective platform for users to record and share their travel experiences during their trips, enabling them to explore and share their travel tracks, and meeting their needs for personalised and socialised travel experiences. This study firstly conducts a competitive analysis of current market applications to gain a comprehensive understanding of the limitations and market pain points of current travel services. In-depth user analysis is conducted to understand user expectations and data collection, and user needs and experience goals are defined in depth through user profiles and user journeys. After defining the problem, this paper designs an intelligent application as the optimal solution, which introduces personalised travel trajectories and community sharing features to recommend high-quality travel trajectories to users, while users can share and exchange their travel tracks in the community to customise personalised travel routes with high efficiency. The application focuses on user-friendliness and efficiency to improve the user travelling experience. Through this research, travel tracks are visually displayed, and the concept of tracks is used to create richer and more interesting travel memories for travel-loving users, injecting new thinking and methods into the field of travel services.

Keywords: User Experience · Travel Service · Travel Tracks · Social Sharing

1 Introduction

Against the backdrop of the trend of the arrival of the self-media era and the development of China's tourism industry, it has become an unstoppable trend for travellers to attach importance to personalised and social experiences during travel [1]. At present, travel services have entered a new channel of rapid recovery, tourism has become a ubiquitous way of life for the people, and tourists' demands show a diversified, personalised and quality diversified stratification trend. The booming development of the tourism industry has given rise to a large number of travel service websites, which provide users with practical tips such as travel route recommendations, and the travel information in these

© The Author(s), under exclusive license to Springer Nature Switzerland AG 2024
C. Stephanidis et al. (Eds.): HCII 2024, CCIS 2118, pp. 149–159, 2024.
https://doi.org/10.1007/978-3-031-61963-2_14

applications is extensive and comprehensive. However, due to the complexity of travel information, there are relatively few travel recommendations that combine personalised recommendation systems with the travel domain [2]. This status quo has low usability for user experience design, and it is difficult for users to efficiently find content that meets their personal needs in a large amount of information to satisfy the demand for a personalised and social travel experience during travel [3]. It takes a lot of time to organise tips that meet their preferences and needs, and the user experience needs to be improved.

How to achieve the sharing of information resources in the tourism industry chain is the core of building a smart tourism platform and applying tourism big data [4]. In order to truly achieve the sharing of information resources in the process of travel services, this study designs a travel service smart application with personalised and socialised experience by introducing personalised travel trajectories and community sharing functions to recommend high-quality travel trajectories to users. The visualisation of travel tracks creates rich and interesting travel memories for travel enthusiasts. The combination of information technology and smart tourism platform improves the convenience, efficiency and intelligence of tourism [5]. This is better able to meet the needs of users than existing travel service platforms, improve the efficiency of user travel, increase user usability and satisfaction, and will also bring better benefits to the tourism industry.

2 Method

2.1 Competitive Analysis

At present, the major travel service brands mainly provide intelligent applications for travel guide recommendations, including recommendations for routes, hotels, travel modes, food and so on. Platforms with a large user base and greater authority were selected for comparative analysis, and the main platforms tested were Tripadvisor, Expedia, Lonely planet and Sixteenfold. These apps typically offer travel route recommendations directly within the platform and organize high-quality travel tips for users to access conveniently, allowing them to easily obtain travel advice and information anytime, anywhere. However, most of these apps lack personalized recommendations and real-time performance. They cannot provide personalized push notifications based on users' preferences and historical behaviors, which could enhance users' sense of participation and overall experience. The competitive analysis is listed in Table 1.

2.2 User Analysis

Personas. The target user is the young adult traveller. Young adults are usually adventurous and enjoy exploring new places and experiencing different cultures. They may seek personalized travel advice and activity recommendations, as well as share and exchange experiences with other travelers through the app. The persona was created through the above analysis as shown in Fig. 1.

Table 1. Comparison of travel service brands advantages and disadvantages.

Brand name	User Group	Advantages	Disadvantages
Tripadvisor	Young adults are overrepresented (25–34 years)	Large user base, bringing together a large number of user reviews to make the travel guide more authentic Wide coverage, users can find a variety of travel information Search and filter function is perfect, which is convenient for users to choose Provide AI support	There are a huge number of travel guides with varying quality High degree of commercialisation and the presence of ads to boot No clear user sharing community
Expedia	Young adults are overrepresented (25–34 years)	Provide a one-stop solution for all your travel booking needs, including air tickets, hotels, attractions, and other booking services Provide membership points system to increase user stickiness Provide special offers to attract users	Over-commercialised, travel recommendations are influenced by advertising No community for sharing and communication
Lonely planet	Young adults are overrepresented (25–34 years)	Highly specialised content, providing comprehensive travel guides with cultural background and more Quality content, providing a wealth of information on travelling destinations	Updates are not timely and do not accurately reflect travel information Insufficient information coverage and possibly insufficient information on some travel destinations No booking service is provided No community for sharing and communication
Sixteen times	Youth are overrepresented (18–24 years)	Intuitive travel route recommendations, using routes and signs to provide a wealth of travel tips Variety of content, multiple route options for the same destination	The interface design is crowded and lacks clarity and conciseness User sharing lacks communication

Name: Ze Lin
Age: 26
Nationality: Shanghai, China
Occupation: Designer

Characteristics: Optimistic, Positive, Curious
Interest: Travel, Outdoor activity
Concerns: Creativity, Quality, Service
Motivations: Attractive, Unique, Simple, Comfortable
Maslow's hierarchy of needs: Self-fulfillment needs

Personal profile:
He is a designer who loves to travel and find inspiration on the road. So whenever he has a holiday, he will travel with his friends. He likes to see the beautiful scenery and feel the humanity. But he doesn't like to do too much walkthrough, and prefers someone to help him make good routes and suggestions to feel what others find interesting.

Fig. 1. The persona detail.

User Journey Map. Define a flowchart of the travel process based on the user profile and organise a journey map of the user's trip (see Fig. 2).

Decide to Travel Phase.   The user may search the web for possible travel destinations.

Before the Travel Phase.   Firstly, the user may use the application to get information about the destination, introduction of attractions, local culture and flavour when planning a trip.

Secondly, users may use the search function to find information on travel routes, hotels, attractions, etc. that match their preferences and needs.

Thirdly, users may read travelogues and tips from other users for inspiration and advice.

Travelling Phase.   Firstly, while travelling, users may need real-time access to map navigation and traffic information in order to reach their destination smoothly.

Secondly, Users can utilize the app to compile and share travel photos, travelogues, reviews, and other content, facilitating communication and interaction with fellow users.

After the travel phase.   Firstly, users may use the app to collate and share travel photos, travelogues, reviews and other content to communicate and interact with other users.

Secondly, users may evaluate and provide feedback on the travelling experience to provide reference and suggestions for other users.

Thirdly, Users may use the application to save travel tracks and footprints as valuable memories and souvenirs.

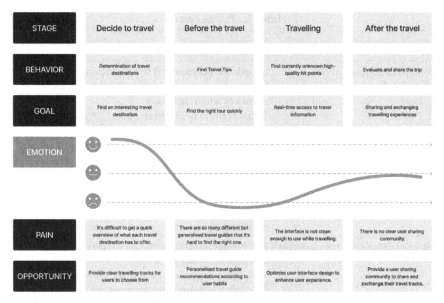

Fig. 2.   The user journey map.

3   Problem Definition

3.1   User Requirements

Based on the above analysis of competitors and users, the user requirements are listed in Table 2.

3.2   Experience Objectives

Based on the above analysis of user needs, the application provides users with personalised travel planning and advice based on existing travel services, Simultaneously, it establishes a sharing community to encourage users to create personal travel tracks and share them with others, creating an open, free and interesting social experience. Through personalised push information, simple and intuitive interactive interface and good visual experience, the app meets users' needs for real-time updated travel information and rich functions, including posting travel plans, travelogues, tips, etc., map function to display destinations and attractions, as well as perfect search function, so as to create an all-around enjoyable travel experience for users.

Table 2. The user needs.

Type	Needs
Emotional experience needs	Experience personalised travel planning and advice You can create your own travel history and share resources with other users Social features to create an open, free and fun social experience
Interactive experience requirements	Personalised push messages, including travel advice, activity track recommendations, etc Interactive interface is simple and clear, with line animation to show the concept of track
Visual experience requirements	Simplified programme interface, easy to operate, providing a good intuitive visual experience
Functional experience requirements	A complete travel information strategy with wide coverage of information With travel experience record and community sharing function, it is convenient for users to collect and share the travel routes they have personally experienced, exchange real travel experience information, and have social attributes Provide map function, clearly displaying the track of travel destinations and interesting places Perfect search and filtering function, support searching related content according to destination, time, theme and other conditions Real-time, regularly updated travel information

4 Prototype Design

4.1 Software Architecture

Based on preliminary market and user research, and after understanding the functional and experiential needs of users, this paper proposes a solution in the form of a smart application. This application introduces personalized travel itineraries and a community sharing function, allowing users to receive recommendations for high-quality travel itineraries, as well as enabling them to share and exchange their own travel experiences within the community. The intelligent application journey is planned to get the information framework diagram as shown in Fig. 3.

4.2 Low Fidelity Interface

The main page of Smart Applications low fidelity is shown in Fig. 4.

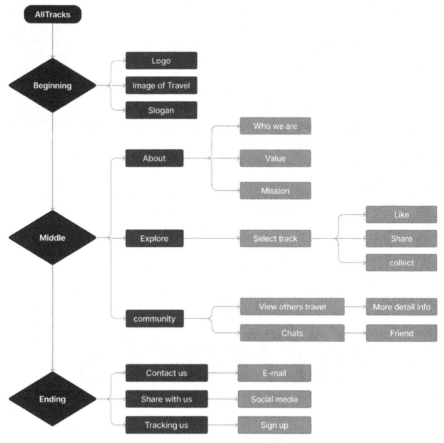

Fig. 3. User Flow.

4.3 Visual Design

The visual design is centred on the concept of trajectory and the logo design clearly demonstrates the concept of trajectory, as shown in Fig. 5. The main colour is bright green, which represents the spirit of energy, vitality and exploration, as shown in Fig. 6. The interface design presents a clear, simple and distinctive interface style, as shown in Fig. 7. Combined with the dynamic effect of lines to show the concept of trajectory, it creates a comfortable and pleasant visual experience, provides users with intuitive perception and enhances their understanding of the travelling path. At the same time, it pays attention to the readability and recognition of the information, through the simple layout and clear fonts, users can easily find the information they need, and improve the user experience and operational efficiency.

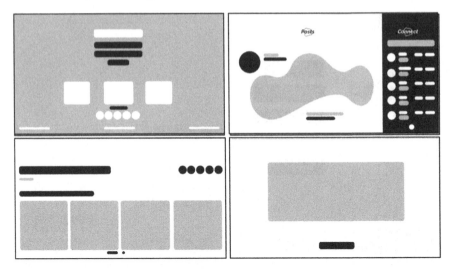

Fig. 4. Main pages of low fidelity prototype.

Fig. 5. The brand logo.

4.4 High Fidelity Interface

Based on the low-fidelity interface, visual design elements were added to design the final high-fidelity interface as shown in Fig. 8. A personalised travel track recommendation and sharing community interface was designed, as shown in Fig. 9.

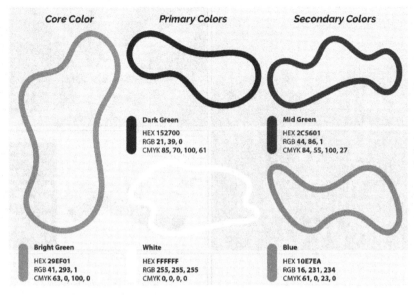

Fig. 6. The brand colour.

Fig. 7. The interface design.

Fig. 8. The interface design.

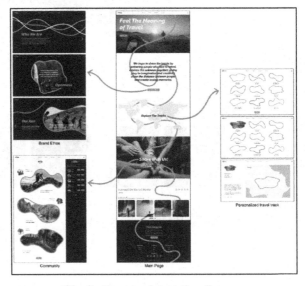

Fig. 9. The page interaction diagram.

5 Conclusion

This paper provides a direction for the design of intelligent applications for travel trajectory recording and sharing. The purpose of this paper is to address the issues of inadequate personalized services, limited social interaction, and insufficient innovative forms present in current intelligent travel service brand applications. It aims to conduct in-depth research and exploration in response to the needs of users lacking an effective platform for recording and sharing their travel experiences. Compared with the existing travel service platforms, this design focuses on introducing personalised travel track and community sharing functions to provide a high-quality travel track and a platform for sharing and communication, so as to provide users with a better travel experience. The significance of this paper lies in its infusion of fresh perspectives into the realm of travel services, offering users a more personalised and socially engaging travel experience. Moreover, it contributes to the advancement and innovation of the travel service industry to a certain extent. Nevertheless, there remain certain limitations within this paper, and the proposed design is conceptual in nature. It serves to address travel-related challenges at the design level and offers insights for future research endeavors.

References

1. Nili, L., Rongkun, L.: Enhancing the quality of tourism services according to the trend of youthfulness and personalization. China Culture Daily **4** (2022). (in Chinese)
2. Hong, S.: Research on tourism application of smartphone APP in the background of smart tourism. Fujian Normal Univ. **2**(5),1–2 (2014). (in Chinese)
3. Chenyue L., Kejian, L., Qingrui, M.: Design and implementation of personalised recommendation system for museums. Softw. Guide **15**(5), 66–68 (2016). (in Chinese)
4. Rundong, Z., Yuefu, Z., Xiao, L.: Construction and countermeasure analysis of tibet territorial wisdom tourism ecosystem platform. J. North China Univ. Sci. Technol. **4**, 27–32+41 (2022). (in Chinese)
5. Xiaoping, Z.: Exploring the enabling effect, development status and countermeasures of smart tourism platforms. J. Guangxi Open Univ. **34**(3), 40 (2023). (in Chinese)

An Investigation of the Perceptual Engineering Theory Based on the Portable Leisure Beverage Experience Space

Hongju Yu[1]([✉]), Rui Xu[2], Changfeng Jiang[1], Danmeng Xu[1], and Ziqiong Yang[1]

[1] School of Art and Design, Fuzhou University of International Studies and Trade,
Fuzhou 350200, China
1578307286@qq.com

[2] The Graduate Institute of Design Science, Tatung University, Taipei, Taiwan

Abstract. With the fast-paced development of human society, people rarely have personal slow-paced leisure time. Because of this, people's perceptual needs are constantly amplified, and a leisure experience space that can bring people's perceptual needs is very important. This article investigates the perceptual needs of users and uses perceptual engineering theory and computer-aided tools to explore the design of movable drink experience spaces. Therefore, perceptual needs are more about the user's emotional response and usage experience of the product, which is regarded as a key element of this design exploration. The research method of this article: After combining these two points, the theory of Kansei Engineering is applied to the movable leisure drink experience space. ①This design research will conduct preliminary research and case analysis on similar products currently on the market at home and abroad. ② Understand the existing pain points between similar products and users and the shortcomings in the application of Kansei Engineering Theory to better locate users' specific needs. The purpose of this article is to combine the obtained data foundation with the theories and tools of some disciplines such as Kansei Engineering Theory and Computer Aided Tools, and take the perceptual needs of users given by the product as the premise, and the goal of the product being able to effectively communicate with users. This provides a better source of clues for solving user behavior problems. The results of this research: Finally, we will examine whether the functions, emotions, and experiences provided by this product can meet the perceptual needs of users, and demonstrate whether the application of perceptual engineering theory in the movable leisure drink experience space can satisfy the existing emotional and experiential needs of users. Needs, and make timely adjustments to achieve user satisfaction with perceptual needs.

Keywords: Perceptual engineering Theory · Perceptual Demand · Movable · Leisure drinking Space · Product Semantics

C. Stephanidis et al. (Eds.): HCII 2024, CCIS 2118, pp. 160–171, 2024.
https://doi.org/10.1007/978-3-031-61963-2_15

1 Introduction

With the continuous development of science and technology, some technologies are slowly entering our lives and changing our lifestyles, such as artificial intelligence, speech recognition, intelligent Internet technology… With the popularization of these technologies, people's lives Quality is also constantly improving and the pace of life is getting faster and faster. On this basis, although people's living standards continue to improve, people's perceptual needs are also constantly amplified because of the fast-paced life. Therefore, a leisure experience space that can bring people's emotional needs can better meet people's needs.

1.1 Research Background

Today's era is an era of perceptual economy, and perceptual factors have become an important factor affecting people's shopping. With the progress of society, people's living conditions are constantly improving. When basic physiological needs are met, people begin to slowly pursue psychological and perceptual needs. Since the birth of design, from the initial satisfaction of survival needs to the pursuit of emotional needs today to the pursuit of higher-level needs in the future, design will always continue to develop and evolve with the development of society and the changes of the times. Variety. After people's needs in a certain area are fulfilled, new needs will also arise. Maslow divided physiological needs to spiritual needs into five levels. Nowadays, the products on the market can basically meet people's functional needs. People's formal beauty and psychological satisfaction are becoming more and more important. Design focus.

1.2 Research Significance

The development of design changes people's lives and promotes social progress. The same complexity of people also brings endless vitality to design. As people's needs change, design also makes carriers that are more in line with people's needs under such circumstances, thereby more accurately meeting people's needs. It can be seen from this that the satisfaction of people's needs in today's leisure drink experience space has gradually faded with the development of society and the changes in people's needs. People are no longer just satisfied with its basic functions, but also pay attention to the feelings and experiences during use. More attention. In summary, it can be seen that after people meet certain needs, they will generate new demand directions and provide new directions for design.

2 Introduction of Kansei Engineering Theory

2.1 Definition of Kansei Engineering

"Kansei Engineering" is the quantitative analysis of various human sensibilities such as vision, hearing, touch, etc. through engineering techniques, and then establishes the functional relationship between human sensibility quantities and various physical quantities used in engineering. This is the basis for engineering research. It can be seen from the above that Kansei Engineering can better obtain users' preferences and needs by digging out people's perceptual psychological needs and conducting quantitative analysis, providing reliable data for design, thereby designing products that meet users' perceptual and psychological needs.

2.2 Research Scope of Kansei Engineering

The foundation of Kansei Engineering is psychology and cognition, and its research areas include: 1. The study of people's feelings, emotions, perceptions, and representations forms the basis of Kansei Engineering; 2. Consumer psychology helps to understand consumption 3. The study of physiology helps to understand human sensibility; 4. The study of semantics helps to study the classification and intention of product semantics.

From the above, it can be seen that research on Kansei Engineering theory requires finding relevant theories and knowledge from various disciplines for statistics and planning.

3 Design Positioning of Movable Leisure Drink Experience Space Based on Kansei Engineering Theory

3.1 Analysis of External Factors

Target Group Positioning

External factors play a strong role in the design process. The design purpose can be clarified to a certain extent in the early stage of design, which can better lay the foundation for the subsequent complex design process. External factors include: users, usage time, usage space, etc. These factors will affect changes in internal factors of the product. It is very important to determine the external factors before starting the design. After research, it is found that the current user population of the beverage experience space is younger, more highly educated, and younger. Among them, the proportion of 25–35 year old reaches 48%; undergraduates. The proportion of those with academic qualifications reached 61%; those with a monthly income of more than 10,000 yuan accounted for 30%. This type of users has become the main consumer group of the beverage experience space. Only by incorporating the needs and feedback of this consumer group into the entire design process can we Achieve design goals better and more accurately (Figs. 1, 2 and 3).

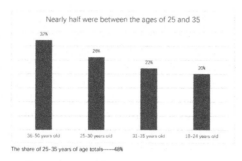

Fig. 1. User demographic characteristics.

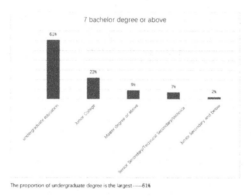

Fig. 2. User demographic characteristics.

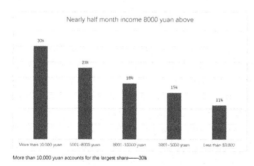

Fig. 3. User demographic characteristics.

Using Time and Space Positioning. People's production and life also affect the use stages of different products. Different products will also be used in different scenarios, behaviors or certain special environments and events. It is rare that a product will follow a person's production and life throughout the day. For example, if you want to drink water, you will use a water cup; if you want to tell the time, you will use a watch; if you want to record, you will use pen and paper. So we can see the difference. Products meet people's special behaviors in different scenarios. Under normal circumstances, people will seek out their leisure and entertainment needs after a day of productive work. Therefore, in order to better comply with people's logic, most of the leisure drink experience spaces on the market are also open at night. Therefore, the positioning of the use time of the final product remains unchanged during the design process.

The current main consumer groups in the leisure drink experience space are characterized by young, highly educated, and youthful. Since the distribution of this type of consumer group is relatively vague, in order to better determine the distribution of the main consumer groups in each tier of cities, thus collecting and sorting out the information on the proportion of consumers in the beverage experience space in each tier of cities, and found that the highest proportion is in the new first-tier cities, which accounts for 24%, followed by the third-tier cities, which accounts for 20%. Based on this, the spatial positioning of product use will be based on cities within these two ranges, and basic research on the environment, humanities, urban layout and other factors of the target area will be conducted to obtain more accurate basic information. Better determine the internal factors of the product and reduce errors in the design process (Fig. 4).

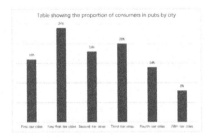

Fig. 4. Proportion of portable leisure beverage experience space users in each tier city.

Pain Point Analysis. The leisure drink experience spaces on the market today have basically met people's leisure and entertainment needs, and people's demand points and pain points have also begun to slowly shift. As shown in the table below, location is the biggest reason why people don't want to go to the leisure drink experience space, accounting for 35%. This reason is analyzed from a behavioral perspective: a lot of time and energy will be consumed on the way there, and on the return trip In the process, there will also be troubles caused by problems such as complicated behavioral procedures due to the long distance. These reasons are also the reasons why people do not choose to go because of the distance problem. In addition, the lack of unique and creative drink experience spaces also accounts for a high proportion, with the proportion as high as 27%. This reason is that most of the leisure drink experience spaces currently on the market are sufficient to meet people's basic needs for leisure and entertainment. Needs, leading people to pursue higher-level needs, that is, emotional and perceptual needs. The remaining factors such as atmosphere, price, environment, food quality, etc. also affect people's interest in casual drink experience spaces. These factors are also the pain points that need to be solved during the design process (Fig. 5).

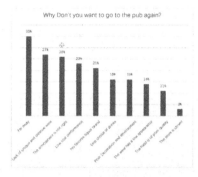

Fig. 5. Analysis of users' pain points for portable leisure beverage experience space.

3.2 Internal Factor Analysis

Function Positioning. As external factors become increasingly clear, the basic elements and directions of internal factors are also confirmed. In order to better solve the problems caused by external factors, in this design study, in terms of function, we made a bold idea to solve the problem of distance, changing the fixed type into a mobile type, and changing the leisure type into a mobile type. The beverage experience space carries out mobile innovation. The mobile version takes various internet celebrity check-in points around the city or across the city as the starting point, and uses the APP to check the location of the mobile beverage experience space, so as to better arrange the pick-up and drop-off. Time and place, reducing the cumbersome and complicated behavioral procedures in the past, and better improving the user experience process.

Appearance Positioning. Most of the existing beverage experience spaces on the market are dominated by dim, warm tones, with relatively single effects and a lack of creativity, which makes it difficult to cater to the changes in the younger consumer groups. In order to better meet the changes in the consumer groups, During the design research process, more color effects and light adjustment functions were added, and the overall style was designed to be more dynamic and cyberpunk style to better cater to the increasingly younger consumer group.

In terms of the basic appearance of the product, in order to meet the placement of infrastructure for the leisure drink experience space and better retain its original basic functions, the basic appearance of the vehicle is based on the urban sightseeing bar as the basic shape of the vehicle (Fig. 6).

Fig. 6. Fieldwork.

Material Selection. The selection of materials for products in different usage scenarios is related to the environment in which the product is located. Taking chairs as an example, outdoor chairs often use corrosion-resistant metal materials to adapt to the challenges brought by the environment. Indoor chairs are indeed made of soft materials that care more about people's experience. The same is true in other different scenes. Different materials will also be used. For example, in hospitals, fast food restaurants, coffee shops and other spaces, the choice of chair materials will be different. Therefore, in order to ensure that the mobile leisure beverage experience space that is used outdoors for a long time can better extend its service life, corrosion-resistant metal or metallic paint will be selected as the material to protect and extend its service life.

4   Product Definition of Movable Leisure Drink Experience Space Based on Kansei Engineering Theory

4.1   Product Size Consideration

In order to ensure the scientific nature of the design, the size of the entire product is determined with reference to the size of sightseeing buses that have been put into production and meet road conditions. The general standard size is 11530 × 2500 × 3040 mm. The design of indoor interior objects follows the basic dimensions of the human body structure, as shown in the table below (Fig. 7).

4.2   Appearance and Color Matching Construction

A total of 4 ideas were made for the basic appearance and color matching of the product, and interviews were used to select the most popular one, and continued design research work was carried out (Figs. 8, 9 and 10).

表2-3 立姿人体尺寸

年龄分组 数据 百分位数/% 项目	男 (18~60 岁)							女 (18~55 岁)						
	1	5	10	50	90	95	99	1	5	10	50	90	95	99
2.1 眼高/mm	1436	1474	1495	1568	1643	1664	1705	1337	1371	1388	1454	1522	1541	1579
2.2 眼高/mm	1244	1281	1299	1367	1435	1455	1494	1166	1195	1211	1271	1333	1350	1385
2.3 肘高/mm	925	954	968	1024	1079	1096	1128	873	899	913	960	1009	1023	1050
2.4 手功能高/mm	656	680	693	741	787	801	828	630	650	662	704	746	757	778
2.5 会阴高/mm	701	728	741	790	840	856	887	648	673	686	732	779	792	819
2.6 胫骨点高/mm	394	409	417	444	472	481	498	363	377	384	410	437	444	459

表2-4 坐姿人体尺寸

年龄分组 数据 百分位数/% 项目	男 (18~60 岁)							女 (18~55 岁)						
	1	5	10	50	90	95	99	1	5	10	50	90	95	99
3.1 坐高/mm	836	858	870	908	947	958	979	789	809	819	855	891	901	920
3.2 坐姿颈椎点高/mm	599	615	624	657	691	701	719	563	579	587	617	648	657	675

年龄分组 数据 百分位数/% 项目	男 (18~60 岁)							女 (18~55 岁)						
	1	5	10	50	90	95	99	1	5	10	50	90	95	99
3.3 坐姿眼高/mm	729	749	761	798	836	847	868	678	695	704	739	773	783	803
3.4 坐姿肩高/mm	539	557	566	598	631	641	669	504	518	526	556	585	594	609
3.5 坐姿肘高/mm	214	228	235	263	291	298	312	201	215	223	251	277	284	299
3.6 坐姿大腿厚/mm	103	112	116	130	146	151	160	107	113	117	130	146	151	160
3.7 坐姿膝高/mm	441	456	461	493	523	532	549	410	424	431	458	485	493	507
3.8 小腿加足高/mm	372	383	389	413	439	448	463	331	342	350	382	399	405	417
3.9 坐深/mm	407	421	429	457	486	494	510	388	401	408	433	461	469	485
3.10 臀膝距/mm	499	515	524	554	585	595	613	481	495	502	529	561	570	587
3.11 坐姿下肢长/mm	892	921	937	992	1046	1063	1096	826	851	865	912	960	975	1005

表2-5 人体水平尺寸

年龄分组 数据 百分位数/% 项目	男 (18~60 岁)							女 (18~55 岁)						
	1	5	10	50	90	95	99	1	5	10	50	90	95	99
4.1 胸宽/mm	242	253	259	280	307	315	331	219	233	239	260	289	299	319
4.2 胸厚/mm	176	186	191	212	237	245	261	159	170	176	199	230	239	260
4.3 肩宽/mm	330	344	351	375	397	403	415	304	320	328	351	371	377	387
4.4 最大肩宽/mm	383	398	405	431	460	469	486	347	363	371	397	428	438	458
4.5 臀宽/mm	273	282	288	306	327	334	346	275	290	296	317	340	346	360
4.6 坐姿臀宽/mm	284	295	300	321	347	355	369	295	310	318	344	374	382	400
4.7 坐姿两肘间宽/mm	353	371	381	422	473	489	518	326	348	360	404	460	478	509
4.8 胸围/mm	762	791	806	867	944	970	1018	717	745	760	825	919	949	1005
4.9 腰围/mm	620	650	665	735	859	895	960	622	659	680	772	904	950	1025
4.10 臀围/mm	780	805	820	875	948	970	1009	795	824	840	900	975	1000	1044

Fig. 7. Human body horizontal size.

First paragraph: Second paragraph:

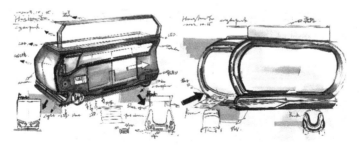

Fig. 8. Homemade hand drawing.

The third paragraph: The fourth paragraph:

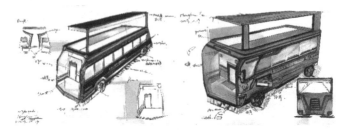

Fig. 9. Homemade hand drawing.

Finally, the most popular one was selected as the fourth one:

Fig. 10. Homemade hand drawing.

4.3 Electronic Model Production

On the basis of determining the appearance, computer-aided tools are used to produce product models (Fig. 11).

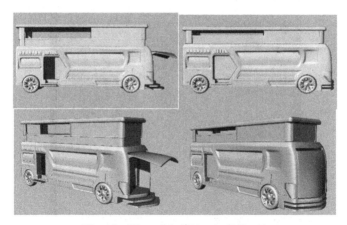

Fig. 11. 3D model making by Rhino7.

4.4 Effect Picture Display

At the end, the product will be rendered and displayed in effect (Figs. 12 and 13).

Fig. 12. Picture by Blender4.0.

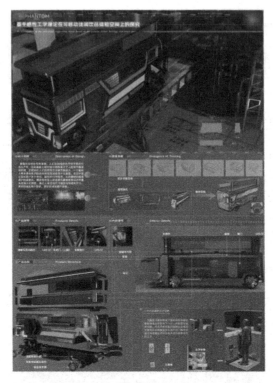

Fig. 13. The final effect of the exhibition board.

5 Conclusion

After people's needs are met, new needs will slowly emerge, thereby increasing the vitality of design and promoting the development of design to a certain level. Apply the theory of Kansei Engineering to the design and development of the entire product, allowing designers to obtain user perceptual and experience data, plus basic analysis of external factors and internal factors. These data make the product more efficient in the design research process. Scientific. This article focuses on the exploration of Kansei Engineering in the leisure drink experience space, and attaches the user's perceptual needs and emotional needs to the entire product design research process, thereby hoping to rationally design and develop a mobile leisure drink experience space that meets user needs.

References

1. Zhang, Y.: A Study on Forecasting Consumer Preferences for Automotive Interiors Based on Perceptual Engineering (2022)
2. Huo, X.: Modeling Design and Optimization of HydrogenEnergy Heavy Truck Based on Kansei Engineeringand CFD, Taiyuan University of Technology

3. Qiu, S.: Study on Design Methods of UrbanElectric Vehicles Based on KanseiEngineering, Hebei University of Technology
4. Maslow, A.H.: A Theory of Human Motivation Psychological Review. Psychological Review, American (1943)
5. Yulan Ding.: Man Machine Engineering. Beijing Institute of Technology Press (2017)

HCI in Mobility and Automated Driving

A Roadmap Towards Remote Assistance: Outcomes from Multidisciplinary Workshop at the 2023 Intelligent Vehicles Symposium

Maytheewat Aramrattana[1]([✉])[iD], Andreas Schrank[2][iD], Jonas Andersson[3][iD], Lin Zhao[4][iD], David Hermann[5], Sanat Mharolkar[6][iD], Marek Vanzura[7][iD], Azra Habibovic[8][iD], and Michael Oehl[2][iD]

[1] The Swedish National Road and Transport Research Institute (VTI), Regnbågsgatan 1, 417 55 Gothenburg, Sweden
maytheewat.aramrattana@vti.se
[2] German Aerospace Center (DLR), Institute of Transportation Systems, Lilienthalplatz 7, 38108 Braunschweig, Germany
{andreas.schrank,michael.oehl}@dlr.de
[3] RISE Research Institutes of Sweden, 417 56 Gothenburg, Sweden
jonas.andersson@ri.se
[4] KTH Royal Institute of Technology, 11428 Stockholm, Sweden
linzhao@kth.se
[5] Technische Universität München, Munich, Germany
david.hermann@tum.de
[6] Nanyang Technological University, 639798 Singapore, Singapore
SANATRAJ002@e.ntu.edu.sg
[7] George Mason University, 4400 University Drive, Fairfax, Virginia 22030, USA
mvanzura@gmu.edu
[8] Scania CV AB, 127 29 Stockholm, Sweden
azra.habibovic@scania.com

Abstract. Remote operation of highly automated vehicles (HAVs) may include occasional assistance from a human remote operator that is located outside the HAVs. Remote assistance typically delegates only high-level guidance tasks to the remote operators such as authorizing a driving maneuver or specifying a new driving path. As remote assistance is fairly unexplored, there are still several research challenges. These challenges were discussed by experts from academia and industry in a multidisciplinary workshop at the 2023 IEEE Intelligent Vehicles Symposium. As a result of the workshop, this paper presents a list of most pressing research questions in the following areas: human-machine interaction and human factors, design of the remote station, design of the HAVs. It also outlines a roadmap for future research on remote assistance of HAV, thereby informing interdisciplinary studies and facilitating the benefits of HAVs before full autonomy can be reached.

Keywords: Remote assistance · Human factors · Remote operation · Autonomous vehicles

1   Introduction

Autonomous driving of road vehicles has been an actively pursued research field in both academia and industry for a long time. In recent years, remote operation capability has become more pronounced as a necessary complement to highly automated vehicles (HAVs) (corresponding to SAE's Driving Automation Level 4 or above [16]). This is largely due to the fact that the real world driving environment is dynamic, with edge cases that HAVs cannot handle or resolve[1]. In this context, the remote operation refers to a scenario in which a human operator, commonly referred to as a *"remote operator"*, operates a vehicle from a location outside the vehicle.

Many terms and definitions have been proposed to classify remote operation of road vehicles and their different modalities. In this paper, we will follow the classification in [1], which categorizes remote operation into three modes: remote driving, remote assistance, and remote monitoring.

Remote driving has been widely considered and discussed both commercially (e.g., Vay[2], Elmo Rent[3]) and within research fields (e.g., in [12,14,15,20,24]). Important challenges and opportunities in remote driving have been identified in [1,24]. On the other hand, remote assistance and remote monitoring have not received as much attention in the research field (see, e.g., [1], Appendix C of [20]). However, commercial stakeholders often consider remote assistance together with remote driving [1].

1.1   Remote Assistance

In recent years, taxonomy on remote operation of road vehicles has been discussed in several documents (e.g., in [3,5,16,22]. However, there is currently no clear consensus. In the context of this paper, *remote assistance* is defined as a remote operation mode where the remote operator only provides input and authorization to an automated driving system (ADS) or an ADS-equipped vehicle without directly performing any part of the dynamic driving tasks (i.e., direct control of a vehicle via acceleration, deceleration, and steering). In other words, a remote operator offers a real-time tactical support by giving inputs (e.g., waypoints), which is then processed and executed by the vehicle. The remote operator, who performs such remote assistance tasks, will be referred to as *"remote assistant"* in this paper. Similar definitions and terms can be seen in documents and standards such as BSI Flex 1890 [5], SAE J3016 [16], and AVSC Best Practice for ADS Remote Assistance Use Case [6]. Within UNECE (WP.1) Global Forum for Road Traffic Safety, remote management is used to refer to "remote operation", which includes remote assistance and remote driving [21,22]. Furthermore, remote assistance could be described as an event-driven class of

---

[1] https://edition.cnn.com/2023/08/14/business/driverless-cars-san-francisco-cruise/index.html.

[2] https://vay.io/.

[3] https://www.elmoremote.com/.

remote operation with a distinct division of tasks between the AV system and the remote operator [13].

1.2   Industrial Perspectives

From a business perspective, remote assistance can accelerate the deployment of HAVs and is recognized as an important element in managing HAV fleets. In recent years, stakeholders such as Waymo [7], Zoox, and Cruise have integrated remote assistance in their robotaxi operations. These operations reveal that HAV commonly request assistance in scenarios beyond their autonomous capabilities, e.g., navigating through unforeseen obstacles, addressing complex traffic situations, or making a certain decision.

Furthermore, the potential of remote assistance goes beyond assisting HAVs on public roads to encompass applications in confined spaces. For example, in spaces such as manufacturing plants and warehouses, remote assistance can be used to guide and relocate vehicles, handle freight, or perform other transportation-related tasks. Another notable application of remote assistance is automated vehicle testing on proving grounds. Here, test vehicles carrying out automated tests can be remotely guided under various test conditions, such as at high velocities, extreme temperatures and difficult terrain.

1.3   Objectives

Although remote assistance of HAVs is employed by several industrial stakeholders in their initial operations, several research gaps persist on this topic that need attention before widespread deployment of HAVs. In particular, it is unknown which human factors challenges might be induced by remote assistance and how these might be addressed to warrant safety and efficiency.

To fill in this gap, this paper discusses research challenges and roadmap towards implementing remote assistance for HAVs. Besides summarizing challenges reported in the literature, this paper also contains main research challenges discussed during interactive sessions of the workshop on Remote Operation of Intelligent Connected and Automated Road Vehicles organized in conjunction with the IEEE Intelligent Vehicle Symposium 2023[4]. During the interactive sessions, invited speakers and workshop participants from academia, industry and administration shared and discussed research challenges related to remote operation.

2   Holistic View on Remote Operation

Design and implementation of remote operation of HAVs require integration of human and technological subsystems [2]. As HAVs are technically complex systems, achieving safe and reliable implementations necessitates consideration of

---

[4] https://www.vti.se/en/research/vehicle-technology-and-driving-simulation/project-redo2/workshop-remote-operation-of-cavs-2023.

software reliability, cybersecurity, and human factors. The success also depends on user acceptance, both from the operator, vehicle users, and other road users. Here, user experience design and human factors engineering lend a key contribution to safety and adoption. In parallel, legal aspects have to be considered to ensure compliance with laws, regulations, and ethical standards.

From a broad perspective, all these factors imply a need for an interdisciplinary perspective to design, evaluation, and implementation of remote operations. In general, research studies are often focused on single dimensions of the socio-technical environment that constitutes a remote operation system rather than the interdependencies *between* sub-systems. In several other domains, the need of a systems perspective in development of control towers or command and control centers is well documented, and remote operation of automated road vehicles has a similar need. *Andersson & Söderman* [2] outlines a systemic view of remote operation by showing how the inter-dependencies between socio-technical factors such as e.g., control modes, vehicle capability, Operational Design Domain (ODD), Human-Machine Interaction (HMI), operator tasks and knowledge requirements, and work organization shape the constraints of operator work. The rapid advancement of AI-technology further stresses the need for a systems perspective since AI is likely to be an increasingly integrated part of future remote operation work systems [23]. Collaboration between the human operator(s) and AI system should be considered as a future pathway for coming research also in remote assistance of road vehicles.

There are several research gaps in understanding the inter-dependencies between human-automation sub-systems in remote assistance of HAVs. One such gap is to understand the communication needs, patterns and feedback mechanisms between actors in the traffic system in order to safely and efficiently operate large numbers of vehicles. This is particularly pronounced during adverse events (e.g., network breakdowns), where understanding inter-dependencies can help in analyses of traffic system resilience.

3   Implementation of Remote Assistance

This section presents overall research challenges with regard to implementation of remote assistance on public roads. These challenges are categorized into three main topics: *i)* HMI and human factors, *ii)* design of the remote operation station, and *iii)* design of HAVs. First, common research challenges among the three topics are presented here. Then, research challenges specific to each topic are presented in their subsection below.

A common research challenge across the three topics is how to ensure that remote assistants have a sufficient **situation awareness (SA)**. The remote assistants need specific information to assess the situation and make decisions when the HAVs require assistance. Therefore, it is crucial to display the most suitable information to enhance the SA of remote assistants. This puts requirements and challenges on all parts of the system. From an HMI and human factors' perspective, challenges lie in the choice of feedback or information that is provided to the remote assistant. Furthermore, HAVs themselves need to be equipped with appropriate sensors in order to provide such information from the vehicle to the remote assistant at the remote operation station. Several feedback modes and their combinations have been considered in remote operation station, e.g., auditory feedback [11], augmented reality (AR) [4], haptic feedback, motion feedback [25], steering force feedback [25], and virtual reality (VR). It is clear from the literature that visual feedback alone may not be enough to create a sufficient SA for the remote assistant; rather, a combination of different feedback modalities is required. However, researchers are yet to reach consensus on a suitable amount and modes of feedback that are required. Another unsolved research question is how to link the SA of the remote assistant and the SA of the HAV. Most HAVs are equipped with systems, that can detect and identify objects in its surrounding. Providing such information to the remote assistant could potentially enhance SA.

Another common research challenge concerns **workload** of the remote assistant. Two unsolved research questions in this context are:

- *How to effectively assess the mental workload of remote assistant?* Different biological measurements such as heart rate and eye movements are typically used for mental workload assessment. However, it still remains unclear what is the threshold for an appropriate mental workload, which will affect how long the remote operator can work daily.
- *How to provide the remote assistants with sufficient information that do not increase their workload?* A well-designed user interface should consider the assistants' workload, ensuring tasks can be completed without remote operation experiencing an information overload.

3.1   HMI and Human Factors

This section focuses on aspects specific to HMI and human factors in remote assistance of HAVs.

The Role of the Remote Assistant: Prior to designing an HMI for remote assistance, a role model has to be ascertained. The purpose is to assign certain tasks to certain roles and specify how these roles collaborate. Once a role model is established, the allocation of tasks and the possibility to delegate these tasks to other roles should be clarified. *Schrank et al.* [17] proposed a model of roles for a remote operation center. Considering specific situations in which remote assistance could be applied, *Kettwich et al.* [8] compiled a catalog with relevant use cases and scenarios.

Requirements: Closely linked to the conceptualization of roles is the question of which requirements are put on the remote assistant, and which tasks are expected to be accomplished by the remote assistant. Examples of requirements are: *i)* having a driving license; *ii)* knowing the tasks of a specific remote operation mode; *iii)* have undergone training for the corresponding remote operation mode; and *iv)* passing a test that checks the necessary skills.

Tasks: Specifying the remote assistant's tasks is a prerequisite for creating a safe and user-friendly HMI. In order to obtain a comprehensive and structured compilation of remote assistant's tasks, it is advised to use a systematic method. *Koskinen et al.* suggest Core Task Analysis as an approach for task compilation in remote assistance [10]. Examples for tasks a remote assistant can be engaged in are: object categorization and wayfinding.

Object categorization means that remote assistants augment the ADS with additional information to categorize particular objects detected in the vicinity of the vehicle. For example, a double-parked car can be interpreted by the ADS as a car waiting at the end of line, which would lead to a wrong decision to wait behind it. A remote operator can re-categorize that double-parked vehicle as an obstacle, which would allow the ADS to execute a proper action.

Wayfinding means that remote assistant suggests the ADS with an optimal trajectory. Typically, when road conditions become too unclear, e.g., because of a road construction, the ADS might get confused and be uncertain how to proceed. In such a case, a remote assistant could draw a route for the ADS, which the vehicle then follows. This route can be created by manually putting waypoints on the map for the ADS to follow.

Open research questions regarding role requirements and tasks include:

- Are there tasks that are not considered in current variants of remote assistance (e.g., the SAE's [16] definition of remote assistance)?
- What are the priorities of a remote assistance?
- How to tailor the HMI to remote assistants' tasks?
- How to ensure communication with relevant actors (e.g., passengers, pedestrians, police officers)?

Training: For a remote assistant to achieve the requirements listed above, standardized training may be needed. This ensures that the remote assistant possesses the required skills for assigned tasks. This could be similar to obtaining commercial driving license (e.g., for trucks or taxis). The following research questions revolve around the training of remote assistants:

- What laws and regulations are relevant for training?
- How long and frequent training is required?
- Which criteria should be utilized for selecting remote assistants, and from which groups should they be recruited (e.g., drivers, gamers)?
- Which operating processes do remote assistants need to know?
- Which scenarios should be used in the training of assistants, and how to assess the training results [26]?

3.2   Remote Operation Station Design

This section explores design of workstations for the function of remote assistance and highlights challenges emerging when HAVs are deployed on a large scale (i.e., at a fleet level).

Seamless Transition Between Different Remote Operation Modes: In a remote operation workstation, it is important to define the information required by remote operators. In remote assistance, remote assistants would initially monitor the vehicle and take action when assistance is requested. Based on this process, it is necessary and reasonable to assume that there will be transitions between different remote operation modes (monitoring, assistance, driving). Therefore, it is important to consider how to achieve a seamless transition between each mode, ensuring that operational performance is not negatively affected. An important question is whether a remote operation station designed for remote assistance can also be used for remote driving and vice versa.

HMI Modalities: Conventional visual monitors are typically used to display HAV information to remote assistants. With respect to this, it should be examined whether AR and VR technologies could offer remote assistants an improved SA as compared to classic monitors. In addition to visual information, the role of other sensory modalities such as auditory and kinesthetic should be further explored.

Handling and Prioritization of Simultaneous Requests: In large-scale deployment of HAVs, a challenge may arise when several HAVs within a fleet require assistance simultaneously, exceeding the capacity of the remote assistant or the system. It is thus necessary to consider how to prioritize and handle such situations.

Examples of Remote Assistance Workstation Design: Following the user-centered design process, *Kettwich et al.* developed a click-prototype for such a workstation and evaluated it systematically [9]. Afterward, *Schrank et al.* constructed a physical workstation for remote assistance and assessed it from a human factors perspective under different levels of cognitive load using a dual-task paradigm [18]. The authors in [19] also explored how augmenting degraded video streams with visualized sensor data may support the remote assistant in assessing traffic situations.

3.3   Vehicle Design

To support remote assistance, HAVs also need to be designed in such a way that the vehicle can provide all necessary information to remote assistants. Here, two major aspects will be discussed: *i)* hardware; and *ii)* software.

Hardware: Human drivers typically rely on three main sensory inputs while operating vehicles—vision, motion, and sound. A remote assistant needs similar inputs to understand the situation and make appropriate decision. Several modes of feedback have been considered in the context of remote assistance. Quality of these feedback modes is highly dependent on the placement of sensors providing the feedback. For instance, while most HAVs are equipped with cameras, these cameras may not always be suitable for remote assistance due to inappropriate placement or resolution. Therefore, it is important to have a high-level approach to designing the camera placements so that both the ADS and remote operation systems can make full use of them. Similarly, in case of auditory feedback, the design of the audio system requires research on optimal placement of microphones and filter design to remove unnecessary noise. In some cases, two-way audio communication may also be required so that the remote assistant can communicate with humans in the vicinity of the vehicle.

Software: Another important aspect to consider is the software design that allows the HAV and the remote operator to function well together. Here, it is crucial to design control and automation systems that effectively support the vehicle's operation while prioritizing guidance rather than remote driving. This involves developing algorithms and frameworks that enable remote assistants to provide timely and accurate inputs for decision-making, enhancing the HAV's capabilities in complex situations. Incorporating redundancy and fault tolerance is also essential to ensure continuous operation even in the event of component failures or communication disruptions, particularly for safety-critical functions. Furthermore, compatibility and integration play a vital role in the design of remote assistance, as they must seamlessly interface with various vehicle platforms, models, and ADS systems. This can be achieved by developing modular architectures and standardized interfaces that facilitate easy adaptation and upgrades across different vehicles.

4   Roadmap for Future Research

For the safe and efficient widespread deployment of Highly Automated Vehicles (HAVs) with remote assistance support, a thorough exploration of remote assistance is necessary from both scientific and practical viewpoints. Based on a literature review and insights from a workshop held in conjunction with the IEEE Intelligent Vehicle Symposium 2023, we present a roadmap to guide further development and research in this area.

- **Adopt a socio-technical perspective**. When designing a remote assistance system it is essential to adopt a socio-technical system perspective, wherein each challenge is considered in conjunction rather than in isolation. Consequently, the future research should focus on various interdependencies between human-automation sub-systems.

- **Define the task of remote assistants**. While current applications of remote assistance may not be particularly complex, remote operators may eventually be faced with more complex and rare situations. A challenge here is to clearly define the task of a remote operator with respect to each remote operation mode, and how to effectively manage rare situations. Related to this, one should also specify co-operation between different remote assistants.
- **Ensure acceptable situation awareness and workload**. Ensuring that a remote assistant can obtain and maintain a sufficient degree of situation awareness is essential. In doing this, it is needed that the remote assistant and HAV build a team with common goals and beliefs, where they strengthen each other's performance. Related to this, future research should investigate dynamics of such teams and define a threshold for acceptable workload for the remote assistants.
- **Facilitate mutual understanding**. In remote assistance, the input from a remote assistant is not directly translated into actions by the HAV; rather, it is interpreted by the HAV's decision system (or automated driving system). Consequently, the remote assistant and HAV need to have a mutual understanding of each other's decision processes. It should be considered whether a feedback loop to the remote assistant is needed to foster learning and improvement.
- **Provide sufficient support tools**. When it comes to the design of the remote operation station, it is particularly important to define the information required by remote operators. The role of new visual tools (e.g., extended reality (XR)) as well as multi-modal HMI in providing such information should be explored. Another topic for future research should be the prioritization of important requests from HAVs.
- **Develop and apply standards and regulations**. While there are some existing standards (e.g., BSI Flex 1886) as well as ongoing efforts (e.g., ISO/CD 7856[5] and ISO/AWI TS 17691[6]), there is a need for further consensus among stakeholders. In particular, it is important for stakeholders not only to advance the development of standards but also to integrate them into their development and operational practices. In parallel, regulatory requirements need to be established and harmonized across regions.

Acknowledgments. This study was funded by Sweden's innovation agency (VIN-NOVA) (grant number 2022-01647).

Disclosure of Interests. Azra Habibovic was employed by Scania CV AB. The rest of authors have no competing interests to declare that are relevant to the content of this article.

---

[5] https://www.iso.org/standard/82951.html.
[6] https://www.iso.org/standard/85037.html.

References

1. Amador, O., Aramrattana, M., Vinel, A.: A survey on remote operation of road vehicles. IEEE Access **10**, 130135–130154 (2022). https://doi.org/10.1109/ACCESS.2022.3229168
2. Andersson, J., Söderman, M.: Navigating the challenges of remote operations of automated road vehicles: a socio-technical perspective. In: Ahram, T., Karwowski, W., Russo, D., Di Bucchianico, G.(eds.) Intelligent Human Systems Integration (IHSI 2024), vol. 119 (2024). https://doi.org/10.54941/ahfe1004466
3. Bogdoll, D., Orf, S., Töttel, L., Zöllner, J.M.: Taxonomy and survey on remote human input systems for driving automation systems. In: Arai, K. (ed.) Advances in Information and Communication, pp. 94–108. Springer International Publishing, Cham (2022). https://doi.org/10.1007/978-3-030-98015-3_6
4. Bout, M., Brenden, A.P., Klingegård, M., Habibovic, A., Böckle, M.P.: A head-mounted display to support teleoperations of shared automated vehicles. In: AutomotiveUI 2017 pp. 62-66. Association for Computing Machinery, New York (2017). https://doi.org/10.1145/3131726.3131758
5. BSI: BSI Flex 1890 Connected and automated mobility - Vocabulary. BSI Flex 1890 v5.0:2023-04, The British Standards Institution (Apr 2023)
6. Consortia SIT: AVSC Best Practice for ADS Remote Assistance Use Case. AVSC-I-04-2023, SAE Industry Technologies Consortia (Nov 2023)
7. Fairfield, N., Seth Herbach, J., Furman, V.: Remote Assistance for Autonomous Vehicles in Predetermined Situations, U.S. Patent US-20150248131-A1, Sept. 3 (2015)
8. Kettwich, C., Schrank, A., Avsar, H., Oehl, M.: A helping human hand: relevant scenarios for the remote operation of highly automated vehicles in public transport. Appl. Sci. **12**(9), 4350 (2022). https://doi.org/10.3390/app12094350
9. Kettwich, C., Schrank, A., Oehl, M.: Teleoperation of highly automated vehicles in public transport: user-centered design of a human-machine interface for remote-operation and its expert usability evaluation. Multimodal Technol. Interact. **5**(5), 26 (2021). https://doi.org/10.3390/mti5050026
10. Koskinen, H., Schrank, A., Lehtonen, E., Oehl, M.: Analyzing the remote operation task to support highly automated vehicles – suggesting the core task analysis to ensure the human-centered design of the remote operation station. In: Proceedings of the 26th International Conference on Human-Computer Interaction (2024)
11. Larsson, P., de Souza, J.B.R., Begnert, J.: An auditory display for remote road vehicle operation that increases awareness and presence. In: The 28th International Conference on Auditory Display, pp. 113–120. Georgia Institute of Technology, Norrköping, Sweden (Jun 2023)
12. Li, S., Zhang, Y., Blythe, P., Edwards, S., Ji, Y.: Remote driving as the failsafe: Qualitative investigation of users' perceptions and requirements towards the 5g-enabled level 4 automated vehicles. Transport. Res. F: Traffic Psychol. Behav. **100**, 211–230 (2024)
13. Majstorović, D., Diermeyer, F.: Dynamic collaborative path planning for remote assistance of highly-automated vehicles. In: 2023 IEEE International Automated Vehicle Validation Conference (IAVVC), pp. 1–6 (2023). https://doi.org/10.1109/IAVVC57316.2023.10328097
14. Mharolkar, S., Kircali, D., Yang, H., Yang, X., Wang, D.: High-fidelity teleoperation for heavy-duty vehicles. In: 2023 IEEE 26th International Conference on Intelligent Transportation Systems (ITSC), pp. 6171–6174 (2023). https://doi.org/10.1109/ITSC57777.2023.10422036

15. Neumeier, S., Wintersberger, P., Frison, A.K., Becher, A., Facchi, C., Riener, A.: Teleoperation: the holy grail to solve problems of automated driving? sure, but latency matters. In: Proceedings of the 11th International Conference on Automotive User Interfaces and Interactive Vehicular Applications, AutomotiveUI 2019, pp. 186-197. Association for Computing Machinery, New York (2019). https://doi.org/10.1145/3342197.3344534, https://doi.org/10.1145/3342197.3344534

16. SAE: Taxonomy and Definitions for Terms Related to Driving Automation Systems for On-Road Motor Vehicles. SAE J3016_202104, SAE International (Apr 2021)

17. Schrank, A., Kettwich, C.: Roles in the teleoperation of highly automates vehicles in public transport. In: Humanist VCE Proceedings of the 7th Humanist Conference (2021). https://www.humanist-vce.eu/_files/archives/ace9ed_64d1f0cf8a164dd185a50e52238fa1a4.zip?dn=Rhodes-2021.zip

18. Schrank, A., Walocha, F., Brandenburg, S., Oehl, M.: Human-centered design and evaluation of a workplace for the remote assistance of highly automated vehicles. Cognition Technol. Work (2024). https://doi.org/10.1007/s10111-024-00753-x

19. Schrank, A., Wendorff, N., Oehl, M.: Assisting the remote assistant: Augmenting degraded video streams with additional sensor data to improve situation awareness in complex urban traffic. In: Proceedings of the 26th International Conference on Human-Computer Interaction (2024)

20. Skogsmo, I., Andersson, J., Jernberg, C., Aramrattana, M.: One2many : remote operation of multiple vehicles. Tech. Rep. 1164A, Swedish National Road and Transport Research Institute, Traffic and road users (2023)

21. UNECE: Informal document No.7 - Remote activities related to driving - (Finland, Germany and the United Kingdom) (September 2023), https://unece.org/sites/default/files/2023-09/ECE-TRANS-WP1-2023-Informal-%20document%20No7e.pdf

22. UNECE: ECE/TRANS/WP.1/2024/3 - Remote activities related to driving - (Finland, Germany and the United Kingdom) (January 2024), https://unece.org/sites/default/files/2024-02/ECE-TRANS-WP1-2024-3e.pdf

23. Veitch, E., Andreas Alsos, O.: A systematic review of human-ai interaction in autonomous ship systems. Saf. Sci. **152**, 105778 (2022)

24. Zhang, T.: Toward automated vehicle teleoperation: vision, opportunities, and challenges. IEEE Internet Things J. **7**(12), 11347–11354 (2020). https://doi.org/10.1109/JIOT.2020.3028766

25. Zhao, L., Nybacka, M., Drugge, L., Rothhämel, M., Habibovic, A., Hvitfeldt, H.: The influence of motion-cueing, sound and vibration feedback on driving behavior and experience - a virtual teleoperation experiment. IEEE Trans. Intell. Trans. Syst., 1–13 (2024). https://doi.org/10.1109/TITS.2024.3353465, https://ieeexplore.ieee.org/document/10414381

26. Zhao, L., Nybacka, M., Rothhämel, M., Habibovic, A., Papaioannou, G., Drugge, L.: Driving experience and behavior change in remote driving - an explorative experimental study. IEEE Trans. Intell. Veh. 1–15 (2023). https://doi.org/10.1109/TIV.2023.3344890

Enhancing Passenger Safety in an Autonomous Bus: A Multimodal Fall Detection Approach for Effective Remote Monitoring

Amey Ajit Dakare[1,2], Yanbin Wu[1], Toru Kumagai[1], Takahiro Miura[3], and Naohisa Hashimoto[1(✉)]

[1] Digital Architecture Research Center, National Institute of Advanced Industrial Science and Technology (AIST), Tsukuba, Japan
{amey.dakare,wu.yanbin,kumagai.toru,
naohisa-hashimoto}@aist.go.jp, s2220817@u.tsukuba.ac.jp
[2] University of Tsukuba, Tsukuba, Japan
[3] Human Augmentation Research Center, National Institute of Advanced Industrial Science and Technology (AIST), Tsukuba, Japan
miura-t@aist.go.jp

Abstract. With the rise of autonomous public transportation, passenger safety in autonomous buses is paramount. This paper introduces a novel Multimodal Long Short-Term Memory (LSTM) network-based fall detection system, to enhance passenger safety by accurately detecting falls, thereby assisting remote supervisors in efficiently monitoring multiple vehicles. It comprises two main processes: feature extraction and fall discrimination. Feature extraction utilizes YOLO (You Only Look Once) v7 for real-time pose estimation, combined with the SORT algorithm for tracking individuals across video frames. Fall discrimination leverages sequential data processing with LSTM networks in the proposed Multimodal approach, which employs a fusion of pose estimation and Inertial Measurement Unit (IMU) sensor data. Evaluations conducted in various fall and non-fall scenarios within a realistic bus setting yielded high recall and F2 scores. Specifically, the model attained 98% recall in single person fall scenarios and 95% in more complex multi-person fall scenarios, significantly surpassing traditional single-modality approaches such as Multilayer Perceptron (MLP) and simple LSTM. The paper also investigates a decision-level fusion approach, balancing predictive accuracy by optimizing the late integration of separate Pose and IMU models, despite its higher computational cost. The impact of varying frame rates on model performance was also explored, addressing practical implications for real-world implementations. The robustness of the model was affirmed even at reduced processing frame rates, ensuring effective real-time processing capabilities crucial for ensuring timely responses in emergency situations. The development of the fall detection system promises a safer and more efficient future for public transportation, especially benefiting elderly individuals.

Keywords: Multimodal Fall Detection · Autonomous Buses · LSTM Networks · Real-time Monitoring

C. Stephanidis et al. (Eds.): HCII 2024, CCIS 2118, pp. 186–196, 2024.
https://doi.org/10.1007/978-3-031-61963-2_17

1   Introduction

In the field of global public transportation, particularly in rural and developing regions, a critical shortage of professional bus drivers has emerged in recent years. This challenge is further compounded by safety concerns, particularly those arising from accidents involving elderly drivers, and low labor costs. The scarcity of drivers not only disrupts daily commutes but also impacts economic activities and isolates vulnerable communities, especially the elderly, due to limited transportation options. Concurrently, growing urban populations worldwide necessitate innovative, efficient, and sustainable transportation solutions. Mobility as a Service (MaaS) emerges as a promising solution to urban mobility challenges [1]. In future, Level 4 autonomous buses, operating independently, can offer a promising solution to these issues while enhancing public transport efficiency and safety. Their introduction could be particularly transformative in rural areas, by providing reliable services and enhancing accessibility for those with mobility limitations.

This research paper focuses on enhancing safety within these autonomous bus services, with a particular focus on the paradigm of remote supervision. This supervision model, where remote supervisors oversee multiple autonomous buses, hinges on effective real-time monitoring systems. A critical aspect of passengers' safety is the detection of passenger falls, especially among the elderly, who are at higher risk of falls and subsequent injuries. Automating the fall detection process reduces the risk of oversight due to human fatigue or error. This enhances safety for all passengers, particularly the elderly and solo travelers, and improves the reliability of autonomous public transport.

Existing fall detection mechanisms in buses primarily use single-modality data, such as pose estimation, and have demonstrated potential. However, they can be hindered by limitations like occlusions, variable lighting [2], and a lack of contextual data, leading to missed incidents or multiple false alarms. This research proposes a multimodal approach that integrates advanced computer vision techniques, such as YOLOv7 [3] for pose estimation combined with the SORT algorithm for tracking individuals across video frames, and Inertial Measurement Unit (IMU) sensor data. The study investigates the enhancement of fall detection in autonomous buses through the application of Long Short-Term Memory (LSTM) [4] networks in concert with multimodal data. This combination aims to address the limitations of single-sensor systems, offering enhanced robustness with improved recall, and faster response times.

This proposed system significantly enhances fall detection accuracy and reliability by analyzing passenger movements more comprehensively by utilizing both visual and kinematic information from the dataset. This advancement in fall detection technology contributes significantly to the development of autonomous transportation solutions, prioritizing passenger safety and remote monitoring operational reliability.

2   Related Work

Since this study involves fall detection with multimodal techniques in a moving environment like bus, existing research in this field could be divided into the following approaches.

2.1 Multimodal Fall Detection

Most LSTM-based fall detection approaches [5, 6] have utilized tri-axial accelerometer devices attached to participants' wrists, leveraging sensor data to detect falls. While effective in controlled environments, the practicality of such device-dependent systems in public bus settings is limited due to the impracticality of equipping passengers with wearable sensors. Furthermore, the research by M. Salimi et al. [7] has advanced fall detection by integrating pose estimation with LSTM networks. This method has shown promise, yet when it comes to the complexities of a bus environment—characterized by its dynamic and crowded nature—such techniques may fall short. Additionally, the requirement for high computational resources in real-time processing poses another challenge, particularly when timely fall detection is crucial.

2.2 Bus Related Fall Detection

In recent years, research specific to fall detection in bus environments has been evolving. Recent works by Zhang et al. [2] and Dakare et al. [8] have proposed methods that recognize falls through human pose estimation, extracting skeletal key points as input for a fall discrimination algorithm. However, these methods encounter significant challenges in bus environments: accurately tracking individuals is difficult in confined and crowded spaces, leading to potential occlusions and misidentified falls. Additionally, the reliance on single frames, rather than sequential data, limits the ability to capture the temporal aspects of falls, which are essential for accurate detection. Our prior study [9] examined the effectiveness of LSTM over Multi-Level Perceptron and achieved improved accuracy compared to processing a single image approach. However, this research did not incorporate additional sensor data from the bus environment, which is vital for prompt and accurate fall detection in an autonomous bus context.

Therefore, the novel approach proposed in this study is pioneering in its exploitation of temporal dynamics—referring to the analysis of movements over time—combined with a multimodal sensor approach within the bus environment.

3 Proposed Method

The simple LSTM model, primarily reliant on visual pose data, sometimes falls short in scenarios where visual cues alone are insufficient to determine a fall, such as in cases of occlusions or poor lighting conditions. The Multimodal LSTM model addresses these limitations by incorporating IMU data of the bus, which provides additional context through readings like accelerations, angular velocities, and orientation.

Our proposed fall detection system leverages a multimodal framework combining pose features with the bus's dynamic information, such as acceleration and speed, to accurately detect falls within a bus environment. This section outlines the system's components, including pose features extraction, IMU features extraction, data synchronization and fusion strategies, and the LSTM fall detection network.

3.1 Pose Features Extraction

In the first stage of our system, we utilize dual models: a YOLOv7-based 2D multi-person pose estimation and object detection network to perform real-time human pose estimation and human detection within the bus. These pre-trained networks are selected for their real-time efficiency and future potential uses in improving passenger safety in an autonomous bus. The pose estimation model identifies 17 keypoints along with a bounding box, while the object detection model provides accurate human bounding boxes. We then integrate a Simple Online and Realtime Tracking (SORT) [10] algorithm to track individuals using bounding box overlap and maintain their identities across frames. The captured keypoints and associated bounding boxes are serialized into JSON format, detailing passenger IDs and frame numbers for subsequent processing.

3.2 IMU Features Extraction

In conjunction with video data, we incorporate real-time Inertial Measurement Unit (IMU) data. An IMU sensor in the bus provides real-time data on angular velocities, accelerations, roll, pitch, azimuth angles, and GPS-derived directional and speed information. This sensor data is pivotal in capturing the nuanced movements associated with falls, thereby enriching the visual pose data. Moreover, the multimodal approach significantly boosts the model's robustness. The integration of IMU data also enables detecting falls in scenarios where visual data might be incomplete. By reducing dependency on a single data source, the model becomes more resilient to variations in visual data quality and can adapt more effectively to diverse fall scenarios and environmental conditions.

3.3 Data Synchronization and Fusion

Precise synchronization of IMU data based on associated frame numbers with estimated tracked pose from video frames ensures temporal alignment essential for meaningful analysis. We address discrepancies in sampling rates and potential latency by aligning timestamps and down sampling the IMU data to match the video framerate.

Early Fusion Strategy. Our system predominantly employs an early fusion approach where IMU and pose data are combined at the feature level, combining both modalities' strengths before feeding them into the LSTM network. This strategy leverages the strengths of each modality and allows the LSTM network to simultaneously process temporal movements from pose data and dynamics from IMU data, enhancing the detection accuracy.

3.4 LSTM Fall Detection Network

Our approach begins with the transformation of JSON-formatted data into structured sequences for the LSTM network. The JSON data, which encapsulates the output from the pose estimation, tracking algorithm and IMU is organized to represent each passenger's movements frame by frame. To effectively analyze the time-series data, we implement a sliding window technique. This method involves creating sequences from frames of a single passenger ID, where each sequence encompasses fused pose and IMU data over a specified frame window. As the window slides frame by frame, the data is not only structured into sequences but also augmented, enhancing the temporal context within each sequence.

Data normalization and scaling are applied to both pose and IMU data to standardize inputs for the LSTM. During prediction, the LSTM processes the constructed sequences to determine the likelihood of a fall at the end of each sequence. The target label for each sequence is whether a fall occurs at the end of that sequence (i.e., last frame). This way, during training, LSTM will learn to discern the intricate relationship between past poses, sensor's data, and the likelihood of a fall in the present frame. The overall flow of inference using this system can be visualized in Fig. 1.

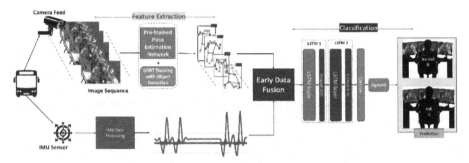

Fig. 1. Overview of the Multimodal Fall Detection System Architecture [Early Fusion]

Late Fusion Strategy. In addition to our primary early fusion strategy, we explored late fusion (decision-level fusion) on an experimental basis. In contrast to early fusion, late fusion involves training separate models for each data modality (pose and IMU) and then combining their outputs at the decision level. This strategy allows each model to independently learn, and extract features relevant to its specific modality before the final decision-making process. The key advantage of late fusion is that it facilitates a more focused and modality-specific learning process, potentially leading to more nuanced detections. However, it may increase computational complexity and require more intricate decision-making logic at the fusion stage. In this research, the optimal weights are determined through an evaluation process of varying the weights assigned to the pose and IMU model outputs and assessing the combined performance using metrics. The optimal weights are chosen which yielded the best performance in terms of the evaluation metrics.

4 Data and Experiments

4.1 Dataset Introduction

The dataset used in this study was self-created, building upon prior work [9], featuring video recordings of fall events within a bus environment, captured using a front-mounted camera. This research enhances the dataset with additional 3-axis IMU data from a sensor placed on the bus floor. The videos capture varied lighting conditions and light passenger densities, simulating real-world bus scenarios, with subjects reacting to sudden braking events- a common cause of falls in buses. The subjects captured in these fall scenarios are the authors themselves, ensuring a controlled and safe environment for data collection. Future expansions of this dataset will seek participation from volunteers, with all studies to be conducted under strict ethical guidelines and safety protocols. The videos were recorded at a frame rate of 28 FPS and downscaled from 1920×1080 to 640×360 pixels for processing efficiency and IMU data originally recorded at 100 Hz down sampled to 28 Hz for frame synchronization.

Our research primarily targets scenarios with fewer passengers or a single traveler in a bus as shown in Fig. 2. In such situations, the risk of unreported falls increases, especially elderly passengers who might struggle to alert the bus supervisor. Also, in scenarios with limited passengers in the moving bus, manually pressing the emergency button in case of a sudden fall is less feasible. Therefore, the datasets were deliberately constructed with fewer individuals to align with our target scenarios. However, our LSTM models are designed to accommodate varying passenger counts. We acknowledge that increased passenger density can lead to extreme occlusion issues, challenging the pose estimation and tracking processes. These extra challenging scenarios need to be tested as a future work of our research.

Fig. 2. a) No-fall b) Single-Person Fall c) Multi-Person Fall Scenes in a moving bus

Each data sequence comprises frame-by-frame pose data and corresponding IMU readings. Specifically, the pose data includes a total of 59 features: 34 for joint coordinates (17 joints with x, y coordinates each), 17 for joint confidence scores, 4 each for tracking and pose bounding boxes. The IMU data contributes an additional 11 features, including angular velocities and accelerations across three axes, roll, pitch, azimuth angles, and GPS-derived direction and speed.

To adequately capture the lead-up to a fall, particularly as falls can occur seconds after significant bus movements, we set the LSTM input sequence length to 224 frames. This length represents 8 s of video data. The training set of our study includes 22 distinct fall events, accounting for 3,434 fall and 22,607 non-fall sequences. The validation set contains 4 unique fall events involving a different individual. Correct measures were implemented to ensure no overlap or data leakage between the training and validation datasets.

4.2 Network Configuration

LSTM network configuration employed in this study consists of two layers with 32 units each, L2 regularization, batch normalization, and dropout layers to combat overfitting. Class weights were used to balance the training dataset, addressing the fall class imbalance. The network was trained with an initial learning rate of 0.0001, a batch size of 64, and 200 epochs. The Adam optimizer [11] and binary cross-entropy loss function were used, with early stopping and ReduceLROnPlateau callbacks for optimal training efficiency.

We performed temporal augmentation: randomly skip, duplicate, or retain on pose data frames to introduce variability in temporal sequences. Other data augmentations included translation, scaling, mirroring of symmetric keypoints, and gaussian noise introduction for pose data. Sensor data augmentation involved warping sequences, applying random 3D rotations, and introducing gaussian noise to replicate real-world data variation.

We also explored the effects of processing speed and frame loss by training the network on two different frame rates: the original 28FPS and a reduced 4FPS (by skipping 7 frames). This exploration aimed to understand the trade-off between processing efficiency and robustness in fall detection.

5 Results and Analysis

We evaluated our model using two distinct test datasets, normalized, and sequenced similarly to the training data for consistent analysis.

5.1 Test Datasets Overview

Single-Person Fall (Dataset A): This dataset includes scenarios with a single individual experiencing a fall. It closely aligns with the training data and serves to assess the model's effectiveness in expected conditions.

Multi-person Fall (Dataset B): For evaluating performance in complex scenarios, Dataset B contains instances of simultaneous falls involving two individuals. These challenging cases test the model's generalization ability beyond the training scenarios.

5.2 Evaluation Methods

Our model's primary focus is on minimizing missed fall events (false negatives), making Recall our key metric. We complement this with the F2 score, which, unlike the F1 score, places greater emphasis on recall over precision

$$F2\ Score = 5 \times \frac{Precision \times Recall}{(4 \times Precision) + Recall} \tag{1}$$

This approach is critical in fall detection scenario, in which case, failing to detect a fall (false negative) is more damaging than incorrectly identifying a non-fall event (false positive). This is because false negatives can lead to missed opportunities for timely assistance in real fall incidents, whereas false positives, albeit inconvenient, can be reviewed and dismissed by a remote supervisor.

5.3 Comparative Analysis

28FPS Performance. In Dataset A, the Multimodal LSTM with Augmentation shows the highest recall of 98% and F2 score of 96%, indicating superior performance in detecting falls. Similarly in Dataset B, the same model demonstrates a high recall of 95%, suggesting effective fall detection in more complex multi-person scenarios although with a slight reduction in precision. This outcome, significantly surpassing the MLP model's 33%, is particularly impressive given that the multi-person fall scenarios were not part of the training dataset. Tables 1 and 2 present a comprehensive quantitative evaluation of the performance metrics for our trained models.

Table 1. Model Evaluation when trained on 28FPS

Model Specifications	Dataset A [Single Person Fall]		Dataset B [Multi-Person Falls]	
	Recall	F2 Score	Recall	F2 Score
MLP [8]	0.91	0.89	0.33	0.38
Simple LSTM [9]	0.92	0.93	0.87	0.85
Multimodal Early Fusion LSTM	0.97	0.95	0.91	0.85
Multimodal Early Fusion LSTM w/ Augmentation	**0.98**	**0.96**	**0.95**	**0.86**

4FPS Performance. Here, the Multimodal LSTM with Augmentation maintains high recall, especially in Dataset B. This indicates robustness in fall detection even with reduced frame rates. Interestingly, the 4FPS models exhibit a tendency to predict falls slightly ahead of the actual event, which is particularly notable in augmented scenarios. This preemptive prediction capability as seen from Fig. 3 is a significant achievement, as it suggests the potential for earlier alerts and interventions in real-world fall scenarios.

In scenarios lacking IMU data, due to issues like sensor malfunctions or occlusions, our study evaluates the system's performance relying solely on pose data, highlighting its adaptability and resilience in real-world conditions. Table 3 demonstrates the ablation study for our Multimodal LSTM models, focusing on non-IMU data. Late Fusion demonstrates notable resilience without IMU data, maintaining high Recall and F2 Score for both datasets, due to its ability to effectively utilize pose data alone through separate processing streams.

Table 2. Model Evaluation when trained on 4FPS

Model Specifications	Dataset A [Single Person Fall]		Dataset B [Multi-Person Falls]	
	Recall	F2 Score	Recall	F2 Score
Simple LSTM [9]	0.95	0.95	0.76	0.79
Multimodal Late Fusion LSTM w/ Augmentation	0.98	**0.97**	0.89	0.80
Multimodal Early Fusion LSTM w/ Augmentation	**1.00**	0.92	**0.95**	**0.86**

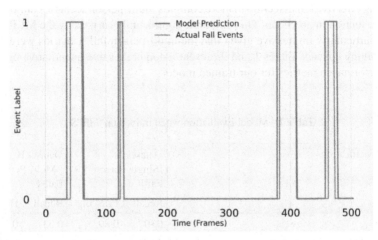

Fig. 3. Fall Prediction Over Time for Test Dataset A

These results indicate the integral role of IMU data in enhancing detection capabilities, especially for complex scenarios. They also highlight Late Fusion's ability to provide effective fall detection with pose data alone, showcasing adaptability critical for real-world deployments.

Table 3. Performance Metrics with Non-IMU Data underscoring the significant impact of IMU data on fall detection

	Non-IMU Dataset A		Non-IMU Dataset B	
	Recall	F2 Score	Recall	F2 Score
Early Fusion	0.66	0.70	0.51	0.55
Late Fusion	**0.97**	**0.97**	**0.84**	**0.85**

In conclusion, when compared with baseline single-modal LSTM network, our Multimodal LSTM model with data augmentation enhances recall across all scenarios and frame rates, suggesting its effectiveness in introducing diverse features that aid in general-izing fall detection. Augmentation appears to make the model more robust to variations and potentially missing frames, which could be beneficial in real-world applications where conditions are not controlled, and data transmission might be unreliable. The performance improvement at 4FPS, especially with augmented data, can be attributed to reduced noise and more focused information processing, as seen in the reduced frame sequences. This states that model judges fall prone situations more efficiently with the help of multimodal information.

6   Future Work

Our future work focuses on optimizing fall detection. Key areas include refining feature selection through feature engineering and enhancing our LSTM model by integrating self-attention mechanisms. Further, we plan to fine-tune our pre-trained pose estimation model specifically for our bus dataset to improve accuracy. Lastly, we aim to implement multi-camera setups for 3D pose estimation to better address issues of occlusions.

While reducing false negatives remains our priority, given the serious consequences of missing a real fall event, we also recognize the importance of balancing false positives with operational efficiency. In line with adaptive learning concepts, we aim to continually improve our model by adapting to new data and scenarios over time. This approach is particularly relevant to Human-Machine Interaction, ensuring our system not only assists humans effectively but also evolves based on interaction patterns and feedback.

7   Conclusion

In conclusion, this study demonstrated a significant advancement in fall detection within an autonomous bus environment through the implementation of a multimodal approach. By integrating pose estimation with IMU sensor data, and analyzing this information through LSTM networks, resulted in improving model's robustness and reliability across a range of situations and frame rates. Preliminary results underscore the effectiveness of our approach, both in single fall as well as complex multi-person fall scenarios, setting it apart from traditional single modality fall detection systems. While our current focus has been on enhancing the accuracy and reliability of fall detection, future efforts will be directed towards incorporating attention mechanisms for refined feature analysis to further optimize the model.

Acknowledgments. This research was supported by the Ministry of Economy, Trade and Industry, Japan and I would like to express my sincere gratitude to them for their generous support in facilitating this research.

Disclosure of Interests. The authors have no competing interests to declare that are relevant to the content of this article.

References

1. Alonso-González, M.J., Hoogendoorn-Lanser, S., van Oort, N., Cats, O., Hoogendoorn, S.: Drivers and barriers in adopting mobility as a service (MaaS) – a latent class cluster analysis of attitudes. Transp. Res. Part a Policy Pract. **132**, 378–401 (2020)
2. Zhang, X., Ji, J., Wang, L., He, Z., Liu, S.: Image-based fall detection in bus compartment scene. IET Image Process. **17**, 118–119 (2023)
3. Wang, C.-Y., Bochkovskiy, A., Liao, H.-Y.M.: YOLOv7: Trainable Bag-of-Freebies Sets New State-of-the-Art for Real-Time Object Detectors. in (2023). https://doi.org/10.1109/cvpr52729.2023.00721
4. Hochreiter, S., Schmidhuber, J.: Long Short-Term Memory. Neural Comput. **9**, 1735–1780 (1997)
5. García, E., et al.: Towards effective detection of elderly falls with CNN-LSTM neural networks. Neurocomputing **500**, 231–240 (2022)
6. Wu, J., Wang, J., Zhan, A., Wu, C.: Fall detection with CNN-casual LSTM network. Information (Switzerland) **12**, 403 (2021)
7. Salimi, M., Machado, J.J.M., Tavares, J.M.R.S.: Using deep neural networks for human fall detection based on pose estimation. Sensors **22**, 4544 (2022)
8. Dakare, A.A., Wu, Y., Hashimoto, N., Kumagai, T., Miura, T.: Fall detection inside an autonomous driving bus: - examination of image processing algorithms. In: Digest of Technical Papers - IEEE International Conference on Consumer Electronics, vol. 2023, January 2023
9. Dakare, A.A., Wu, Y., Kumagai, T., Miura, T., Hashimoto, N.: Advancing fall detection in an autonomous bus: examination of LSTM technique. In: Proceedings of the International Conference on Mechanical and Robotics Engineering (ICMRE 2024). IEEE (2024, to be published)
10. Bewley, A., Ge, Z., Ott, L., Ramos, F., Upcroft, B.: Simple online and realtime tracking. In: Proceedings - International Conference on Image Processing, ICIP 2016-August, pp. 3464–3468 (2016)
11. Kingma, D.P., Ba, J.L.: Adam: a method for stochastic optimization. In: 3rd International Conference on Learning Representations, ICLR 2015 - Conference Track Proceedings (2015)

Hierarchical Task Analysis for Collision Avoidance Warnings in Driving

Madeline Easley and Jung Hyup Kim[✉]

Department of Industrial and Systems Engineering, University of Missouri, Columbia 65211,
USA
mge6pp@mail.missouri.edu, kijung@missouri.edu

Abstract. The objective of this study is to investigate the effects of collision avoidance warnings in driving by employing a Hierarchical Task Analysis (HTA) technique. HTA dissects complex tasks into smaller, more manageable sub-tasks arranged hierarchically. The main goal of HTA for collision avoidance warnings is to understand the driving behavior patterns in response to collision avoidance warnings. The driving process was segmented into three primary sub-processes: perception, cognition, and motor processes. The perception and cognition processes were evaluated based on physiological responses, while physical actions were analyzed to understand motor processes. The results indicated that the driver's decisions significantly impacted the process pattern.

Keywords: Hierarchical Task Analysis · Driving Performance · Collision Avoidance Warnings

1 Introduction

Prior research has shown that collision avoidance warnings can greatly alter drivers' behavior [1–5]. Drivers who receive alerts about a potential collision are more likely to alter their position on the road, speed, or any other evasive action to avoid an accident. Collision avoidance warnings, such as forward collision warnings (FCW) and lane departure warnings (LDW), are specifically designed to alert drivers to hazards on the road. These collision avoidance warnings can positively influence driver's behavior by increasing their awareness and attention to their surroundings. Informing drivers about the potential hazards, these collision avoidance warnings can cause drivers to be more cautious and proactive while driving, therefore reducing the possibility of accidents. The efficiency of these warnings can be influenced by various factors, such as the type and frequency of warnings, driver experience and training, and the design and implementation of the collision avoidance system. However, some drivers become overconfident in their skills and ignore the given warnings, which results in an increased risk of accidents. With new advancements in collision avoidance technology, vehicle safety has been significantly improved. To fully understand the effects of collision avoidance technology on driver's performance and safety, it is essential to understand how collision avoidance warnings influence driving behavior.

© The Author(s), under exclusive license to Springer Nature Switzerland AG 2024
C. Stephanidis et al. (Eds.): HCII 2024, CCIS 2118, pp. 197–202, 2024.
https://doi.org/10.1007/978-3-031-61963-2_18

To study how drivers react to collision avoidance alerts, it's essential to first evaluate each driver's hazard and perception threshold. This research used the Signal Detection Theory (SDT) framework to examine the sensitivity of various warning signals [6]. Despite the difficulty in understanding the cognitive processes behind a driver's decision-making during warning responses, a participant's decision could be categorized into four different outcomes: effective warning, false warning, aware warning, and ignored warning. The first of these is an effective warning (EW), which is defined as the presence of a physiological response (i.e., eye movement) along with a motor response (such as braking, accelerating, or turning). This shows that the driver trusts the warning and follows with necessary action to avoid any collision. EW is the most favorable outcome, as the warning alerts drivers to potential threats and gives them time to prevent a collision. The second response is when neither a motor response nor a physiological response is detected. This is categorized as an aware warning (AW). In this scenario, the driver had already seen the potential hazard before the alarm was triggered. Despite not providing any extra information, the warning prompted the driver to re-evaluate their decision-making and adjust their motor response to minimize the risk of collision. Third, a false warning (FW) is categorized as an instance when there was only a physiological response and no motor response. In this case, a driver did not identify any potential dangers in the vicinity of the vehicle after the alarm was triggered. Lastly, if a driver had neither physiological nor motor responses to the warning, it was classified as an ignored warning (IW).

To develop hierarchical task analysis (HTA) charts for collision avoidance warnings in driving, we focused on the sequence of events for effective warnings (EW), aware warnings (AW), and false warnings (FW). This framework provides a starting point for analyzing and improving drivers' behavior in response to FCW and LDW warnings.

2   Method

The study involved 20 students from the University of Missouri-Columbia, all of whom had at least two years of driving experience, held a valid driver's license, and did not require prescription lenses for driving. All participants were male, with an average age of 20.52 years and a standard deviation of 1.47. Participants navigated a vehicle over a 9.3-mile course that covered various roads in Columbia, Missouri, following a pre-established route (Fig. 1).

The route was designed to cover a diverse range of driving environments. The drive took approximately 20 min under light traffic conditions and was designed to assess the collision avoidance capabilities of selected driver assistance technologies. The test began in the Conley Avenue Parking lots of Mizzou and continued to Providence (a major road), Interstate 70, Highway 63, and Tiger Avenue on campus. This route was designed to include periods of rest, city driving, and campus driving. It was anticipated to generate low to medium workload levels—the chosen route aimed to include common stressful situations encountered by the average driver. The driving sessions were scheduled during expected low traffic, specifically mid-morning (10:00 am–12:30 pm) or mid-afternoon (2:00 pm–4:30 pm) periods. Each driving session lasted 15 to 20 min, varying with traffic conditions. Before beginning each test, drivers received instructions and a concise summary of the route they would be taking.

Fig. 1. Overview of Driving Path [7].

The drivers were joined by two research assistants, who were seated in the back seat of the car. The research assistants were tasked with observing participant's driving and the occurrences during the route. Four trials were conducted with each participant, with a 10-min break between each trial. The first trial was a control group without collision avoidance warnings, while the subsequent three trials were conducted with the warnings. The testing from beginning to end lasted approximately 2–2.5 h for each participant. This included the 30-min briefing of instruction, 20 min of baseline data collection without the warning signals, an hour of three trials with the tested warning signals, and 30 min of break time. For this experiment, a 2008 Chevrolet Malibu was used as the test vehicle. To track eye movements while driving, participants wore Tobii Glasses with a 100 Hz sampling rate. Tobii Glasses are wearable eye trackers that can provide a wireless live view. A high-definition camera was mounted on the right window of the vehicle to record the driver's physical actions. Additionally, a 360-degree camera was installed on the vehicle's roof to document the surrounding driving conditions.

3 Result

3.1 Plan 0: Responding to the Warnings

Plan 0 was completed through the fulfillment of three sub-goals:

- Gather data from the driving environment.
- Analyze the collected data.
- Activate the motor response.

Figure 2 illustrates the driver's response to warnings, with effective warnings (EW) prompting the execution of Plans 1 and 2 in loops until an appropriate motor response is made (Plan 1 $\longleftrightarrow$ Plan 2 $\rightarrow$ Plan 3 $\rightarrow$ END). If an emergency is detected during Plans

1 or 2, the driver would then immediately move to Plan 3. With aware warnings (AW), drivers already perceive potential hazards and respond without cognitive processing (Plan 1 → Plan 3 → END). For the false warning (FW), the drivers evaluated the causes of warnings and decided on no motor response (Plan 1→ Plan 2 → END).

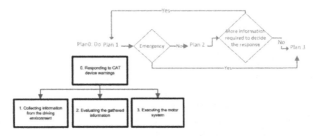

Fig. 2. Plan 0 – Overall Hierarchical Task Analysis.

3.2   Plan 1: Gather Data from the Driving Environment

The primary objective of Plan 1 is to gather information from the entire surrounding area to detect potential hazards. It requires constant vigilance without any interruptions throughout Plan 1. A detailed diagram of Plan 1 is presented in Fig. 3.

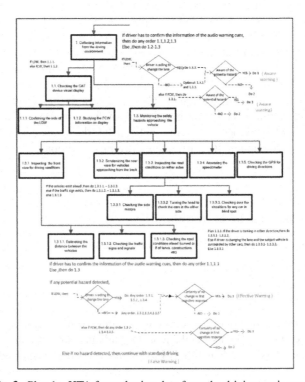

Fig. 3. Plan 1 – HTA for gathering data from the driving environment.

3.3 Plan 2: Analyze the Collected Data

Once drivers collect information, they must analyze and comprehend the implications of this data, particularly regarding the potential risks that could result in a collision. This step is crucial in avoiding poor decision-making. Figure 4 provides a detailed depiction of Plan 2.

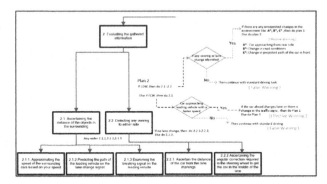

Fig. 4. Plan 2 – HTA for analyzing the collected data.

3.4 Plan 3: Activate the Motor Response

Based on their decision, drivers may opt for various motor actions, including slowing down the vehicle, applying the brake pedal, or steering the wheel as part of their response (refer to Fig. 5).

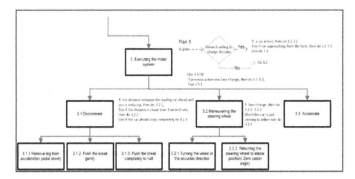

Fig. 5. Plan 3 – HTA for activating the motor response.

4   Discussion

Through this study, hierarchical task analysis charts for collision avoidance warning were developed through observation. The findings of this study provide valuable insights into enhancing our understanding of the driving task and potential hazards. These insights can contribute to the development of more effective collision avoidance systems. These outcomes also offer opportunities to create guidelines and regulations related to collision avoidance systems in vehicles.

This study has a few potential limitations worth noting. First, all subjects who participated in this study were male college students. In future studies, it could be beneficial to widen the participant pool to include diverse age groups or female drivers to obtain a more comprehensive understanding. Secondly, the use of HTA charts may not fully capture the dynamic aspects of driving such as weather conditions [8], traffic, and road construction. Lastly, the HTA charts used in this study do not account for the possibility of driver errors, either in actual collisions or in near-crash accidents.

References

1. Zhang, Y., et al.: Effect of warning system on interactive driving behavior at unsignalized intersection under fog conditions: a study based on multiuser driving simulation. J. Adv. Transp. **2020**, 1–16 (2020)
2. Harder, K.A., Bloomfield, J., Chihak, B.J.: The Effectiveness of Auditory Side-and Forward-Collision Avoidance Warnings on Snow Covered Roads in Conditions of Poor Visibility (2003)
3. Chen, J., et al.: Effectiveness of lateral auditory collision warnings: should warnings be toward danger or toward safety? Hum. Factors **64**(2), 418–435 (2022)
4. Chen, W.-H., Zeng, J.-J., Kao, K.-C.: Effect of auditory intersection collision avoidance warnings on driving behaviors in different distracted driving conditions. In: 19th International Technical Conference on the Enhanced Safety of Vehicles, Washington, DC (2005)
5. Yang, X., Kim, J.H.: Pupil and electromyography (EMG) responses to collision warning in a real driving environment. In: Kurosu, M. (ed.) Human-Computer Interaction. Technological Innovation. HCII 2022. LNCS, vol. 13303. Springer, Cham (2022). https://doi.org/10.1007/978-3-031-05409-9_32
6. Kim, J.H.: The effects of collision avoidance warning systems on driver's visual behaviors. In: HCI in Mobility, Transport, and Automotive Systems. Automated Driving and In-Vehicle Experience Design: Second International Conference, MobiTAS 2020, Held as Part of the 22nd HCI International Conference, HCII 2020, Copenhagen, Denmark, 19–24 July 2020, Proceedings, Part I 22. Springer (2020). https://doi.org/10.1007/978-3-030-50523-3_21
7. Yang, X., Kim, J.H.: The effect of visual stimulus on advanced driver assistance systems in a real driving. In: IIE Annual Conference. Proceedings. Institute of Industrial and Systems Engineers (IISE) (2017)
8. Tang, R., Kim, J.H.: Evaluating rear-end vehicle accident using pupillary analysis in a driving simulator environment. In: Advances in Human Factors and Simulation: Proceedings of the AHFE 2019 International Conference on Human Factors and Simulation, 24–28 July 2019, Washington DC, USA, vol. 10 (2020). Springer. https://doi.org/10.1007/978-3-030-20148-7_17

An Initial Exploration of Usability Evaluation for Physical and Virtual Automotive Multimedia Interfaces

Shih-Cheng Fann[✉] and Shang-Yuan Chang

National Yunlin University of Science and Technology, Yunlin, Taiwan
fann72515@gmail.com

Abstract. As technology matures, the use of virtual interfaces to operate products has become one of the current design trends. This study focuses on the usability evaluation of physical and virtual interfaces using the example of the automotive multimedia control system interface. The research utilizes the Thinking Aloud method and interviews to investigate user perceptions of these interfaces. Participants were separately tasked with performing operational tasks using both physical and virtual interfaces for the automotive multimedia control system. The study aims to understand how users evaluate and utilize these interfaces while driving, exploring how different interface designs impact user interactions. After recording each participant's interaction process and verbal feedback, interviews were conducted to gain deeper insights into user experiences and opinions regarding both interface types. The experimental results are comprehensively discussed to identify current usability issues and to provide recommendations for preferred automotive interface designs and future design considerations based on user preferences.

Keywords: Interface design · User research · Kansei Engineering · Thinking Aloud

1 Introduction

With the advancement of technology, the current design trend is shifting towards replacing physical user interfaces with virtual operating interfaces. However, the tangible feel of a product remains crucial; the actual tactile experience may differ from the psychological perception. Many designers focus heavily on the visual aspects of design, often overlooking the importance of haptic feedback in evaluating user behavior within the operational interface. The absence of the tactile sensations associated with physical interactions can lead to significant changes in product design and has a direct impact on the design of interfaces or systems that eliminate real sensory interactions, thereby influencing the design of automotive dashboards. Many physical operation interfaces emphasize on how to achieve the operation purpose simply, intuitively and safely in a short period of time by using the senses of touch and hearing. Physical objects possess weight, materiality, and appearance, constituting a tangible presence. The sensory system plays a significant role in occupying a substantial portion of human cognition.

© The Author(s), under exclusive license to Springer Nature Switzerland AG 2024
C. Stephanidis et al. (Eds.): HCII 2024, CCIS 2118, pp. 203–210, 2024.
https://doi.org/10.1007/978-3-031-61963-2_19

Sensory experiences, through continuous exploration of the environment and interaction with the world, are integral. Products need to fully leverage such interactions, incorporating elements like touch, smell, hearing, and more. (Norman, D. A. 2004). Although computers offer abstract virtual actions, they eliminate the joy derived from tactile sensations and physically manipulating objects during real interactions. The presented ideas and concepts lack the materiality of physical objects. In the context of this research, the usability evaluation of physical and virtual operating interfaces is explored using the Thinking Aloud method and interviews. Participants are instructed to perform operational tasks on the car dashboard using both types of interfaces. The study records the process and verbal feedback of each participant, supplemented by interviews to gain a deeper understanding of their experiences and opinions regarding the two interfaces on the car dashboard. The experimental results are comprehensively discussed to identify current usability evaluation issues and usability problems. The study aims to propose preferred designs for car dashboard interfaces based on user preferences and provide recommendations for future designs.

2   Method

This research focuses on the affective usability evaluation of participants towards physical and virtual operational interfaces. The experiment utilizes the in-car central multimedia system interface as a sample, conducting thinking-aloud experiments on both interfaces separately. Post-experiment, semi-structured interviews are conducted to understand participants' real-time usage evaluations and situations when operating the two interfaces on the car dashboard. The goal is to explore how the design of two different operational interfaces influences participants' usage conditions, verbal feedback, and preferences. The study synthesizes the experimental results to draw conclusions and provide recommendations.

2.1   Thinking Aloud Experiment

In this research, participants were asked to operate both the physical and virtual interfaces while driving a car in order to gain insights into the actual behavior of the participants when actually operating the two interfaces. The experiment will involve participants driving a vehicle and performing tasks with two different interfaces. To ensure the safety of the participants, they will not be driving an actual car. Instead, they will use the Serafim R1 steering wheel and pedal controller (Fig. 1) in conjunction with the CarX Highway Racing software (Fig. 2), The participants will be asked to simulate driving a car on a computer, in order to elicit more pronounced user experiences and evaluations, this study will set up driving scenarios that are more extreme. The simulation will involve participants driving a vehicle on an unlimited-speed highway, with the entire route being a straight line and no other vehicles present. During the operation, participants will be unable to use the steering wheel control keys, and the vehicle's gear shifting and acceleration will be automatically controlled. Participants will be able to control the direction of the vehicle using the steering wheel and apply brakes using the pedal.

The physical interface used in the experiment is the Clarion car audio system, as shown in (Fig. 3). The experimental scenario is illustrated in (Fig. 4), and the overall

Fig. 1. Serafim R1 steering wheel and pedal controller

Fig. 2. CarX Highway Racing software.

duration of the experiment is approximately 30 min. The tasks involve common function-alities of car audio systems. 1. Power on from standby mode. 2. Switch to broadcasting function. 3. Switch radio channels. 4. Adjust volume. 5. Switch to CD playback function. 6. Change tracks. 7. Pause and play. 8. Power off and return to standby mode.

Fig. 3. Clarion car audio system

Fig. 4. Participants conduct experiments

The experimental sample for the virtual interface is the Coral Vision RX10 system, as shown in (Fig. 5). The experimental scenario is depicted in (Fig. 6), and the overall experiment duration is approximately 30 min. The operational tasks encompass common functions of the in-car multimedia system. The functionalities covered in the virtual interface tasks include: 1. Power on from standby mode. 2. Switch to music playback function. 3. Change the playlist. 4. Change the track. 5. Fast forward and rewind. 6. Adjusting Volume 7. Switch to podcast function 8. Change the podcast program. 9. Pause and play. 10. Power off and return to standby mode.

Fig. 5. Coral Vision RX10

Fig. 6. Participants conduct experiments

2.2 Semi-structured Interview

This research involved 20 expert participants who performed tasks using two differ-ent interfaces. Following the tasks, a semi-structured interview was conducted as part of the experiment to gain insights into the participants' detailed evaluations and ver-bal feedback regarding the actual use of the two operational interfaces while driving. The interview questions were as follows: There are two questions in the unstructured interview section: 1. Please describe in detail your overall feelings after completing the two experiments. 2. Did you encounter any difficulties in this experimental opera-tion? Structured Interview Questions 10 questions in total: 1. Which interface is faster to accomplish operational tasks? 2. In your current driving experience, what functions do you often use when operating the center console? 3.In the subjective experience of the participant, what are the advantages of the physical interface? 4. In the subjective experience of the participant, what are the disadvantages of the physical interface?5. In the subjective experience of the participant, what are the advantages of the virtual interface? 6. In the subjective experience of the participant, what are the disadvantages of the virtual interface? 7. What kind of control function interfaces need to be physically designed? 8. What control function interfaces can be designed virtually? 9. Can the tac-tile and motion feedback of the physical interface be simulated or replaced by vibration in the virtual interface? What type of central control interface design does the participant prefer for future car purchases? The interview process will be recorded via video, and all participants' feedback will be transcribed verbatim. The transcripts will be subjected to content analysis to assess reliability, followed by comprehensive organization and analysis to gather detailed preferences and opinions from the participants.

3 Results

After conducting experiments using the thinking Aloud method and Semi-Structured Interview, this research recorded the results of experiments involving two different inter-faces. The experimental design was documented, and data were categorized and filtered. The analysis focused on participants' operational behaviors and verbal feedback dur-ing the experiments, aiming to understand their cognitive activities. it is evident that participants faced difficulties in confirming functional mode switches during the phys-ical interface operation experiment. For example, when switching radio stations, more time was needed to confirm the current channel. Similarly, in the CD functional mode, participants had to verify if the playing song matched the task-specified track, check the correctness of the functional mode settings, and as the vehicle speed increased, par-ticipants felt increased pressure. However, participants also pointed out that the tactile feedback from physical buttons made the operation feel intuitive for users.

In the virtual interface operation experiment, the participants pointed out that the task of searching for music tracks by touch control while the vehicle is moving requires attention and time to confirm the position of the touch keys, and it requires more atten-tion and time to search for the targets with foreign language display. When manipulating the touch menu, it was easy to experience excessive scrolling, necessitating repeated back-and-forth sliding during the search. Furthermore, this experiment's device encoun-tered issues with operational response and feedback time delays, leading to potential mistouches and causing hesitation for the participants. Participants also mentioned in the experiment that they felt that looking at the screen to operate the interface while driving was a dangerous behavior and would cause a lack of concentration while driving. However, participants also pointed out that the virtual interface had the advantage of displaying most information in different functional modes. Moreover, its usage was similar to smartphones, making participants feel familiar with the interface.

This research conducted semi-structured interviews with expert participants. Afterward, the structured interview section was examined using content analysis to calculate the "mutual agreement value" and "reliability R value." The "mutual agreement value" was found to be 0.72, and the "reliability R value" was 0.98 (98%), exceeding 85%. After comprehensive analysis, the following results were obtained:

1. Please describe your overall feelings after completing the two experiments: The test subject indicates that they experience a certain degree of fatigue while driving a car and believes that distraction is a considerably dangerous behavior. All participants have previously used electronic products (3C products), and they feel that learning is faster when using virtual interfaces. However, physical interfaces can provide more tactile feedback, and buttons and knobs are also preferred control methods by participants in certain operational tasks. In the task of searching for a specific song, participants find that diverting attention to locate the song is a relatively challenging aspect of the operational task.

2. Did you encounter any difficulties during the experimental procedure this time? When driving a car, navigating through the physical interface to find a specific song or switch functions can be challenging. The operation involves multiple layers of settings, and if you don't frequently use them, it may feel difficult to navigate. Additionally, successfully executing specific tasks may require some time and thought. The virtual interface, particularly when adjusting the volume function, is less intuitive. In contrast, the physical interface's use of a rotary knob for adjusting the volume is very intuitive and user-friendly.

3. Which interface can complete tasks more quickly? In this research, participants believed that using a physical interface allows for a quicker completion of tasks. However, participants also noted that they initially expected virtual interfaces to achieve tasks more quickly before the experiment. After the operation, they chose the physical interface because of its clear button and knob functions, fixed positions, and the ability to provide tactile feedback. In contrast, virtual interfaces are more prone to accidental touches and lack the tactile feedback present in physical interfaces.

4. In your driving experience so far, which functions of the central console do you frequently use while operating the vehicle? The participants frequently use navigation, music playback, and answering phone calls while operating the central console in their driving experience so far.

5. In the participants' subjective experiences, what are the advantages and disadvantages of physical interfaces? Participants mentioned that the advantages of physical interfaces include the ease of operation after learning to use them simply relying on memory to press buttons and turn knobs. They also expressed a preference for the tactile feedback provided by physical buttons. The drawbacks mentioned by the participants include the perceived traditional design of the experimental machine,

limited content on the interface, difficulty in understanding the English abbreviations used in the interface, leading to reluctance among participants to use it. Additionally, the abundance of buttons, some with unclear functions, resulted in confusion for the participants.

6. In the participants' subjective experiences, what are the advantages and disadvantages of virtual interfaces? Participants noted that the advantages of virtual interfaces include clear icons and colors, providing a visually intuitive experience. Due to their familiarity with using electronic devices (3C), they found it easy to adapt to virtual interfaces without investing much time in learning. Participants highlighted that the virtual interface in this experiment has a clean and well defined layout. However, its drawbacks include the lack of tactile feed-back, leading to potential confusion and distraction during operation, posing safety concerns while driving. Additionally, there were perceived hardware and software issues, contributing to a sense of delayed responsiveness according to the participants.

7. What control functions on the car's central console need to be designed physically, and which ones can be designed virtually? The participants find that "knobs" and "buttons" are user-friendly for adjusting functions related to quantities, such as volume and air conditioning temperature. These controls provide an intuitive operational experience, and tactile feedback is deemed important when manipulating such functionalities. Other functions that can be better recognized with visual icons can use the virtual interface.

8. Can the tactile feedback from physical interfaces be simulated or replaced by vibrations in virtual interfaces? This research conducted interviews with participants regarding the common use of haptic feedback in virtual interfaces, aiming to simulate or replace physical interfaces through vibration. Participants expressed that while haptic feedback could partially simulate or replace the tactile sensations of physical interfaces, they still preferred tangible interfaces, such as the actual rotation of knobs or the displacement of buttons, when operating a vehicle.

9. What type of central control interface design do participants prefer for future car purchases? The participants expressed a preference for a hybrid interface design for future car purchases, incorporating both physical elements (such as the air conditioning interface) and virtual elements (such as the multimedia and navigation interface). They suggested that the central control functions should not be overly complicated but should include smartphone connectivity and navigation capabilities. Additionally, they emphasized the importance of a user-friendly interface that can be quickly learned, with an ideal scenario being a system with robust voice control functionality.

4 Conclusion

In this research, the results are summarized and suggestions for future research are made. The research samples cover both physical and virtual interfaces, and the users' behaviors and evaluations are analyzed when operating the two types of interfaces through practical tasks and interviews, and references and suggestions are made for fu-ture designers and researchers to design and study automotive center control interfaces to meet the needs of contemporary users. The results of this research found that.

1. User preferences continue to lean towards the design of a virtual interface for car dashboards in the future. They express that virtualized interfaces are more modern compared to traditional ones, and the learning curve for using them is shorter, as many current consumer electronics products share similar interfaces. Currently, the virtualization of physical interfaces remains a design trend. However, it is recommended to make trade-offs for different functions, and a hybrid interface is considered to be more ideal.

2. The virtual interface can comprehensively display information, icons, and symbols related to functions, clearly informing users about the context of use. The physical interface is not intuitive to understand due to the abbreviation of buttons and functions, resulting in a longer learning time. It is suggested that the physical interface can use icons to replace the abbreviation of ambiguous text, so that the user can easily and intuitively understand its functions while retaining the sense of tactile feedback of the physical interface.

3. Physical interfaces, due to their tactile feedback, may require a longer learning and adaptation period. However, once users become familiar with the operations, they can quickly perform functions relying on tactile memory. Virtual interfaces, while offering enhanced visual information perception, lack tactile memory feedback, which can potentially lead to driver distraction.

4. Physical knobs and buttons provide an intuitive tactile feedback that cannot be replicated by virtual interfaces or vibration functions. Especially when users want an easy way to control quantities, it is recommended that designers retain some physical knobs and buttons when designing functions that require tactile memory.

Due to this study serves as a preliminary investigation, due to safety and experimental scale limitations, this study was unable to conduct experiments on actual roadways, and there may be discrepancies between the experimental conditions and real-world usage. It is recommended that future researchers, provided that safety can be ensured in the experimental environment, conduct user surveys that are closer to real-world scenarios. This approach should yield more design and research information that aligns with user needs and using a driving simulator for experiments is one of the subsequent goals of this study. The results of this study can serve as a reference for future designers and researchers when developing and studying automotive central control interfaces. This will aid in designing interfaces that meet the needs of modern and future users. In addition to fulfilling basic usage requirements and enhancing users' positive experiences, these interfaces can also contribute to improved driving safety.

References

1. Amini, P., Falk, B., Schmitt, R.: Quantitative analysis of the consumer perceived value deviation. In: Proceedings of the 24th CIRP Design Conference, Milano:CIRP, pp. 14–16 (2014)
2. Chan, C.-S.: Can style be measured? Des. Stud. **21**(3), 277–291 (2000)
3. Chan.: Exploring individual style in design. Environ. Plann. B. Plann. Des. **19**(5), 503–523 (1992)
4. Desmet, P.M.A.: A multilayered model of product emotions. Des. J. **6**(2), 4–13 (2003)

5. Graneheim, U.H., Lundman, B.: Qualitative content analysis in nursing research: concepts, proce-dures and measures to achieve trustworthiness. Nurse Educ. Today **24**(2), 105–112 (2004)
6. Kassarjian, H.H.: Content analysis in consumer research. J. Consumer Res. **4**(1), 8–18 (1977)
7. Krippendorff, K.: Content analysis: An introduction to its methodology. Sage Publications Inc, Thousand Oaks, CA (2012)
8. Levy, P.: Beyond kansei engineering: the emancipation of kansei design. Inter. J. Des. **7**(2), 83–94 (2013)
9. Nagamachi, M.: Kansei engineering: a new ergonomic consumer-oriented technology for product de-velopment. Int. J. Ind. Ergon. **15**(1), 3–11 (1995)
10. Osgood, C.E.: Psycholinguistic relativity and universality. Acta Physiol (Oxf.) **19**, 673–678 (1961)
11. Schmitt, R., Falk, B., Stiller, S., Heinrichs, V.: Human Factors in Product Development and Design Advances in Production Technology, pp. 201–211. Springer Publishing, New York (2015)
12. Thyme, K.E., Wiberg, B., Lundman, B., Graneheim, U.H.: Qualitative content analysis in art psychotherapy research: concepts, procedures, and measures to reveal the latent meaning in pictures and the words attached to the pictures. Arts Psychother. **40**(1), 101–107 (2013)
13. Weber, R.P.: Basic content analysis, quantitative applications in the social sciences, vol. 19, pp. 24–26 (1990)

Event Graph Study of Typical Battery Electric Vehicle User Experience Based on Online Comments

Quan Gu, Jie Zhang[✉], Ruiguang Tan, Yuchao Cai, and Chenlu Wang

School of Art Design and Media, East China University of Science and Technology,
Shanghai 200237, China
zjecust2022@163.com

Abstract. Battery electric vehicles (BEVs) as representatives of environmentally friendly and future transportation have gained extensive attention. Research on user experience in the electric vehicle field has become increasingly important as it directly influences the market acceptance and sustainability of electric vehicles. This study aims to explore the user experience of typical battery electric vehicles and gain a deeper understanding of user perceptions, needs, and pain points using an event graph research method based on online comments. In the literature review, we examine the current state of battery electric vehicles and user experience research, identifying shortcomings in existing studies, particularly in dealing with challenges related to online comment data. Our approach involves data collection, data preprocessing, and event graph construction, utilizing natural language processing and data mining techniques to automatically extract user experience information from online comment data. By building an event graph of battery electric vehicle user experience, we can identify key events in different stages such as purchase, driving, maintenance, and charging, along with the emotions, satisfaction, and recommendations associated with these events. The results reveal that the user experience event graph not only aids in understanding users' overall perceptions of battery electric vehicles but also uncovers detailed user requirements, such as improvements in charging infrastructure, increased driving range, and vehicle performance enhancements. In the discussion section, we analyze the significance of the research findings and explore how battery electric vehicle manufacturers and government agencies can use this information to enhance products and policies. We also emphasize the limitations of this study, including data sources and event graph construction methods, and suggest future research directions, such as cross-cultural comparisons and user experience research for a broader range of vehicle types. In conclusion, the findings of this study provide valuable insights for the development of the battery electric vehicle industry and user satisfaction, offering useful guidance for future electric vehicle research and design.

Keywords: Online comments · user experience · event graph · battery electric vehicle · natural language processing

C. Stephanidis et al. (Eds.): HCII 2024, CCIS 2118, pp. 211–222, 2024.
https://doi.org/10.1007/978-3-031-61963-2_20

1 Introduction

Battery electric vehicles (BEVs) have emerged as a revolutionary technology in today's automotive industry, offering a critical solution for sustainable mobility. The market share of electric vehicles continues to expand, and investments from governments and manufacturers are increasing to drive the future of electric mobility. However, to achieve long-term sustainability and success in the electric vehicle industry, apart from the technical and infrastructure challenges, user experience must be at the forefront.

User experience is one of the key indicators of measuring the success of a product or service because it directly affects user satisfaction, loyalty, and word-of-mouth. For electric vehicles, user experience encompasses not only the comfort and performance during the driving process but also the experiences in various stages such as purchasing, charging, maintenance, and more. Understanding how users perceive electric vehicles, along with their needs and pain points, is crucial, as it can aid manufacturers in improving their products, governments in formulating policies, and potential buyers in making informed decisions.

The objective of this study is to gain a deep understanding of the user experience of typical battery electric vehicles, especially as reflected in user viewpoints and emotions within online comments. Online comments have become a valuable source of information because they represent the authentic voices of a vast community of electric vehicle users. By analyzing these comments, we can construct an event graph to showcase the key events, emotions, and recommendations that users encounter during their use of electric vehicles. To achieve this goal, this study employs natural language processing and data mining techniques to extract information related to user experience from extensive online comment data. Through the creation of an event graph of battery electric vehicle user experience, our research not only contributes to understanding user expectations and needs but also helps uncover potential issues and avenues for improvement, ultimately contributing to the sustainable development of the electric vehicle industry and enhancing user satisfaction.

2 Literature Review

2.1 History and Relevant Theories of Battery Electric Vehicles and User Experience Research

The history of battery electric vehicles (BEVs) can be traced back to the late 19th and early 20th centuries when early electric cars made appearances on city streets. Ferdinand Porsche's "Lohner-Porsche Mixte Hybrid" in 1900 became the first mass-produced hybrid electric car. However, early electric vehicles were constrained by immature battery technology and a lack of charging infrastructure, which prevented them from achieving widespread success in the market. Over time, internal combustion engine vehicles became the dominant source of power in the automotive market. Nevertheless, in the early 21st century, a series of factors rekindled interest in electric vehicles. These factors include continuous advancements in battery technology, growing concerns about climate change and environmental issues, high fuel prices, and government environmental policies. These trends are particularly evident in some regions, with the European

Union proposing a comprehensive ban on new gasoline cars starting in 2035 to expedite the transition to zero-emission vehicles. To combat the worsening environmental conditions, many scholars and inventors worldwide have shown interest in the design of electric vehicles (EVs). In an effort to reduce CO2 and other greenhouse gas emissions, many developed countries' governments are promoting the use of electric vehicles.

Theories and frameworks related to user experience play a significant role in the field of user experience research. Donald Norman's "Emotional Design" theory emphasizes the importance of emotions and emotional factors in user experience. He categorizes user experience into three dimensions: visceral, behavioral, and reflective. The visceral dimension covers the product's appearance, sensations, and tactile qualities, the behavioral dimension involves user interactions and operations with the product, and the reflective dimension encompasses users' emotions and satisfaction. This theory is highly useful for understanding users' perspectives on the appearance, operation, and emotional response to electric vehicles (Norman, 9). However, despite significant advancements in electric vehicle technology and market development, user experience research remains challenging. User experience spans various areas, including purchasing, driving, charging, maintenance, and more. Understanding how users perceive and evaluate these aspects is crucial for electric vehicle manufacturers and policymakers. Some studies have conducted surveys and analyses related to user experience, emphasizing the environmental advantages of electric vehicles and users' appreciation of clean energy and contributions to reducing climate change. However, other studies have highlighted challenges such as limited battery range, inadequate charging infrastructure, and the high cost of electric vehicles. Although these limitations exist, researchers and automobile manufacturers worldwide have developed various electric vehicle technologies, with room for further development.

While some research on battery electric vehicle user experience has been conducted, some studies have methodological limitations. For example, some studies may rely solely on surveys and lack in-depth user comments and viewpoints. Additionally, previous research may not have fully leveraged online comment data, which can provide more comprehensive user perspectives and emotions. Therefore, this study aims to address these research gaps by constructing an event graph of battery electric vehicle user experience based on online comment data to gain a deeper understanding of user needs, expectations, and pain points.

2.2 The Role of Online Comments in User Experience Research

In today's digital era, the prevalence of the internet and social media has led users to increasingly share their opinions, experiences, and emotions on online platforms. This trend has elevated online comments as a valuable source of information for understanding user experiences, not only in the realm of battery electric vehicles but across various industries.

Traditionally, scholars often relied on subjective reporting methods to extract user emotional experiences and functional experiences. This approach has been particularly evident in situations related to products and services, often entailing controlled experiments and questionnaires. In recent years, researchers have ventured into mining user emotional experiences from user-generated textual content. For instance, Lee et al. (18)

conducted sentiment analysis to investigate variances in multimedia consumer ratings and reviews. Additionally, Son and Kim (20) devised a methodology to categorize user experiences in online customer reviews, with a primary focus on e-commerce platforms. Their analysis of 10,482 reviews from Best Buy revealed the effectiveness of their model in extracting user experience insights from text, encompassing vocabulary usage, sentiment expressions, and more. This methodology aids in comprehending the emotional aspects of user experiences.

Incorporating online comment data into the study of user experiences in the context of battery electric vehicles grants a comprehensive view of user needs and expectations from the users' standpoint. This approach is instrumental for manufacturers to enhance their products, for policymakers to formulate informed strategies, and for potential car buyers to make well-informed decisions. Thus, online comment data plays a pivotal role in user experience research.

3   Research Methodology

3.1   Framework

The purpose of this study is to utilize text mining techniques based on big data and natural language processing (NLP) to compare textual user experiences of typical Battery Electric Vehicle (BEV) users. This comparison aims to construct a causal graph that represents the corresponding user experience, thereby establishing a framework for understanding these user experiences. The overall workflow is depicted in Fig. 1 and involves several steps: data collection, data filtering, event identification based on dependency syntax, and the final visualization of the user experience event graph.

- **Step 1: Data Collection** -The study initiates with data acquisition. Using web scraping software, comments and feedback regarding user experiences with the target BEV product are gathered from online platforms.
- **Step 2: Data Filtering and Text Mining** - The collected user comments are in unstructured text format. To enhance data analysis efficiency, these comments undergo data preprocessing, including noise reduction.
- **Step 3: Data Analysis** - Dependency syntax analysis is applied to extract trigger words related to event relationships.
- **Step 4: Data Visualization** - Event graph visualization is carried out to understand user experience through the temporal relationships among events, including sequential, causal, and conditional relationships. This visualization is accomplished using specialized software.

3.2   Data Collecting

Web scraping software is utilized to collect and organize online comments related to product user experiences from various online platforms. In order to capture a comprehensive understanding of the product usage process, longer texts are preferred over short ones. Therefore, the question-and-answer platform Zhihu is selected as the data source.

Text information is collected and organized using web crawlers and APIs, which are commonly used technologies for data collection from social media platforms, including

Zhihu. The web crawlers simulate human login and search for Zhihu posts based on specific keywords. The HTML of the web page is then collected and parsed to extract relevant information such as the published content and username.

3.3 Data Preprocessing

Data Filtering. In the data cleaning phase, the primary goal is to remove irrelevant comments and noise from the comments relevant to the study. Mining text from free information systems like Zhihu is inherently noisy and may generate a substantial amount of errors. Text data cleaning is essential in such cases and can be implemented using open-source Python scripting language. However, manual corrections might still be necessary, depending on data structure, quality, or research objectives. In this study, before formal analysis, we performed a series of data cleaning steps. We manually removed interfering data in the raw data that was not relevant to the selected user experiences, such as special characters, blank information, URL links, and more. This was achieved by constructing a professional dictionary, eliminating stop words, and employing text filtering. For instance, informal words like "please," "still," "too," and so on were set as stop words, while frequently separated fixed combinations like "range," "driving experience," "monthly sales volume," were designated as specialized terms.

3.4 Event Graph Construction

An event graph is a directed graph that describes the logical evolution of event relationships, including sequential, causal, conditional, and hierarchical relationships between events. Analogous to the definition of a knowledge graph, an event graph can be formally defined as follows (1):

$$Event\ Graph\ =\ (E,\ R,\ S) \tag{1}$$

where, $E = \{e1, e2, ..., e|E|\}$ represents the set of events in the event graph, $R = \{r1, r2, ..., r|R|\}$ represents the collection of relations in the event graph that denote logical relationships like sequential, causal, conditional, and hierarchical, and S is a subset of $E \times R \times E$, signifying the set of event triples in the event graph.

4 Event Graph Construction and Analysis

In this section, we will present a case study to illustrate how we effectively identify experiential user experience text from product online reviews using the proposed method and visualize them for better comprehension of these user experiences.

4.1 Case

Sample Selection: Sample selection is crucial to ensure data representativeness. We chose currently popular battery electric vehicles (BEVs) that belong to the same vehicle type and have similar price ranges. These vehicles include the Tesla Model 3 representing the international electric vehicle brand Tesla, the BMW i3 representing the international traditional brand BMW, the Han EV representing the Chinese traditional brand BYD, and the ET5 representing the emerging Chinese electric vehicle brand NIO. Specific information is provided in Table 1.

Table 1. Information Table of Data Collection Objects

Typical BEV Photos				
Car Model Information	Model 3	Han EV	ET5	I3
Manufacturer	Tesla	BYD	NIO	BMW
L*W*H(mm)	4694*1850*1443	4980*1910*1495	4790*1960*1499	4872*1846*1481

To investigate the user experience of these selected BEVs and filter out irrelevant information, specific search queries were designed for each model, such as "Han EV experience" "Model 3 experience" "ET5 experience" and "i3 experience". The collected raw data for each model is presented in Table 2.

Table 2. Typical table of collected raw data.

提问题目	ID	ID描述	回答点赞数	回答内容	回答时间
特斯拉 Tesla Model 3 的驾驶体验和实际续航到底如何?	Sam哥	腐国汽车工程师一枚	13 人赞同了该回答	我平时也是小特app社区，b站和youtube来关注一些跟tesla相关的问题，特别是现在国产model3价格降低了之后，大家似乎关注最多的就是续航的问题。简单的答案当然是取决于你如何使用，具体要跟温度，速度，路况，使用方法都密切的关系。先引入一个新的衡量标准，我觉得会更简单直接一些。因为大部分的疑虑都在于为什么车上显示的剩余里程 和 我跑掉的里程 加在一起 跟一开始不一样。主要的原因是，里程的显示永远都是动态的，是综合计算出来的。而真正比较好理解的方式（当然需要一点计算）是只关注 电量（kw*h，度）和 能耗 （tesla惯用 wh/km）。model3现在中国可以买到的也就只有大约53度（国产，也有50度的说法）和 75度（进口，全驱和性能），能耗的话我觉得正常情况可能是在120-250wh/km（越低越好，极限的我见过60多wh/km，等下具体会讲）。可以看出来能耗的范围很大，所以这个车的里程完全取决于你怎么用。对于满电量的长续航75度电，你的续航可能会在600km到300km，这是比较实际的估算。接下来我就来说一下实际使用，多个因素对续航的具体影响究竟又多大。1.1 速度从原理上来说，速度对能耗主要的影响有两点电机输出的力矩输出的电流是直接相关的，高力矩需求=大电流=能耗大高速风阻占大头，而且风阻提高的很快，所以维持高速和高速时候请求加速需要的力矩就然增加，根据上一条，能耗增加具体能观看如下：`<img src="https://picd.zhimg.com/50/v2-ad6d03ff54517556ba07c2c463a27cba_720w.jpg?source=1940ef5c" data-size="normal" data-rawwidth="1185" data-rawheight="728" data-default-watermark-src="https://pic1.zhimg.com/50/v2-`	发布于 2020-02-06 15:53

Text mining from free information systems like Zhihu inherently contains noise and errors (Hecht et al. 24; Grimaldi 25). Thus, a series of preprocessing steps was performed before formal analysis. This involved manual removal of irrelevant data such as special characters, blank information, and URL links. Tokenization and part-of-speech tagging were then applied, followed by noise reduction processing. For instance, colloquial words like "please," "still," and "too" were treated as stop words, and fixed collocations such as "mileage," "driving experience," and "monthly sales volume" were treated as special words.

4.2 Event Graph Generation and Analysis

Event graph generation and analysis are essential data mining tasks, particularly when dealing with online review data. They assist in extracting valuable information from large-scale text data. The following outlines the primary components of event graph generation and analysis:

Event Identification. Event identification serves as the initial step in constructing an event graph, involving the recognition and extraction of event descriptions from online review data. This process is achieved through event extraction based on dependency syntax analysis. The Fig. 3 illustrates a dependency syntax analysis arc diagram based on the LTP language technology platform.

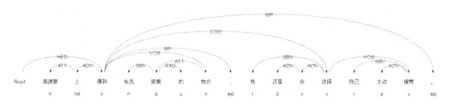

Fig. 1. Dependency Syntax Analysis Arc Diagram

Event Relationship Establishment. The core of the event graph lies in establishing relationships between events. In studies of natural language sentence pattern matching, sentence types can be categorized into consecutive events, conditional events, and causal events, allowing the determination of corresponding formats for different sentence patterns.

Consecutive Relationships. Consecutive relationships denote temporal sequencing between events, indicating that one event occurs after another. These relationships can be established by analyzing contextual and temporal information in comments, aiding in the construction of event timelines.

Causal Relationships. Causal relationships indicate how one event leads to the occurrence of another. Identifying causal relationships often requires in-depth linguistic analysis, including the analysis of sentence structures and logical connections. For instance, by detecting language patterns, it is possible to determine that one event happened as a result of another, contributing to the construction of causal chains between events.

Conditional Relationships. Conditional relationships signify dependencies between events, where the occurrence of one event depends on the presence or occurrence of another event. Identifying conditional relationships may involve analyzing context and keywords to ascertain the conditional links between events. For example, if a comment mentions that a certain event occurred due to specific conditions, it can be regarded as a clue to a conditional relationship (Table 3).

Table 3. Typical Relationship Words for Event Relationships

Relationship	Typical Association Words
Causal Relation-ships	因为(because), 由于(due to), 所以(so), 因此(therefore), 导致(result in), 从而(thus), 致使(leading to), 故(hence), 故而(consequently), 既然(since)
Consecutive Re-lationships	其次(next), 然后(then), 接着(followed by), 随后(afterward), 接下来(coming next)
Conditional Re-lationships	如果(if), 只要(as long as), 除非(unless), 当(when), 假如(suppose), 假使(assuming that), 设若(provided that), 倘若(in case), 既然(given that)

Event Graph Construction. Constructing an event graph involves organizing the identified events and their relationships into a graph structure. Events serve as nodes, while relationships function as edges that connect these nodes, thereby forming a graph. Graph databases or graph representations can be used to store and query event graph data for subsequent analysis and applications. Constructing an event graph allows for the extraction of crucial information about events from online review data, which aids in better understanding the connections and impacts between events.

In this study, the Gephi tool was employed for visualizing the construction of causal event graphs. Each node represents an event, with source nodes corresponding to respective topics. The directed arrows between two nodes represent causal relationships between events. For example, in the notation "node1 → node2," node1 represents the causal event, while node2 represents the resultant event. A typical event graph for battery electric vehicles (BEVs) is depicted in Fig. 2.

5 Discussion

5.1 Analysis and Interpretation of Research Results

Through the construction and analysis of the event graph of user experiences with battery electric vehicles (BEVs), we have gained an in-depth understanding of user experiences. In our study, we identified some interesting patterns and trends:

User Satisfaction: The majority of users expressed satisfaction with battery electric vehicles in their comments. They often emphasized the environmental friendliness, energy efficiency, and reduced fuel consumption of electric vehicles.

Issues and Challenges: Users also mentioned some issues and challenges, including concerns about battery range, insufficient charging infrastructure, and long charging times. These findings align with previous research results.

Relationships Between Events: Our event graph revealed relationships between different events, such as the connection between purchasing and charging. These relationships can help manufacturers better understand user needs and concerns.

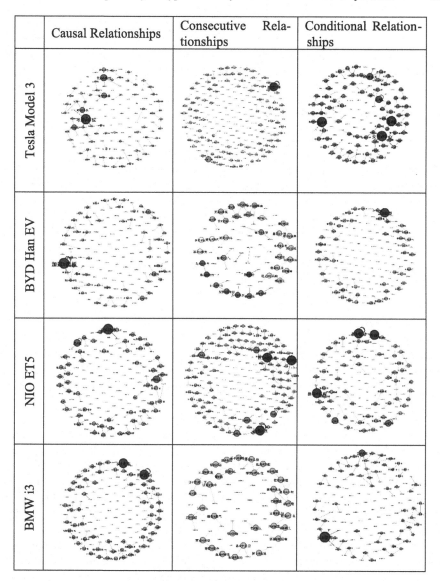

	Causal Relationships	Consecutive Relationships	Conditional Relationships
Tesla Model 3			
BYD Han EV			
NIO ET5			
BMW i3			

Fig. 2. Typical Event Graph for BEVs

5.2 Potential Impact on Manufacturers and Consumers

Impact on Manufacturers: Battery electric vehicle user experience event graphs provide valuable user feedback to manufacturers. They can gain a better understanding of the fundamental reasons for user satisfaction and dissatisfaction. This helps manufacturers improve their products, enhance user satisfaction, and drive the development of the electric vehicle market. Additionally, event graphs can guide manufacturers to make wiser decisions regarding product design and market positioning.

Impact on Consumers: Battery electric vehicle user experience event graphs also have the potential to impact potential buyers. They can analyze the event graph to understand the experiences of other users, enabling them to make more informed purchase decisions. This enhances consumer satisfaction and reduces regrets.

5.3   Innovations and Limitations

Innovations: The innovation of this study lies in constructing the event graph of user experiences with battery electric vehicles using online comment data. This approach allows us to gain a deep understanding of multidimensional user experiences. Furthermore, the construction and analysis of event graphs provide practical guidance and insights for both automotive manufacturers and consumers.

Limitations: One of the main limitations of the study is the source of data, which may be influenced by selection bias. Additionally, sentiment analysis and event relationship establishment may still face accuracy challenges, especially when dealing with complex textual data. Moreover, the construction of event graphs is a complex process that requires a substantial amount of time and resources.

6   Conclusions

In conclusion, this study aimed to construct an event graph of user experiences with battery electric vehicles based on online comments and conduct an in-depth analysis of this graph to reveal patterns and trends in user experiences. Through this research, we have made the following key findings and contributions:

We found that the majority of battery electric vehicle users hold positive views of their experiences, particularly regarding environmental friendliness, energy efficiency, and reduced fuel consumption. However, users also raised some issues and challenges, such as battery range, insufficient charging infrastructure, and long charging times.

By constructing and analyzing the event graph of user experiences with battery electric vehicles, we successfully revealed the key factors of user satisfaction and dissatisfaction and identified the relationships between significant events and their impact.

The innovation of this study lies in using online comment data to construct the event graph, providing practical user feedback and guidance for automotive manufacturers and consumers. It not only helps manufacturers improve their products and enhance user satisfaction but also assists potential buyers in making informed decisions.

This study holds significant potential for practical applications. For automotive manufacturers, understanding critical aspects of user experience can help optimize product design, improve charging infrastructure, and formulate smarter marketing strategies. For potential buyers, the event graph offers valuable user feedback to help them choose the battery electric vehicle that suits their needs. For policymakers, this research provides a basis for crafting policies that support the promotion of electric vehicles.

Future research can further enhance data analysis techniques, expand the range of data sources, and investigate differences among user groups. Additionally, studying the evolution of event graphs will contribute to a better understanding of how user experiences change over time. These efforts will further advance the study of battery electric vehicle user experiences and provide more support for the development of electric vehicle technology and user satisfaction.

Acknowledgments. This work was supported by the National Social Science Fund of China under [21&ZD215]. The research team would like to express great appreciation to the editor and the relevant reviewers for the advises and suggestions on this research paper.

References

Breed, A.K., Speth, D., Plötz, P.: CO2 fleet regulation and the future market diffusion of ze-ro-emission trucks in Europe. Energy Policy (2021)

EU proposes effective ban for new fossil-fuel cars from 2035 | Reuters. https://www.reuters.com/business/retail-consumer/eu-proposes-effective-ban-new-fossil-fuel-car-sales-2035-2021-07-14/. (Accessed 30 April 2023)

Huang, C.-J., Hu, K.-W., Chen, H.-M., Liao, H.-H., Tsai, H.W., Chien, S.-Y.: An Intelligent energy management mechanism for electric vehicles. Appli. Artifi. Intell. **30**, 125–152 (2016)

Karmaker, A.K., Ahmed, Md.R., Hossain, Md.A., Sikder, Md.M.: Feasibility assessment & design of hybrid renewable energy based electric vehicle charging station in Bangladesh. Sustain. Cities Soc. **39**, 189–202 (2018)

Grande, L.S.A., Yahyaoui, I., Gómez, S.A.: Energetic, economic and environmental viability of off-grid PV-BESS for charging electric vehicles: case study of Spain. Sustain. Cities Soc. **37**, 519–529 (2018)

Xue, F., Gwee, E.: Electric vehicle development in Singapore and technical considerations for charging infrastructure. Energy Procedia **143**, 3–14 (2017)

Khan, U., Yamamoto, T., Sato, H.: Understanding attitudes of hydrogen fuel-cell vehicle adopters in Japan. Int. J. Hydrogen Energy (2021)

Ajanovic, A., Haasl, R.: Prospects and impediments for hydrogen and fuel cell vehicles in the transport sector. Int. J. Hydrogen Energy (2021),

Norman, D.A.: Emotional Design: Why We Love (or Hate) Everyday Things. Basic Books (2004)

Waseem, M., Sherwani, A.F., Suhaib, M.: Integration of solar energy in electrical, hybrid, autonomous vehicles: a technological review. SN Appl Sci **1**, 1459 (2019)

I. Alvarez-Meaza, E. Zarrabeitia-Bilbao, R.M. Rio-Belver, G. Garechana-Anacabe. Fuel-cell electric vehicles: Plotting a scientific and technological knowledge map. Sustainability (Switzerland) (2020),

M. Waseem, M. Suhaib, A.F. Sherwani. Modelling and analysis of gradient effect on the dynamic performance of three-wheeled vehicle system using Simscape. SN Appl Sci (2019),

Waseem, M., Sherwani, A.F., Suhaib, M.: Driving pattern-based optimization and design of electric propulsion system for three-wheeler battery vehicle. International Journal of Performability Engineering **16**, 342–353 (2020)

Godovykh, M., Tasci, A.D.: The influence of post-visit emotions on destination loyalty. Tourism Rev. **76**(1), 277–288 (2021)

Jiang, Z., Benbasat, I.: Virtual product experience: effects of visual and functional control of products on perceived diagnosticity and flow in electronic shopping. J. Manag. Inf. Syst. **21**(3), 111–147 (2004)

Alomari, H.W., et al.: A User Interface (UI) and User eXperience (UX) evaluation frame-work for cyberlearning environments in computer science and software engineering education. Heliyon **6**(5), Article e03917 (2020)

Haugeland, I.K.F., Følstad, A., Taylor, C., Bjørkli, C.A:. Understanding the user experience of customer service chatbots: an experimental study of chatbot interaction design. Int. J. Hum. Comput. Stud., 161, Article 102788 (2022)

Lee, S.W., Jiang, G.B., Kong, H.Y., Liu, C.: A difference of multimedia consumer's rating and review through sentiment analysis. Multimedia Tolls Appli. **80**, 625–642 (2020)

Zhao, L., Li, J.L.: The effect of user-generated image pixel quality on user experience: a scenario-based experiment in social media. Int. J. Psychol. Behav. Sci. **17**(5), 1–6 (2021)

Y. Son, W.K.: Development of methodology for classification of user experience (UX) in online customer review. J. Retailing Consum. Serv. **71**, Article 103210 (2023)

Xiang, Z., Du, Q., Ma, Y., Fan, W.: A comparative analysis of major online review platforms: Implications for social media analytics in hospitality and tourism. Tour. Manage. **58**, 51–65 (2017)

Liu, X., Hu, W.: Attention and sentiment of Chinese public toward green buildings based on Sina Weibo. Sustain. Cities Soc. **44**, 550–558 (2019)

Liu, Y., Wu, B., Wang, B., Li, G.: SDHM: A hybrid model for spammer detection in Weibo. In: Paper presented at the 2014 IEEE/ACM International Conference on Advances in So-cial Networks Analysis and Mining (ASONAM 2014). IEEE, Piscataway, NJ (August 2014)

Hecht, B., Hong, L., Suh, B., Chi, E.H.: Tweets from Justin Bieber's heart: the dynamics of the location field in user profiles. In: Proceedings of the SIGCHI Conference on Human Factors in Computing Systems, pp. 237–246 (2011)

Grimaldi, D.: Can we analyse political discourse using Twitter? Evidence from Spanish 2019 presidential election. Soc. Netw. Anal. Min. **9**(1), 1–9 (2019). https://doi.org/10.1007/s13278-019-0594-6

Sorgente, A., Vettigli, G., Mele F.: Automatic extraction of cause-effect relations in natural language text. In: Proceedings of the 13th Conference of the Italian Association for Artificial Intellgence, Rome, Italian, pp. 37–48 (2013)

Scenarios Exploration: How AR-Based Speech Balloons Enhance Car-to-Pedestrian Interaction

Xinyue Gui[1]([envelope]) [ORCID], Chia-Ming Chang[1] [ORCID], Stela H. Seo[2] [ORCID], Koki Toda[1] [ORCID],
and Takeo Igarashi[1] [ORCID]

[1] The University of Tokyo, Tokyo, Japan
xinyueguikwei@gmail.com, info@chiamingchang.com,
toda.koki@mail.u-tokyo.ac.jp, takeo@acm.org
[2] Kyoto University, Kyoto, Japan
stela.seo@i.kyoto-u.ac.jp

Abstract. Previous studies considered the text-based external human-machine interface (eHMI) as the most effective method for self-driving vehicles. However, classic eHMIs (LED displays, windshields, and grounded projectors) cannot meet these requirements because of various limitations (e.g., placement, space, and limited communication channels). With rapid improvements in the Internet of Things, there are more options to improve communication between self-driving vehicles and pedestrians. We introduce our novel eHMI concept, the AR-based speech balloon, which displays text in a balloon shape and floats around self-driving vehicles through smart glasses. In this paper, we present future research scenarios of people wearing smart glasses. We define the mockups, describe the three main problems, and explain how an AR-based speech balloon can alleviate them in six corresponding scenarios.

Keywords: AR Comic · Car-to-Pedestrian Interaction · Scenario-based design

1 Introduction

Regarding technological convergence, various types of technologies collaborate and improve each other to keep up with cutting-edge innovations. Technological development is a long process; therefore, in the distant future, we foresee a situation in which pedestrians interact with mixed traffic consisting of manual and self-driving vehicles [1]. Current external human- machine interface (eHMI) design has emerged with the development of self-driving vehicles to improve pedestrian safety and communication efficiency in car-to-pedestrian interactions. In the classic eHMI, researchers have investigated different types of communication modalities (e.g., text, animated gestures, eyes, and facial expressions) [2], implemented them on a display or physically on a car, and evaluated them.

© The Author(s), under exclusive license to Springer Nature Switzerland AG 2024
C. Stephanidis et al. (Eds.): HCII 2024, CCIS 2118, pp. 223–230, 2024.
https://doi.org/10.1007/978-3-031-61963-2_21

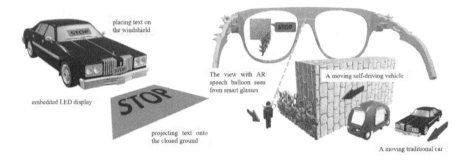

Fig. 1. The classic text-based eHMIs, and our proposal: the self-driving vehicle will stop after detecting an pedestrian, while the traditional car may not. The self-driving vehicle should notify the pedestrian of this potential danger from the blind spot.

According to extensive survey study and comparison experiments, text-based eHMI has been proven to be the most effective approach [3].

However, as technology advances and more information need to be presented, the classic text-based eHMI may not be able to meet this demand. The main problem is the conflict between information complexity and device constraints. The current implementation for displaying text is shown in Fig. 1 left. We define them as "classic text-based eHMIs" through this paper. With advances in technologies, such as the Internet of Things (IoT), object and event detection and response (OEDR), and wireless networks, self-driving vehicles in a network can gather, filter, sort, and selectively display messages for different pedestrians. However, this leads to three major problems for classic text-based eHMIs.

First, there are hardware limitations. Potential dangers, such as an approaching car from a blind spot, can be detected and identified by the sensor system of the self-driving vehicle. However, existing classic text-based eHMIs have limitations (e.g., placement and visibility in bad weather). They cannot provide information to pedestrians in time, particularly when the self-driving vehicle is not visible. Second, information asymmetry exists. As pedestrians cannot see what the self-driving vehicle senses (with robust sensing systems), it may be difficult for pedestrians to trust information from the vehicle. Third, when there are multiple pedestrians or cars, the classic text-based eHMI cannot send these processed messages to the appropriate pedestrian. A self-driving vehicle must pitch specific information to a specific individual. In this paper, we further discuss these problems with six corresponding scenarios and introduce our solution, an AR-based speech balloon that can improve the classic text-based eHMI in car-to-pedestrian interactions.

In manga culture, the speech balloon is a typical comic that can convey different message types (speaking and thinking) and even emotions by employing various balloon shapes [4]. Furthermore, speech balloons can progressively break up long informative words into shorter ones, thereby enhancing communication effectiveness [5]. As AR technology advances, such a futuristic implementation is nearing its realization. For example, AR technology assigns an unique ID to every party in the digital world. Using these IDs, AR objects can be placed on a person with scalable, flexible, and spatial placements. Hence, we used speech balloons with text, which is the most effective modality for self-driving vehicles, as revealed by a previous study.

In this study, we identified problems with the classic text-based eHMI and explained them by illustrating six scenarios. We then described how AR speech balloons could alleviate these problems in these scenarios. Each scenario contained two components: the overall view and smart glasses view. The overall view provided a general explanation of the scenario, including how the cars and pedestrians tend to move. We took a picture from the third-person omniscient perspective. We then added 3D models to illustrate the storyline. The smart glass view displayed the scene through the glasses from the pedestrian's perspective. To create this view, we took an appropriate picture of each scenario from the first-person perspective (pedestrian perspective) in the real world. We then added a speech balloon. In these two perspectives, self-driving vehicles differ (3D model in overall view and real car in smart glasses view).

We created a mockup of the AR speech balloon and used the "basic" bubble shape from comic books, an oval with a "tail" [6]. The tail of the bubble points toward the speaker or sound source so that the person can tell which car is communicating with them. Further, we applied the holographic effect (using Adobe Photoshop) to the basic bubble by adding various levels of motion blur to several layers and rendering with a halftone pattern filter and displacement maps (Figures in the Scenario Illustration section). Because the speech balloon should not interfere with the pedestrian's sight, we chose to make it translucent so that the pedestrian could see other objects in the surrounding environment through the speech balloon using AR glasses. The balloon's color and size should be modified to increase the visibility of the text.

2   Scenario Illustration

In introduction, we lists three problems. For each problem, we explained by two scenarios and the corresponding solution based on the proposed concept.

2.1   Discussion on Problem One: Display Information Both Spatially and in Advance

In terms of placement limitations, classic text-based eHMIs show information in front of the car. However, there are instances in real life where bystanders pass by the car's side or back without seeing the information displayed in front of the vehicle (Fig. 2, upper left). Classic text-based eHMIs are firmly attached to vehicles, leading to two problems. First, the font size and text length cannot exceed vehicle size. Second, the LED display cannot show text separately from the self-driving vehicle. If the vehicle is not visible to the pedestrian, the message on the eHMI is invisible. For S1 (Fig. 2, upper right), a solution (see bottom) can be used to display the speech balloon with the phrase "A car is coming" in front of the pedestrian (the back of the self-driving vehicle).

Fig. 2. The problem and solution for S1 and S2

In scenario S2 (Fig. 2, bottom left), a self-driving vehicle detects a person emerging from the tunnel as it draws near. The pedestrian is unaware of the self-driving vehicle because the wall blocks it. The windshield or LED display cannot separate information from the car. Projectors can display text away from the car. However, projectors have two restrictions. 1) It requires a clear screen or plate to project; thus, the existing eHMI is limited to projection onto the ground. 2) It has strict lighting requirements. To date, experiments with projected eHMIs have been conducted in a dark environment. In our solution (Figure 2, bottom right), self-driving vehicle urges the pedestrian to halt in advance by floating the speech balloon far enough, providing a clearly understandable message, and making it visible to the pedestrian. The text in the speech balloon could be the descriptive word: "A car is coming from left."

2.2 Discussion on Problem Two: Information Asymmetry and the Need to Display Complex Information

In addition to using AR features to address the restrictions of the device (LED and projector), the features of speech balloons have valuable features for optimizing the typical problems in car-to-pedestrian interaction in two major aspects.

Fig. 3. The problem and solution for S3

First, a self-driving vehicle must convey complex information messages to address information asymmetry in a complex scenario.

Fig. 4. The solution for S4 (from left to right): The self-driving vehicle conveys its advisory, description, perception, commanding using a normal-shape, rectangular, cloud-like bubble and jagged-edged shape balloon respectively.

In S3 (Fig. 3, left), when a driving self-driving vehicle planning to go straight detects a wall blocking an approaching traditional car, the latter collides with a walking pedestrian. The pedestrian observes that the self-driving vehicle does not use the turning signal and thus believes that it is safe to proceed to the cross. However, displaying a simple "STOP" as some classic eHMIs may confuse pedestrians, letting them think the self-driving vehicle is malfunctioning. Therefore, the self-driving vehicle should display a command message with an explanation. However, it takes time to read long sentences. Studies have shown that speech balloons can break long sentences into short portions and communicate information more efficiently [5]. By implementing the speech balloon's properties, the self-driving vehicle can display the content in a multi-line format list in order of priority (Fig. 3, right). If time is short, the pedestrian can read only the prior part of them. At the same time, this can reduce the information gap between pedestrians and self-driving vehicle.

To illustrate the second aspect, we need to explain a concept called "message type." Dey et al. [3] discovered several types (intention, instruction, situational awareness, warming, and advisory) and their combinations. Colley and Rukzio [7] constructed a design space with two large groups (explicit and implicit), with each group containing eight message types. Based on this background, we propose an argument that shows only message content without indicating the message type, which is not sufficient for pedestrians. People who have experienced watching anime or manga have a common understanding that different balloon types can convey varying states or messages, such as a character's commands, thoughts, or even emotions. These features can help solve the message ambiguity in car-to-pedestrian interactions (Fig. 4).

2.3   Discussion on Problem Three: Pitch the Message to Specific Pedestrians

This section discusses the interactions between a self-driving vehicle and multiple pedestrians, multiple self-driving vehicles and one pedestrian, and multiple self-driving vehicles and multiple pedestrians (labeled 1-to-N, N-to-1, and N-to-N, respectively) [8].

Individual differences resulted in a 1-to-N situation. For example, there is no absolute "right," "left," "slightly," or "sharply" when the self-driving vehicle displays "I will turn left slightly." The relative position is altered as the pedestrian stands at a new location. In addition, pedestrians from different backgrounds (e.g., nations or ages) may have different preferences for how they want to be informed (i.e., personalization). This can improve communication effectiveness, as users understand and respond faster when reading their native language (such as movie subtitles). Users can set their data in the digital ID, and the smart glasses can display the information corresponding to the user's preferences, such as changing the language display (Fig. 5).

Fig. 5. The solution for S5

In the N-to-1 case, the pedestrian typically receives a filtered message. Using the classic eHMI, the self-driving vehicle in the IoT network can process the message and send it to the pedestrian. The drawback is that the displayed message has a high probability of being blocked when there is a cluster of self-driving vehicles or mixed traffic in the N-to-1 case. In the first section, we discuss a solution: a self-driving vehicle can float speech balloons where pedestrians can see them.

The combination of these two cases (1-to-N, N-to-1) results in an N-to-N condition. We explain this by showing a future self-driving vehicle taxi service application in S6 (Fig. 6). Railway stations, airports, and hotels have designated exits for taxi services. A disorganized taxi service may lead to pandemonium when many customers stream into a parking lot. The IoT system can allocate taxis according to the amount of a customer's luggage, the order in which they arrive at the location, and where they are standing in the parking lot. The vehicles then communicate with the designated customers for the most efficient diversion. Each consumer will only see the speech balloon of the assigned self-driving vehicle to reduce confusion with other vehicles.

Fig. 6. The solution for S6

3   Conclusion

This paper explores the application scenario in a distant setting with fully developed IoT systems, self-driving vehicles, and AR technology. We began with a text-based eHMI, introduced the concept of an AR speech balloon for self-driving vehicles communicating with pedestrians, and created a holographic-style mockup. We identified three problems with the classic text-based eHMI and constructed six scenarios to illustrate how AR speech balloons can alleviate these problems.

All of the discussions in this paper assume that smart glasses are as ubiquitous as mobile phones. Thus far, there has been little demand from public users for smart glasses. For example, Magic Leap, a famous smart glasses manufacturer, saw only 6,000 sales in its first year of availability, much below the "at least" 1 million units anticipated [9]. In addition to being used by the industry, smart glasses have few customers because of their high price and complicated operation. Nevertheless, we believe that with the development of technology, people's acceptance and demand for new things (AR glasses and autonomous driving) will increase accordingly, such as the recently popular Quest3. We anticipate that AR glasses for traffic might be first adopted by professional road users, such as taxi drivers and delivery drivers (cars, motorbikes, and bicycles). Professional road users spend a long time on the road, and safety and efficiency are critical for their jobs. AR glasses that facilitate communication with autonomous vehicles may be an attractive tool for them.

References

1. Lee, J., Park, W., Lee, S.: Discovering the design challenges of autonomous vehicles through exploring scenari via an immersive design workshop. In: Designing Interactive Systems Conference 2021, DIS 2021. pp. 322–338. Association for Computing Machinery, New York (2021). https://doi.org/10.1145/3461778.3462119
2. Mahadevan, K., Somanath, S., Sharlin, E.: Communicating awareness and intent in autonomous vehicle-pedestrian interaction. In: Proceedings of the 2018 CHI Conference on Human Factors in Computing Systems, CHI 2018, pp. 1–12. Association for Computing Machinery, New York (2018). https://doi.org/10.1145/3173574.3174003
3. Dey, D., et al.: Taming the eHMI jungle: A classification taxonomy to guide, compare, and assess the design principles of automated vehicles' external human-machine interfaces. Trans. Res. Interdiscipl. Perspect. **7**, 100174 (2020)
4. Yamanishi, R., Tanaka, H., Nishihara, Y., Fukumoto, J.: Speech-balloon shapes estimation for emotional text communication. Inform. Eng. Express **3**(2), 1–10 (2017)
5. Kurahashi, T., Sakuma, R., Zempo, K., Mizutani, K., Wakatsuki, N.: Retrospective speech balloons on speech-visible ar via head-mounted display. In: 2018 IEEE International Symposium on Mixed and Augmented Reality Adjunct, ISMAR-Adjunct 2018, pp. 423–424. Institute of Electrical and Electronics Engineers (IEEE), Piscataway, NJ, USA (2018). https://doi.org/10.1109/ISMAR-Adjunct.2018.00127
6. Anime   Outline.   https://www.animeoutline.com/how-to-draw-manga-speech-bubbles/, (Accessed 14 Feb 2024)
7. Colley, M., Rukzio, E.: A design space for external communication of autonomous vehicles. In: 12th International Conference on Automotive User Interfaces and Interactive Vehicular Applications, Automotive. UI 2020, pp. 212–222. Association for Computing Machinery, New York (2020). https://doi.org/10.1145/3409120.3410646
8. Jensen, K.B., Helles, R.: Speaking into the system: social media and many-to-one communication. Eur. J. Commun. **32**(1), 16–25 (2017)
9. VR   Times.   https://virtualrealitytimes.com/2019/12/06/report-magic-leap-sold-6000-ar-headsets-in-6-months/, (Accessed 14 Feb 2024)

Mobility Demand Estimation: Integrating Population Distribution and Mobility Data

Toru Kumagai[✉] [iD]

National Institute of Advanced Industrial Science and Technology (AIST), 1-1-1 Umezono, Tsukuba 305-8568, Ibaraki, Japan
kumagai.toru@aist.go.jp

Abstract. This study presented an approach for estimating mobility demand using area mobility models based on a relatively small dataset of mobility data and population distribution estimates. This method assumes that the mobility of each individual is a function of their address. It estimates the mobility model for a hypothetical individual at a given address by utilizing the mobility data of nearby individuals. By sampling mobility occurrences based on these models and weighting and aggregating the sampled data according to the population density of each address, the method generates area-wide mobility data. The method was applied to real data, specifically to estimate mobility demand for elderly individuals residing in suburban areas. The results show that elderly individuals visit shopping districts from 4 km to 7 km apart. Validation is performed by comparing the results with data from other reliable sources.

Keywords: Mobility Model · Mobility Data · GPS data · Mobility Demand · Public Transportation · Mobility as a Service · Elderly Individuals

1 Background

In many regions of Japan, traditional public transportation fails to adequately serve individuals who lack alternative means of mobility, particularly those without driver's licenses, as well as younger and older demographics. Furthermore, as Japan grapples with an aging and declining population, there is a decrease in transportation demand and a shortage of public transportation providers, necessitating the reorganization of transportation systems to improve efficiency and convenience. This reorganization requires consensus-building among various stakeholders, including local governments, transportation operators, Mobility-as-a-Service (MaaS) operators, residents, and related service providers [1–3]. Objective analysis based on mobility data representing the region's transportation demand is crucial for informing such considerations.

Methods for understanding regional mobility demand include approaches based on mobile phone base stations, utilization history of electronic payment services encompassing transportation and purchase data, methods involving the installation of GPS recording apps on mobile phones, distribution of GPS devices, participant-recorded

C. Stephanidis et al. (Eds.): HCII 2024, CCIS 2118, pp. 231–236, 2024.
https://doi.org/10.1007/978-3-031-61963-2_22

movement histories, and interview-based methods. These methods have both advantages and disadvantages, and it is not feasible for any single method to comprehensively capture all aspects of mobility demand. While the method utilizing mobile phone base stations allows observation of the movements of a large number of people, the data obtained from a privacy standpoint is limited. Interview-based methods require cost and time, and the number of participants is limited; however, they enable understanding of reasons for travel, satisfaction levels, and potential mobility needs. Therefore, it is necessary to carefully consider how to construct the regional transportation system and conduct purposeful information gathering to understand the transportation demand of the region.

Among the methods mentioned above, distributing GPS devices to residents targeted for transportation services and recording their movements offers particular advantages. By actively selecting the target population for data collection, this approach facilitates the acquisition of more relevant information directly applicable to the specific needs of transportation system redesign. However, it inherently faces limitations in terms of the number of subjects that can be measured, thereby making it challenging to capture the overall demand in an area.

2 Object

This study introduced an approach to estimate mobility demand using area mobility models derived from a relatively small dataset of mobility data and population distribution estimates. Subsequently, we applied this method to estimate travel demand between residences and nearby commercial facilities for elderly residents in suburban areas with limited commercial amenities. To validate our approach, we compared its results with Origin-Destination (OD) data obtained through alternative means.

3 Method

The proposed approach builds upon methods from existing studies [4] and comprises three main steps.

The first step involves formalizing the mobility model of hypothetical individuals residing in a specific location as a function of their residential address. This assumption is deemed reasonable since individuals typically frequent facilities close to their homes. This holds particularly true for elderly individuals who have retired and no longer commute, potentially having limited physical capabilities for long-distance travel.

The second step involves approximating the mobility model of hypothetical individuals residing in a specific location by sampling with replacement the movement data of subjects with neighboring addresses. If sufficient data is available, it can be obtained through some machine learning techniques. However, in the context of this study, such ample data is not available. In cases where data is insufficient, parameter identification may be possible if a parametric model can be assumed, but it is also challenging to assume a parametric model. Therefore, we conduct sampling with replacement of the movement data of neighboring subjects, similar to how the bootstrap method approximates the population by sampling with replacement.

The third step involves weighting and aggregating the hypothetical mobility models obtained through the aforementioned procedure based on population density. This enables the derivation of an area mobility model from a relatively limited number of subject data. Even if the subjects exhibit regional biases, this approach allows us to derive a mobility model that aligns with the population density distribution of the area. Furthermore, in scenarios with abundant data, biases in the subject profile can be corrected by weighting them according to factors such as the age distribution of the area.

4 Data

This study employed personal mobility data from individuals aged 70 and above, gathered through the Smart Mobility Challenge Project [5] and made available by the Smart Mobility Promotion Council [6]. The dataset comprised GPS mobility data collected from 77 individuals residing in or around Tsukuba, Japan, over a span of four weeks, with GPS positions recorded every 3 min. Figure 1 (Left) illustrates a plot of all movement data superimposed on a map of Tsukuba.

Additionally, the study utilized the National Land Information System Geographical System (NLIS) [7], which contains diverse geographic information, including population, transportation, and land use data. Specifically, the study examined the population distribution around Tsukuba, Japan (Fig. 1 (Right)). The region with high population density in the southeast corresponds to the center of Tsukuba.

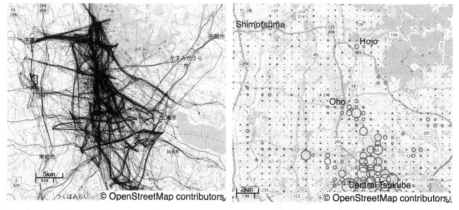

Fig. 1. (Left) Plot of all movement data superimposed on a map of Tsukuba. **(Right)** Population distribution around Tsukuba, Japan. Circles represent the population size of each grid cell, with a cell size of approximately 500 m by 500 m. The map is based on data from OpenStreetMap and is licensed under the Open Database License [7]. Map data was obtained from 'a.tile.openstreetmap.org' using the Mapping Toolbox [8].

5 Application and Results

The proposed method was utilized to estimate the travel demand among elderly individuals aged 70 and above living in suburban areas with limited access to retail facilities. By addressing the specific requirements of elderly residents in suburban settings, often characterized as "shopping refugees," this application directly confronts the challenges faced by regional public transportation systems.

Figure 2 depicts the mobility data generated by the proposed method, alongside the movement frequency derived from reliable Origin-Destination (OD) data. This experiment simulated the travel patterns of residents within the black square, using their residential locations as the point of origin.

The results reveal that the proposed method identified three nearby destinations: Hojo, Shimotsuma, and Oho. Similarly, the frequency of movement derived from OD data indicates substantial mobility to these same locations. Hojo is situated approximately 4 km to the east, Shimotsuma approximately 7 km to the west, and Oho around 7 km to the south-southeast. Hojo serves as the historical center of this region, boasting a relatively dense population and a traditional shopping district. In contrast, Shimotsuma features a large commercial facility, while Oho, being a newly developed area, hosts a commercial district with various shops, including supermarkets, home centers, and other businesses. This finding suggests that elderly residents residing in areas with limited retail options often travel to nearby commercial districts. Given that many individuals over 70 have relinquished their driver's licenses and lack personal transportation, they depend on public transit or rides from family members to access these commercial areas.

The proposed method fails to estimate mobility to areas adjacent to the origin in the northeast, as indicated by the frequency of movement based on OD data. The inability of the proposed method to estimate this movement is likely attributable to the limitations of the GPS data used, which was recorded every three minutes and thus could not capture short-distance movements effectively.

Table 1 presents the estimates of monthly movements to Hojo, Shimotsuma, and Oho generated by the proposed method, alongside the values obtained from OD data. The proposed method estimates demand through sampling without replacement; therefore, 12 simulations were conducted, and the means and standard deviations are displayed in the table. Both results are of comparable magnitude, indicating the validity of the proposed estimation method. However, the close values observed for Hojo and Oho may be coincidental, warranting further investigation. Given that the proposed method relies on a limited number of subjects for estimation, it is inevitably influenced by the specific behaviors of these subjects. In particular, Shimotsuma demonstrates considerable deviation in values.

When applying the proposed method to real-world scenarios, it is crucial to use data from individuals intended to accurately represent the target users of transportation services. Constructing models that are useful in service design depends on the sufficient utilization of data from these intended users.

6 Conclusion

In conclusion, this study presented an approach for estimating mobility demand using area mobility models based on a relatively small dataset of mobility data and population distribution estimates. The method was applied to estimate travel demand between residences and nearby commercial facilities for elderly residents in suburban areas with limited commercial amenities. By comparing the results with Origin-Destination (OD) data obtained through alternative means, the validity of the proposed method was assessed.

The application of the proposed method revealed significant mobility to nearby commercial districts such as Hojo, Shimotsuma, and Oho. The method accurately estimated travel patterns, though it failed to capture movements to areas adjacent to the origin in the northeast, likely due to limitations in GPS data capturing short-distance movements.

Overall, the proposed method provided valid estimates of travel demand, with results comparable to OD data. However, further investigation is warranted. As the method relies on a limited number of subjects, it is essential to ensure that the data used adequately represents the target users of transportation services in real-world scenarios.

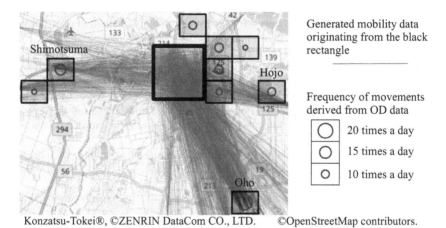

Konzatsu-Tokei®, ©ZENRIN DataCom CO., LTD.   ©OpenStreetMap contributors.

Fig. 2. Comparison between mobility data generated using the proposed method and the frequency of movements derived from other reliable OD data. The mobility data of individuals aged 70 and over was generated and analyzed, while the frequency of movements was derived from the aggregated yearly OD data. This OD data was obtained from Konzatsu-Tokei®. Konzatsu-Tokei® data is data processed comprehensively and statistically by NTT DOCOMO from cell phone location information sent by consenting users of NTT DOCOMO applications. The location information is GPS data (latitude and longitude information) measured every five minutes at a minimum and does not contain personally identifiable information.

Table 1. Comparison of estimated monthly movements to Hojo, Shimotsuma, and Oho between the proposed method and OD data.

Destination	Demand Estimation Per Month Mean ± SD	Frequency of Movement Per Month Derived from OD data
Hojo	354.2 ± 26.4	354.25
Shimotsuma	214.7 ± 7.6	361.8
Oho	623.5 ± 20.7	624.6

Acknowledgments. This study was supported by Ministry of Economy, Trade and Industry, Japan. We would like to acknowledge Smart Mobility Challenge Promotion Council for providing the mobility data used in this research.

References

1. Ministry of Economy, Trade and Industry, Japan, Smart Mobility Challenge Project Launched (2019). https://www.meti.go.jp/english/press/2019/0618_005.html (Accessed 2024)
2. Ministry of Economy, Trade and Industry, Japan, METI Compiles a Collection of Knowledge Useful for Public Implementation and Future Directions Based on the Results and Challenges of the FY2020 Smart Mobility Challenge Project (2021). https://www.meti.go.jp/english/press/2021/0402_002.html (Accessed 2024)
3. Smart Mobility Challenge Promotion Council: Creating Smart Mobility, Lessons from Five Years of Case Studies (2024). https://www.mobilitychallenge.go.jp/knowledge/ (Accessed 2024) (in Japanese)
4. Kumagai, T.: Estimation of mobility model using limited mobility data. In: HCII2023 Proceedings. CCIS, vol. 1835, pp. 497–502 (2023). https://doi.org/10.1007/978-3-031-36001-5_64
5. Smart Mobility Challenge Promotion Council Homepage (2019). https://www.mobilitychallenge.go.jp (Accessed 2024)
6. National Land Information Division, National Spatial Planning and Regional Policy Bureau, National Land Information System (NLIS). https://nlftp.mlit.go.jp/index.html (Accessed 2023)
7. OpenStreetMap, Copyright and License. https://www.openstreetmap.org/copyright (Accessed 2024)
8. The MathWorks, Inc., "Mapping Toolbox". https://jp.mathworks.com/help/map/ (Accessed 2024)

Design Elements Analysis of Cabin Atmosphere Lamp of Intelligent Vehicle Based on Kansei Engineering

Miao Liu[ID] and Wanxia Lu[✉]

East China University of Science and Technology, Shanghai 200237, People's Republic of China
lwxdaily@163.com

Abstract. The interior atmosphere light is a kind of interior light applied in the interior of the car, which is used to highlight the interior environment of the car. The user can set the color and brightness of the atmosphere light according to the needs, which has a good user experience effect. Car cabin atmosphere light generally through the color, brightness adjustment and the application of rhythm scheme, passenger-car emotional interaction, enhance the user's driving experience. Based on kansei engineering, this paper studies and analyzes the current situation of intelligent car cockpit atmosphere lights in the market, and establishes an evaluation system of perceptual vocabulary for intelligent car cockpit atmosphere lights. Based on the analysis results of image scale map, the design elements and corresponding physical characteristics are extracted from the presentation mode, brightness and color of the intelligent car cabin atmosphere light. Finally, the design scheme of automobile cabin atmosphere lamp which meets the psychological needs of users is obtained.

Keywords: Automobile atmosphere lamp · Kansei Engineering · Driving experience

1 Introduction

Interior space is an important area for intelligent vehicle design and display of product perceived quality. Automotive interior atmosphere lights are generally installed in the ceiling, instrument panel, center control board, door trim panel and other positions, through the dimming controller adjustment, can achieve dimming, switching and rhythmic effects [1]. The design of automobile interior atmosphere light is very important to the driving experience, and it is the main carrier for lighting designers to convey information. On the other hand, the interior atmosphere lights play a good role in the safety of driving at night. The environment that surrounds a driver and passengers provides not only the functional ability to operate the vehicle safely but also elicits both positive and negative emotional responses [2]. However, at present, there are relatively few researches on the design elements of intelligent car cabin atmosphere lights based on the perspective of kansei engineering to improve users' emotional experience.

C. Stephanidis et al. (Eds.): HCII 2024, CCIS 2118, pp. 237–246, 2024.
https://doi.org/10.1007/978-3-031-61963-2_23

The purpose of this paper is to apply Kansei engineering to the research and development process of intelligent car cabin atmosphere light. Through the investigation of consumer groups, explore the image characteristics of each element of the cabin atmosphere light, so that designers can accurately grasp the design elements of the "people-oriented" intelligent car cabin atmosphere light.

2   Relevant Review Studies

2.1   Research on Kansei Engineering

"Kansei Engineering" is a comprehensive interdisciplinary subject between design, engineering and other disciplines. It is a product development technology and research method that takes people's perceptual needs as the first element and can transform them into design elements.

Foreign scholars started their research on Kansei engineering earlier. The first Japanese research paper on Kansei engineering was Mitsuki Nagamachi's "Research on Emotional Engineering" published in Ergonomics in 1975. In 1986, "Kansei engineering" was proposed and applied to automobile design by Kenichi Yamamoto, former chairman of Mazda Motor Group in Japan.Subsequently, the Kansei Engineering Automotive Research Institute was established to apply Kansei engineering in automotive design and development [3]. At present, Kansei engineering in Japan has a very wide range of applications. In addition to applied psychology, computer science, business administration, ergonomics and other fields, it is also applied and developed in tourism, food engineering, acoustics and other fields [4]. The study of Kansei engineering in the United States is also relatively in-depth, and it is combined with relevant theories for the development of intelligent products. Ishaan Pakrasi et al. [5] uses Laban Movement Analysis paired with the Kan-sei Engineering iterative design approach to dissect movement and visual traits of archetypal characters and marry them to features of the robot to guide the design.

At present, the research of Kansei engineering in China is mainly concentrated in the field of design, attaching importance to the application of this method, and the research hotspots include image, user experience, product design, cultural and creative products, etc. [6]. Xie Xuanhui from Tsinghua University [7] used the method of combining NCS system and perceptual image theory to study the interior color design of subway vehicles. Yang Dongmei et al. [8] combined the perceptual image method to study the product design preference of the elderly. Tang Yile et al. [9] applied data analysis in Kansei engineering to the evaluation system of cultural and creative products to improve the efficiency of design evaluation of cultural and creative products.

In the research of design elements of intelligent car cabin atmosphere light in this paper, Kansei engineering can help designers understand the emotional needs of users in order to improve user experience satisfaction.

2.2   Research on the Impact of Car Atmosphere Lights on Car Experience

With the development of cars towards the third space of life, more and more consumers begin to pay attention to the construction of interior texture. The application of atmosphere lights in automobiles is increasing day by day, attracting the attention and high recognition of most consumers [10]. The rise of automotive interior atmosphere lights has become the biggest highlight of automotive interior and the standard of new energy vehicles [11].

The atmosphere lights at different installation locations can present different lighting effects according to the driver's individual needs, bringing a pleasant and relaxing feeling to the driving experience [12]. By adjusting brightness and color, optical devices can affect the emotions of drivers and passengers, make them feel relaxed and comfortable or excited, and improve the cognitive ability of drivers, prevent fatigue driving, and help drivers concentrate [13].

3   Research Process

3.1   Sample Collection and Screening

Collect Sample Pictures. A total of 65 pictures were obtained by extensively collecting sample pictures of intelligent car cabin atmosphere lights through big data. The sample picture is analyzed and screened to form the sample database. In order to ensure the accuracy of the experiment, interference factors such as people, watermarks and trademarks on the sample map were removed, and the size of the sample map was unified. After preliminary screening, 40 images of intelligent car cabin atmosphere lights with high clarity were obtained. After screening, classification and comparison by the review team, 7 representative samples were finally obtained for the final research. They are sample 11, sample 19, sample 22, sample 25, sample 28, sample 31 and sample 39, as shown in Table 1.

Table 1. Representative samples

S11	S19	S22	S25	S28	S31	S39
Benz	Rolls-Royce Wraith	Audi A4L B&O	BYD Auto	NIO EC7	BMW i7	BMW 120i

Collect Emotional Vocabulary. A total of 103 evaluation words of intelligent car cabin atmosphere lights were collected by web crawler. The collected words are integrated, and the words with a wide range of images and high semantic complexity are selected layer by layer. The attributes of 103 semantic description words are classified by KJ method, 10 perceptual words are selected, and these words are paired with antonyms as representative pairs and numbered to form a perceptual vocabulary.

3.2   Establishment and Classification of Difference Word Pairs

In order to obtain the final key emotional vocabulary of the intelligent car cabin atmosphere light, 5 automotive interior design professionals were invited to combine and delete the emotional vocabulary to further optimize the vocabulary. Through cluster analysis, the key perceptual words are divided into three groups, and finally 12 adjectives, namely 6 groups of perceptual words, are established from them, as shown in Table 2.

Table 2. Establishment and classification of perceptual word pairs

Atmosphere light design elements	Perceptual word pair
Presentation mode	Traditional - Technological Static - Rhythmic
luminance	Soft - Stimulating Uniform - Gradient
Color	Single - Colorful Quiet - Warm

3.3   Visual Image Direction

In 1957, Osgood proposed semantic difference analysis [14]. As a common research method of Kansei Engineering, it can transform users' perceptual cognition of products into accurate data, thus establishing a prerequisite for exploring the mapping relationship between perceptual cognition and design elements [15].

In this study, the semantic difference method was used to quantify the subjects' perception of the elements of 7 samples of intelligent car cabin atmosphere lights. In order to establish the visual image direction, 7 representative samples of intelligent car cabin atmosphere light were selected and combined with perceptual image vocabulary to establish the semantic scale of Likert 7-level scale (-3–3), and perceptual vocabulary was divided into levels, representing different degrees. The two ends of the semantic scale are image words of relative meaning, and the closer the value is to one end, the more it fits the image words of this end. Participants rated based on subjective feelings, with seven numbers representing different levels of perceptual imagery. For example, the option of "single - colorful" takes the score value of $-3, -2, -1, 0, 1, 2, 3$, respectively, representing very single, relatively single, not too single, can not distinguish, not too colorful, more colorful and very colorful.

A total of 85 people were selected for the perceptual semantic experiment, and 76 valid questionnaires were finally collected, including 40 men and 36 women. The subjects were made up of people with random social identities, including drivers, teachers, freelancers, doctors, students, and so on. They were all between 20 and 45 years old, with an average age of 31.5 years. All subjects had intelligent car driving experience, normal vision and no color deficiency disorder. The subjects first selected one of their favorite atmosphere lights from the 7 representative samples, and then scored the perceptual elements of the 7 samples.

Reliability analysis is an effective analysis method to measure whether a comprehensive evaluation system has certain stability and reliability [16]. Reliability analysis can be used to evaluate the validity of the scale. In order to verify the validity of the measurement results of this study, SPSS software was used to test 76 questionnaires, and the Klonbach α coefficient was 0.867, which was above 0.7 and between 08–0.9, proving that the reliability of the questionnaire was high. The mean value of the questionnaire data was processed, and the 6 groups of perceptual image evaluation tendency of each representative sample were finally obtained (Table 3).

Table 3. Table of mean scores of perceptual intention semantics

	Traditional-Technological X1	Static-Rhythmic Y1	Soft-Stimulating X2	Uniform-Gradient Y2	Single-Colorful X3	Quiet-Warm Y3
S11	0.2	−1.3	−1.1	−0.8	−2.3	−2.1
S19	1.2	1.9	−1.2	2.1	−1.2	−2.4
S22	−0.6	−1.9	2.1	2.3	1.9	1.1
S25	2.4	2.6	−1.6	2.7	0.3	−1.9
S28	1.8	0.3	−2.3	1.0	−1.2	1.6
S31	1.9	2.6	1.7	2.4	2.7	1.5
S39	−1.1	−1.9	−2.2	−2.6	−2.4	−2.4

According to the presentation mode, brightness and color image value of the intelligent car cabin atmosphere lamp sample, the intention scale map is drawn. Each element corresponds to two groups of perceptual words, which are set as the X axis and the Y axis respectively, and the perceptual words are placed at both ends of the X and Y axes respectively. Take the presentation of the atmosphere lamp as an example, the two ends of the X1 axis are traditional and technological, and the two ends of the Y1 axis are static and rhythmic. According to statistics, it can be seen from Table 3.3 that X1 of sample 11 is 0.2 and Y1 is −1.3. X2 is −1.1,Y2 is −0.8; X3 is −2.3 and Y3 is −2.1. That is, the image coordinates of the presentation mode of sample 11 are (0.2, −1.3), the brightness image coordinates are (−1.1, −0.8), and the color image coordinates are (−2.3, −2.1). According to this method, the intention coordinate values of the other 6 sample elements can be obtained, and then the image scale map of presentation mode, brightness and color can be drawn, as shown in Fig. 1 to 3.

3.4 Extraction of Atmosphere Lamp Design Elements

According to the statistical results of the purchase intention data of the smart car cabin atmosphere lamp samples, users have the strongest purchase desire for samples 19 and 31, and also show strong intention for sample 25. Sample 11 and sample 22 have lower

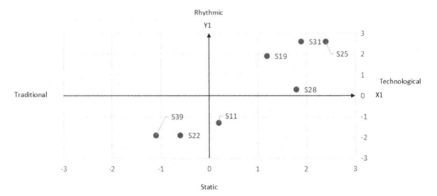

Fig. 1. Image scale diagram of presentation mode

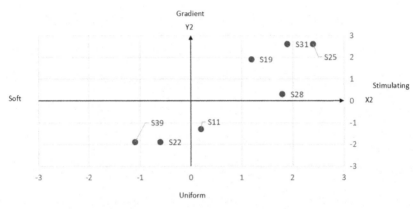

Fig. 2. Scale diagram of brightness image

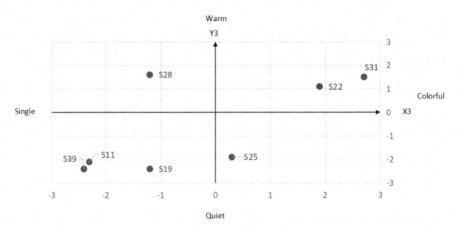

Fig. 3. Scale diagram of color image

purchase desire. According to the scale diagram of each element, samples 19, 25 and 31, which are strongly desired by users, are all located in the positive axis of X1 and Y1. All are located in the first quadrant area, showing the intention of technology and rhythm. However, samples 39 and 22, which were selected less, were located in the third quadrant, presenting a traditional and static impression. In terms of the brightness of the atmosphere lamp, samples 19 and 25 in the four-quadrant scatter plot are located in the negative axis of the X2 axis, showing a soft feature. For the Y2 axis, samples 19, 25, and 31 are all located in the forward part of the Y2 axis, showing a gradient intention. In terms of color, the intention scale diagram of each element corresponding to the atmosphere light sample can be seen that sample 25 and sample 31, which have a strong desire to buy by users, are located in the positive axis part of the X3 axis, that is, the corresponding perceptual word is "colorful". For the Y3 axis, most of the scattered points corresponding to the samples are located in the negative axis of the Y3 axis, including samples 19 and 25, which are more selected by users, showing a quiet intention.

Based on the comprehensive appeal analysis, the design elements corresponding to the perceptual intention words are extracted according to the sample features with high intention scores, and the design strategies in the following three aspects are obtained:

Design strategy 1. In terms of presentation mode, according to the survey results, it can be learned that the user's preferred presentation mode is "Technological" and "Rhythmic". Based on the scale diagram of intention, it can be seen that the two samples whose presentation mode is closest to the "Technological" and "Rhythmic" intention are samples 25 and 31. According to the common features of the two automobile atmosphere light samples, the design elements are extracted. The atmosphere light should have irregular light strips and dynamic light changes.

Design strategy 2. In terms of brightness, "Soft" and "Gradient" lighting is favored by users. The samples closest to the "Soft" intention in the brightness evaluation are samples 28 and 39, and the samples corresponding to "Gradient" are samples 25 and 31. By referring to the common features of the two automobile atmosphere light samples to extract the design elements, we can see that the light waterfall surround atmosphere light with low brightness and diffuse soft lighting can reflect the perceptual word "soft". The "gradual" is mainly reflected in the change of color brightness.

Design strategy 3. In terms of color, the design output should be displayed as "Colorful" and "Quiet". Similarly, samples whose colors are closest to the "Colorful" feature are sample 22 and sample 31. Both of them are mixed with different colors and accompanied by hue changes. The samples whose color is closest to the "Quiet" feature are samples 19 and 39. Combined with the sample characteristics, the design strategy of mixing different cool tones is obtained.

4 Design Application and Evaluation

4.1 Basic Attribute Analysis

Based on the analysis results of the image scale map, the basic properties of the intelligent car cabin atmosphere light that meet the psychological needs of users can be obtained. According to the above design elements of the atmosphere lamp strategy, from the presentation mode, brightness, color three aspects, further analysis and application. 5 experts with more than 2 years of experience in automotive interior design and 2 enthusiasts of automotive atmosphere lights were invited to conduct focus group discussions. Expand the analysis of three different attributes from the perceptual layer down, and extract the physical characteristics matching the design elements and inferences, as follows:

Presentation Method. According to strategy 1, irregular light strips are used in the presentation of atmosphere lights. Personalized lighting Settings according to user preferences and needs. The light pulsates with changes in the sound of the car cabin, such as human voices, music, etc. The rhythm of the light changes according to the user's music choice. Change the original light mode, transform into an interesting interactive change of the atmosphere light, enhance the interaction of the interior lighting system, so as to present a scientific and technical, rhythmic effect.

Brightness. Safety first. The brightness of the atmosphere lamp should be carefully designed, not too bright to affect driving, and not too dark to affect the normal activities of drivers and passengers. According to strategy 2, soft low-brightness, light cascade surround ambient lights are used for soft lighting. At the same time, the color brightness changes to achieve the effect of gradual change.

Color. According to the strategy 3 elements, the color of the atmosphere light should present a colorful effect, and it is necessary to avoid stimulating the light color of the driver. In order to ensure the driver's driving safety and reduce excited emotions, the use of quiet cold color light source to adjust the driving atmosphere. The specific color selection is close to the natural sky blue color, and the combination of higher brightness and lower purity purple, showing a mysterious and quiet intention.

4.2 Design and Application

Based on the analysis results, this study designed an intelligent car cabin atmosphere light (Fig. 4). The experimental results are verified by simulated driving experiments. Different schemes are used to simulate driving experiments. After the end of the experiment, the satisfaction survey of the subjects was carried out, and the results showed that the design scheme of the intelligent car cabin atmosphere light improved based on the analysis results had a higher satisfaction, accounting for 83%. It shows that the results meet the psychological needs of users.

The appropriate car cabin atmosphere light can ensure the driver's mood and attention while enhancing the atmosphere inside the car and improving the car driving experience. At the same time, the results of the simulated driving experiment also show that inappropriate light color and flicker pattern may have a negative effect on the driver's emotion and attention. For example, red lights can cause drivers to be impulsive, reducing their concentration and reaction speed. Frequent flashing lights may cause glare and visual fatigue, further interfering with the driver's ability to drive. This is consistent with one of the conclusions of Grimm (2003) [17] 's main research work in this field, that is, the interior environmental lighting system has the potential to affect comfort, but its potential impact depends largely on the color, intensity and size of the light source and other factors.

Fig. 4. Improved design scheme of intelligent car cabin atmosphere lamp

5 Conclusion

Guided by the theory of Kansei Engineering, this paper studies the design elements of the intelligent car cabin atmosphere light, adopts the semantic difference method, and quantifies the design of the intelligent car cabin atmosphere light through perceptual images. Based on the analysis results of image scale map, the user's preference for smart car cabin atmosphere light is obtained. The relationship between the user's perceptual meaning and the design elements of the intelligent car cabin atmosphere light is established, and the design strategy of the intelligent car cabin atmosphere light is improved. Guide the design of intelligent car cabin atmosphere lights to develop in a more humane and more in line with consumer needs, thus improving the user experience. Through the selective use of light, the safety of driving can be enhanced, that is, while ensuring the passenger's ride experience, it can provide a more comfortable driving environment for the driver, reduce visual interference, and ensure driving safety. The score of the subjects in this experiment is still subjective, and the shortcomings will be improved in the subsequent research.

References

1. Wang, Y.: Discussion on automotive interior atmosphere lamp. In: Henan Automotive Engineering Society. Proceedings of the 15th Henan Provincial Automotive Engineering Technology Symposium, p. 2 (2018)

 2. Stylidis, K., et al.: Understanding light. A study on the perceived quality of car exterior lighting and interior illumination. Procedia CIRP **93**, 1340–1345 (2020)
 3. Qu, Y.: Consideration on the styling design of domestic automobile under the framework of kansei engineering. Design **32**(18), 96–97 (2019)
 4. Li, Y., Liang, C., Liu, X.: The perceptual engineering research present situation and the enlightenment. J. Decoration **6**, 92–95 (2016)
 5. Pakrasi, I., Chakraborty, N., LaViers, A.: A design methodology for abstracting character archetypes onto robotic systems. In: Proceedings of the 5th International Conference on Movement and Computing (MOCO 2018), Article 24, pp. 1–8 .Association for Computing Machinery, New York (2018)
 6. Wang, Y.: Research hotspot and trend analysis of domestic Kansei engineering based on citespace knowledge graph. Heilongjiang Sci. **15**(01), 55–58 (2019)
 7. Xie, X.: Color design method of subway vehicle interior based on NCS and perceptual image. Mech. Design Res. **37**(05), 159–164 (2021)
 8. Yang, D., Zhang, J., Ding, M., et al.: Color design method of aged products based on perceptual image. Mech. Des. **35**(03), 110–113 (2018)
 9. Tang, Y., Peng, L., Shen, J.: Research on scene application of design evaluation based on Kansei engineering in cultural and creative industry. Screen Printing **12**, 69–72 (2021)
10. Sheng, H., Ma, L., Li, Z., et al.: Structure design and development trend of Automotive Interior atmosphere light. Automotive Electr. Appli. (04), 63–64 (2020)
11. Li, Z.: Application technology of Optical fiber in Automotive Interior atmosphere light. Times Automobile **15**, 135–137 (2023)
12. Xu, Y.-y., Cai, H.: Research on lighting uniformity of automotive interior atmosphere lights. China Lighting Electr. Appli. (01), 13–18 (2022)
13. Wondratschek, B.: Atmosphere lights: A new element of automotive splendor. Automotive Accessories **17**, 54–55 (2022)
14. Meng, L., Xing, Y.: Research on design of bedside lamp based on Kansei engineering. Indust. Des. **06**, 49–51 (2023)
15. Li, X., Zhang, X.: Research on lower limb rehabilitation gait machine design based on Kansei engineering. Indust. Des. **12**, 81–84 (2023)
16. Zhang, H., Tian, M.: Application of reliability analysis in questionnaire design. Statist. Decision **21**, 25–27 (2007)
17. Grimm, M.: Requirements for an ambient interior lighting system for motor vehicles. Utz, Wiss (2003)

Gesture-Based Machine Learning for Enhanced Autonomous Driving: A Novel Dataset and System Integration Approach

Sven Milde[✉], Stefan Friesen, Tabea Runzheimer, Carlos Beilstein,
Rainer Blum, and Jan-Torsten Milde

Department of Applied Computer Science, Fulda University of Applied Sciences,
Fulda 36037, Germany
{sven.milde,stefan.friesen,tabea.runzheimer,carlos.beilstein,
rainer.blum,jan-torsten.milde}@cs.hs-fulda.de

Abstract. This paper describes a new multi-modal dataset for human pose recognition and its use for gesture interaction with autonomous driving vehicles for the purpose of fine positioning them. The dataset consists of 422,036 images grouped into 6 classes representing typical poses for giving instructions to robot vehicles. For each image RGB data, depth data and skeletal data was collected with multi-modal data fusion in mind. It should be emphasised that the entire data set was recorded by a single person, bearing in mind that the combination with depth and skeletal data may mask physical and ethnic characteristics of the subject. For evaluation of the dataset a ResNet101 was used to perform a t-SNE analysis as well as some hidden layers were used from the network to perform a cosine similarity calculation to find duplicates in our dataset.

Keywords: Pose recognition · Dataset · Multi-modal Data

1 Introduction

This paper describes the work for creating a new multi-modal dataset containing poses for fine positioning of the so-called CityBot vehicle. The project our work is part of involves the development of the CityBot, an automated driving robot vehicle with modular extensions for specific use cases. The CityBot can perform multiple everyday tasks (e.g. transport of passengers or collection of waste) and get to desired destinations automated. Changing the modular extensions in the so-called maintenance area requires fine positioning (e.g. to be able to attach the passenger trailer) which the CityBot might lack even if the CityBot uses a different sensors for localisation. Therefore there needs to be an option for the CityBot to be controlled manually. In the vision of implementing a CityBot fleet for a domain like a city quarter or an airport it is recommended, that this manual controlling is possible without additional devices, apart from the

C. Stephanidis et al. (Eds.): HCII 2024, CCIS 2118, pp. 247–256, 2024.
https://doi.org/10.1007/978-3-031-61963-2_24

CityBot's internal devices. Since gestures are a frequently used method in traffic, it makes sense to use them for fine positioning.

In our previous work [24], two studies were conducted to take a deeper look at gestures that are intuitively used by test persons for given tasks inside of a virtual reality environment. To achieve this, the test persons had to define a couple of gestures themselves to use with the CityBot without giving them detailed sample gestures. They were asked to perform a fine positioning task (e.g. navigate the CityBot to a parking slot) with the CityBot afterwards, using the gestures, they just defined. From this, a set of gestures was selected for controlling the CityBot and taken as the template to create a dataset for a machine learning model.

2   Related Work

Detecting gestures for the purpose of interaction with automated driving vehicles is part of human-robot interface area. A range of studies exist looking at different topics on communicating with automated driving vehicles. Faber et al. [11] looks at different problems that may occur communicating with a vehicle. He concluded that a vehicle needs context knowledge to interpret communication in traffic situations in a correct way. Chivarov et al. [7] investigated different aspects of human-robot interfaces for mobile robots whereas Chang et al. [6] first has a special interest in using eyes as part of the human-robot interface and later [5] has a look at different visual components that can be used as part of the user interface.

Automated driving vehicles need a user interface capable of different modalities. For this reason we took a deeper look at the research with different modalities and multi-modality. Dumas et al. [8] made a review on principles, models and frameworks for creating multi-modal interfaces. Salem et al. [34] investigate a natural way to communicate with a robot. He concludes, that gestures are best suited, but multi-modality should be preferred. In the work of Higham et al. [14] the multi-modal communication of animals is analysed and references are made to human communication. Speech and gestures are typical elements in multi-modal user interfaces, but there are also approaches using additional devices to include more modalities (e.g. an ultra wide band sensor, a time of flight sensor) [1,12,16,28,35,46].

Wang et al. and Mitra et al. [25,43] both made reviews on the topic of human-robot interfaces to get an overview of the actual state of the art. Popov et al. [31] describe gesture recognition and classification can happen in a general way. Ma et al. [22] focused on gestures for automated driving vehicles in case of traffic police command detection. These gesture are also instructing the vehicle in which way it has to move or stop.

To be able to detect and classify gestures with machine learning models fairly large datasets for training are needed. Ruffieux et al. [33] did a survey to collect different datasets and their metadata to compare them and to give a key-access point for researchers for creating their own datasets. Schak and Gepperth [37,38] conducted a survey on existing gesture datasets and created their own dataset.

For collecting the data they used a RGB-D camera and an additional motion sensor attached to the hand to get multi-modal data. Lucking et al. [19,20] also created a new gesture dataset combined with speech therefore multi-modal data. Also Escalera et al. [9] created a large dataset combining gestures and speech for multi-modality and Zhang et al. [45] created a dataset with an egocentric view on the gestures instead of third-person view. Cadoni et al. focused on traps that may appear if gestures are created in a user centered design process (e.g. gestures that are too simily to each other to be detected by machine learning models) whereas Muller et al. [27] focused on identifying mislabed instances in their dataset.

For recognition of gestures in multi-modal data streams different machine learning models are used. Long short-term models are used to learn time dependent information of videos [18,36,44]. An alternative are 3D convolutional neural networks, where the third dimension is used to depict the time dependency of the data [17,26,40,41]. There are also other approaches in the literature like using a convexity approach [3], product manifolds [21] and a K-Ary tree hashing classifier [2] as well as recurrent and temporal convolution [29], key frame extraction [39] and local descriptors for action recognition [4]. For evaluating the models Pisharady et al. [30] designed a new gesture recognition performance score and Wang et al. [42] checked local spatio-temporal features to evaluate action recognition. Yang et al. [10] mentioned a new form of network for action recognition which is faster, smaller and better than frequently used models.

During the reported here, two problems were found for detecting gestures. The first problem is the time needed to perform a certain gesture. In a random situation it might not always be the same. Therefore, the input data for our machine learning algorithm differs in size and the exact dimensions are unknown. The second problem is to determine the beginning of a gesture, which needs to be found in a multi-modal data stream. Different solutions to these problems can be found in existing research, but are is most cases achieved by reducing the frame rate significantly. For these reasons, gestures will be detected via poses identifiable from single frames in this work.

3   Dataset

The dataset actually consists of 422036 elements recorded by one well instructed person. With this approach the conducted poses are performed correctly and consistently over the dataset. In addition this leads to small variability of each pose class. Every pose image is extracted from a video recording a gesture performed by one person. The data is recorded using the ZED 2i camera and the ZED API saving the data with all sensor information in one file.

3.1   Setup

For capturing the sequences a fixed setup was used ensuring the same distance and position of the camera. The person recording the sequences had a marked area on the ground, so the setup for each run was the same. In every run the person repeated the same gesture for thirty seconds, then changing to the next gesture. For some variability all gestures are recorded respectively with each single hand and with both hands together. To impede monotony the person did not record all these three ways of one gesture one after the other, but rotated between the used hand and the gestures. After about 60 h of recording the different data types were extracted as described in Sects. 3.3 to 3.5.

3.2   Gesture Classes

The dataset consists of six classes for moving the CityBot in different directions.

- **Forward** The first class is a forward gesture to make the CityBot move forward. Using one or both hands facing the palm to the body with the fingers *pointing to the sky* and repeatedly moving the hands to the body.
- **Backward** The second class is a backward gesture to make the CityBot move backward. Using one or both hands facing the palm to the body with the fingers *pointing to the ground* and repeatedly moving the hands away from the body.
- **Turn left** The third class is a gesture to make the CityBot turn to its left side. Using the right arm and lift it on the side of your body until it is nearly parallel to the ground. Additionally the left arm can be used in front of the body, moving to the same direction.
- **Turn right** The fourth class is a gesture to make the CityBot turn to its right side. Use the left arm and lift it on the side of your body until it is nearly parallel to the ground. Additionally the right arm can be used in front of the body, moving to the same direction.
- **Stop** The fifth class is a more static class to make the CityBot stop any movement. Use one or both hand facing the palm away from the body with the arms stretched out in front of the body.
- **Nothing** The sixth class is needed for training the model and contains different body poses showing none of the other classes.

In Fig. 1 the distribution of the different classes in the dataset is shown.

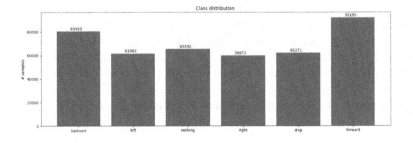

Fig. 1. Distribution of the classes in the dataset

3.3   RGB Data

To get the RGB data the video stream was processed from the ZED 2i stereo-scopic camera and extracted the left images in Full HD. After that the images were cropped to the middle part where the person is depicted to 213×240 pixels. During the machine learning task some image data augmentation is applied randomly to the images. Translation, scaling, rotation and shearing is applied in small units. Also the images are resized to 150×150 pixels to be loaded to tensors.

3.4   Depth Data

To record the depth data the ZED API was used to calculate the images depending on the two video streams from the camera. Left and right images are calculated depending on the calibration of the camera to get depth images. The depth images are also Full HD and cropped to 213×240 pixels per image. During loading of the data some image data augmentation is applied like mentioned in Sect. 3.3.

3.5   Skeletal Data

The skeletal-data is extracted from the recordings using a machine learning model integrated in the ZED API. With the model 34 body joints are extracted each containing nine values. Three values for the position of the body joint in the world with respect to the camera. Four values for a Quaternion describing the rotation of the body joint with respect to the camera and two values describing the two-dimensional position of the body joint in the picture with respect to the left camera image. Of these body joints only 22 body joints containing to the upper body are used for further work. The lower body is not important for the poses because only arms and hands are used

3.6   Annotation

Due to the process of the recording each run of the recordings contains multiple classes of gestures. To be able to use supervised machine learning algorithms the data needed to be annotated. This was done manually by sorting the single images.

4   Evaluation

To check the accuracy of the annotated data two methods where applied on the dataset. First a ResNet101 [13] was used where the last layer was extracted to be able to use the features from the model. With these features a t-SNE algorithm [15,23] was used to be able to visualize the dependencies between the data like shown in Fig. 2. It can be seen that some gestures are well separated from the others whereas some gestures are totally mixed up. Turning left and right are well separated even though there are multiple subareas. Gestures like forward, stop and backward where the hands are in front of the body may be a problem in detection because the differences in the features are too small for a good differentiation.

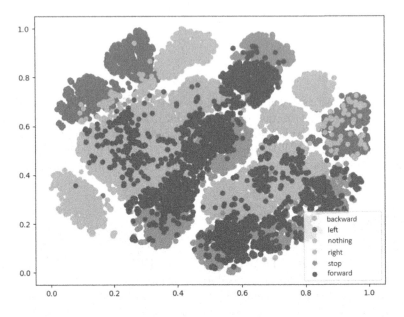

Fig. 2. Class distribution using t-SNE [15,23] algorithm with last layer of ResNet101 network [13]

Due to the high frame rate in the videos, some images might be duplicates of each other. For this the work of Rahutomo et al. [32] was used. The ResNet101 was used to extract features from an early layer of the model to reduce the complexity of the input images. With these features the cosine similarity between all images is calculated to show which images are equal. A threshold of 0.98 was used to eliminate the duplicates.

5   Conclusion and Future Work

In this paper a new multi-modal dataset is provided for gesture recognition containing 422,036 images. The dataset consists of RGB images, depth-images and skeletal data of the upper body of the person in the images. The dataset can be used to create machine learning models able to identify gestures, intended in this research to instruct automated driving vehicles. In a first step a t-SNE algorithm was used to visualize the class dependencies of the images. Also the cosine similarity was applied to find duplicates in the data caused by the high frame rate in the video.

As future work the annotation of the dataset needs to be finished, because actually only 75% are annotated. When annotation is finished the t-SNE visualisation must be done again as well as the cosine similarity to find duplicates. Additionally the work of Müller et al. [27] must be used to find mislabeled data. With the finished dataset different machine learning models should be trained for gesture recognition and classification to find the best suited one for the task. For the learning procedere also the question of data fusion needs to be answered, if early, late or a hybrid way might be the best for accuracy.

Acknowledgments. This work is part of the Campus FreeCity project, which is funded with a total of 10.9 million euros by the German Federal Ministry for Digital and Transport (BMDV).

References

1. Ahmed, S., Wang, D., Park, J., Cho, S.H.: Uwb-gestures, a public dataset of dynamic hand gestures acquired using impulse radar sensors. Sci. Data **8**(1), 1–9 (2021)
2. Ansar, H., Ksibi, A., Jalal, A., Shorfuzzaman, M., Alsufyani, A., Alsuhibany, S.A., Park, J.: Dynamic hand gesture recognition for smart lifecare routines via k-ary tree hashing classifier. Appl. Sci. **12**(13), 6481 (2022)
3. Barros, P., Maciel-Junior, N.T., Fernandes, B.J., Bezerra, B.L., Fernandes, S.M.: A dynamic gesture recognition and prediction system using the convexity approach. Comput. Vis. Image Underst. **155**, 139–149 (2017)
4. Bilinski, P., Bremond, F.: Evaluation of local descriptors for action recognition in videos. In: Crowley, J.L., Draper, B.A., Thonnat, M. (eds.) ICVS 2011. LNCS, vol. 6962, pp. 61–70. Springer, Heidelberg (2011). https://doi.org/10.1007/978-3-642-23968-7_7
5. Chang, C.M., Toda, K., Igarashi, T., Miyata, M., Kobayashi, Y.: A video-based study comparing communication modalities between an autonomous car and a pedestrian. In: Adjunct Proceedings of the 10th International Conference on Automotive User Interfaces and Interactive Vehicular Applications, pp. 104–109 (2018)
6. Chang, C.M., Toda, K., Sakamoto, D., Igarashi, T.: Eyes on a car: an interface design for communication between an autonomous car and a pedestrian. In: Proceedings of the 9th International Conference on Automotive User Interfaces and Interactive Vehicular Applications, pp. 65–73 (2017)
7. Chivarov, N., Chikurtev, D., Pleva, M., Ondas, S.: Exploring human-robot interfaces for service mobile robots. In: 2018 World Symposium on Digital Intelligence for Systems and Machines (DISA), pp. 337–342. IEEE (2018)
8. Dumas, B., Lalanne, D., Oviatt, S.: Multimodal interfaces: a survey of principles, models and frameworks. In: Lalanne, D., Kohlas, J. (eds.) Human Machine Interaction. LNCS, vol. 5440, pp. 3–26. Springer, Heidelberg (2009). https://doi.org/10.1007/978-3-642-00437-7_1
9. Escalera, S., et al.: ChaLearn looking at people challenge 2014: dataset and results. In: Agapito, L., Bronstein, M.M., Rother, C. (eds.) ECCV 2014. LNCS, vol. 8925, pp. 459–473. Springer, Cham (2015). https://doi.org/10.1007/978-3-319-16178-5_32

10. Yang, F., Sakriani Sakti, Y.W., Nakamura, S.: Make skeleton-based action recognition model smaller, faster and better. In: ACM International Conference on Multimedia in Asia (2019)
11. Färber, B.: Kommunikationsprobleme zwischen autonomen fahrzeugen und menschlichen fahrern. In: Autonomes Fahren, pp. 127–146. Springer Vieweg, Berlin, Heidelberg (2015)
12. Gu, Y., Do, H., Ou, Y., Sheng, W.: Human gesture recognition through a kinect sensor. In: 2012 IEEE International Conference on Robotics and Biomimetics (ROBIO), pp. 1379–1384. IEEE (2012)
13. He, K., Zhang, X., Ren, S., Sun, J.: Deep residual learning for image recognition. In: Proceedings of the IEEE Conference on Computer Vision and Pattern Recognition, pp. 770–778 (2016)
14. Higham, J.P., Hebets, E.A.: An introduction to multimodal communication. Behav. Ecol. Sociobiol. **67**(9), 1381–1388 (2013)
15. Hinton, G.E., Roweis, S.: Stochastic neighbor embedding. Adv. Neural Inform. Process. Syst. **15** (2002)
16. Jiang, S., Sun, B., Wang, L., Bai, Y., Li, K., Fu, Y.: Skeleton aware multi-modal sign language recognition. In: Proceedings of the IEEE/CVF Conference on Computer Vision and Pattern Recognition, pp. 3413–3423 (2021)
17. Köpüklü, O., Gunduz, A., Kose, N., Rigoll, G.: Real-time hand gesture detection and classification using convolutional neural networks. In: 2019 14th IEEE International Conference on Automatic Face & Gesture Recognition (FG 2019), pp. 1–8. IEEE (2019)
18. Lefebvre, G., Berlemont, S., Mamalet, F., Garcia, C.: BLSTM-RNN based 3D gesture classification. In: Mladenov, V., Koprinkova-Hristova, P., Palm, G., Villa, A.E.P., Appollini, B., Kasabov, N. (eds.) ICANN 2013. LNCS, vol. 8131, pp. 381–388. Springer, Heidelberg (2013). https://doi.org/10.1007/978-3-642-40728-4_48
19. Lücking, A., Bergman, K., Hahn, F., Kopp, S., Rieser, H.: Data-based analysis of speech and gesture: the bielefeld speech and gesture alignment corpus (saga) and its applications. J. Multimodal User Interfaces **7**(1), 5–18 (2013)
20. Lücking, A., Bergmann, K., Hahn, F., Kopp, S., Rieser, H.: The bielefeld speech and gesture alignment corpus (saga). In: LREC 2010 workshop: Multimodal Corpora–advances in Capturing, Coding and Analyzing Multimodality (2010)
21. Lui, Y.M.: Human gesture recognition on product manifolds. J. Mach. Learn. Res. **13**(1), 3297–3321 (2012)
22. Ma, C., Zhang, Y., Wang, A., Wang, Y., Chen, G.: Traffic command gesture recognition for virtual urban scenes based on a spatiotemporal convolution neural network. ISPRS Int. J. Geo Inf. **7**(1), 37 (2018)
23. Van der Maaten, L., Hinton, G.: Visualizing data using t-sne. J. Mach. Learn. Res. **9**(11) (2008)
24. Milde, S., et al.: Studying multi-modal human robot interaction using a mobile vr simulation. In: International Conference on Human-Computer Interaction, pp. 140–155. Springer (2023). https://doi.org/10.1007/978-3-031-35602-5_11
25. Mitra, S., Acharya, T.: Gesture recognition: a survey. IEEE Trans. Syst. Man Cybernet. Part C (Appli. Rev.) **37**(3), 311–324 (2007)
26. Molchanov, P., Yang, X., Gupta, S., Kim, K., Tyree, S., Kautz, J.: Online detection and classification of dynamic hand gestures with recurrent 3d convolutional neural network. In: Proceedings of the IEEE Conference on Computer Vision and Pattern Recognition, pp. 4207–4215 (2016)

27. Müller, N.M., Markert, K.: Identifying mislabeled instances in classification datasets. In: 2019 International Joint Conference on Neural Networks (IJCNN), pp. 1–8. IEEE (2019)
28. Patsadu, O., Nukoolkit, C., Watanapa, B.: Human gesture recognition using kinect camera. In: 2012 Ninth International Conference On Computer Science and Software Engineering (JCSSE), pp. 28–32. IEEE (2012)
29. Pigou, L., Van Den Oord, A., Dieleman, S., Van Herreweghe, M., Dambre, J.: Beyond temporal pooling: recurrence and temporal convolutions for gesture recognition in video. Int. J. Comput. Vision **126**(2), 430–439 (2018)
30. Pisharady, P.K., Saerbeck, M.: Gesture recognition performance score: a new metric to evaluate gesture recognition systems. In: Jawahar, C.V., Shan, S. (eds.) ACCV 2014. LNCS, vol. 9008, pp. 157–173. Springer, Cham (2015). https://doi.org/10.1007/978-3-319-16628-5_12
31. Popov, P.A., Laganière, R.: Long hands gesture recognition system: 2 step gesture recognition with machine learning and geometric shape analysis. Multimedia Tools Appli., 1–32 (2022)
32. Rahutomo, F., Kitasuka, T., Aritsugi, M.: Semantic cosine similarity. In: The 7th International Student Conference on Advanced Science and Technology ICAST, vol. 4, p. 1 (2012)
33. Ruffieux, S., Lalanne, D., Mugellini, E., Abou Khaled, O.: A survey of datasets for human gesture recognition. In: Kurosu, M. (ed.) HCI 2014. LNCS, vol. 8511, pp. 337–348. Springer, Cham (2014). https://doi.org/10.1007/978-3-319-07230-2_33
34. Salem, M., Kopp, S., Wachsmuth, I., Rohlfing, K., Joublin, F.: Generation and evaluation of communicative robot gesture. Int. J. Soc. Robot. **4**(2), 201–217 (2012)
35. Sarkar, A., Gepperth, A., Handmann, U., Kopinski, T.: Dynamic hand gesture recognition for mobile systems using deep LSTM. In: Horain, P., Achard, C., Mallem, M. (eds.) IHCI 2017. LNCS, vol. 10688, pp. 19–31. Springer, Cham (2017). https://doi.org/10.1007/978-3-319-72038-8_3
36. Schak, M., Gepperth, A.: Robustness of deep LSTM networks in freehand gesture recognition. In: Tetko, I.V., Kůrková, V., Karpov, P., Theis, F. (eds.) ICANN 2019. LNCS, vol. 11729, pp. 330–343. Springer, Cham (2019). https://doi.org/10.1007/978-3-030-30508-6_27
37. Schak, M., Gepperth, A.: Gesture mnist: a new free-hand gesture dataset. In: International Conference on Artificial Neural Networks, pp. 657–668. Springer (2022). https://doi.org/10.1007/978-3-031-15937-4_55
38. Schak, M., Gepperth, A.: Gesture recognition on a new multi-modal hand gesture dataset. In: ICPRAM, pp. 122–131 (2022)
39. Tang, H., Liu, H., Xiao, W., Sebe, N.: Fast and robust dynamic hand gesture recognition via key frames extraction and feature fusion. Neurocomputing **331**, 424–433 (2019)
40. Tran, D.S., Ho, N.H., Yang, H.J., Baek, E.T., Kim, S.H., Lee, G.: Real-time hand gesture spotting and recognition using rgb-d camera and 3d convolutional neural network. Appl. Sci. **10**(2), 722 (2020)
41. Vaswani, A., et al.: Attention is all you need. Adv. Neural Inform. Process. Syst. **30** (2017)
42. Wang, H., Ullah, M.M., Klaser, A., Laptev, I., Schmid, C.: Evaluation of local spatio-temporal features for action recognition. In: Bmvc 2009-British Machine Vision Conference, pp. 124–1. BMVA Press (2009)
43. Wang, W., Zhang, Y.D.: A short survey on deep learning for skeleton-based action recognition. In: Proceedings of the 14th IEEE/ACM International Conference on Utility and Cloud Computing Companion. pp. 1–6 (2021)

44. Yuanyuan, S., Yunan, L., Xiaolong, F., Kaibin, M., Qiguang, M.: Review of dynamic gesture recognition. Virt. Real. Intell. Hardware **3**(3), 183–206 (2021)
45. Zhang, Y., Cao, C., Cheng, J., Lu, H.: Egogesture: a new dataset and benchmark for egocentric hand gesture recognition. IEEE Trans. Multimedia **20**(5), 1038–1050 (2018)
46. Zhao, X., Li, X., Pang, C., Zhu, X., Sheng, Q.Z.: Online human gesture recognition from motion data streams. In: Proceedings of the 21st ACM International Conference on Multimedia, pp. 23–32 (2013)

Towards Sustainable Mobility - Public Acceptance of Automated Last-Mile Deliveries

Virpi Oksman$^{(\boxtimes)}$ ⓘ and Minna Kulju ⓘ

VTT Technical Research Centre of Finland, Tampere, Finland
`virpi.oksman@vtt.fi`

Abstract. This paper examines the significance of public acceptance in the integration of automated last-mile delivery technologies, such as drones and delivery robots. To evaluate the public perception of automated last-mile deliveries, an online survey was conducted in Finland, comprising of 500 respondents. The findings of the survey revealed that the respondents displayed positive or neutral attitudes toward automated last-mile deliveries, emphasizing the advantages of affordability, efficiency, delivery tracking, and environmental sustainability. Notably, nearly half of the respondents expressed the importance of environmental friendliness in deliveries facilitated by drones or delivery robots. Overall, the respondents exhibited a predominantly positive or neutral attitude toward the proliferation of automated deliveries in their residential areas. In the specific Nordic context, drones were found to be slightly more favored than delivery robots although individuals residing in city centers or inner cities displayed lower inclination to utilize drone services compared to respondents residing in suburban or sparsely populated areas. The respondents indicated a preference for using delivery robots or drones primarily for home delivery of meals and grocery shopping. The study also underscores the necessity for intuitive designs and the consideration of privacy concerns in future research endeavors. Moreover, the paper elucidates the implications of HCI theoretical frameworks employed to comprehend users' acceptance.

Keywords: Drones · delivery robots · public acceptance · trust · survey

1 Introduction

The rapid advancement of technology has revolutionized various aspects of our lives, including the way goods are delivered to our doorsteps. Various technological solutions have emerged to address the logistical challenges of modern society, such as emissions, congestion, and the need for speedy delivery. One such technological development is the use of drones and delivery robots for various purposes, including last-mile delivery services [1–3]. As technology continues to advance, the potential for fully automated delivery systems becomes increasingly feasible. Yet, the successful implementation of such systems heavily relies on public and social acceptance. The acceptance and adoption of these technologies by users are crucial for their successful integration into society.

© The Author(s), under exclusive license to Springer Nature Switzerland AG 2024
C. Stephanidis et al. (Eds.): HCII 2024, CCIS 2118, pp. 257–266, 2024.
https://doi.org/10.1007/978-3-031-61963-2_25

Large cities and urbanized countries are particularly interested in exploring these technologies due to the challenges they face in traditional delivery methods [3]. These challenges include traffic congestion, limited parking spaces, and the rising demand for faster and more efficient delivery services. Automated last-mile delivery systems have the potential to alleviate these issues by bypassing congested road networks and delivering goods directly to customers' doorsteps [3]. Moreover, in locations, where traditional delivery methods may be less efficient or inaccessible in remote areas or islands, the acceptance of drones is less researched although they may offer several benefits for the users. The acceptance of such systems is heavily influenced by the context in which they are employed. For instance, the public in numerous countries exhibits the highest degree of willingness to embrace drone technology when it is utilized for health and welfare purposes, such as emergency medical services [4, 5]. Moreover, Nordic countries perceive the primary advantage of these systems as improved accessibility in harsh weather particularly in remote and hard-to-reach areas like islands [6]. Understanding these local and cultural nuances is crucial for industry stakeholders and policymakers to tailor their strategies and foster public acceptance.

The concept of using drones and delivery robots for last-mile delivery is gaining traction globally. Both drones and automated delivery robots offer unique advantages and face specific limitations in the context of last-mile delivery. On the one hand, drones excel in overcoming geographical barriers and reducing delivery time, but their payload capacity and susceptibility to various weather conditions remain challenges. On the other hand, automated delivery robots demonstrate versatility in handling larger packages than drones and navigating various terrains but require careful consideration of safety and battery limitations.

Previous research has primarily focused on the reception of a single automated last-mile delivery system in large cities and highly urbanized nations [3, 7–11]. Many studies on public acceptance of delivery robots have been conducted in countries with high population density due to health factors and strict distancing measures during the pandemic [1, 2]. These studies have provided insights into the factors that influence users' acceptance of drones or delivery robots, such as perceived usefulness, perceived ease of use, trust, privacy concerns, and user experience [7]. However, there still exists a research gap regarding the public perception of diverse contexts and across different demographics. Furthermore, further investigation is warranted to ascertain individuals' preferences for specific automated solutions under varying circumstances and locations, should they be provided with the opportunity to choose.

This paper studies the public acceptance of automated last-mile delivery systems, focusing on drones and delivery robots, and sheds light on perceived benefits, trust, and concerns associated with both delivery methods in different use contexts and by different users. Various theoretical frameworks are used as a basis to understand public acceptance and they are often based on Technology Acceptance Model (TAM) [12]. However, the traditional TAM model necessitates augmentation with additional frameworks and concepts, such as trust theory [13], and sustainable design theory [14]. In the era of automation, trust has emerged as a significant concept that characterizes human-technology interaction and especially AI-powered transportation, trust is a critical aspect of adoption and acceptance [15]. Furthermore, sustainability design theory enhances our comprehension of the transformation of human behavior and technological products toward a more ecological approach. Altogether, these theoretical concepts offer new insights into users' acceptance of drones and delivery robots.

The structure of this paper is as follows: In the next section, a theoretical framework for understanding public acceptance of automated delivery systems will be described. The subsequent section will introduce our methodology and survey results will be presented. Following that, the findings will be summarized and discussed, and conclusions will be drawn.

2 Theoretical Frameworks for Understanding Public Acceptance

Understanding public acceptance of drones is crucial for harnessing the full potential of this technology while addressing the concerns and challenges it presents. Some theoretical frameworks provide valuable tools for analyzing and comprehending the complex social dynamics that influence public attitudes and behaviors toward drones and delivery robots.

The Technology Acceptance Model (TAM) is widely utilized as a basis for a theoretical framework within the field of Human-Computer Interaction (HCI) research to elucidate the factors influencing users' acceptance and adoption of novel technologies. It posits that users' intention to utilize technology is contingent upon two primary determinants: perceived usefulness and perceived ease of use [12]. In principle, in the context of this particular study, TAM can be employed to comprehend users' acceptance of drones and delivery robots through an examination of perceived usefulness, encompassing aspects such as convenience, efficiency, and feasibility for the intended purpose. TAM also highlights perceived ease of use, addressing user-friendly interfaces and intuitive controls. However, it is important to note that in the present stage of our research, perceived ease of use was not incorporated due to the absence of actual use demonstrations in the study. Furthermore, we anticipated that most respondents still lacked prior experience with the user interfaces of drones or automated delivery robots, thereby rendering them unable to evaluate the actual user experience.

Moreover, trust theory can be applied to explore the factors that influence individuals' trust in technology. Trust is a cognitive and behavioral perception that has been empirically demonstrated to positively influence consumers' inclination to adopt a particular technology. Traditionally, it can be conceptualized as the confidence an individual has in the responsible conduct of the other party involved, coupled with the expectation that the party will refrain from capitalizing on the user's vulnerabilities [13]. In the context of this study, trust theory can be used to examine users' trust in drones and delivery robots, including factors such as the reliability of the deliveries, safety aspects, privacy, and other concerns. Understanding users' trust is particularly imperative to acknowledge associated with AI-powered automated technologies, as users often express apprehensions about trust in such non-human-actor systems. Respectively, trust significantly influences users' willingness to adopt and engage with these technologies [16].

In addition, sustainable design theory explains how technologies can be designed to minimize negative environmental impacts and promote sustainability [14]. In our study, sustainable design theory can be applied to examine users' attitudes and preferences towards drones and delivery robots as environmentally friendly delivery options. This can include factors such as whether the users perceive sustainability as an important factor when they are choosing delivery options and perceptions of ecological benefits, and potential environmental concerns associated with these technologies.

3   Methodology

Online Survey Conducted in Finland and the Study Participants. An online survey in the Northern part of Finland was conducted to study the public perception of automated last-mile deliveries. In this study, two automated delivery options as a part of home delivery of various purchases such as groceries and prepared meals were defined and compared: delivery robots operating on roadsides and sidewalks, and drones flying in lower U-Space. The TAM-based assessments of public perception were conducted to gain an understanding of perceived benefits. Trust theory-based estimations were included in question considering the user concerns and the trust for the technology being able to perform delivery tasks and being safe also for bystanders such as pedestrians. The sustainable design theory approach was applied to questions regarding how important the users perceive the sustainability of these new systems and what kind of ecological impacts they associate them with. The multiple-choice questions used a 5-point Likert scale (Totally agree – Totally disagree). With the open-ended questions in the questionnaire, we aimed to gain an understanding of the reasons behind related concerns, perceived benefits, and preferred uses. The survey included an exclusive question of whether respondents had ever ordered purchases from an online store. If they had not ordered and were not interested in the future to do so, they were excluded from the survey. In total, there were 31 excluded respondents.

Altogether there were 500 respondents to the online survey of which 51% were female and 48% male. The majority (93%) lived in urban or suburban areas, while about 7% lived in sparsely populated areas. The respondents were quite evenly from all age groups, from 18 to 84-year-olds, although there was a clear minority of people over 75 years old. Well over half (70%) of the respondents lived alone or with a spouse, and about a quarter of them were families with children.

4   Results

4.1   Assessment of Automated Last-Mile Deliveries

The survey results revealed that respondents had a generally positive or neutral attitude towards the increase in automated deliveries in their residential area. Specifically, 15% expressed a very positive view, while 39% were rather positive and 39% remained neutral. Notably, factors such as gender, age, or residential area did not significantly impact this overall attitude. Drones were slightly more favored for deliveries than delivery robots (36.2% vs. 34.6%), although respondents residing in a city center or inner city were slightly less likely to use drone services than respondents living in suburban or sparsely populated areas. In addition, respondents in the age group 35–44 had a higher likelihood of using last-mile delivery solutions, especially when compared to respondents over the age of 65.

The respondents expressed an intention to use delivery robots or drones primarily for home delivery of meals and grocery shopping of food. Conversely, they were less likely to use these automated last-mile deliveries for delivering baby accessories or toys together with decoration accessories and dishes. When comparing the residential area and the intention to use delivery robots and drones for delivering specified items, it seems that there is no big difference between different areas. Instead, the younger age groups (18–24 and 25–34) would be more likely to use delivery robots or drone deliveries, especially for food deliveries from grocery shops or restaurants. However, in open-ended responses, it was also suggested that *"Shopping with a transport robot would be a really positive thing for older people as well."*

The respondents perceived the punctual deliveries, the possibility to select the most suitable delivery time, delivery to the door, together with the speed of the delivery as meaningful features of the automated deliveries. These were benefits for over half of the respondents (Fig. 1.). According to open-ended responses, automated solutions were expected to be *"Much more flexible when it comes to choosing the delivery time"*. Moreover, the respondents expected that automated transport will benefit users with faster and more affordable transport methods than currently available.

Additionally, nearly half of the respondents perceived environmental friendliness as an advantage in deliveries facilitated by drones or delivery robots. For all respondents, the environmental friendliness of these novel last-mile deliveries seems to be more important compared to traditional deliveries. In addition, environmental friendliness was significantly more important for female respondents than male respondents. Approximately 55% of female respondents expressed that last-mile deliveries should be environmentally friendly, whereas 39% of male respondents shared this view. Instead, respondents' residential areas (urban, suburban, or rural) did not exert a substantial influence on their opinions regarding the importance of environmental friendliness. However, it seems that environmental friendliness is slightly more important for respondents under 35 years than for others (52% vs. 45%).

4.2   Concerns Related to Drones and Delivery Robots

The concerns of respondents regarding automated last-mile deliveries were investigated in the study. Figure 2 below presents respondents' perceptions of different concerns related to delivery robots and drones. Delivery falling into the wrong hands emerged as the most significant concern among respondents, particularly in the context of delivery robots. Also, in open-ended questions some respondents expressed apprehension that packages might be stolen during the last-mile delivery process: *"My residential area is the so-called restless, so I would worry about thieves and vandalism. Otherwise, robot delivery would be great!"*.

In addition, privacy and safety were specific concerns for some respondents. They worried about potential collisions between delivery robots or drones and pedestrians and cars on the street or buildings along the delivery route: *"A small delivery robot on the*

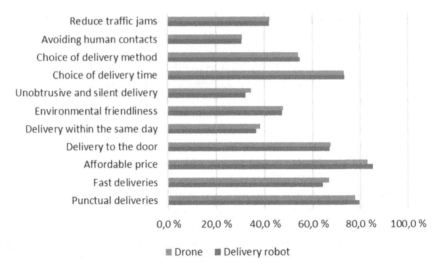

Fig. 1. Perceived benefits: a comparison between drones and delivery robots.

street can be a traffic risk for cars in the detached house area (on narrow roads, lots of parking). The slushy weather of winter is a problem."

Nevertheless, respondents were less troubled by noise or visual disturbances caused by these automated systems. Additionally, they expressed concern about the local environment. Specifically, they worried that automated last-mile deliveries, especially drone deliveries, could harm small animals like birds and insects.

Based on the survey results it seems that female respondents exhibited slightly higher levels of concern regarding environmental, safety, and privacy issues related to automated last-mile deliveries. In addition, respondents in the youngest age group, 18–24, appeared less concerned than other age groups. Instead, the place of residence had minimal impact on respondents' concerns being consistent across different residential areas. However, the data suggests that individuals residing in rural areas expressed a slightly higher level of concern regarding privacy infringements associated with drones, in contrast to delivery robots. Specifically, approximately 38% of respondents from rural areas expressed being very concerned about their privacy with drones. In comparison, among suburban and urban respondents, these figures stood at 31% and 28%, respectively. In the case of delivery robots, the number of respondents being very concerned about their privacy in rural areas was 35%, in suburban areas 27%, and in urban areas 29%. One participant explained in open-ended section: *"I oppose them. Let them drive in city centers if someone wants them. I want to be free, especially of the drones."*

4.3 Technology Trust and Safety Concerns

The study explored respondents' perceptions of technology trust and safety concerning automated last-mile deliveries. Figure 3 illustrates that overall respondents were quite confident about their safety. Notably, their trust was slightly higher in the case of delivery robots. Respondents highlighted weather conditions as a potential hazard for

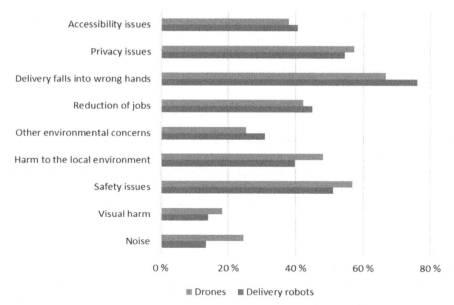

Fig. 2. Number of respondents who were concerned or very concerned about different issues related to delivery robots or drones.

both delivery robots and drones. Furthermore, concerning drones, there was a prevailing worry that increased adoption of drone deliveries might lead to collisions between drones themselves.

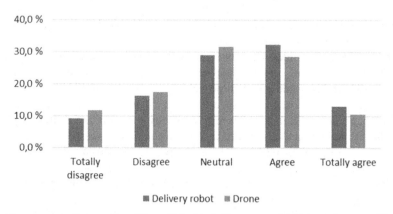

Fig. 3. Responses to the question: "I would feel safe if automated delivery robots would operate along roadsides and sidewalks or automated drones were flying overhead."

Significant gender differences emerged in safety concerns related to automated last-mile deliveries. Female respondents exhibited notably higher levels of apprehension, particularly regarding drones, but also to some extent with delivery robots. Almost 36%

of female respondents disagreed with the statement "I would feel safe if automated drones were flying overhead". In contrast, 22% of male respondents expressed disagreement with the same statement. However, the respondent's age or place of residence did not significantly influence safety concerns.

5 Discussion

The findings of this study provide insights into the public acceptance of automated last-mile deliveries, specifically focusing on drones and delivery robots. Overall, the respondents displayed positive or neutral attitudes toward automated last-mile deliveries, emphasizing the advantages of affordability, efficiency, delivery tracking, and environmental sustainability. These findings align with previous research that has highlighted the potential benefits of automated delivery systems, such as reducing traffic congestion, improving delivery efficiency, and minimizing carbon emissions. [1–3] The positive attitudes toward affordability and efficiency indicate that respondents recognize the potential cost savings and time benefits associated with automated deliveries. This is particularly important in urban areas where traffic congestion and limited parking spaces pose challenges for traditional delivery methods. The respondents' emphasis on delivery tracking suggests that they value transparency and visibility in the delivery process, which can help build trust and confidence in automated systems.

Notably, nearly half of the respondents expressed the importance of environmental friendliness in deliveries facilitated by drones or delivery robots. This finding highlights the growing awareness and concern for sustainability in last-mile deliveries. The use of drones and delivery robots has the potential to reduce carbon emissions and contribute to a more environmentally friendly transportation system. This aligns with sustainable design theory, which emphasizes the importance of minimizing negative environmental impacts and promoting sustainability [14]. It is encouraging to see that the public recognizes and values the environmental benefits of automated deliveries.

In general, the respondents exhibited a predominantly positive or neutral attitude toward the proliferation of automated deliveries in their residential areas. This indicates a willingness to embrace and accept these technologies as part of their daily lives. However, it is important to note that attitudes may vary depending on the specific context and location. For instance, individuals residing in city centers or inner cities displayed a slightly lower inclination to utilize drone services compared to respondents residing in suburban or sparsely populated areas. This difference may be attributed to factors such as population density, infrastructure, and familiarity with new technologies. Understanding these local and cultural nuances is crucial for industry stakeholders and policymakers to tailor their strategies and foster public acceptance. The study also revealed that respondents exhibited a preference for using delivery robots or drones primarily for home delivery of meals and grocery shopping. This aligns with the growing trend of online food and grocery delivery, especially in urban areas. The convenience and time-saving benefits of automated last-mile deliveries for these specific purposes are highly valued by respondents.

The study also identified several concerns and trust issues influencing public acceptance of automated last-mile deliveries. Theft emerged as the most significant concern among respondents, particularly in the context of delivery robots. This highlights the need for robust security measures and safeguards to protect packages during the last-mile delivery process. Privacy and safety were also specific worries for respondents, indicating the importance of addressing these concerns to build trust and confidence in automated systems. Respondents expressed concern about potential collisions between delivery robots or drones and pedestrians or buildings, emphasizing the need for safe and reliable operation. Additionally, respondents were concerned about the potential environmental impact of automated deliveries, particularly about harm to small animals and insects. These concerns underscore the importance of sustainable design and responsible implementation of automated delivery systems.

Moreover, trust theory was applied to explore the factors that influence it. Trust emerged as a significant factor influencing users' acceptance of drones and delivery robots. The study found that respondents were quite confident about their safety in the presence of delivery robots and drones, although women exhibited slightly higher levels of safety concerns compared to men. This suggests that building trust and addressing safety concerns are crucial for the successful integration of automated delivery systems. Trust in AI-powered technologies, in particular, is a critical aspect of future automated delivery adoption and acceptance.

Acknowledgments. This research has been supported by the Business Finland DROLO and DROLO II project (Grant 41170/31/2020 and Grant 4002/31/2023).

Disclosure of Interests. The authors have no competing interests to declare that are relevant to the content of this article.

References

1. Koh, L.Y., Yuen, K.F.: Consumer adoption of autonomous delivery robots in cities: Implications on urban planning and design policies. Cities **133**, 104125 (2022). https://doi.org/10.1016/j.cities.2022.104125
2. Yuen, K.F., Cai, L., Lim, Y.G., Wang, X.: Consumer acceptance of autonomous delivery robots for last-mile delivery: technological and health perspectives. Front. Psychol. **13**, 1–17 (2022). https://doi.org/10.3389/fpsyg.2022.953370
3. Khan, R., Tausif, S., Javed Malik, A.: Consumer acceptance of delivery drones in urban areas. Int. J. Consum. Stud. **43**(1), 87–101 (2019). https://doi.org/10.1111/ijcs.12487
4. EASA, Study on the societal acceptance of Urban Air Mobility in Europe, pp. 1–162 (2021). https://www.easa.europa.eu/full-report-study-societal-acceptance-urban-air-mobility-europe
5. Westendorp, C.F.: Improving AED availability: a framework to support decision-making on where to develop AED drone networks (2019). https://feb.studenttheses.ub.rug.nl/22794/
6. Oksman, V., Kulju, M.: Nordic Study on public acceptance of autonomous drones. In: HCI International 2022 – Late Breaking Posters (2022)
7. Wang, N., Mutzner, N., Blanchet, K.: Technology in Society Societal acceptance of urban drones: A scoping literature review. Technol. Soc. **75**, 102377 (2023). https://doi.org/10.1016/j.techsoc.2023.102377
8. Sabino, H., et al.: A systematic literature review on the main factors for public acceptance of drones. Technol. Soc. **71**, 102097 (2022). https://doi.org/10.1016/j.techsoc.2022.102097

9. Lin Tan, L.K., Lim, B.C., Park, G., Low, K.H., Seng Yeo, V.C.: Public acceptance of drone applications in a highly urbanized environment. Technol. Soc. **64** (2021). https://doi.org/10.1016/j.techsoc.2020.101462

10. Talley, S.: Public acceptance of AI Technology in self-flying aircraft. J. Aviat. Educ. Res. **29**(1) (2020). https://doi.org/10.15394/jaaer.2020.1822

11. Eißfeldt, H., et al.: The acceptance of civil drones in Germany. CEAS Aeronaut. J. **11**(3), 665–676 (2020). https://doi.org/10.1007/s13272-020-00447-w

12. Davis, F.D.: Perceived usefulness, perceived ease of use, and user acceptance of information technology. MIS Q. Manag. Inf. Syst. **13**(3), 319–339 (1989). https://doi.org/10.2307/249008

13. Schnall, R., Higgins, T., Brown, W., Carballo-Dieguez, A., Bakken, S.: Trust, perceived risk, perceived ease of use and perceived usefulness as factors Related to mHealth technology use. Study Heal. Technol. Inf. **216**(4), 467–471 (2015)

14. Baldassarre, B., Keskin, D., Diehl, J.C., Bocken, N., Calabretta, G.: Implementing sustainable design theory in business practice: a call to action. J. Clean. Prod. **273**, 123113 (2020). https://doi.org/10.1016/j.jclepro.2020.123113

15. Lukyanenko, R., Maass, W., Storey, V.C.: Trust in artificial intelligence: from a foundational trust framework to emerging research opportunities. Electron. Mark. **32**(4), 1993–2020 (2022). https://doi.org/10.1007/s12525-022-00605-4

16. Omrani, N., Rivieccio, G., Fiore, U., Schiavone, F., Agreda, S.G.: To trust or not to trust? an assessment of trust in AI-based systems: concerns, ethics and contexts. Technol. Forecast. Soc. Change **181**, 121763 (2022). https://doi.org/10.1016/j.techfore.2022.121763

Understanding Mobility Needs and Designing Inclusive CCAM Solutions: A Literature Review and Framework

Madlen Ringhand[(✉)] , Juliane Anke , and David Schackmann

Chair of Traffic and Transportation Psychology, TUD – Dresden University of Technology, Hettnerstr. 1-3, 01069 Dresden, Germany
madlen.ringhand@tu-dresden.de

Abstract. In our increasingly interconnected world, ensuring inclusive and reliable mobility is paramount. Cooperative, Connected, and Automated Mobility (CCAM) solutions can play a pivotal role in addressing the diverse needs of people with mobility challenges. Through an extensive literature review, this paper constructs a theoretical framework to understand mobility needs within the context of CCAM comprehensively. It delves into individual characteristics, including socioeconomic, psychological, cognitive, and physical factors influencing mobility needs and behaviors. Using an extended version of Ajzen's Theory of Planned Behavior and models on motives and needs, it describes the dynamics between user characteristics, CCAM service characteristics, and the formation of intentions that subsequently affect the actual usage. The framework covers three levels: 'Mobility Needs,' 'CCAM Design Requirements,' and 'Intention & Use.' In conclusion, this theoretical framework offers practical utility by informing the design of CCAM solutions to foster higher adoption rates and heightened mobility satisfaction across diverse user groups. The gathered results can be directly applied to evolve future CCAM solutions by researchers, service providers, and manufacturers.

Keywords: CCAM · mobility · inclusion · mobility framework

1 Introduction

Inclusive and reliable mobility is becoming increasingly important in a more connected world. Mobility innovations, particularly Cooperative, Connected, and Automated Mobility (CCAM) solutions, hold immense potential to consider the unique transportation needs of people with mobility challenges. However, in the past, the design and quality of many public transport services and car manufacturers focused on the average user and developed standardized mobility solutions (Deakin 2022). In recent years, equity and accessibility have become increasingly crucial in transport research, and transport service providers aim to make public transport more inclusive (Martens 2016). To account for the needs and requirements of people with mobility challenges, it is first necessary to understand these needs. Therefore, this paper presents the results of

C. Stephanidis et al. (Eds.): HCII 2024, CCIS 2118, pp. 267–274, 2024.
https://doi.org/10.1007/978-3-031-61963-2_26

an extensive literature review, resulting in a theoretical framework on mobility needs and CCAM, which can be used for further research and development. It highlights the importance of understanding the specific user requirements to ensure the development of equitable and inclusive CCAM solutions. It builds a theoretical foundation for the EU project SINFONICA (Anke & Ringhand 2023), aiming to capture the mobility needs of European citizens through a bottom-up approach, with particular attention to the needs of people with mobility challenges and under-researched groups. The paper is structured as follows: Sect. 2 presents the literature review results to identify mobility needs, motives, and theories on intention and behavior formation. These build the foundation for the framework presented in Sect. 3 and the conclusion in Sect. 4.

2 Empirical and Theoretical Foundation for the Framework

2.1 Needs, Motives, and Motivation

In an everyday understanding, needs describe basic human requirements that need to be fulfilled, or if not, one would like to satisfy. Therefore, needs are strongly associated with a person's intrinsic motivation. Focusing on understanding human motivation and well-being, the basic psychological needs theory by Ryan and Deci (2017) proposes three basic needs that must be satisfied to enable self-determination. According to this theory, the first need is *competence*, which describes the experience of efficacy in interactions. The second need, *autonomy*, describes the ability to effectively interact with the environment, master challenges, and feel a sense of achievement. Finally, *relatedness* expresses the desire to connect to others and to be part of a social group (Ryan & Deci, 2017). According to the theory, if all these needs are met, people are likelier to experience a sense of self-determination, intrinsic motivation, and general well-being.

When these needs are not fulfilled, it can lead to frustration and decreased motivation. Other theories consider further needs, such as physical thriving, influence, self-actualization/meaning, self-worth, popularity, security/safety, and pleasure/stimulation (Sheldon et al. 2001). Needs can act as dynamic motivational forces that direct and energize behavior, influencing individuals' choices and actions (Sheldon & Gunz 2009). These processes are described as motives, which provide a more dynamic perspective, representing the individual and varied reasons behind goal-directed behavior. They shed light on the individual and situational factors that lead individuals to take specific actions to satisfy those needs (Nuttin 1984).

In the context of mobility, several motives are influential regarding mode choice and the adoption of new mobility services, such as CCAM. Regarding mode choice, instrumental motives, such as speed and accessibility, have been identified as influential (Correia & van Arem, 2016), and symbolic motives, for instance, the prestige and social position associated with a vehicle (Steg et al. 2001). On the other hand, the attitude towards new mobility solutions is influenced, amongst others, by the perceived travel time savings and additional comfort they offer (Pigeon et al. 2021). Therefore, considering needs and motives is integral to understanding the intention to use CCAMs and the attitude toward them.

To achieve equity in transport, four essential user requirements are identified in transport literature that must be addressed based on the user needs mentioned above. These are availability, accessibility, affordability, and acceptability (Arup, Urban Transport Group, 2022; Cirella et al. 2019; Dabelko-Schoeny et al., 2021). To meet the availability requirement, CCAM solutions must be accessible to users regardless of location or mobility constraints and provide timely and connected services with simplified information. Accessibility includes CCAM design and infrastructure to ensure freedom from barriers. Affordability requires transparent cost information, easy access to pricing, and seamless payment options. Finally, acceptance requires CCAM solutions to be convenient, secure, comfortable, and responsive to user needs.

2.2 Individual Differences in Mobility Needs

We define mobility needs as 'all physical or psychological user-related requirements towards mobility solutions, like CCAM, that arise from users' individual psychological motives, characteristics, and situational factors and determine the (intention to) use.' (Anke & Ringhand 2023, p. 18) From the perspective of user characteristics, people can differ in terms of their socioeconomic and sociodemographic, psychological, cognitive, and physical characteristics.

Socioeconomic and sociodemographic factors (such as age, gender, income, etc.) have been found to influence mode choice and travel behavior. For instance, people in more deprived neighborhoods are likelier to walk and use public transport (Rachele et al. 2015). Furthermore, needs and motives are affected by certain socioeconomic and sociodemographic factors, such as gender. A study in the UK has found in this context that women show a higher need for safety and security than men (Innovate UK, 2022). Finally, challenges arise from factors such as age, as older people face more cognitive and physical challenges than younger people (GOAL 2013).

Psychological factors, in turn, relate more to intrapersonal factors, such as personality traits and the subjectively weighted importance of motives and needs. These factors can also influence mobility behavior. For instance, a study revealed an association between a more agreeable and not conscientious personality and increased public transport use (Roos et al. 2022). When it comes to future mobility options, trust in technology has been found to influence the adoption of driverless cars, as well as having a positive attitude toward them and perceiving them as safe (Kaur & Rampersad, 2018; Launonen et al., 2021).

The *cognitive characteristics* of a person cover their skills, intelligence, experiences, knowledge, mental models, and literacy. Certain services requiring skills, such as language proficiency and digital skills, have been identified in studies as potential barriers to public transport (Dabelko-Schoeny et al., 2021). Furthermore, research on the acceptance of autonomous vehicles indicates that a greater understanding of the technological facets of autonomous driving is correlated with increased acceptance or intention to use autonomous mobility (Charness et al. 2018).

Finally, *physical characteristics* such as health and physical constitution can lead to mobility challenges. This is especially the case for people with disabilities. When walking, hearing, or seeing are impaired, people often need assistance to travel, which is frequently lacking and thus hinders their community participation (Bezyak et al. 2020).

Besides the user characteristics, situational factors also play an essential role in forming mobility needs. These can be the living environment, vehicle availability, trip purpose, cultural characteristics, and environmental conditions like weather and time of the day. All these factors characterize not only individuals but also allow groups with similar characteristics to be considered regarding mobility specifics. Groups that might be considered are low-income and unemployed people, older people, people with disabilities, migrants, ethnic minorities, people with language barriers, young people and children, women and queer people, people living in rural areas and digitally non-connected people. This selection is not exhaustive but is intended to consider people whose needs and motives might be underrepresented in current research (for a detailed description of groups with mobility challenges see Anke & Ringhand 2023; Di Gregorio & Renzi 2023).

2.3   Intention and Behavior Formation

One prominent theory about the formation of intentions and the subsequent eventual behavioral execution is the Theory of Planned Behavior (Ajzen 1991). It proposes that a person's intentions precede their behavior. These intentions are shaped by three primary predictors: attitudes, subjective norms, and perceived behavioral control. Attitudes are influenced by behavioral beliefs that associate certain consequences with the desirability of a behavior. Positive attitudes increase the likelihood of forming an intention to engage in that behavior. On the other hand, subjective norms reflect the perceived social pressure and sense of belonging to a peer associated with conforming to a particular behavior (Ajzen 1991). These norms are influenced by normative beliefs, which represent the expectations of others regarding the behavior. Finally, perceived behavioral control involves the perceived ease or difficulty of performing a behavior, including self-efficacy and controllability. According to the theory, the interplay of these three prerequisites may lead to the formation of intentions, which can lead to behavior. Whether intentions lead to behavior depends on the actual behavioral control. It refers to factors that objectively facilitate or hinder behavior execution (Ajzen 1991). Within the context of inclusive mobility, those factors, for instance, might be the low availability of a service or personal prepositions, which impede the use of mobility services. The Theory of Planned Behavior provides a comprehensive framework for understanding and predicting mobility behavior in various contexts and is included in the CCAM framework as a theoretical foundation focusing on actual and perceived behavioral control.

3   The CCAM Framework

Based on the research results, a theoretical framework focusing on the mobility needs of CCAM was developed (see Fig. 1). The framework consists of three levels. The first level of the framework (highlighted in purple) revolves around forming mobility needs, combining individual user characteristics and situational factors. These determine requirements for CCAM service characteristics, which, in turn, affect the users' mobility behaviors. For instance, a digitally non-connected user with low-tech affinity may prioritize easy information acquisition and interface design, while a physically disabled user may emphasize the service's accessibility. These individual characteristics interact with situational factors, such as trip purpose or the environment. Therefore, mobility needs are dynamic and influenced by changing situational factors and individual characteristics. The framework includes exemplary user groups with mobility challenges.

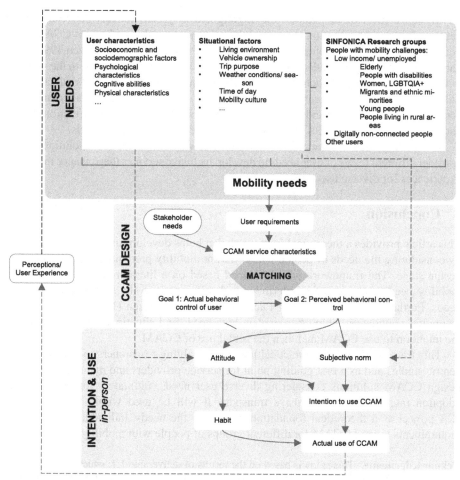

Fig. 1. Framework on mobility needs regarding CCAM having three levels – 'User Needs', 'CCAM Design Requirements', and 'Intention & Use' (Anke & Ringhand 2023).

The second level (highlighted in orange) is the centerpiece of the framework, as it deals with how people's requirements and the respective CCAM characteristics come together to enable people to use CCAM. The CCAM service characteristics are determined by the users' mobility needs and corresponding requirements, but stakeholder requirements are also considered. The CCAM design process should aim to improve the user's actual and perceived behavioral control. This is achieved when all the conditions necessary for the user to perform the behavior (using a CCAM service) are met and perceived as such. The matching between service characteristics and user needs influences the level of actual behavioral control. For example, high intention to use may be hindered if the service network is unavailable, leading to low actual behavioral control and making CCAM use impossible.

The third level of the framework (highlighted in green) reflects the relationship between forming an intention to use and the subsequent real-world use of CCAM services, incorporating components of the Theory of Planned Behavior (Ajzen 1991) and habits (Fu 2021). The formulation of an intention to use is influenced, next to the various individual and situational factors, by attitudes and subjective norms. The realization of this intention depends on nuanced factors such as the perceived behavioral control, the actual behavioral control, and pre-established habits. Besides these interrelations, user and situational characteristics also influence attitudes and subjective norms.

In summary, the structure of this framework shows that future CCAM solutions must consider different levels of user needs to develop inclusive services that enhance mobility experiences for diverse user groups.

4   Conclusion

This article provides a theoretical framework that helps develop future CCAM services by considering the needs of people with different mobility prerequisites right from the design stage. The framework was developed based on a literature review identifying mobility needs and respective interindividual differences in the importance of those needs. Furthermore, the Theory of Planned Behavior by Ajzen (1991) was used as a theoretical foundation, helping to explain how needs and situational factors influence the intention to use CCAM and then the actual use of CCAM.

This framework provides practical utility by enabling researchers to conduct user-centric studies and as a first guiding point for service providers and manufacturers that design CCAM solutions considering diverse user needs, ultimately fostering higher adoption rates and more inclusive transport. It will be used within the SINFON-ICA project as a theoretical foundation to capture the needs, individual factors, and requirements toward CCAM for different groups of people with mobility challenges.

Acknowledgements. This study is based on the results of deliverable 1.1, which was produced as part of the SINFONICA project (Anke & Ringhand, 2023). The SINFONICA project (Grant Agreement n° 101064988) was funded by the European Union under the Horizon Europe Research and Innovation Programm. Views and opinions expressed are however those of the authors only and do not necessarily reflect those of the European Union or the European Commission. Neither the European Union nor the granting authority can be held responsible. The authors thank Jens Schade for his contributions to the SINFONICA project proposal, which made this study possible.

Disclosure of Interests. The authors have no competing interests to declare that are relevant to the content of this article.

References

Ajzen, I.: The theory of planned behavior. Organ. Behav. Hum. Decis. Process. **50**(2), 179–211 (1991). https://doi.org/10.1016/0749-5978(91)90020-T

Anke, J., Ringhand, M.: SINFONICA Deliverable 1.1: Mobility needs and requirements of European citizens. Technische Universität Dresden, Professur für Verkehrspsychologie (2023). https://sinfonica.eu/wp-content/uploads/2023/07/D1.1-Mobility-needs-and-requirements-of-European-citizens.pdf

Arup, Urban Transport Group. Equitable Future Mobility: Ensuring a just transition to net zero transport (2022). https://www.urbantransportgroup.org/system/files/general-docs/Arup%20UTG%20Equitable%20Mobility_final.pdf

Bezyak, J.L., Sabella, S., Hammel, J., McDonald, K., Jones, R.A., Barton, D.: Community participation and public transportation barriers experienced by people with disabilities. Disabil. Rehabil. **42**(23), 3275–3283 (2020). https://doi.org/10.1080/09638288.2019.1590469

Charness, N., Yoon, J.S., Souders, D., Stothart, C., Yehnert, C.: Predictors of attitudes toward autonomous vehicles: the roles of age, gender, prior knowledge, and personality. Front. Psychol. **9**, 2589 (2018). https://doi.org/10.3389/fpsyg.2018.02589

Cirella, G.T., Bąk, M., Kozlak, A., Pawłowska, B., Borkowski, P.: Transport innovations for older people. Res. Transp. Bus. Manag. **30**, 100381 (2019). https://doi.org/10.1016/j.rtbm.2019.100381

de Almeida Correia, G.H., van Arem, B.: Solving the user optimum privately owned automated vehicles assignment problem (UO-POAVAP): a model to explore the impacts of self-driving vehicles on urban mobility. Trans. Res. Part B: Methodol. **87**, 64–88 (2016). https://doi.org/10.1016/j.trb.2016.03.002

Dabelko-Schoeny, H., Maleku, A., Cao, Q., White, K., Ozbilen, B.: "We want to go, but there are no options": Exploring barriers and facilitators of transportation among diverse older adults. J. Transp. Health **20**, 100994 (2021). https://doi.org/10.1016/j.jth.2020.100994

Deakin, E.: A Brief History of Transportation Policies and Institutions. UC Berkeley: Institute of Transportation Studies at UC Berkeley (2022). https://doi.org/10.7922/G2GX48WF

Di Gregorio, P., Renzi, G.: SINFONICA - MS3. Creation and organization of Group of Interest: Internal Report on the activities carried out within Work Package 1, T1.4. UNIMORE Università degli Studi di Modena e Reggio Emilia (2023). https://sinfonica.eu/wp-content/uploads/2023/06/SINFONICA-Creation-and-organization-of-Groups-of-Interest.pdf

Fu, X.: How habit moderates the commute mode decision process: integration of the theory of planned behavior and latent class choice model. Transportation **48**(5), 2681–2707 (2021). https://doi.org/10.1007/s11116-020-10144-6

GOAL. GOAL (GOAL: Growing Older, stAying mobiLe: The transport needs of an ageing society): Final report summary (2013). https://cordis.europa.eu/docs/results/284924/final1-goal-final-report.pdf

Innovate UK. Lived experiences of women and girls in relation to everyday journeys (2022). https://ttf.uk.net/wp-content/uploads/2022/11/7448-Innovate-AT-Report-Long-3.pdf

Kaur, K., Rampersad, G.: Trust in driverless cars: Investigating key factors influencing the adoption of driverless cars. J. Eng. Tech. Manage. **48**, 87–96 (2018). https://doi.org/10.1016/j.jengtecman.2018.04.006

Launonen, P., Salonen, A.O., Liimatainen, H.: Icy roads and urban environments. Passenger experiences in autonomous vehicles in Finland. Transport. Res. F: Traffic Psychol. Behav. **80**, 34–48 (2021). https://doi.org/10.1016/j.trf.2021.03.015

Martens, K.: Transport Justice. Routledge (2016). https://doi.org/10.4324/9781315746852

Nuttin, J.: Motivation, planning, and action: A relational theory of behavior dynamics. Studia psychologica. Leuven Univ, Press (1984)

Pigeon, C., Alauzet, A., Paire-Ficout, L.: Factors of acceptability, acceptance, and usage for non-rail autonomous public transport vehicles: A systematic literature review. Transport. Res. F: Traffic Psychol. Behav. **81**, 251–270 (2021). https://doi.org/10.1016/j.trf.2021.06.008

Rachele, J.N., Kavanagh, A.M., Badland, H., Giles-Corti, B., Washington, S., Turrell, G.: Associations between individual socioeconomic position, neighborhood disadvantage, and transport mode: Baseline results from the HABITAT multilevel study. J. Epidemiol. Community Health **69**(12), 1217–1223 (2015). https://doi.org/10.1136/jech-2015-205620

Roos, J.M., Sprei, F., Holmberg, U.: Traits and transports: the effects of personality on the choice of urban transport modes. Appl. Sci. **12**(3), 1467 (2022). https://doi.org/10.3390/app12031467

Ryan, R.M., Deci, E.L.: Self-Determination Theory: Basic Psychological Needs in Motivation, Development, and Wellness. Guilford Press (2017). https://doi.org/10.1521/978.14625/28806

Sheldon, K.M., Elliot, A.J., Kim, Y., Kasser, T.: What is satisfying about satisfying events? Testing 10 candidate psychological needs. J. Pers. Soc. Psychol. **80**(2), 325–339 (2001). https://doi.org/10.1037/0022-3514.80.2.325

Sheldon, K.M., Gunz, A.: Psychological needs as basic motives, not just experiential requirements. J. Pers. **77**(5), 1467–1492 (2009). https://doi.org/10.1111/j.1467-6494.2009.00589.x

Steg, L., Vlek, C., Slotegraaf, G.: Instrumental-reasoned and symbolic-affective motives for using a motor car. Transport. Res. F: Traffic Psychol. Behav. **4**(3), 151–169 (2001). https://doi.org/10.1016/S1369-8478(01)00020-1

An Online Guide System for Improving Driving Skills on the Race Track: Visual Feedback Approach

Kunhee Ryu[1]([envelope]), Jinsung Kim[1], Jongtaek Han[1], Jonghak Bae[2],
Bogyeong Suh[2], Jaehyun Lim[2], and Jongeun Choi[2]

[1] Vehicle Control Technology Development Team, Division of Advanced Vehicle Platform, Hyundai Motor Company, Hwaseong-si, Republic of Korea
{ryuhhh,jinsung.kim,hanjongtaek}@hyundai.com
[2] School of Mechanical Engineering, Yonsei University, 50 Yonsei-ro, Seodaemun-gu, Seoul, Republic of Korea
{jonghakbae,suh1129,ashestoashes,jongeunchoi}@yonsei.ac.kr

Abstract. Racing instruction often involves instructors riding along in the vehicle, providing coaching on aspects such as acceleration, braking points, and handling techniques, primarily through verbal instruction. In this paper, we propose an online racing guide system designed to partially emulate the role of a human instructor. The proposed system comprises a guide algorithm and a driver feedback interface. By employing model predictive control techniques, the guide algorithm generates optimal torque and steering guidance based on the vehicle state and pre-collected track data. The computed optimal guidance is conveyed to the driver through visual feedback. This paper covers the overall system setup, algorithm, experimental results, and future plans.

Keywords: Racing Guide System · Visual Feedback · Model Predictive Control

1 Introduction

In the recent automotive industry, facilitating software technology has been emphasized, and manufacturers are trying to provide user-friendly features such as driving assistance, in-car entertainment, and overall convenience by using the technology. Enhancing driving skills is also one of the interesting features, which can be accomplished through facilitating software technology and it has been researched [1, 4, 5, 8].

The authors in [1] introduced a driving simulator designed to educate drivers on eco-driving rules. The impact of a feedback interface on driver behavior in automated driving was explored through a user study in [4]. In [5], a haptic interface for automated driving was proposed to assist drivers in gradually resuming manual control during takeovers. Additionally, [8] presented results from a user

© The Author(s), under exclusive license to Springer Nature Switzerland AG 2024
C. Stephanidis et al. (Eds.): HCII 2024, CCIS 2118, pp. 275–282, 2024.
https://doi.org/10.1007/978-3-031-61963-2_27

study examining the types of HUD (Head-Up Display) information that enhance the intuitive understanding of drivers.

In this paper, we propose an online driving guide system for enhancing driving skills on race track. The proposed system provides drivers with optimal guidance in real-time based on the current vehicle state, and the guidance is conveyed to the driver via visual feedback. By doing this, the proposed system can partially perform the role of human instructors, and one can expect to lower the entry barriers to racing, which may provide customers with a fun-driving experience. The objective of this paper is to present the design, implementation, and experimental results of the proposed system. Section 2 outlines the overall system architecture and methods. Experimental results are provided in Sect. 3, and Sect. 4 concludes the paper.

2 Method

The proposed system consists of two parts; i) an online guide algorithm and ii) a feedback interface, as depicted in Fig. 1.

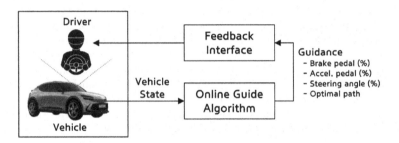

Fig. 1. Overall architecture of the online guide system

The guide algorithm provides the optimal guidance with respect to the acceleration and braking pedal, and steering based on the current vehicle state. The optimal guidance delivered to the driver via the visual feedback interface. In what follows, we present the details of the proposed system.

2.1 Generation of Optimal Guidance

In the proposed system, the guidance signal is calculated based on the current vehicle state and track information by the guide algorithm. We employ the MPCC (model predictive contouring control) problem [2,3,6] to generate the optimal guidance.

We consider the single-track vehicle dynamics in the curvilinear coordinate, which is given by

$$\dot{x} = \begin{bmatrix} \frac{1}{1-\kappa(s)e_c}(v_x \cos e_\psi - v_y \sin e_\psi) \\ v_x \sin e_\psi + v_y \cos e_\psi \\ \omega - \frac{\kappa(s)}{1-\kappa(s)e_c}(v_x \cos e_\psi - v_y \sin e_\psi) \\ \frac{1}{m}(F_t^f \cos \delta - F_s^f \sin \delta + F_t^r) + v_y \omega \\ \frac{1}{m}(F_t^f \sin \delta + F_s^f \cos \delta + F_s^r) - v_x \omega \\ \frac{1}{I_z}(l_f F_s^f \cos \delta - l_r F_s^r) \end{bmatrix} \tag{1}$$

$$=: f_{\text{curv}}(x, u)$$

where $x = [s, e_c, e_\psi, v_x, v_y, \omega]^\top$, the arc-length along the track center line is denoted by s, $\kappa(s)$ is the curvature at s on the center line, e_c is the error of lateral position to the center line, and e_ψ is the error of yaw angle. v_x, v_y, and ω are the longitudinal and lateral velocity, and yaw rate, respectively. F_t^i and F_s^i are the longitudinal and lateral tire forces of wheel $i \in \{f, r\}$, respectively. For the lateral tire model, we use the simplified PMF (Pacejka's magic formula) [7]. Each longitudinal tire force of the front and rear tires is modeled as a function of τ, considering the braking and accelerating, and r_w denotes the effective radius of the tire. The control input u is defined as $u = [\tau; \delta]$.

With the vehicle model (1), we solve the following optimization problem to obtain the optimal guidance, known as the MPCC problem [3], which is given by

$$\underset{\substack{x_{1:N} \\ u_{0:N-1}}}{\text{minimize}} \quad e_N^\top Q e_N + \sum_{i=0}^{N-1} e_i^\top Q e_i + u_i^\top R u_i \tag{2a}$$

$$\text{subject to} \quad x_0 = x(kT_s) \tag{2b}$$

$$x_{i+1} = x_i + \int_0^{T_s} f_{\text{curv}}(x_i, u_i) \tag{2c}$$

$$\underline{u} \le u_i \le \overline{u} \tag{2d}$$

$$-d \le e_{c,i} \le d \tag{2e}$$

$$\underline{\alpha} \le \alpha_i^j \le \overline{\alpha}, \quad j \in \{f, r\} \tag{2f}$$

where $e_i = [e_{s,i}; e_{c,i}]$, $e_{s,i} = s_i - \bar{s}_i$, $\bar{s}_i$ denotes the reference with respect to the arc-length progress s, and $Q = \text{diag}\{q_s, q_c\} \ge 0$ and $R = \text{diag}\{r_\tau, r_\delta\} > 0$ are weight matrices. The prediction horizon is denoted by N and T_s is the sampling time. In equations (2c) to (2f), the overline and underline denote the upper and lower bounds of variables, respectively.

It is noted that adjusting parameters, Q and R, allows for personalized guidance that suits the skill level of the driver. Table 1 shows the selection of the weights according to the driving styles. Since $e_{s,i}$ represents the track progress error, high values of q_s and low values of q_c imply a greater emphasis on progress, corresponding to aggressive driving. Conversely, low values of q_s and high values of q_c imply a focus on generating optimal input that follows the center-line of the track, corresponding to conservative driving.

Table 1. Driving styles according to the weight values.

Driving style	q_s	q_c
Aggressive	High	Low
Moderate	Medium	Medium
Conservative	Low	High

Figure 2 shows the vehicle trajectories obtained from the simulation based on vehicle specifications of Hyundai IONIQ 5, corresponding to the aggressive and conservative driving styles. In the left figure of Fig. 2, Q is selected for conservative driving, resulting in a trajectory that follows the center-line of the track as close as possible. On the other hand, for a driving trajectory corresponding to aggressive driving, not only is the overall average driving speed high, but corners are approached using an out-in-out strategy rather than following the center-line. This distinction becomes particularly evident in sequential cornering sections. The lap times for each scenario are approximately 50.35 seconds for the conservative style and 45.65 seconds for the aggressive style, respectively. Hence, the driving style can be modified by tuning the weight of the cost function, and an optimal control input tailored to the driving skills of individuals can be generated.

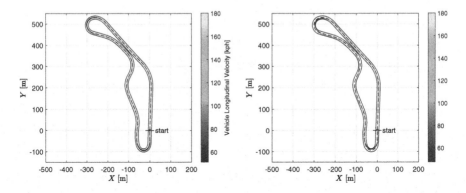

Fig. 2. Vehicle trajectories according to the driving styles: conservative (left), and aggressive (right)

2.2   Optimal Guidance Feedback to the Driver

The resulting optimal guidance, acceleration and braking pedal percentages, and steering angle are conveyed to the driver through the feedback interface. Recently, HUDs have gained recognition as effective interfaces for driver assistance, providing features such as route guidance, warning alarms, and vehicle speed information. One of the primary advantages of HUDs is their ability to

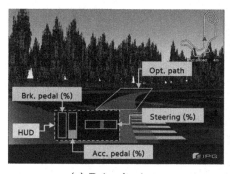 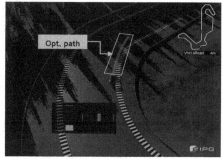

(a) Driver's view.   (b) Bird-eye view.

Fig. 3. Demonstration of the visual feedback interface on CarMaker.

allow drivers to access information while keeping their focus on the road. This advantage becomes even more crucial in a racing environment, where driving situations change rapidly. Therefore, we utilize the HUD as a feedback interface for delivering optimal guidance in racing scenarios.

Visual feedback has the advantage of clarity over guidance delivered through the voice of a human instructor. In particular, conveying details about the optimal path through verbal instructions is challenging, however, using visual feedback can make it apparent.

The guidance values displayed on the HUD include i) the current and guided acceleration pedal percentages, ii) the current and guided braking pedal percentages, and iii) the current and guided steering wheel angle percentages. These values are represented using three gauge bars, as illustrated in Fig. 3. The guidance for acceleration and braking pedals is presented through vertical gauge bars, primarily corresponding to the longitudinal dynamics of the vehicle. In contrast, steering guidance, which mainly corresponds to lateral dynamics, is provided via a horizontal gauge bar.

3 Proof of Concept

This section presents the experiment results. The primary objective of this experiment was to ensure the reliability of the online guidance algorithm. To conduct experiments with the real vehicle, we implemented specific modifications to the vehicle. By integrating the output of a high-precision GNSS (Global Navigation Satellite System) and internal sensor data, we construct the vehicle state information to address the MPCC problem (2). Figure 4 shows the hardware configuration of the test vehicle for the proof of concept. Two GNSS antennas are installed on the roof. The GNSS receiver and edge computing device are installed in the cargo space.

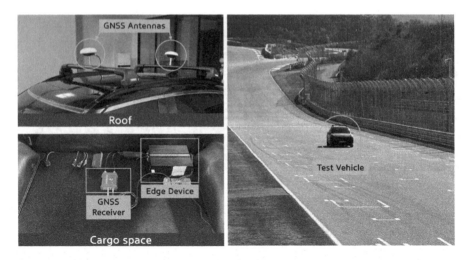

Fig. 4. Hardware configuration of the test vehicle (left), and the test vehicle running on the track (right).

Figure 5 depicts the configuration of the proof of concept. The edge device plays a role in transmitting signals which are from the GNSS receiver and Control Area Network (CAN) of the vehicle to the algorithm via ethernet communication. With the signals from the edge device, the online guide algorithm, operating on a laptop, generates the optimal guidance. The state and optimal guidance are logged during the test race. Notably, the optimal guidance was not conveyed to the driver in this experiment.

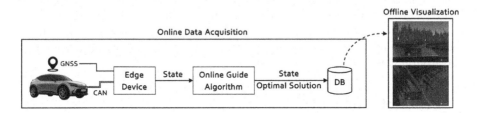

Fig. 5. Configuration of the proof of concept.

Figure 6 depicts snapshots of the logged data visually reconstructed on the map using CarMaker, a commercial software for vehicle simulation. The test race corresponds to aggressive driving. In the sequential corner section, one can observe that the guidance signals and optimal path are aligned with the out-in-out strategy as shown in the right of Fig. 2.

Through this experiment, we confirmed that the optimal guide algorithm, one of the key components of the proposed system, operates based on actual vehicle signals. The user study to validate the effectiveness of the proposed system will be left for future work.

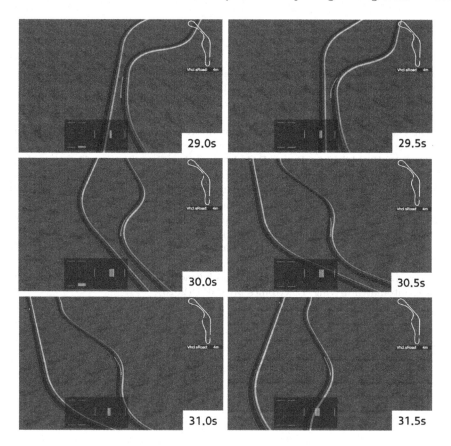

Fig. 6. Snapshots of experimental results.

4   Conclusion and Future Work

This paper introduces an online guidance system for track driving. The proposed system solves the model predictive control problem to generate optimal driving guidance in real-time and delivers it to the driver through visual feedback interfaces such as HUDs. Guidance for acceleration, braking pedal, and steering angle is provided to the driver through three gauge bars, aiming to emulate the role of a human instructor partially. As future works, we plan to implement the driver feedback interface on the test vehicle and conduct user studies to verify the effectiveness of improving driving skills.

Disclosure of Interests. The authors have no competing interests to declare that are relevant to the content of this article.

References

1. Beloufa, S., et al.: Learning eco-driving behaviour in a driving simulator: contribution of instructional videos and interactive guidance system. Transport. Res. F: Traffic Psychol. Behav. **61**, 201–216 (2019)
2. Kabzan, J., et al.: Amz driverless: the full autonomous racing system. J. Field Robot. **37**(7), 1267–1294 (2020)
3. Lam, D., Manzie, C., Good, M.: Model predictive contouring control. In: 49th IEEE Conference on Decision and Control (CDC), pp. 6137–6142. IEEE (2010)
4. Lau, C.P., Harbluk, J.L., Burns, P.C., El-Hage, Y.: The influence of interface design on driver behavior in automated driving. CARSP, Victoria, BC (2018)
5. Lv, C., et al.: Human-machine collaboration for automated driving using an intelligent two-phase haptic interface. Adv. Intell. Syst. **3**(4), 2000229 (2021)
6. Metzler, M.: Automotive applications of explicit non-linear model predictive control. Ph.D. thesis, University of Surrey (2020)
7. Pacejka, H.B., Bakker, E.: The magic formula tyre model. Veh. Syst. Dyn. **21**(S1), 1–18 (1992)
8. Park, K., Im, Y.: Ergonomic guidelines of head-up display user interface during semi-automated driving. Electronics **9**(4), 611 (2020)

Assisting the Remote Assistant: Augmenting Degraded Video Streams with Additional Sensor Data to Improve Situation Awareness in Complex Urban Traffic

Andreas Schrank[✉] , Nils Wendorff , and Michael Oehl

German Aerospace Center (DLR), Institute of Transportation Systems, Lilienthalplatz 7, 38108 Braunschweig, Germany

{andreas.schrank,nils.wendorff,michael.oehl}@dlr.de

Abstract. Remotely operating highly automated vehicles (HAVs, SAE 4 [1]) bears the potential to boost their large-scale deployment. A human operator supports the vehicle automation remotely in situations that exceed the automation's capabilities. A high-quality video stream displaying the HAV's environment is key for the remote operator to obtain and maintain situation awareness. One of the major technical obstacles is the frequent and serious limitation of connectivity between the remote operator and the HAV, particularly a drop of bandwidth. This results in a severely degraded video resolution. As a remedy, we propose the use of data transmitted from the HAV's additional onboard sensors to augment a low-resolution video stream. A significantly lower bandwidth suffices to transmit sensor compared to video data, enabling their transmission even when the video resolution is degraded. This could help the remote operator gain situation awareness, particularly in remote assistance, a variant of remote operation in which the operator provides high-level advice to the vehicle [2]. To confirm the need for a sensor data augmented view of the traffic situation, an experimental online user study ($N = 117$) was conducted. The study presented short video clips of complex naturalistic urban road traffic to participants. The objective was to examine if overlaying the video stream with visualized sensor data improves a remote assistant's situation awareness and whether the effect of overlaid sensor data depends on the video resolution. Results revealed a significant effect of video resolution on objective situation awareness. Additionally, an interaction effect between resolution and sensor-data overlay became evident on the perception level of situation awareness. Hence, sensor data augmentation of degraded video streams may support the remote assistant's situation awareness by increasing the salience of relevant elements in a traffic situation. Future research will investigate sensor data augmentation in a standardized simulation environment.

Keywords: Remote operation · remote assistance · human-machine interaction · highly automated vehicles

© The Author(s), under exclusive license to Springer Nature Switzerland AG 2024
C. Stephanidis et al. (Eds.): HCII 2024, CCIS 2118, pp. 283–294, 2024.
https://doi.org/10.1007/978-3-031-61963-2_28

1 Introduction

Remote operation is a gateway to highly automated and connected driving. New legal regulations both on national and EU level make remote operation a prerequisite for the deployment of highly automated vehicles (HAV, SAE 4 [1]) on public roads. As stated in the 2021 German Road Traffic Act [3], a "technical supervisor" is required to oversee automated driving operations and intervene if necessary. In its remote implementation, the technical supervisor's role overlaps with SAE's [1] definition of a "remote assistant" (RA), a specific variant of a remote operator. Given the legal constraints, it is strongly assumed remote assistance is currently the only legally permissible implementation of remote operation, at least in Germany.

Kettwich et al. [4] proposed a human-machine interface (HMI) for the RA's workplace in line with these legal requirements and proved it to be effective and user-friendly. Schrank et al. [5] showed that this workplace HMI is viable even under increased levels of induced cognitive load. In addition to performance, these studies confirmed that establishing and maintaining situation awareness (SA) is key for safe and effective remote assistance (see also [6]). A valid representation of the traffic environment around the supervised HAV that enables the RA to perceive the relevant elements in the situation precisely (SA level 1 [7]) needs to be conveyed to the RA. Only if the perception of all relevant elements is ensured, a valid wholistic representation of the situation may emerge (SA level 2) which allows an accurate prediction of how the situation will unfold (SA level 3). Thus, it is pivotal for the remote assistance of HAVs to ensure the RA has sufficient SA. [4]'s HMI mainly relies on the video stream transmitted from the HAV to the RA. This is common for remote operation HMIs in general [8]. However, in real-world operations, connectivity restraints in mobile networks such as low bandwidth may degrade the quality of the video stream, e.g., by lowering its resolution. This can be detrimental for the RA's SA as the perception of relevant elements may be impaired, deteriorating SA overall.

In order to maintain a sufficient degree of SA even in the event of poor connectivity, strategies to compensate for these restraints are needed. We suggest that additional sensor data, e.g., from Light Detection and Ranging (LiDAR) or radar sensors, be visualized to augment the video stream. This comes with at least three advantages: First, sensor data serve as an additional source of information that may shed light on objects in an environment that the RA might not have detected otherwise, increasing the RA's SA. For instance, this could be the case in unfavorable light or weather conditions. Second, the bandwidth required to transmit sensor data is considerably lower than for transmitting high-resolution video streams. Even when network performance is poor, sensor data may still be transmissible when high-resolution video streams are not. Third, sensor data from HAVs are readily available. Since the HAV's perception of the environment relies on sensor data, sensors that produce visualizable output are often part of an HAV's standard hardware equipment. Alternatively, sensor data originating from infrastructure, e.g., from road-site units, could be utilized.

For the effective and efficient use of sensor data in remote assistance, however, a user-centered visualization of the sensor data and their interplay with the video stream data is pivotal. This visualization could be the cornerstone of a novel HMI for remote assistance. Figure 1 presents an exemplary visualization of LiDAR data as an overlay of the video stream to aid the RA's SA.

Fig. 1. Example for visualization of sensor data from real traffic environment. Data from vehicle's LiDAR sensor are laid over video stream with low resolution as a point cloud. Algorithms were applied to classify the LiDAR points in the traffic environment. Relevant object classes are color-coded as follows: vehicles in blue and vulnerable road users (pedestrians and cyclists) in yellow, for example.

To ascertain if the augmented view helps users obtain SA, an online user study was conducted. In addition to the question whether augmenting the video stream with visualized sensor data improves SA in general, it is conceivable that such an augmentation might affect SA particularly positively when the resolution of the video stream is lower, e.g., due to connectivity issues. It is argued that by overlaying a degraded video stream with visualized sensor data, a compensatory effect may become evident: Remote assistants may be able to obtain the required visual information from the sensor data in lieu of the video stream, compensating for the lack of higher resolution.

Previous research has indeed shown that lower video stream quality impedes the remote operator's SA [9]. However, the study focused on remote driving and did not specify what specific driving scenarios were used. To the authors' knowledge, whether a degraded video stream of real driving scenarios negatively affects SA in remote assistance has not yet been investigated in the literature. Additionally, no research for remote assistance on the effects of an interplay between an augmented video stream and different video resolutions could be found in the literature.

Therefore, this paper aims to evaluate the effect of augmenting the video stream that is displayed to the remote assistant's workplace with visualized sensor data on situation awareness. Stimuli are complex urban situations recorded in real-world traffic that are relevant for remote assistance. As it is hypothesized that augmenting the video stream is particularly beneficial for situation awareness in situations with lower resolution, i.e., when the video stream is degraded, the resolution of the video stream will be systematically varied.

2 Methods

2.1 Participants and Experimental Design

117 participants (39 female, $M_{age} = 36.19$, $SD_{age} = 15.40$, 18 to 82 years) completed an experimental online study. Participants had to be at least 18 years and possess a valid driver's license. The study applied a between-subject design with each participant randomly assigned to one of the four conditions of Augmentation × Resolution (Fig. 2).

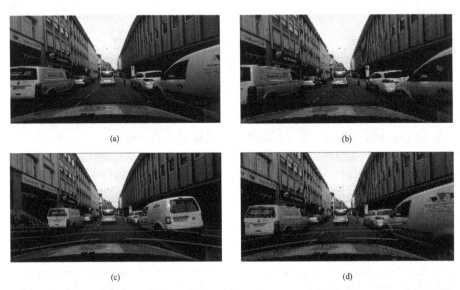

Fig. 2. Screenshot from the video sections (recorded at 20 Hz) of complex, urban, real traffic situation presented to participants. Note the pedestrian on the right shoulder trying to cross the street, highlighted in yellow in the Augmentation conditions. (a) High Resolution – No Augmentation condition with the recorded resolution of 2046 × 1024 pixel; (b) Low Resolution – No Augmentation condition with the resolution reduced to 10 percent and then re-upscaled to its original resolution without interpolation; (c) High Resolution – Augmentation condition with overlaid LiDAR point cloud as described in Fig. 1; (d) High Resolution – Augmentation condition.

2.2 Materials

The presented videos were recorded by cameras mounted onto a research vehicle [10] during test drives in real urban traffic. The video stream was searched for sections with complex and ambiguous traffic situations that may require the intervention of a RA. Each section was ten seconds long. Seven sections were selected, one of which was used for training purposes. Depending on condition, resolution and/or augmentation were adjusted (Fig. 2).

2.3 Measures

To measure situation awareness (SA) objectively, a query-based questionnaire was created, inspired by the Situation Awareness Global Assessment Technique (SAGAT) [11]. In SAGAT, a situation is "frozen" and questions about it are asked, which are then used to measure three levels of SA as defined by [7]. Unlike in SAGAT, the video sections here stopped playing 10 s after onset for each video and did not resume. In addition, the Situation Awareness Rating Technique (SART) was applied as a measure for subjective SA [17].

Individual responses for SA levels 1 and 2 were developed for each of the six video sections, which participants had to rate as correct or incorrect. One point was awarded for each correct response, and a response was considered correct only if a true statement was checked or a wrong statement was not checked [12]. For SA level 3, responses were the same throughout all video sections. Each participant's SA score was determined by the number of correct responses [13].

Table 1 lists questionnaire items, respective responses and the maximum number of points for each SA level. In total, participants could score 11 points for each of the six video sections. Following [7]'s theory of SA, items for level 1 queried the participant's perception of relevant elements in the traffic environment, for level 2 the understanding of the situation, and for level 3 the projection, operationalized as the future behavior of the monitored vehicle "to reach the destination quickly and safely".

2.4 Procedure

First, participants were informed about the general scope and objectives of the study. Second, participants indicated their demographical data including age and gender. Third, the notion of remote assistance, an exemplary workplace for remote assistance, and the task they had to complete were presented to participants. Participants were prompted to imagine to work as a remote assistant (RA). They were told that the video sections they were presented showed different traffic situations recorded by an automated vehicle. This vehicle requested assistance from them because it could not solve a certain complex urban traffic situation. Their task was to view the video section recorded ten seconds prior to the request and answer questions about the traffic situation. After viewing the video section and assisting the vehicle, it would resume the automated mode. This prompt was based on the notion that viewing a short video clip of the period before an automated vehicle's request for assistance may improve SA of remote operators [14]. Fourth, participants were randomly assigned to one of the four conditions of Augmentation × Resolution. A test trial was run in the assigned condition. Just as the following experimental trials, it consisted of a 10-s video section of a traffic situation (see "Materials") and the developed SA questionnaire (see "Measures"). Each videos section could be viewed only once. After each video section ended, participants had unlimited time to respond to the respective SA questionnaire. Fifth, participants ran through the six randomized experimental trials with one video section each and completed the respective questions.

Table 1. Items and responses of developed questionnaire to measure objective situation awareness.

SA Level	Item	Responses[1]	Maximum of Points Granted
1	What did you observe in the situation?	The road had a solid line	6 (multiple responses may be correct; 1 point for every correctly checked or unchecked response)
		A person was standing on the road	
		A vehicle was blocking a lane	
		The traffic light was yellow	
		Pedestrians were waiting at the pedestrian light to cross the street	
		The vehicle in front was using the direction indicator (turn signal)	
2	What did you observe in the situation?	The vehicle ahead had to change lanes at least once	4 (multiple responses may be correct; 1 point for every correctly checked or unchecked response)
		The monitored vehicle was able to change to the right lane at any time	
		The monitored vehicle could not turn right at the traffic light because a vehicle was blocking the lane	
		The monitored vehicle had to pass a vehicle that was blocking a lane	
3	How should the monitored vehicle behave to get to its destination quickly and safely for all road users?	Continue driving	1 (only one response is correct)
		Go over a green light	

(*continued*)

Table 1. (*continued*)

SA Level	Item	Responses[1]	Maximum of Points Granted
		Change to the right lane	
		Change to the left lane	
		Turn right	
		Turn left	
		Overtake vehicle in front of me	
		Brake and continue driving at reduced speed	
		Brake and bring the vehicle to a stop	

[1] Responses are examples only for SA levels 1 and 2 as on these levels, responses are tailored to each distinct video section. For Level 3, responses are the same across video sections.

3 Results

The following section reports the statistical analyses regarding objective and subjective situation awareness (SA).

In terms of objective situation awareness, descriptive results are presented in Table 2. A two-way analysis of variance (ANOVA) revealed a significant effect of condition on the overall objective SA score (Table 3). The only significant factor was Resolution. Pairwise post-hoc comparisons showed that the only significant effect between conditions was between the two conditions High Resolution and Low Resolution, each without Augmentation ($M_{Diff} = 0.850$, $p = .022$).

Table 2. Descriptive statistics of objective situation awareness overall.

Condition	M	SD
High Res. – No Augm	8.227	1.157
High Res. – Augm	7.975	1.104
Low Res. – No Augm	7.377	0.948
Low Res. – Augm	7.806	1.033
Total	7.841	1.085

Res. = Resolution; Augm. = Augmentation. Range: [0; 11].

Table 3. The effect of condition on the score of objective situation awareness overall in two-way analysis of variance (ANOVA).

Condition	Sum of Squares	df	Mean Square	F	p
Corrected Model	11.343	3	3.781	3.410	.020
Intercept	6964.430	1	6964.430	6281.259	.000
Augmentation	.013	1	.013	.012	.914
Resolution	9.500	1	9.500	8.568	.004
Resolution × Augmentation	2.132	1	2.132	1.922	.168
Error	125.290	113	1.109		
Total	7328.944	117			

$R2 = .083$ (corrected $R2 = .059$).

Table 4 presents descriptive statistics for scores of level 1 objective situation awareness. As shown in Table 5, A two-way ANOVA yielded a global significant effect of condition on the level 1 score of objective SA. However, unlike in the overall objective SA score, not only Resolution was shown to have a significant main effect on the level 1 score but also the interaction effect between Resolution and Augmentation reached significance (Table 5). Again, pairwise post-hoc comparisons showed that this effect was driven by a single significant difference between High-Resolution and Low-Resolution conditions, each without Augmentation ($M_{Diff} = 0.626$, $p = .002$). On SA levels 2 and 3, no significant differences between conditions were found.

Table 4. Descriptive statistics of objective situation awareness at level 1.

Condition	M	SD
High Res. – No Augm	4.626	0.625
High Res. – Augm	4.407	0.736
Low Res. – No Augm	4.000	0.525
Low Res. – Augm	4.294	0.605
Total	4.356	0.658

Res. = Resolution; Augm. = Augmentation. Range: [0; 6].

Regarding subjective situation awareness measured by SART scores, no significant effects of condition on SART score were observed (Table 6).

Table 5. The effect of condition on the score of objective situation awareness at level 1 in two-way analysis of variance (ANOVA).

Condition	Sum of Squares	df	Mean Square	F	p
Corrected Model	5.527	3	1.842	4.658	.004
Intercept	2141.140	1	2141.140	5413.919	.000
Augmentation	0.040	1	0.040	0.102	.750
Resolution	3.900	1	3.900	9.862	.002
Resolution × Augmentation	1.876	1	1.876	4.745	.031
Error	44.690	113	0.395		
Total	2270.389	117			

$R2 = .110$ (corrected $R2 = .086$).

Table 6. The effect of condition on the score of subjective situation awareness (SART) in two-way analysis of variance (ANOVA).

Condition	Sum of Squares	df	Mean Square	F	p
Corrected Model	9.673	3	3.224	1.366	.257
Intercept	2161.298	1	2161.298	915.721	.000
Augmentation	0.187	1	0.187	0.079	.779
Resolution	5.991	1	5.991	2.538	.114
Resolution × Augmentation	4.178	1	4.178	1.770	.186
Error	266.704	113	2.360		
Total	2528.852	117			

$R2 = .035$ (corrected $R2 = .009$).

4 Discussion and Outlook

This user study investigated the effect of a video stream for a remote assistant of highly automated vehicles that is augmented with visualized sensor data on both objective and subjective situation awareness (SA). In addition, the resolution of the video stream was varied. It was found that video resolution had a significant effect on objective SA. When looking at level 1 of objective SA, there was an additional interaction effect of resolution and augmentation. No significant effect of condition was found either on the other levels of objective SA or on subjective SA. In the following paragraphs, two interesting findings will be highlighted.

First, the effect on SA level 1 is in line with the hypothesis that an added value of the augmentation is to be expected for this level of SA since it pertains to the perception of relevant elements in the situation. The color-coded highlighting of other road users proved to facilitate SA in conjunction with the video resolution by increasing the road users' salience in the traffic situation. Thus, these results point into the direction of a compensatory effect of augmentation: Particularly when the video resolution is degraded, the use of sensor data augmentation has a beneficial effect on the perception level of SA. However, as no influence of augmentation on SA levels 2 and 3 was found, the enhanced perception did not affect integration and projection levels of SA.

Second, a discrepancy between effects on objective and subjective SA became evident. Neither augmentation nor resolution had a significance effect on subjective SA. This finding is interesting as it shows that even though perception was objectively improved (SA level 1), this effect did not spill over to the reported *subjective* SA. This result is in line with Endsley's [15, 16] finding that subjective SA indicators, such as SART, and objective SA indicators, such as SAGAT, measure distinct psychological constructs: While subjective SA measures were found to be correlated with confidence, they were not correlated with objective SA measures. Conclusively, objective SA measures, though self-reported, may not be immediately articulatable by participants but may rather need to be collected in a systematic, query-based approach. Our findings on objective SA also resonate with Georg et al.'s [9] outcomes in their remote driving study, underlining that video stream quality is both relevant for remote driving and remote assistance. Beyond this methodological perspective, the discrepancy between objective and subjective SA may also bear practical implications for safety. As being aware of what is happening in the traffic situation is a necessary prerequisite for assessing the situation correctly, ensuring safety, the objective improvement of SA may be desirable even when it is not reflected in a similar subjective impression.

The study comes with some limitations. First, the statistical analyses showed a high degree of dispersion. This may be due to the use of real-world video streams and visualization algorithms with limited accuracy, as is nevertheless the state of the art in object identification and classification algorithms. The lack of accuracy and resulting ambiguous visualizations might have led to confusion in identifying relevant road users in the augmented conditions. Thus, an added value of augmentation became evident only in the low-resolution conditions. Second, the video resolution was still relatively good even in the low-resolution condition. Objects could still be identified by participants in most cases. This ceiling effect might conceal a more pronounced effect of the augmentation on SA. Third, as participants were not asked to give advice to the HAV, a lack of involvement is possible which might mask effects. In future research, the resolution of the video stream could be degraded even more to discover potential positive effects of visualized sensor data. This may increase ecological validity further as a lower resolution is a common issue in real-world data transmission. Additionally, the effect of increased accuracy of the mentioned algorithms could be investigated, reflecting technological progress.

Overall, the data gives indications for further pursuing and investigating HMIs for remote assistance that are augmented by additional sensor data. Future research could refine this framework by including features to aid attentional guidance. By increasing the salience of objects that are crucial for a traffic situation, safety and performance of HAV remote assistance could be further enhanced.

Acknowledgments. This project has received funding from the European Union's Horizon 2020 research and innovation programme under grant agreement No. 101006664. The authors would like to thank all partners within Hi-Drive for their cooperation and valuable contribution. Furthermore, the authors would like to express their gratitude to Jörg Schäfer and Philipp Schmälzle for their aid in the augmentation of the videos and to Kai Sklorz for supporting conceptualization and data collection.

Disclosure of Interests. The authors have no relevant competing interests to declare.

References

1. Society of Automotive Engineers Taxonomy and Definitions for Terms Related to Driving Automation Systems for On-Road Motor Vehicles (SAE J 3016–202104) (2021). https://www.sae.org/standards/content/j3016_202104. Accessed 02 Jul 2021
2. Automated Vehicle Safety Consortium AVSC Best Practice for ADS Remote Assistance Use Case (AVSC-I-04–2023) (2023)
3. Straßenverkehrsgesetz: Betrieb von Kraftfahrzeugen mit autonomer Fahrfunktion; Widerspruch und Anfechtungsklage: StVG § 1e (2021)
4. Kettwich, C., Schrank, A., Oehl, M.: Teleoperation of highly automated vehicles in public transport: user-centered design of a human-machine interface for remote-operation and its expert usability evaluation. MTI **5**, 26 (2021). https://doi.org/10.3390/mti5050026
5. Schrank, A., Walocha, F., Brandenburg. S., et al.: Human-centered design and evaluation of a workplace for the remote assistance of highly automated vehicles. Cogn Tech Work (2024). https://doi.org/10.1007/s10111-024-00753-x
6. Linkov, V., Vanžura, M.: Situation awareness measurement in remotely controlled cars. Front. Psychol. **12**, 592930 (2021). https://doi.org/10.3389/fpsyg.2021.592930
7. Endsley, M.R.: Toward a theory of situation awareness in dynamic systems. Hum. Factors J. Hum. Factors Ergon. Soc. **37**, 32–64 (1995). https://doi.org/10.1518/001872095779049543
8. Amador, O., Aramrattana, M., Vinel, A.: A survey on remote operation of road vehicles. IEEE Access **10**, 130135–130154 (2022). https://doi.org/10.1109/ACCESS.2022.3229168
9. Georg, J-M., Putz, E., Diermeyer, F.: Longtime effects of video quality, video canvases and displays on situation awareness during teleoperation of automated vehicles*. In: 2020 IEEE International Conference on Systems, Man, and Cybernetics (SMC), pp. 248–255 (2020)
10. DLR Transport FASCar – research vehicle for automated driving (2023). https://verkehrsforschung.dlr.de/en/fascar-research-vehicle-automated-driving. Accessed 26 May 2023
11. Endsley, M.R.: SAGAT: A methodology for the measurement of situation awareness, Northrop C, Hawthorne, CA (1987)
12. Endsley, M.R., Bolté, B., Jones, D.G.: Designing for Situation Awareness: An Approach to User-Centered Design. Taylor & Francis, Boca Raton, London, New York (2003)
13. Gregoriades, A., Pampaka, M.: Enhancing drivers' situation awareness. In: Stanton, N.A., Landry, S., Di Bucchianico, G., et al. (eds.) Advances in Human Aspects of Transportation, vol. 484, pp. 301–312. Springer International Publishing, Cham (2017)
14. Mutzenich, C., Durant, S., Helman, S., et al.: Updating our understanding of situation awareness in relation to remote operators of autonomous vehicles. Cogn. Res. Princ. Implic. **6**, 9 (2021). https://doi.org/10.1186/s41235-021-00271-8
15. Endsley, M.R., Selcon, S.J., Hardiman, T.D., et al.: A comparative analysis of Sagat and Sart for evaluations of situation awareness. In: Proceedings of the Human Factors and Ergonomics Society Annual Meeting, vol. 42, pp. 82–86 (1998). https://doi.org/10.1177/154193129804200119

16. Endsley, M.R.: The divergence of objective and subjective situation awareness: a meta-analysis. J. Cogn. Eng. Decis. Making **14**, 34–53 (2020). https://doi.org/10.1177/155534341 9874248

17. Taylor, R.M.: Situation awareness rating technique (SART): the development of a tool for aircrew systems design (AGARD-CP-478). In: Situational Awareness in Aerospace Operations, pp. 3/1–3/17. NATO-AGARD, Neuilly Sur Seine, France (1990)

Passenger's Preference on Internal Interface Design in Driverless Buses: A Virtual Reality Experiment

Yanbin Wu(✉) ⓘ, Fumie Sugimoto ⓘ, Ken Kihara ⓘ, Takemasa Yokoyama ⓘ, Motohiro Kimura ⓘ, Yuji Takeda ⓘ, and Naohisa Hashimoto ⓘ

National Institute of Advanced Industrial Science and Technology (AIST), Higashi 1-1-1, Tsukuba 3059566, Japan
wu.yanbin@aist.go.jp

Abstract. Driverless buses are anticipated to enhance mobility services. Nevertheless, addressing passenger concerns about safety and information provision becomes crucial when there is no driver or onboard authority. Cabin services, such as emergency information, are handled by a remote operator via an internal human machine interface (iHMI). Integrating passengers' preferences into the iHMI design while dealing with issues related to remote monitoring is an underexplored area in current research. This study aims to examine the content and methods of information presentation for iHMI in driverless buses, with a specific focus on whether projecting the appearance of the remote operator onto the iHMI can enhance the acceptability and trust in driverless buses. To facilitate efficient development and assessment, a virtual reality environment was constructed to replicate the situation inside a driverless bus. In the experiment, 60 participants were recruited and divided into three groups. They experienced both normal driving scenarios and abnormal driving scenarios involving emergency events. Group A experienced the iHMI without the appearance of the remote operator in both normal and abnormal scenarios; Group B experienced the iHMI with the appearance of the remote operator only in abnormal conditions; Group C experienced the iHMI with the appearance of the remote operator in both normal and abnormal scenarios. The results, however, revealed that presenting the remote operator on the iHMI did not significantly affect passenger's subjective experience, indicating that further exploration and refinement might be needed for optimal passenger experience.

Keywords: Driverless Vehicle · Mobility Service · Human Machine Interface · User experience · Remote Operation

1 Introduction

Integrating automated driving technology into public transportation systems is expected to address mobility challenges such as the shortage of professional drivers [1]. To facilitate the wider adoption of driverless bus services, it's imperative that both driving and

C. Stephanidis et al. (Eds.): HCII 2024, CCIS 2118, pp. 295–301, 2024.
https://doi.org/10.1007/978-3-031-61963-2_29

non-driving tasks traditionally carried out by bus drivers transition to automated technology. Passengers are cognizant of the multifaceted roles fulfilled by bus drivers, extending beyond mere vehicle operation to include providing information, ensuring safety, and managing unforeseen circumstances. However, the absence of a driver or onboard authority in driverless buses can lead to passenger insecurity and inconvenience [2, 3].

The absence of a tangible human presence at the helm creates cognitive dissonance for passengers. Familiar cues, such as a driver's attention demeanor, subtle adjustments during driving, and reassuring nods, are noticeably absent. This void raises concerns about safety, acceptance, and overall trust. While automated systems are meticulously engineered, they lack the intuitive human judgment upon which passengers have come to rely. Previous research indicated that passengers expressed concerns about information provision, preventing incivilities, and addressing automation failures [4]. Beyond insecurity, passengers encounter inconveniences. In a driverless bus, there is no friendly voice announcing the next stop, no reassuring eye contact during fare collection, and no empathetic acknowledgment of a passenger's request for assistance. The absence of these seemingly mundane interactions disrupts the essence of the passenger experience. Passengers may feel adrift, uncertain about emergency protocols, and inconvenienced by the absence of a human touch.

To mitigate these challenges, a well-designed internal Human-Machine Interface (iHMI) emerges as a critical bridge. For instance, during demonstration rides, passengers have expressed a preference for multiple screens to compensate for the absence of a human driver [5]. Beyond serving as an information display, the iHMI must facilitate seamless communication with remote operators [6]. In a survey investigating passenger's preferences on iHMI regarding remote support [7], while texts and humanoid voices were deemed sufficient for displaying information in normal situations, presenting the remote operator's face was found to enhance passengers' sense of safety during abnormal situations. To enhance acceptance in driverless buses, iHMI must be designed to align with passenger needs. Given the limitations of real-world experiments, virtual reality (VR) simulations of driverless bus scenarios have been utilized to refine the design and evolution of HMI [8].

This study aimed to examine the content and methods of information presentation on iHMI in driverless buses. Specifically, it sought to verify whether the presentation of the face of a remote operator would enhance the trust and acceptance towards driverless buses. To achieve this objective, a VR environment replicating the interior of a driverless bus was constructed. Participants experienced both (1) normal driving scenarios and (2) driving scenarios including emergency events in VR. Following the experience, subjective evaluations were measured.

2   Methods

2.1   Apparatus and Scenarios

The HTC VALVE INDEX head-mounted display (HMD) was used to construct a VR experiment system that could replicate various driving scenarios inside a driverless bus. As shown in Fig. 1, we aimed to faithfully reproduce the interior of the Isuzu Elega Mio bus. Within the bus, two monitors were installed to display information for the passengers, allowing various forms of information presentation as part of the iHMI. We designed two scenarios to emulate (1) normal driving conditions and (2) driving conditions involving abnormal events in the driverless bus. In these scenarios, we manipulated the information presentation on the in-vehicle HMI, alternately displaying the face of the remote administrator (Fig. 1a) and not displaying it (Fig. 1b).

The normal driving scenario encompassed various events typical of bus travel, including a greeting announcement, departure, right turn, sudden braking, announcement of the next bus stop, and arrival at the bus stop. Corresponding visual information of these events was displayed on the in-vehicle monitors, along with simulated auditory information resembling onboard announcements. In the condition without displaying the remote operator's face, text and illustrations depicting "departure," "turning," "acceleration/deceleration," and "getting on and off" were presented along with onboard announcements (Fig. 1a). Conversely, in the condition displaying the remote operator's face, the image of the remote operator replaced the illustrations, and the announcements were delivered by the remote operator (Fig. 1b). The abnormal driving scenario was essentially the same as the normal driving scenario but included an event where another passenger suddenly fell down at end of the scenario. Both scenarios lasted approximately 5 min and 30 s.

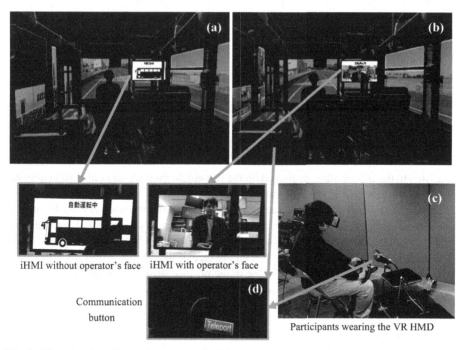

iHMI without operator's face   iHMI with operator's face

Communication
button

Participants wearing the VR HMD

Fig. 1. The virtual reality environment of a driverless bus; (a) with an illustration-based iHMI; (b) with remote operator's face presenting on the iHMI (b); and (c) a participant wearing the HTC HMD was riding on the driverless bus in VR, and (d) a button for connecting to the remote operator was set in both VR and real-world.

2.2 Participants, Conditions, and Instructions

A total of 60 participants (20 to 60 years old, 30 females) were recruited from the local community. To be eligible, each potential participant was required to hold the experience of using route-bus services, be in good health, and have normal vision. Approval for the study was granted by the National Institute of Advanced Industrial Science and Technology (AIST) Safety and Ethics committee, and each participant provided written informed consent before participating in the experiment. Participants were compensated for their involvement.

The participants were allocated into three groups as shown in Table 1. An equal distribution of age and gender were ensured with 20 participants each in the three groups, combining the driving scenarios (normal driving scenario and abnormal driving scenario) and the method of information presentation (without displaying the face of the remote operator and displaying the face). Participants first experienced the normal driving scenario and then the abnormal driving scenario.

Table 1. Experiment conditions.

Group	Normal Driving Scenario	Abnormal Driving Scenario
A (N = 20)	Without face	Without face
B (N = 20)	Without face	With face
C (N = 20)	With face	With face

The participants in the experiment were seated in the seats of the VR experimental space and equipped with VR HMD and controllers. After wearing the equipment, they confirmed being in a seated position as passengers on the seats of a driverless bus before starting the scenario presentation. Participants were instructed to:

1. Listen to the information displayed on the in-vehicle monitor and onboard announcements while seated in the bus seats.
2. In case of any abnormal event, press the emergency call button located on the back of the front seat (Fig. 1c) and report the abnormal event orally to the remote operator via the communication interface also located on the back of the front seat (participants reported abnormal events verbally, with the face of the remote operator visible in the face display condition and not visible in the no-face display condition).
3. Answer the questionnaires regarding the driverless bus and the iHMI after the completion of the drive.

2.3 Measures

To quantitatively measure participants' preferences regarding the different designs of the iHMI, participants were asked to rate their subject trust on a 7-point scale and their acceptance on a 5-point scale. The trust scale consisted of 12 questions adopted from [9], while the acceptance scale consisted of nine questions adopted from [10]. The average score of the 12 questions on the trust scale and the nine questions on the acceptance scale were used as the measures of trust and acceptance, respectively. Additionally, to measure participant's performance in responding to the abnormal event, participants reaction times were defined as the duration from the moment when a passenger fell down to when participants completed reporting the condition to the remote operator.

3   Results

Figure 2 illustrates the participants' trust scores, with a score of one indicating complete lack of trust in the driverless bus, and a score of 7 indicating full trust. Across both normal and abnormal scenarios, the average scores for all three groups were above the neutral baseline (i.e., 4). While it appeared that the trust levels of Group B and C were slightly higher than those of Group A, the two-way Analysis of Variance (ANOVA) did not reveal any significant differences.

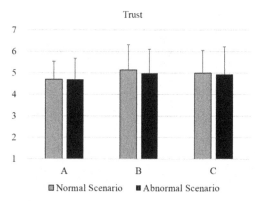

Fig. 2. Subjective trust of the three groups under normal and abnormal scenarios; error bars indicate the standard deviations.

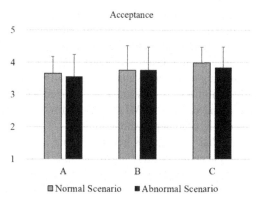

Fig. 3. Acceptance of the three groups under normal and abnormal scenarios; error bars indicate the standard deviations.

As shown in Fig. 3, the results of participant's acceptance were similar to that of trust. Across both normal and abnormal scenarios, the average scores for all three groups exceeded the neutral baseline (i.e., 3). While there appeared to be slightly higher acceptance levels in Group B and C compared to Group A, the two-way ANOVA did not yield any significant differences.

Figure 4 shows the results of reaction times during the passenger-falling event. On average, Group A reported the event to the remote operator within approximately 14.2 s, while Group B and C reacted within 12.6 s and 12.4 s, respectively. However, the one-way between-subject ANOVA did not detect any significant differences among the three groups.

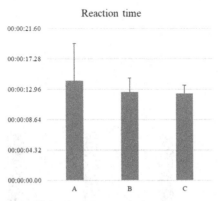

Fig. 4. Average reaction times of the three groups during the passenger-falling event; error bars indicate the standard deviations.

4 Discussions

By conducting a VR-based experiment, this study investigated how passenger's trust and acceptance varied under different scenarios and iHMI designs. Because driverless buses are not yet reliably operational on public roads, posing challenges for collecting empirical evidence to optimize the design of iHMIs. VR technology has emerged as a potent solution for simulating experiences that are currently unfeasible or prohibitively expensive in real-world conditions. In this study, we utilized VR to construct an immersive platform for testing and refining iHMI designs, allowing us to explore scenarios without the constraints of physical deployment.

The findings indicate that participants generally trust and accept driverless buses, as their levels of trust and acceptance were above neutral. However, in the experiment, displaying the face of the remote operator on the iHMI did not notably improve passenger trust or acceptance toward driverless buses. Additionally, considering that maintaining this feature can be seen as burdensome for bus operators, it seems that the benefits of this effort do not outweigh the associated burden. This highlights the necessity of exploring alternative strategies to enhance passenger trust and acceptance, such as investigating different design elements or communication channels, which may yield more effective outcomes.

Acknowledgments. This work is supported by Ministry of Economy, Trade and Industry Japan and Ministry of Land, Infrastructure, Transport and Tourism Japan.

Disclosure of Interests. The authors have no competing interests to declare that are relevant to the content of this article.

References

1. Balaban, O., Puppim de Oliveira, J.A.: Finding sustainable mobility solutions for shrinking cities: the case of Toyama and Kanazawa. J. Place Manag. Dev. **15**(1), 20–39 (2022)
2. Bellone, M., Ismailogullari, A., Kantala, T., Mäkinen, S., Soe, R.M., Kyyrö, M.Å.: A cross-country comparison of user experience of public autonomous transport. Eur. Transp. Res. Rev. **13**(1), 19 (2021)
3. Turnbull, K.F.: Enhancing mobility with automated shuttles and buses. In: Meyer, G., Beiker, S. (eds.) Road Vehicle Automation 10. ARTSymposium 2022, pp. 72–78. Lecture Notes in Mobility. Springer, Cham (2023). https://doi.org/10.1007/978-3-031-34757-3_7
4. Shen, J., Liu, Q., Ye, Z., Jiang, W., Ma, C.: Autonomous bus services: current research status and future recommendations. Digit. Transp. Saf. **2**(3), 229–240 (2023)
5. López-Lambas, M.E., Alonso, A.: The driverless bus: an analysis of public perceptions and acceptability. Sustainability **11**(18), 4986 (2019)
6. Miller, K., Chng, S., Cheah, L.: Understanding acceptance of shared autonomous vehicles among people with different mobility and communication needs. Travel Behav. Soc. **29**, 200–210 (2022)
7. Wu, Y., Konishi, N., Kihara, K., Kimura, M., Takeda, Y., Hashimoto, N.: Passenger's preference on internal interface design in automated buses: a survey. In: Adjunct Proceedings of the 15th International Conference on Automotive User Interfaces and Interactive Vehicular Applications, pp. 162–167 (2023)
8. Stadler, S., Cornet, H., Huang, D., Frenkler, F.: Designing tomorrow's human-machine interfaces in autonomous vehicles: an exploratory study in virtual reality. In: Jung, T., tom Dieck, M.C., Rauschnabel, P.A. (eds.) Augmented Reality and Virtual Reality. PI, pp. 151–160. Springer, Cham (2020). https://doi.org/10.1007/978-3-030-37869-1_13
9. Jian, J.Y., Bisantz, A.M., Drury, C.G.: Foundations for an empirically determined scale of trust in automated systems. Int. J. Cogn. Ergon. **4**(1), 53–71 (2000)
10. Van Der Laan, J.D., Heino, A., De Waard, D.: A simple procedure for the assessment of acceptance of advanced transport telematics. Transp. Res. Part C Emerg. Technol. **5**(1), 1–10 (1997)

A Conceptual Design for Threat Detection System in UAM Vertiport Using Video Recognition and Flight Data

Donghyun Yoon[1] , Juho Lee[1] , Jinyong Lee[1] , and Youngjae Lee[2(✉)]

[1] K-FAM (KAFA Future Air Mobility) Lab, Korea Airforce Academy, 635 Danjae-ro, Sangdang-gu, Cheongju, Republic of Korea
tloveu4949@gmail.com, wngh577@korea.ac.kr

[2] KADA (Konkuk Aerospace Design·Airworthiness Institute) Lab, Konkuk University, 120 Neungdong-ro, Gwangjin-gu, Seoul, Republic of Korea
slaser01@nate.com

Abstract. In this research, our research team propose an AI & Flight data-based threat detection system that can identify potential threats that may occur during the takeoff and landing stages at Urban Air Mobility (UAM) Vertiports. This system has been developed to detect threats that are currently difficult to detect based on current radar system by image object recognition and its own flight data, and we present a specific methodology that the proposed system can be used for Vertiport. The resulting methodology will provide a threat detection framework for UAM Vertiports, which will improve the overall safety and efficiency of takeoff and landing phase operations in Vertiport if more diverse threats are used to deep learning in the future.

Keywords: UAM Vertiport · Take-off and Landing Threat Detection System · Object Recognition · ADS-B

1 Introduction

Urbanization is intensifying around major cities worldwide, leading to saturated urban transport networks, increased carbon emissions, and deteriorating living conditions, which collectively diminish the suitability of cities for habitation. Amid these challenges, UAM is recognized as a revolutionary transportation system that could transform the existing paradigm [1]. To commercialize it, the Vertiport is an important facility for the landing and takeoff of UAM. One of the essential ground support infrastructures required for safe takeoff and landing at the Vertiport is surveillance systems. These systems detect and act against unauthorized aerial vehicles, birds, drones, and other threats approaching the Vertiport. Particularly in urban settings, there are various threats like micro and non-metallic unmanned aerial vehicles. Due to the location of the of Vertiports in city center with the density of high-rise building, radar shadow zones exist, creating blind spots where threats like birds can emerge suddenly. Also, there is limitation of radar. To solve this problem, our team propose a threat detection system based on video recognition and flight data with the human-operated 'Runway Control Tower (referred to as Rwy Control)' concept.

2 Related Work

2.1 UAM Vertiport with Surveillance System

Vertiports, essential infrastructure for the takeoff and landing of UAM (Urban Air Mobility) aircraft, play a crucial role in the UAM industry. One of the critical ground support infrastructures necessary for safe operations at vertiports is surveillance facilities, which detect and manage unauthorized aircraft, birds, drones, and other potential threats as they approach the vertiport. Given the urban setting, various threatening aerial objects, including small, non-metallic unmanned aircraft, can be present, and the high-altitude positioning of vertiports in urban areas can lead to radar blind spots where sudden threats like birds can emerge. Therefore, given the goal of automating UAM operations, vertiport surveillance requires radar and optical-based object recognition and tracking AI technologies [2].

Current Airport Surveillance Systems. Current airport surveillance systems play a crucial role in ensuring the safe and efficient operation of air traffic. These systems' primary functions can be broadly categorized into three main areas: aircraft monitoring function(monitoring aircraft movements on the ground and in the vicinity of the airport, including runways, taxiways, and in the air near the airport), environmental monitoring function(monitoring meteorological conditions including wind speed and direction, visibility, temperature, and precipitation) and security monitoring function(monitoring airport security zones to control access to equipment used for safe takeoffs and landings and maintain overall physical security).

Limitations of Current Airport Surveillance System Adapting to Vertiports. Despite the proven efficiency and effectiveness of existing airport surveillance systems, various limitations may arise when applying them to UAM vertiports.

First, in terms of aircraft design and operation, conventional airport surveillance systems are designed for fixed-wing aircraft that take off and land horizontally. In contrast, UAM employs Vertical Takeoff and Landing (VTOL) techniques, necessitating a different type of monitoring system tailored to the vertiport's vertical operation.

Second, in terms of traffic, the frequency of UAM operations between vertiports is expected to be much higher than that of conventional air traffic systems. This necessitates a more sophisticated surveillance system to ensure safe and efficient operations.

Third, from an operational perspective, UAM requires a higher level of automation compared to traditional air traffic systems. Unlike current airports located in provincial cities, vertiports will be situated in urban environments characterized by buildings, heavy traffic, and dense populations. This will significantly reduce the available space for equipment installation and personnel, increasing complexity. The following table compares the areas of conventional airports and vertiports [3].

Table 1. Difference in Area Between Airport and Each Type of Vertiport

No	Type	Area (m^2)
1	A smallest Domestic Airport in Korea (Yeosu)	1,330,930
2	2 X Apron, 16 X FATO&TLOF Vertiport	19,173
3	1 X Apron, 5 X FATO&TLOF Vertiport	110,728
4	1 X Apron, 4 X FATO&TLOF Vertiport	8,497

When compared to Yeosu Airport, the smallest domestic airport in South Korea in terms of land area, the largest type of vertiport is approximately 69 times smaller, and the smallest type of vertiport is about 156 times smaller. Therefore, to implement surveillance systems of the same performance as current airports in the much smaller vertiports, the design must be based on unmanned automation using smaller-scale sensors and the data derived from them.

Given these limitations, for the safe operation of UAM, a more precise and automated surveillance system is needed, especially for the takeoff and landing phases, where most accidents occur in existing air traffic systems. In military airports, due to the complexity and increased risk of accidents during mass takeoffs and landings in short periods, particularly during wartime, there is a need for more sophisticated advice and surveillance concerning bird activity, weather, runway conditions, and other hazards during these phases. Hence, A human based monitoring system 'Rwy Control Tower' is employed in military airports. Considering the frequency of takeoff and landing phases, it is believed that there are more similarities between the operational methods of military airports and UAM vertiports than between civilian airports and UAM vertiports.

2.2 Deep Learning-Based Image Object Recognition

Deep learning is one of the types of machine learning based on artificial neural networks, designed as a mathematical model with multiple layers of neurons, mimicking the mechanism of human neurons. It consists of an input layer, hidden layers, and an output layer. Through the connections' weights and activation functions between neurons, it can process and transmit information, enabling the learning of complex patterns.

Deep learning-based object recognition in images has gained significant attention in the field of computer vision. Object recognition involves detecting, identifying, and tracking specific objects within an image or video. The primary goal in this field is to improve the accuracy and speed of object detection. Deep learning has shown considerable progress in feature extraction and learning/detection speed and is widely used in object recognition tasks today. Deep learning-based object recognition can be divided into two main approaches: two-stage object recognition algorithms and one-stage object recognition algorithms [4].

Two-stage object recognition algorithms first identify potential object regions using a 'Region Proposal' algorithm, followed by a 'Classification' algorithm to determine the types of objects. In contrast, one-stage object recognition algorithms perform region proposal and classification simultaneously. Generally, one-stage algorithms are faster but less accurate compared to two-stage algorithms, which are slower but more precise. The commonly used algorithms are listed in the table below (Table 2) (Table 1).

Table 2. Popular Object Recognition Algorithms

Category	Algorithm	Release Year
2-Stage	SPPNet	2014
	Fast R-CNN	2015
	Faster R-CNN	2015
1-Stage	YOLO(First Version)	2015
	SSD	2015
	RetinaNet	2017

3   Method

In this research, we aimed to propose a system for threat detection and surveillance that could be applicable to Vertiports by adopting the Rwy Control concept found in military airports. In Rwy Control, veteran observers with specialized expertise are stationed to monitor the conditions of the takeoff and landing zones and the ground situation using radar, CCTV, and visual inspection to detect threats. With this in mind, we proposed surveillance system using optical cameras and object recognition based on deep learning to ensure that there are no threats in the aircraft's takeoff and landing zones. This information is then matched with flight status data based on ADS-B. To implement this, we proceeded with the following research steps (as shown in Fig. 1).

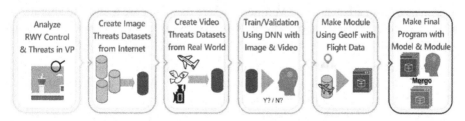

Fig. 1. Research Process

4 Research Process

4.1 Analysis of Rwy Control Operation and Threat Factors

In the case of Rwy Control, veteran operators with expertise are stationed to prepare for potential hazards during aircraft takeoff and landing. They observe the environment and ground conditions in the landing area through radar, CCTV, and visual observation. Their role involves directly communicating with approaching and departing aircraft to ensure safe operations. This setup is primarily deployed at military airports and can detect various multi-faceted threats that may not be advised by the control tower during takeoff, landing, and final approach phases.

To analyze and select potential threats for the UAM Vertiport, we have introduced the concept of current operational risk factors. According to the International Civil Aviation Organization (ICAO), risk factors are conditions or objects that can cause or potentially lead to aircraft accidents and related incidents.

Among these factors, Rwy Control can detect some natural factors and organizational/personal factors. Natural factors primarily encompass weather conditions, geographical conditions, environment, and public health. Organizational/personal factors include communication, tasks, personnel, operations, and regulations. From these factors, we have identified the following as potential threat factors:

(1) Natural Factor: 'Birds and Wildlife (Environmental Factor)' (2) Organizational/Personal Factor: 'Drones (Regulatory Factor)' 'Unauthorized Aircraft (Operational Factor)'.

4.2 Creation of Threat Datasets from Internet Image

To train the selected deep learning model, we defined and gathered suitable images of Vertiport landing threat factors from publicly available sources to construct the dataset. To discern landing threat factors, this research established four major assumptions:

- Objects categorized under prohibited acts as specified in the Republic of Korea Airport Facilities [5].
- Objects with significantly low Radar Cross Section (RCS), making detection challenging by radar-based aircraft monitoring systems.
- Objects capable of quickly moving from radar shadow areas caused by radar installations in urban areas to Vertiports, where they can pose a threat to aircraft.
- Objects observed by humans (optical) through Runway Control currently operational at the airport.

Based on these assumptions, landing threat factors were selected as follows: aircraft, birds, and drones passing through the landing airspace (vertical airspace and FATO). The results are shown in Table 3(with sample image).

4.3 Creation of Threat Datasets from Real World Video

To verify whether the deep learning model trained on the image dataset is suitable for surveillance in the actual Vertiport monitoring environment, various threat factors near

Table 3. Labels in Internet Image Dataset with samples

Labels	Train (81%)	Valid (11%)	Test (8%)	Total (100%)	
Airplane	5109	721	476	6306	Drone
Bird	5111	722	476	6309	Airplane
Drone	5112	728	469	6309	Bird

the airfield were captured using optical cameras and compiled into a video dataset. The recording environment and result of dataset (Table 4) are as follows:

- **Location of Camera Installed**

  Within a 2 km radius of the runway, altitude of 100 m above sea level.

- **H/W Specification of Camera Installed**

  Supports 4K resolution with 8 million pixels, recording at 3840 × 2160/7 fps (Tables 5, 6 and 7).

- **Recording Time**: At least 5 s (after objects were detected)

Table 4. Labels in Real World Video Dataset with samples

Labels	Number	Type	
Airplane (within 1Km)	35	Abnormal (Threat)	
Airplane (over 1Km)	116	Abnormal (Threat)	
Birds	22	Abnormal (Threat)	
Clear (No objects)	30	Normal	

4.4 Training Object Recognition Model

Using the annotated image dataset, training of the deep learning model was conducted. In this paper, we employed the latest version of the one-stage object recognition algorithm, 'YOLO (You Only Look Once),' named 'YOLOv8 [6]. YOLOv8 provides a wide range of models tailored to the training environment by adjusting the scale of parameters, ranging from lightweight models pretrained on the COCO (Common Objects in Context)

Table 5. Internet Image Dataset Recognition Result

Label	Objects	Precision	Recall	mAP (50)	mAP (50–95)
Airplane	948	0.925	0.869	**0.919**	0.731
Bird	1155	0.96	0.958	**0.979**	0.811
Drone	753	0.952	0.943	**0.935**	0.596
ALL	2856	**0.946**	**0.923**	**0.944**	**0.713**

Table 6. Real World Video (Threats) Dataset Recognition Result

Label	Objects	Detection	Miss	True-Positive
Airplane (within 1 km)	35	31 (88.5%)	4 (11.5%)	29 (82.8%)
Airplane (over 1 km)	116	116 (100%)	0 (0%)	116 (100%)
Bird	22	20 (90.9%)	2 (9.1%)	0 (0%)
ALL	**173**	**167 (96.5%)**	**6 (3.5%)**	**145 (83.8%)**

Table 7. Real World Video (Non-Threat) Dataset Recognition Result

Label	Number of Videos	Normal (clear)	Abnormal (detect threats)
Clear Sky	30	26 (86.6%)	4 (13.4%)

dataset to base models (YOLOv8m) and enhanced models (YOLOv8l, YOLOv8x). In this research, the YOLOv8x model, which showed the highest object recognition performance based on mean average precision (mAP), was applied for transfer learning (utilizing a pretrained model based on a large-scale dataset to adapt to new tasks). A Transfer learning take advantage to prevent overfitting that may occur with small-scale datasets. Moreover, using existing weights enables rapid model development [7].

The development environment used, and training parameters includes:

- **Hardware:** CPU (Intel i9-13900K), GPU (GeForce RTX 4090), RAM (128GB)
- **Libraries:** Pandas, Numpy, Pytorch, OpenCV, Ultralytics (YOLOv8 model), etc.
- **Epochs:** 1000 (number of times the entire dataset is passed forward and backward through the neural network during training)
- **Patience:** 40 (number of epochs with no improvement after which training will be stopped early)
- **Batch Size:** 16 (number of samples used in one iteration to update the model)

4.5 Development of Flight Operation Data Utilization Module

Development of a Module for Alerting the Monitoring System Upon Entry of Aircraft into a Specific Surveillance Area Using Flight Operation Data. The development environment is as follows:

- **Development Language/Main Libraries:** Python/folium, shapely
- **Flight Operation Data:** Flight Tracker based on ADS-B

4.6 Development of an Integrated Threat Detection

The final step involved integrating the module (software) equipped with the object detection model and the aircraft monitoring module (software) utilizing flight data to develop the threat detection system. Real-time optical cameras (hardware) were installed to provide videos to the object recognition model and the ADS-B tracker (software) was designed to input data into the flight surveillance module. Based on these modules, an administrator can view warning messages, real-time monitoring video, and logs (Fig. 2).

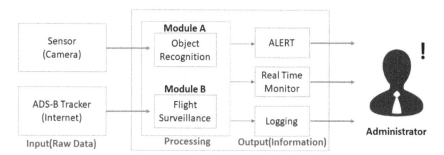

Fig. 2. Flowchart of Threat Detection System

5 Results

We conducted an evaluation of the trained deep learning model using the threats test dataset (image, real world video), as described below tables. Considering the 'mAP' results (image) and 'detection ratio' result (real world video), the effectiveness in utilizing the threat detection system was confirmed.

On the other hand, the several problems were founded.

- Although this system was detected as a threat object, there were cases where it was not possible to accurately distinguish what kind of object it was (see True-Positive).
- There were some situations in which clouds were detected as a threat object even though there was a clean sky without a threat object (see Abnormal counts).
- In most cases of birds, it was recognized as a threat object, but the type was classified as an airplane. It is assumed that this appeared by learning a still image of a sitting bird, not a flying bird when learning the model.

As a result of the research, the need to improve the system in the direction of (1) improving the performance of classifying the types of threat objects and (2) reducing the percentage of false positives was found. These improvements will be studied later.

Acknowledgments. This research was funded by the Hyundai Motors Company (HMC) and KT.

Disclosure of Interests. The authors have received research grants from Hyundai Motors Company (HMC) and KT.

References

1. KPMG.: Spread out in the sky, Mobility revolution, UAM. KPMG Insight **70**(1), 3 (2020)
2. Lee, Y.J., et al.: UAM Concept of Operations, 1st edn. Konkuk University, Seoul (2020)
3. Molit, R.O.K.: K-UAM Technology Roadmap. 1st edn. R.O.K Goverment, Sejong (2021)
4. Zou, Z., et al.: Object detection in 20 years: a survey. Proc. IEEE **111**(3), 258 (2023)
5. Molit, R.O.K.: Airport Facility Law, 14th edn. R.O.K Government, Sejong (2023)
6. Hussain, M.: YOLO-v1 to YOLO-v8, the rise of YOLO and its complementary nature toward digital manufacturing and industrial defect detection. MDPI Mach. **11**(7), 677 (2023)
7. Zhuang, F., et al.: A comprehensive survey on transfer learning. Proc. IEEE **109**(1), 43−76 (2021)

Intelligent Navigation Light Design for Night Riding Enthusiasts

Haotian Zhuang[✉]

East China University of Science and Technology, Shanghai 201424, People's Republic of China
isazhuanghaotian@gmail.com

Abstract. Night cycling is gaining popularity in China, especially among urban professionals due to its simplicity and compatibility with busy schedules. Through literature research and user surveys, this study reveals existing market problems such as single-direction lighting, equipment management difficulties, integration challenges with home environments, and limited usage scenarios.

Based on the understanding of these existing problems, this study proposes and designs a multifunctional intelligent cycling lighting device aimed at addressing the aforementioned challenges. Research methods include desktop research, competitive analysis, questionnaire surveys, and user interviews to gain insights into the needs and pain points of night cycling users. Through the analysis of user workflow and the integration of design opportunities, the study primarily focuses on hardware design, presenting a multifunctional intelligent cycling light product specifically designed for suburban night cycling enthusiasts. Covering both indoor and outdoor usage scenarios, the product enhances practicality through the interconnectedness of hardware and software, thereby achieving a multifunctional intelligent cycling equipment design solution that meets outdoor night cycling needs.

The main contributions of this study lie in the breakthrough and innovation of the current market's homogenized product design, expanding the product's usage scenarios and achieving multi-directional lighting. By effectively integrating the functions of other cycling auxiliary devices such as navigation, cycling odometer, weather forecast, and timing, the study enhances the product's convenience and efficiency, thus improving user experience. The application of this product can reduce the redundancy caused by the single functionality and numerous quantities of different cycling auxiliary devices, providing a demonstration for the sustainable development of the bicycle industry.

Keywords: Industrial Design · Suburban Night Cycling · Bicycle Lighting Equipment · Sports Gear

1 Introduction

Recently, urban areas have witnessed a surge in the popularity of outdoor cycling, serving as both recreation and exercise. This trend has captivated urban white-collar workers in China who seeks to diversify leisure activities and social interactions through sports.

C. Stephanidis et al. (Eds.): HCII 2024, CCIS 2118, pp. 311–321, 2024.
https://doi.org/10.1007/978-3-031-61963-2_31

Night cycling has emerged as a favored activity among this demographic, offering convenience, relaxation, and accessible aerobic exercise. Urban centers like Shanghai have seen a notable surge in post-80s and post-90s generations engaging in night cycling, solidifying its status as a burgeoning trend in outdoor sports, particularly among urban white-collar workers, fostering broader participation in outdoor activities.

With the rise of the night cycling trend, the domestic market for smart cycling products in China is experiencing significant growth opportunities. Over the past two years, the number of participants in cycling activities has been increasing annually nationwide. According to data from the China Bicycle Association, the current number of bicycles in China exceeds 200 million [1].

A study on the characteristics of urban residents' leisure cycling behavior has shown that infrastructure and supporting equipment are important factors restricting the development of cycling [2]. Although night cycling has gained increasingly widespread recognition and popularity among urban populations in China, corresponding cycling accessories are relatively scarce in the domestic market, failing to meet the diverse needs of current cycling enthusiasts.

In terms of safety, the current social environment and legal regulations in China do not yet mandate the use of lighting devices for bicycles at night. In 2020, there were 23,123 traffic accidents nationwide caused by electric bicycles. Accidents peaked during the morning and evening rush hours, especially during the evening rush hours (18:00–21:00) [3]. Most bicycles do not have lights when traveling at night, sharing non-motorized lanes with electric bicycles, posing risks to cyclists' safety.

Therefore, cycling lights play a crucial role in night cycling. They not only improve the cyclist's visibility but also enhance pedestrians' and other vehicles' awareness of cyclists. Suitable cycling light equipment can not only enhance the safety of night cycling but also effectively prevent potential traffic accidents [4].

In conclusion, night cyclists face various issues regarding the diversity and safety of equipment, necessitating better solutions to enhance the cycling experience. Thus, this study aims to analyze the current status and usage cases of bicycle riding lights in China, understand the development of the domestic market for smart cycling products, and deeply analyze the gaps and limitations of cycling light products in the market, providing a theoretical basis and practical guidance for the development of smart cycling products that better meet the needs of night cyclists.

2   Research Methodology

This study aims to design a safer intelligent outdoor night cycling light through innovative enhancements to existing products. Development direction was determined via desktop research and competitive analysis. Methods including questionnaire surveys and user interviews were used to understand the needs of outdoor night cyclists. Design techniques such as user journey mapping identified design opportunities and requirements. A product design framework was established to determine solutions, functionalities, and expressions. Finally, an interaction information framework was constructed to explore software and hardware design, achieving a safer, more convenient, and efficient intelligent navigation cycling light.

2.1 Desktop Research

The cycling light (see Fig. 1) is an illumination device designed specifically for cyclists to enhance visibility and safety during night or low-light riding conditions. Typically mounted on the front of bicycles (see Fig. 2), cycling lights illuminate the path ahead for users. LED technology is commonly employed in most cycling lights. The design of cycling lights typically takes into consideration the specific requirements of night riding, such as illumination range, waterproof performance, and ease of installation and removal. These lights are often powered by batteries or USB charging.

Fig. 1. Basic form of cycling light   **Fig. 2.** State of cycling light in use.

In different cycling scenarios, users have various demands for cycling lights. Urban outdoor night riders typically encounter three main cycling scenarios: "Urban Cycling," "Suburban Cycling," and "Rural Cycling."

- In urban cycling scenarios, cyclists face dense traffic and busy streets, requiring higher demands for cycling lights such as turn signal lights and brake indicator lights on to enhance visibility to surrounding pedestrians and motorists.
- Suburban cycling areas lie between urban and rural regions, featuring wider roads with less traffic. However, poorly lit roads may exist, necessitating cycling lights with strong illumination capabilities to adapt to diverse environments.
- In rural cycling, roads may be muddy and bumpy with limited lighting. Riders prioritize stable and long-lasting lighting along with increased visibility to prevent accidents.

In summary, cyclists in different scenarios should choose suitable lights based on their skill level and preferences while maintaining safety awareness and adhering to proper cycling practices.

2.2 Competitive Analysis

This article focuses on the design improvements of cycling lights, which comes in various forms, applications, functions, and colors. By researching representative products from the top ten ranked and best-selling cycling light brands domestically and internationally, a comparative analysis of different types of cycling lights was conducted, resulting in the following findings (see Fig. 3).

The trends in the future development direction of cycling lights are summarized based on the above table analysis.

Currently, most front cycling lights suffer from the following design issues: firstly, there is a lack of coverage in the illumination range, as it only covers the front area,

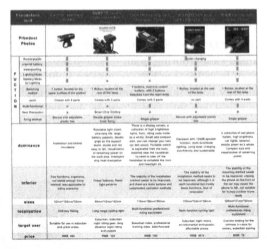

Fig. 3. Competitor Analysis.

neglecting variations in road conditions, thereby limiting the applicability of the equipment. Regarding operation modes, the mainstream market still relies on button switches and manual adjustment of cycling lights, which are not conducive to operation while riding. The practicality of multifunctional cycling lights needs to be reconsidered. Therefore, improvements in illumination modes, operation modes, and functional diversity require further research.

Based on the existing issues, this design aims to address them by expanding the illumination range. This will involve adopting adjustable brightness, multi-mode switching, and other illumination modes to adapt to different environmental requirements. In terms of operation modes, screen touch and slide switching will be added to reduce user operation difficulty. Functionally, integration with other cycling accessories will meet user needs, enhance product cost-effectiveness and usability, and optimize the overall user experience.

2.3 User Research

Questionnaire Research

Survey population. The subjects of this research are urban outdoor night cyclists, primarily comprising young and middle-aged individuals. Their cycling routes mainly include urban roads, suburban roads, and rural roads.

Purpose of the Study. This study examines the usage experiences of target users regarding bicycle riding light products and equipment for outdoor night cycling. It utilizes a combination of online questionnaire surveys and offline user interviews to systematically investigate users' demands and preferences. By delving into the routines of night cycling enthusiasts, it captures key information and pain points in the night cycling experience, aiding in accurately depicting user profiles and journey maps. This approach guides the design direction to better meet user expectations.

Research Methodology. The questionnaire content was drafted online using the "Wen-juanxing" platform. The questionnaire covered respondent information, night cycling experience, and equipment usage. It was distributed in seven active WeChat cycling groups, yielding 153 valid responses.

Research and Analysis. The survey included demographic information such as gender and age. Results revealed a balanced gender distribution, with 57.52% male and 42.48% female respondents. The age group of 26–30 years old had the highest participation at 29.18%, followed by the 18–25 age group at 22.22%. These two age groups accounted for over half of the total respondents, indicating significant involvement from young and middle-aged individuals in cycling activities.

The distribution of time spent participating in cycling activities among the respondents was varied (see Fig. 4). Among them, the highest proportion was those who had been participating in cycling activities for about 1 year, accounting for 32.03%. The next highest proportion was among those who had been cycling for approximately six months, accounting for 28.1%. The proportion of those who had been cycling for more than 2 years was 14.38%.

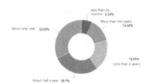
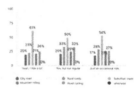

Fig. 4. Distribution of users' riding age.   **Fig. 5.** Distribution of users' riding route preference.

In order to focus the design direction, it was necessary to explore which route types are most frequently ridden by cyclists among those who have maintained a stable cycling habit over time. Analysing the data obtained from the research (see Fig. 5), among the three categories of "regular riders", "no regular frequency" and "occasional riders", the most frequently chosen route type for cycling enthusiasts was suburban roads, irrespective of the frequency of cycling. Regardless of the frequency of cycling, the most common route type chosen by cycling enthusiasts was suburban roads. More than half, 61%, of those who ride regularly choose suburban routes. Road cycling is the next most likely choice, after suburban roads.

Based on the analysis above, we have decided to focus on suburban roads as the primary reference scenario. Subsequently, we will prioritize considering the needs and characteristics of cycling on suburban roads to enhance the practicality and user experience of the product. We will design lighting modes and luminaire features more suitable for suburban cycling, as well as product functionalities that better adapt to the suburban road environment.

Through investigating the preferred positions for placing smartphones during cycling (see Fig. 6), we found that most users tend to place their phones in safer locations such as "clothing pockets" or "personal backpacks". Further discussions with users during interviews revealed that this practice stems from the high risk of phones falling during cycling due to the bumpy nature of the ride and potential accidents like collisions, tire

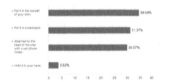

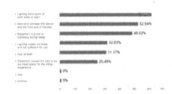

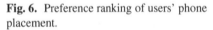

Fig. 6. Preference ranking of users' phone placement.

Fig. 7. Users' trouble ranking with products.

blowouts, or overturns, especially during high-speed cycling. However, when users need to use their phones for navigation, they have to take certain risks by either holding the phone or placing it on the handlebar phone mount. Thus, this analysis inspired the idea: Can cycling light products be compatible with navigation functions, replacing the need for smartphones, thereby reducing the risk of phone damage and providing users with effective services?

To investigate the issues with existing front-mounted cycling light products (see Fig. 7), we invited users to select the difficulties they encountered while cycling at night through a multiple-choice method. The results showed that the majority of users (62.09%) experienced the problem of "blind spots on both sides" while cycling in suburban areas at night. This indicates that existing front-mounted cycling lights only consider forward illumination during design, neglecting the users' need for side illumination, which causes inconvenience and unease.

Next, 52.94% of users considered "device installation and compatibility with the handlebar" to be a problem that troubled them. This suggests shortcomings in the installation and compatibility of existing cycling light products, leading to difficulties for users during use.

The third most common issue, with a percentage of 49.02%, was "device loosening during cycling." This indicates a lack of stability in existing front-mounted cycling lights during use, which may affect the user's cycling experience and safety. To address these issues, it is necessary to design front-mounted cycling light products that are more comprehensive, stable, and compatible, to enhance the user's cycling experience and safety.

During user interviews, one user who no longer regularly cycles due to physical reasons mentioned that after giving up cycling, they were unsure how to deal with their previous cycling equipment, and were reluctant to discard it and wanted to keep it as a memento.

In addition, our questionnaire surveys revealed that cycling enthusiasts who seek cycling data records currently face challenges with scattered and independent data recording devices. Carrying multiple devices for each cycling trip leads to cumbersome equipment management, increases the risk of forgetting or losing devices, and results in incomplete data. This inconvenience and trouble discourages users. Additionally, the scattered nature of these devices complicates data aggregation and analysis, posing a barrier for novice cyclists.

2.4 Summary of the Research Section

Persona. The design targets young and middle-aged individuals who prefer solo outdoor night rides in suburban areas, based on user research findings from interviews and questionnaires. A user persona for this group was developed by extracting their characteristics. (see Fig. 8).

Fig. 8. Persona.

After conducting thorough research on outdoor night riding enthusiasts through online and offline channels, user behavior was categorized into three phases: "pre-ride," "during ride," and "post-ride." A user journey map (see Fig. 9) was created to depict potential challenges and user behavior. By incorporating the user's emotional fluctuations, the system identified the user's current riding process and potential touchpoints throughout the entire journey.

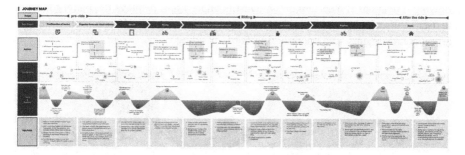

Fig. 9. User Journey Diagram.

Problem Definition: Based on the above analysis, the following comprehensive user pain points and user needs table (see Fig. 10) were compiled, focusing mainly on three aspects: "use of riding equipment," "riding safety," and "data recording."

In terms of device usage, cycling lights are often only used outdoors and are frequently idle in indoor household settings. Users emphasize the stability of the device when worn and its waterproof performance for comfort and safety. They hope for stable usage in various weather and road conditions. Additionally, users prefer devices that are compact, portable, and easy to carry to save time on equipment setup before traveling

In terms of safety, users seek improved lighting performance and longer battery life for extended night rides. They also value cycling devices with data recording and navigation features, particularly ones that are portable. Feedback on sports data serves as a significant motivator for users to maintain their cycling habits.

3   Design Result - KUMI LIGHT Intelligent Cycling Lights

3.1   Product Design Practices for Hardware

Design Positioning. The hardware design of the intelligent lighting cycling device for suburban outdoor night riding in this study is based on the existing design of cycling lights and the development of navigation devices for cycling. The aim is to design an outdoor cycling light that inspires users to ride.

Product Features Overview and Usage. The usage effect diagram of the intelligent lighting riding device for suburban outdoor night riding is shown in Fig. 11. In outdoor environments (left side of Fig. 11), users can connect this product to the fixed bracket installed on the bicycle head by inserting it and then press and hold the circular button on the right side of the device for 3 s to start the device. Before use, ensure that the device is connected to the phone via Bluetooth. Simply press and hold the circular button on the left side of the body for 5 s until the button light ring starts flashing to enter Bluetooth pairing mode. Once pairing is successful, users can output riding data in real-time on the smart riding device and receive weather forecasts and other information.

In indoor environments (middle of Fig. 10), the body and charging base adopt wireless magnetic suction charging. The charging base's design provides support for the body, allowing it to stand at a certain angle. During charging, it displays the battery level and the user's current accumulated riding mileage, resembling a medal, recording the user's current achievements, and encouraging outdoor riding.

Fig. 10. KUMI LIGHT Intelligent Cycling Lights at different time periods.

The lighting area of the device includes the front, left, and right sides (Fig. 10 right). For this product, users have two ways to turn on the riding light while cycling. One is to double-tap the center of the screen on any interface, and the other is to press the side button of the product once to switch it on or off. This dual activation method prevents the device from being accidentally touched when it rains. With lighting areas in different directions, users can improve the clarity of the surrounding environment, better predict road conditions and traffic situations, thereby reducing the occurrence of traffic accidents.

In a home environment, the intelligent riding lighting device needs to be charged. This product uses wireless magnetic suction charging technology, where electromagnetic induction wireless charging transfers energy through coil coupling. In terms of production costs, electromagnetic induction technology is lower in cost compared to other wireless charging technologies, providing certain economic advantages [5]. The charging base is connected to the plug through a data cable to provide power.

3.2 Software Component

Functional Framework Construction. Based on user needs, the software component of the device primarily records and displays information during cycling journeys (refer to Fig. 11). The device interface comprises five main functions: Home, Route Navigation, Physiological Monitoring, Cycling Data, and Settings.

1. Home: Provides a quick way to understand the current environmental conditions, such as time, weather, temperature, and wind direction, helping users determine whether the current environment is suitable for cycling in a timely manner.
2. Route Navigation: Helps users plan the best route, avoid congestion or dangerous areas, and improve cycling safety and efficiency.
3. Physiological Monitoring: Monitors users' physical condition, helps users understand their exercise status, adjust cycling intensity, and improve health and cycling performance.
4. Cycling Data: Records and displays users' cycling data, helps users understand their cycling habits and performance, and provides references and guidance for future cycling plans and training.
5. Settings: Allows users to personalize and adjust device settings, improving device applicability and user satisfaction.

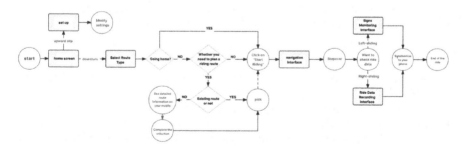

Fig. 11. KUMI LIGHT product usage procedure.

Interface Design. After organizing the structure and functions of the cycling light device, the software product's interaction interface is designed, considering aspects such as font style, image usage, functional layout, and button placement to complete the main function pages. Firstly, the primary interfaces and their contents for device interaction are determined, and the functions within each primary interface are arranged to align with the user's logical usage. There are a total of 5 primary interfaces (see Fig. 12), namely Home, Route Navigation, Physiological Monitoring, Cycling Meter, and Settings.

Fig. 12. Device Hi-Fi Interface Design.

The selection of font color for the device interface also requires attention during design. Fonts and pages are interdependent, so the choice of font color should not only consider its contrast with the background but also avoid being too stark. Suitable font colors can prevent visual fatigue, thereby increasing the usability of the interface [6].

Research in the United States has shown that under dim lighting conditions, using dark backgrounds with light-colored fonts can provide a clearer visual advantage [7]. Therefore, in this interface design, a dark gray color is used as the background color, which is more eye-friendly and reduces visual fatigue, especially in nighttime usage, highlighting white text information and other colored data.

According to human eye habits, in areas of the interface where emphasis is needed, colors with clear hue and high brightness can reflect the vitality and dynamism of the movement. Flexibly adjusting the transparency of colors within the same color scheme can help differentiate information. Furthermore, using color gradients to depict data changes can provide positive psychological cues to users. For the main information display in this interface, vibrant gradient colors with high saturation are selected as the primary hue, ensuring clarity even during nighttime use. High saturation colors can accurately guide the user's gaze, allowing for quick information extraction even while cycling. Additionally, bright and vivid colors like yellow, red, and green are chosen for secondary icons to enrich the software's palette, imbuing it with a youthful and energetic sports vibe.

4 Summary

This study focuses on addressing the issues of limited visibility, safety concerns, and equipment usability during night cycling. It delves deep into the needs of domestic night cycling enthusiasts and proposes an intelligent cycling lighting product that covers both outdoor and indoor usage scenarios based on user behavior patterns.

The primary innovation of this product lies in its departure from standardized designs, expanding its usage scenarios, and offering multi-directional lighting. By integrating functions of other cycling auxiliary devices such as navigation, cycling odometer, weather forecast, and timer, the product enhances convenience and efficiency, thus elevating user experience. Its application can reduce redundancy and improve cycling efficiency among various cycling auxiliary devices, thus promoting the transformation and upgrade of the cycling product market towards intelligence.

In the future, we will continue to explore and refine product functionalities, expand application scenarios, and develop social applications tailored for cyclists based on existing hardware products. This will facilitate communication and experience sharing among users, further enriching the night cycling experience and promoting the development of night cycling. With user experience at the core, we will integrate cutting-edge technologies such as artificial intelligence navigation and intelligent lighting control to meet personalized user demands, thus elevating the intelligence level of the product to a higher level.

References

1. Ziwei, F.: Bicycle industry rides on the wind as cycling moves hundreds of billions of yuan of industry. China City News (2023). https://doi.org/10.28056/n.cnki.nccsb.2023.000874
2. Xiaohai, H., Aiyun, C., Yan, L.: Research on the characteristics of urban residents' bicycle riding leisure behaviour. Contemp. Sports Sci. Technol. 7(36), 240–241+243 (2017)
3. Xinyu, Z., Zhaoming, C., Jianan, Z., et al.: Analysis of the causes of electric bicycle traffic accidents and countermeasures in China. Urban Traffic 19(06), 64–70 (2021)
4. Guang, Z., Yuping, H., Yuling, D.: A kind of bicycle smart light design based on safety guide. Mod. Inf. Technol. 5(12), 59–63 (2021)
5. Juncheng, W., Xiaoqian, M., Xiang, L., et al.: Analysis of the development status of global wireless charging industry. High Technol. Commun. 26(03), 299–305 (2016)
6. Jin, M.: Visual Guidelines-Research on Running Sport Interface Design Methods. China Academy of Art, Beijing (2017)
7. Erickson, A., Kim, K., Bruder, G., Welch, G.F.: Effects of Dark mode graphics on visual acuity and fatigue with virtual reality head-mounted displays. In: 2020 IEEE Conference on Virtual Reality and 3D User Interfaces (VR), pp. 434–442. Atlanta, GA, USA (2020)

Research on the Correlation of User Evaluation on the Interaction Features Between the Central-Control-Screen and Voice in the Automobile Cockpit

Yuanyang Zuo[1]([✉]) [ID], Jun Ma[1,2] [ID], Huifang Du[1], Meilun Tan[3], and Qi Yang[1]

[1] College of Design and Innovation, Tongji University, Shanghai, China
zuo.yy@qq.com
[2] School of Automotive Studies, Tongji University, Shanghai, China
[3] Academy of Arts and Design, Tsinghua University, Shanghai, China

Abstract. The purpose of this study is to investigate the user experiences of the two mainstream interaction modes, voice interaction and central control screen (CCS) interaction, in intelligent cockpits. A vocabulary library for sensory words in the two modes is established by collecting sensory imagery vocabulary based on the theory of sensory engineering. Questionnaire design is used to collect users' subjective feelings, resulting in user experience scores for the two modes. The research results identify the most favored user experiences in both voice and CCS interactions, as well as strongly correlated user perceptions and clustering results obtained through principal component analysis. The findings provide targeted guidance for automakers and designers to meet user interaction needs in both voice and CCS interactions, thereby enhancing the interactive experience and safety of automotive intelligent cockpits.

Keywords: Automobile Cockpit · Central Control Screen Interaction · Voice Interaction · User Experience

1 Introduction

The widespread application of automobiles and the continual enhancement of user experiences have made automotive interaction design [1–3] and multimodal interaction [4, 5] ongoing focal points of research. More studies are concentrating on the development trends of multimodality and the application and integration of new modes within the driving cockpit [6, 7]. Ma et al. assessed the impact of interaction modes and secondary task categories on driver distraction from vehicle information systems [8]. Their previous research also analyzed the distracting effect of human-machine interface (HMI) displays on driving in vehicles [9]. In the field of voice and touch interaction in intelligent cockpits, more attention is paid to the experiential differences within individual modal interactions, as well as research on the driving experience and performance brought

C. Stephanidis et al. (Eds.): HCII 2024, CCIS 2118, pp. 322–328, 2024.
https://doi.org/10.1007/978-3-031-61963-2_32

about by combining with other modal forms. Ji et al. conducted research on the interaction design of information type and speaker gender in autonomous driving vehicles, with results indicating that female voices were perceived as more trustworthy, acceptable, and pleasant compared to male voices. This is attributed to participants' greater familiarity with female voices, which are widely used in intelligent devices and navigation systems [10]. Pfleging et al. analyzed the impact of multimodal interaction combining gestures and voice on driving performance, concluding that while the use of speech and gestures was slower than using buttons, driving performance remained similar, and there was reduced visual demand when using speech and gestures [11]. Zhang et al. found that different positions and user interfaces of displays significantly affected the comfort level of drivers [12]. Currently, voice interaction and touch interaction are the mainstream interaction input methods in intelligent car cabins. However, there is a lack of comparative research. User evaluations play a particularly crucial role in assessing these two modes. The research question in this study is whether there is a correlation in user perspectives on traditional mainstream interaction modes in automobiles. What conclusions can be drawn through a study of correlation? This study conducts a survey targeting users' perspectives on the two interaction channels of voice interaction and CCS, aiming to draw conclusions and explore key findings related to correlation. Correlation studies contribute to a deeper understanding of user interaction preferences in specific environments, enhance the intuitiveness, efficiency, and user satisfaction of interactions, and enable safer designs, thereby reducing distractions and attention dispersion during the driving process.

2   Method

This study, based on the theory of sensory engineering [13], collected sensory imagery words to establish a sensory word library in two dimensions: voice interaction and CCS interaction. The study utilized clustering analysis to eliminate intention words with similar meanings. Subsequently, a comparison was made within intention words to describe CCS interaction and voice interaction. Finally, subjects with higher frequencies were matched with corresponding imagery words, resulting in a total of 6 pairs of sensory engineering word pairs: Size-Cool; Interior-Simple; Function-Rich; Operation-Convenient; Driving-Focused; Steps-Efficient. After conducting interviews with 8 testers (interaction designers, automotive engineering, and users), it is found that the most frequent words in CCS interaction are "unable to find functional location", "content interference", and "system stability". The most frequent words in voice interaction interviews are "recognition errors", "unsatisfactory execution", and "difficulty in conceptualizing language". Additionally, a quantitative survey has been conducted on 6 word pairs and 6 high-frequency interview words through questionnaire with 12 questions (See Appendix) (Sample size: 210; Method: Online questionnaire; Source: Users of intelligent cockpit cars in first-tier cities in China). The interactive features of the CCS and voice are scored with Likert 5-point scale, and principal component analysis and correlation analysis have been performed on the data. The whole research method flowchart is shown in Fig. 1.

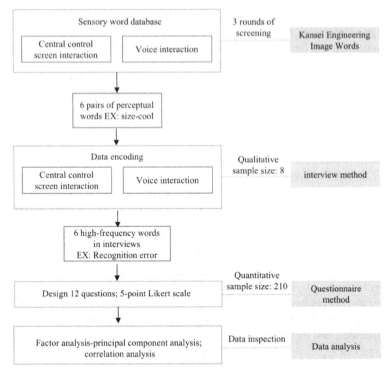

Fig. 1. Research method flowchart.

Table 1. Kaiser-Meyer-Olkin Bartlett's Test of Sphericity.

KMO sampling suitability q		0.860
Bartlett's test of sphericity	Approximate chi-square	1038.269
	degrees of freedom	66
	Significance	0.000

3 Results

The validity evaluation [14] of the results is shown in Table 1. The KMO value 0.86 which is greater than 0.7 is considered acceptable, indicating that the data is suitable for factor analysis. The p-value of Bartlett's sphericity test is 0.000 which is smaller than 0.050, indicating that the questionnaire has a validity structure. The correlation matrix is not an identity matrix, and there is correlation between data. In the questionnaire, the perceptual engineering questions that interact with the CCS are A1−A3 (positive questions), while the frequency of interviews is related to A4−A6 (negative questions). The perceptual engineering questions related to voice interaction in the questionnaire are B1−B3 (positive questions), while the frequency of interviews is related to B4−B6 (negative questions). In the average values of 210 CCSs, A3 (Rich function of CCS) is the most favored by users (4.22). In the average value of voice interaction, B2 (Voice interaction making drivers more attentively compared to the CCS) and B3 (Voice interaction improving efficiency) get the highest score (4.26). On the whole, B6 (Troublesome to construct voice command) gets the lowest score (2.32). As shown in Fig. 2, three principal components have been extracted after conducting principal component analysis on the data. A1−A3 and B1−B3 show a clustering relationship, mainly based on the survey results of perceptual engineering intentions. A4−A6 and B4−B6 show a clustering relationship, mainly based on the survey results of high-frequency words in the interview.

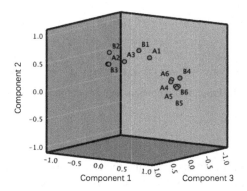

Fig. 2. Principal component analysis component diagram.

It can be found that there is a strong clustering relationship between A2 & B3 and A5 & B6. Figure 3 shows the correlation coefficients of data with Pearson correlation study [15, 16]. There exists strong correlation between B5 (Unsatisfied voice command) and B6 (Troublesome to construct voice command), which only represents degree relationships of the same changes rather than causal relationships.

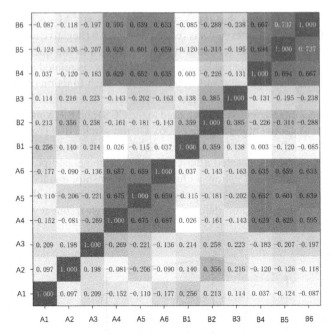

Fig. 3. Principal component analysis component diagram.

4 Conclusion

This paper explores the concerns regarding the central control screen and voice interaction in the automobile cockpit through the extraction of affective engineering terms and interviews. It is found that users prefer rich functionality in central control screen interaction, while in voice interaction, more users agree with the views that "voice interaction makes users more focused than the CCS interaction" and "voice interaction can improve efficiency". Correlation analysis reveals a strong correlation between "dissatisfaction with voice commands" and "difficulty in constructing voice commands". The results of this study can provide insights for the integrated interaction design of voice and central control screens in automobile intelligent cockpits, contributing to enhancing the user driving interaction experience.

Disclosure of Interests. The authors have no competing interests to declare that are relevant to the content of this article.

Appendix

Number	Questions	Scale
A	Please rate your opinions on the following characteristics of the CCS:	

(continued)

(*continued*)

Number	Questions	Scale
A1	The large size of the CCS looks very cool	1. Completely disagree; 2. Disagree somewhat; 3. Neutral; 4. Agree somewhat; 5. Completely agree
A2	The CCS makes the interior look very sleek	
A3	The CCS makes the functions inside the car more abundant	
A4	The CCS makes it difficult for me to find the location of some functions	
A5	The content on the CCS distracts me while driving	
A6	I have concerns about the stability of the CCS (such as crashes)	
B	Please rate your opinions on the following characteristics of voice interaction:	
B1	Voice commands eliminate the need for me to remember many opening paths for functions	1. Completely disagree; 2. Disagree somewhat; 3. Neutral; 4. Agree somewhat; 5. Completely agree
B2	Using voice commands while driving makes me more focused on driving compared to operating the CCS	
B3	Voice commands save me a lot of operational steps, making my operations very efficient	
B4	The car often misunderstands what I say	
B5	The car often does not satisfy me with the results of my voice commands	
B6	I often find it troublesome to come up with voice commands	

References

1. Breitschaft, S.J., Pastukhov, A., Carbon, C.C.: Where's my button? Evaluating the user experience of surface haptics in featureless automotive user interfaces. IEEE Trans. Haptics **15**(2), 292–303 (2022)
2. de Clerk, M., Dangelmaier, M., Schmierer, G., Spath, D.: User- centered design of interaction techniques for VR-based automotive design reviews. Front. Robot. AI **6**, 13 (2019)
3. François, M., Osiurak, F., Fort, A., Crave, P., Navarro, J.: Automotive HMI design and participatory user involvement: review and perspectives. Ergonomics **60**(4), 541–552 (2017)
4. Burke, P.W., Burke, B.: Information Graphics: Innovative Solutions in Contemporary Design. Thames and Hudson (1999)
5. Papanek, V.J.: Design for the Real World. China Citic Press, Beijing (2012)

6. Park, J., Ebert, S.M., Reed, M.P., Hallman, J.J.: A statistical model including age to predict passenger postures in the rear seats of automobiles. Ergonomics **59**(6), 796–805 (2016)
7. Clabaugh, C., Matarić, M.: Robots for the people, by the people: personalizing human-machine interaction. Sci. Robot. **3**(21), eaat7451 (2018)
8. Ma, J., Li, J., Gong, Z.: Evaluation of driver distraction from in-vehicle information systems: a simulator study of interaction modes and secondary tasks classes on eight production cars. Int. J. Ind. Ergon. **92**, 103380 (2022)
9. Ma, J., Gong, Z., Tan, J., Zhang, Q., Zuo, Y.: Assessing the driving distraction effect of vehicle HMI displays using data mining techniques. Transp. Res. F: Traffic Psychol. Behav. **69**, 235–250 (2020)
10. Ji, W., Liu, R., Lee, S.H.: Do drivers prefer female voice for guidance? An interaction design about information type and speaker gender for autonomous driving car. In: Krömker, H. (ed.) HCII 2019. LNCS, vol. 11596, pp. 208–224. Springer, Cham (2019). https://doi.org/10.1007/978-3-030-22666-4_15
11. Pfleging, B., Schneegass, S., Schmidt, A.: Multimodal interaction in the car: combining speech and gestures on the steering wheel. In: Proceedings of the 4th International Conference on Automotive User Interfaces and Interactive Vehicular Applications, pp. 155–162 (2012)
12. Zhang, R., Qin, H., Li, J.T., Chen, H.B.: Influence of position and interface for central control screen on driving performance of electric vehicle. In: Krömker, H. (ed.) HCII 2020. LNCS, vol. 12212, pp. 445–452. Springer, Cham (2020). https://doi.org/10.1007/978-3-030-50523-3_32
13. Wang, W.M., Li, Z., Tian, Z.G., et al.: Mining of affective responses and affective intentions of products from unstructured text. J. Eng. Des. **29**(7), 404–429 (2018)
14. Bryman, A.: Social Research Methods. Oxford University Press (2016)
15. Dawson, B., Trapp, R.G., Trapp, R.G.: Basic & Clinical Biostatistics. McGraw-Hill Medical (2004)
16. Pearson, K.: On the criterion that a given system of deviations from the probable in the case of a correlated system of variables is such that it can be reasonably supposed to have arisen from random sampling. Phil. Mag. **50**(302), 157–175 (1900)

HCI in Psychotherapy and Mental Health

Design of Magnetic Levitation Therapy Pillow in DHM Model Supported Healthcare Field

Suer Fei$^{(\boxtimes)}$ and Cong Gu

China Academy of Art, Hangzhou 311100, China
3190200014@caa.edu.cn

Abstract. The advent of the digital medical era has accelerated the creation of Digital Human Models (DHM) in the healthcare industry. The fast-paced lifestyle and increasing stress in the modern world have also led to difficulties in falling asleep and poor quality of sleep among the masses, and the demand for therapy pillows has risen significantly. Concurrently, the author revealed that using magnetic levitation technology in pillow structures can efficiently fit to the human cervical spine. As a result, this paper proposes a therapy pillow design centered around magnetic levitation technology. Referencing the research of other scholars. The paper summarizes the stress conditions of different users' cervical regions during sleep, guiding the layout and intensity adjustment of the magnetic levitation system. Through specific experiments, the feasibility of applying magnetic levitation technology in intelligent therapeutic pillows is verified, resulting in the final solution. This study aims to explore the possibility of alleviating cervical discomfort during sleep based on the DHM model. It provides new insights into the application of magnetic levitation technology and holds certain referential value for the research of health therapy products.

Keywords: Magnetic Levitation · Therapy Pillow · Digital Human Models · Healthcare · Sleep Health

1 Introduction

1.1 Background of DHM Research in Healthcare Field

Digital Human Modeling (DHM), is the formation of databases from real human measurements in order to simulate human interaction with products or workplaces in a virtual environment. This assessment method is crucial for creating products that are centered on user needs. It integrates aspects of ergonomics and user psychology to help designers incorporate human factors into their design concepts at the early stages of design, which not only reduces the time required for design, but also effectively improves the overall quality of the product.

Currently, DHM is widely used in the healthcare field. "HADRIAN" [1] is a software for surveying and analyzing anthropometric data needs, which records anthropometric data, range of motion data, range of extension data, and daily mobility data for more

C. Stephanidis et al. (Eds.): HCII 2024, CCIS 2118, pp. 331–341, 2024.
https://doi.org/10.1007/978-3-031-61963-2_33

than one hundred respondents. The respondents included elderly people with age-related impairments and special disabled people (covering multiple disabilities), and these data are useful for healthcare products for special populations. Morotti, Colombo [2] and other scholars explored the possible causes of gait anomalies during prosthetic fitting and interface modeling by simulating and analyzing the walking styles of patients with lower-limb amputations, and ultimately developed a novel lower-limb prosthetic sleeve design system. In the field of assistive tools, an ergonomic evaluation of the design of a bathing system using a DHM model for the elderly was conducted, and the most appropriate bathing posture was also determined [3, 4]. These applications not only improve the quality of life of the users, but also provide a better understanding of the needs and conditions of the patients, thus providing more personalized healthcare services.

1.2 Background of Smart Therapy Pillow in the Field of Sleep Health

In the post-epidemic era, the home sleep therapy equipment market is booming. In China, it's expected to exceed RMB 439.9 billion by 2025. This growth is due to factors like a large population, aging society, poor sleep quality, and increased demand for private therapy. Government support for medical innovation and the rise of "artificial intelligence+" in home medical devices also contribute. Smart therapy pillows, are gaining traction for their ability to improve sleep quality and ease cervical spine problems. They're also affordable to use, showing great market potential in the expanding sleep therapy sector.

1.3 Rationale for the Application of Maglev Technology in Healthcare Field

The Review of Safety in the Use of Maglev Technology. Electromagnetic waves are formed by the perturbation of an electromagnetic field, and because of the action of the electromagnetic field, electromagnetic waves propagate, and the magnetic field that generates electromagnetic waves is also known as a "changing magnetic field". When the movement of the magnetic levitation device becomes a "changing magnetic field", its effect on the human body is also minimal. Electromagnetic levitation devices are usually marketed with a magnetic induction strength of no more than 0.35 T, and magnetic field attenuation in air is so severe that the effects of magnetic fields are generally negligible at a distance of about one meter from a strong magnetic field. International Commission on Non-Ionizing Radiation Protection on moving the human body in a fixed magnetic field in the document shows: human movement can withstand changes in magnetic field induction strength of 2 T (Tesla) more than 3 tons of nuclear magnetic resonance device, in the operation of its magnetic induction strength is also basically between 0.35–3 T, according to the investigation of the majority of the hospitals used in most of the nuclear magnetic resonance device magnetism is only 0.5 T.

Therefore, the magnetic levitation physical therapy pillow is designed to alleviate cervical discomfort through the height and angle of the fine-tuning, the need for power is extremely small, so the magnetic levitation technology in the design of the human body is basically harmless.

The Cases for Maglev Technology in Healthcare Field. The third-generation magnetically levitated artificial heart, called the China Heart VAD, jointly developed by

China's Suzhou Concentric Heart and Fu Wai Hospital, has been hailed as one of the most advanced artificial hearts in the world (see Fig. 1). The artificial heart expands the scope of the surgical procedure by reducing magnet power requirements, minimizing size while ensuring effectiveness, and is suitable for implantation in women and children. Fu Wai Hospital is conducting real-time aging tests on the artificial heart, which have been underway for more than three years. The artificial heart has passed the large animal reporting test of the China Food and Drug Administration Research Institute and is currently in the clinical trial stage [5].

Fig. 1. China Heart VAD (Image Source: "Advances in Maglev Technology for Medical Device Development")

In 2010, Dai Min et al. proposed a novel magnetically levitated artificial joint design, which utilizes the magnetic repulsion between the concave and convex surfaces of the joint by placing NdFeB permanent magnets in the prosthesis to reduce the load on the load-bearing surfaces of the joint [6]. The results of the study show that the artificial magnetic levitation joint design is feasible and safe, which can increase joint elasticity and effectively reduce the risk of prosthesis loosening.

Lv Yi et al. proposed a magnetic levitation cervical spine traction device in 2018, which has the functions of axial traction, horizontal rotation, and magnetic therapy, and can break through the limitations of the existing cervical spine traction device on the patient's head movement (see Fig. 2 and Fig. 3). This device has completed the cooperation between industry, academia and research, and in March 2020, it will be transformed and promoted in Shaanxi Province. It is expected to be applied to clinical treatment in the future [7].

2   Aim

Utilizing DHM to analyze human head and neck morphology in a sleep context, this study explores the development and implementation of a novel magnetic levitation therapy pillow. This integration of the DHM model into health-related physical therapy advances the field's capabilities significantly.

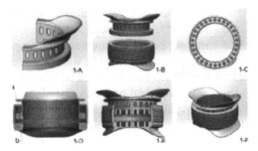

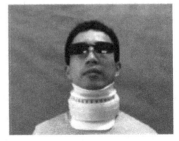

Fig. 2. Structure of magnetic levitation cervical traction device

Fig. 3. Use of magnetic levitation cervical traction device (Image source: "Design and application research of a magnetic levitation cervical spine traction device")

Magnetic levitation technology, characterized by its non-wearing, frictionless nature, and high degree of autonomy, is ingeniously integrated into the therapy pillow's structure. This innovation allows for a dynamic equilibrium, achieving a levitation effect that aligns with the human body's natural sleeping curvature. By continuously adapting to this curvature, the pillow effectively alleviates pressure on the head and neck, thus fostering a state of relaxation and stabilization. Consequently, this integration significantly enhances sleep quality, representing a breakthrough in physical therapy applications related to sleep health.

3   Methodology

3.1   Literature Review

Literature on Head and Neck DHM Modeling During Sleep. The human-machine aspect data of physical therapy pillow design is mainly for the analysis of the cervical spine morphology of people in different sleep positions, as well as the analysis of the state of the head and neck pressure, to form a DHM model about the human head and neck morphology in the sleep scenario (see Fig. 4). Thus, it is used to determine the structure, shape in, hardness, height and other parameters of the therapy pillow.

Finding the literature and understanding the cervical spine morphology mainly through Visible Body website (https://www.visiblebody.com/t). Zixiao Zhang [5] et al. analyzed the cervical spine morphology from by collecting cervical spine physiological data from 632 Chinese volunteers and classified them into different groups according to age. Eventually, it was found that cervical spine morphology varied with age and gender, and the higher the age, the more likely to induce cervical spine disease; cervical spine C2–7 angle was the primary outcome indicator, while other angles were secondary outcome indicators.

The appropriate pillow height during sleep is 6–7 cm behind compression for supine sleepers and 7–8 cm behind compression for lateral sleepers. Scholar Wang Lu Ye [6] found that both supine and lateral pillow heights were significantly higher in people

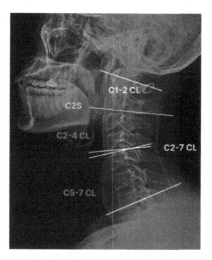

Fig. 4. DHM modeling of the cervical spine

with cervical spondylosis than in people without cervical spondylosis. Ren, S. C. [7] found that elevated pillow heights significantly increased the mean and peak pressures of the cranial and cervical regions as well as cervical spine extension and lordosis. The results of this study are summarized in the following table. Craniocervical pressure and cervical alignment are correlated with height and weight, and they are thought to reflect the quality of the cervical spine, providing a quantitative and objective assessment of the biomechanical effects of pillow height on the human body.

The resulting correlated DHM model is as follows:

Head and Neck Height in Different Sleeping Positions. In the lying position, the ideal pillow height is to keep the head and neck low, usually at a height of 7–10 cm in a horizontal line. In the side-lying position, the pillow height should be elevated to allow the head and neck to remain horizontal and to avoid excessive twisting and pressure on the neck, and the height should generally be between 10 and 14 cm (see Fig. 5 and Fig. 6).

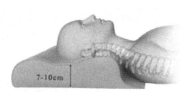
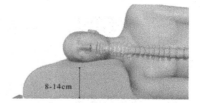

Fig. 5. Head and neck heights in the lying position

Fig. 6. Head and neck heights in the side lying position

Head and Neck Pressure Distribution in Different Sleeping Positions. When sleeping on the back, head pressure is around 10% of body weight (e.g., 25−50N for a 50 kg person) and neck pressure is about 5% (10−25N for 50 kg). Side sleeping results in head pressure of about 6% of body weight (12−30N for 50 kg) and neck pressure is roughly 3% (9−15N for 50 kg). (see Fig. 7 and Fig. 8).

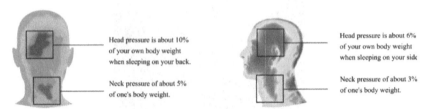

Fig. 7. Sleep on the back pressure distribution   **Fig. 8.** Sleep on the side pressure distribution

3.2   Experimental Research

Experimental Purpose. The aim is to evaluate the stability of both single and multiple magnetic levitation systems in controlling a levitated object, replicating head and neck pressure on a smart pillow. This involves manually pressing the object and varying its weight in a small magnetic levitation system to assess dynamic balance, understanding the relationship between levitation height and various variables, and experimenting with magnetic force size and position to evaluate support and comfort, establishing the working principle of the magnetic levitation therapy pillow.

Experimental Procedure. ①. Use a small TPU pillow model (120 mm × 65 mm × 60 mm, 800 g). Set up two identical magnetic levitation systems (800−1000 g capacity, 120 mm wide, 20 mm high) to mimic a therapy pillow's levitation, and connect the systems to a 220 V power supply for experimental documentation. ②. In the first experiment, place the object on the magnetic levitation system, aligning its center of gravity with the stator's center. The goal is to achieve stable mid-air levitation. The second experiment involves positioning the object above two magnetic levitation systems, ensuring uniform levitation and centering the object's gravity between the systems. Record the initial levitation height. ③. Manually press the levitated object to test stability, measuring and recording the levitation height and stabilization time (see Fig. 9 and Fig. 10) ④. Recruit ten volunteers to replicate these steps, ensuring the experiment's accuracy and reliability.

Fig. 9. Hand-pressure magnetic levitation object single magnetic levitation system

Fig. 10. Hand-pressing of magnetic levitation objects with multiple magnetic levitation systems

Experimental Result. Number of experiments (n)sults and observation records, the ability and stability of the maglev system to control the object were analyzed (see Table 1).

Table 1. Magnetic levitation system levitation height and stability

Number of maglev systems(n)	Number of experiments (n)	Average suspension height		Average steady state		
		Pressing before (cm)	Pressing after (cm)	Pressing before	Pressing after	Time of pressing after (s)
1	10	2.2	1.8	Stable, no wobble	Sway easily	95
2 (spacing 7.5cm)	10	2.5	2.2	Stable, no wobble	Stable, no wobble	205

We chose to use multiple magnetic levitation system control as the core working system of the magnetic levitation physical therapy pillow. The reasons are as follows:

Control Flexibility. Multiple magnetic levitation systems offer greater control over the position and orientation of the pillow. This enhanced control allows for better adjustment to the user's needs, providing more precise support and comfort. Single maglev systems, on the other hand, are constrained by their internal structure, which may lead to stability issues.

Resistance to Disturbances. Multiple magnetic levitation systems can independently manage disturbances in different directions. This feature ensures a higher level of stability, especially when faced with external perturbations. Conversely, a single maglev system's capability to counteract disturbances is limited due to its inherent physical limitations, making it less adaptable to varying conditions.

4   Result

The following section describes the detailed design methodology of the magnetic levitation therapy pillow in order to refine the functionality of the product.

Based on the physical therapy pillow size research in the market, the overall size of the product was determined to be 500 mm × 370 mm × 100 mm (see Fig. 11).

4.1   Multi-Point Support Based on Multiple Maglev Systems

The advantages of multiple magnetic levitation systems controlling a single object are analyzed through experiments in the above content, and at the same time, the pressure distribution of multiple cervical vertebrae under sleep scenes, and the head-neck-shoulder

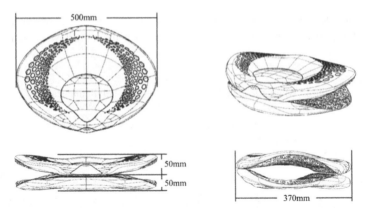

Fig. 11. Physical Therapy Pillow Size

relationship of different sleeping postures, the most suitable cervical vertebrae state is also different under different scenes before going to sleep, in physical therapy, and during sleep. Therefore, in the internal structure design of the intelligent physiotherapy pillow, we choose to use multiple magnetic levitation systems to control the product, so that the weight of the head and neck is dispersed to a larger support surface, to reduce the pressure of the pillow on the cervical vertebrae, and to achieve the purpose of the head and neck multi-point support.

In order to keep the lever in balance, it is necessary to satisfy the equal magnitude of the moments acting on both ends of the lever. See Eq. (1)

$$F1 \times L1 = F2 \times L2 \tag{1}$$

The relative distance between the magnets is constant, but the magnetic force is intelligently adjusted in response to changes in the user's sleeping position. Therefore, we can derive the formula for the force applied by the rear magnets as F back = F bearing force - L1/L2, and the formula for the left and right sides is F left - L3 = F right - L4. Where F bearing force is about 3% to 5% of the body weight, and the magnetic force of the left and right sides is about 6% of the body weight.

According to the pressure distribution of human sleeping posture, we layout three magnetic levitation systems in the left and right side sleeping area and neck support area respectively; in order to achieve the effect of dynamic balance of the magnetic force, we add one magnetic levitation system in the symmetrical side of the center axis of the neck support area, so there are a total of four magnetic levitation systems controlling the work of the intelligent physical therapy pillow. According to the principle of lever balance, the transformation of magnetic force and gravity can be seen, the left and right side sleeping area needs to provide 6% of the head weight of the magnetic force, the cervical support area needs to be 3%−5% of the head weight of the magnetic force, and the rear balance area needs to take the example of a 50 kg person, the head weight of the person is about 10 kg, so the left and right side sleeping area needs to be supplied with the magnetic force of 6N, and the cervical support area and the rear balance area need to be supplied with the magnetic force of 3−5N (see Fig. 12 and Fig. 13).

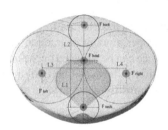

Fig. 12. Multi-point bracing works

Fig. 13. The relationship between the user and bracing points

4.2 Adaptive Height Adjustment for Different Sleeping Positions

According to the previous introduction, it is known that people lie flat and lie on their sides at different support points and need different appropriate heights. After the intelligent physical therapy pillow captures the user's sleeping height data in the early stage, when it monitors the user's sleeping posture change, it will carry out the adaptive adjustment of the data. The initial height of the pillow is 6 cm, when sleeping on the back, the pillow can be lifted up to 4 cm, and the overall pillow height is 7−10 cm; when sleeping on the back, the pillow can be lifted up to 8 cm, and the overall pillow height is 8−14 cm (see Fig. 14 and Fig. 15).

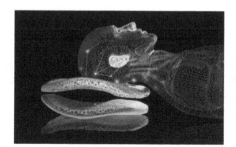

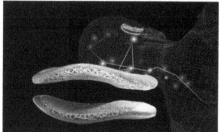

Fig. 14. Therapy pillow levitation effect when sleeping on the back

Fig. 15. Therapy pillow levitation effect when sleeping on the side

4.3 Combination with Cervical Traction Under Magnetic Levitation Technique

We cite the concept of Chinese traction, through the patient's head and neck to improve the appropriate traction massage to the cervical disc herniation and other diseases, to the magnetic levitation of the multi-point floating cervical traction driven relaxation. Intelligent formulations are made from the three dimensions of the strength, angle and time frequency of traction to avoid the uncontrollable factors brought about by manual labor.

The study by Wu Zhongdong [8] guided the specific traction angles required for different cervical spine conditions. For example, anterior cervical lordosis requires 5°

to 15° of forward flexion, while posterior cervical lordosis requires $-15°$ to $-5°$ of backward flexion. Chen Wei-Yeh [9] emphasized that the duration of traction is critical and is recommended to vary depending on the intensity of the traction force.

Therefore, the Maglev Pillow can provide the proper amount of traction for TCM traction, thus enhancing the therapeutic effect. This force can be adjusted by the magnetic levitation technology of the pillow. Magnetic levitation pillows can be customized for different levels of cervical pain and fatigue, providing different massage modes and intensities to meet individual needs.

5 Conclusion

This study introduces the design strategy of magnetic levitation physiotherapy pillow. On the one hand, the construction of the DHM model of the human head and neck during sleep is realized through literature review, which provides a kind of theoretical support for utilizing the DHM model. On the other hand, based on the DHM model, the working principle of the magnetic levitation physiotherapy pillow was established through the experimental research method to form a technical support. The final result optimizes user experience and enhances medical professionalism through the functions of levitation height adaption, multi-point support, and intelligent traction. It provides an effective and forward-looking solution for the healthcare field.

References

1. Marshall, R., et al.: Multivariate design inclusion using HADRIAN. In: Digital Human Modeling for Design and Engineering Conference and Exhibition. 2008–01–1899 (2008). Accessed 10 Sept 2017
2. Morotti, R., Rizzi, C., Regazzoni, D., Colombo, G.: Digital human modeling to analyse virtual amputee's interaction with prosthesis. In: Proceedings of the ASME 2014 International Design Engineering Technical Conferences and Computers and Information in Engineering Conference IDETC/CIE (2007)
3. Hanson, L., Hogberg, D., Lundstrom, D., Warell, M.: Application of human modeling in healthcare industries. In: Dufyf, V.G., (ed.) Digital Human Modeling. ICDHM 2009, LNCS 5620. Springer, New York (2009)
4. Maurya, C.M., et al.: Digital human modeling (DHM) for improving work environment for specially-abled and elderly. Sn Appl. Sci. **1**(11) (2019)
5. San, L., Zhang, N., Ma, F., et al.: Progress in the application of magnetic levitation technology in medical device research and development. China Med. Dev. **35**(08), 11–15 (2020)
6. Zhang, Z.X., et al.: A novel classification that defines the normal cervical spine: an analysis based on 632 asymptomatic Chinese volunteers. Eur. Spine J. (2023)
7. Ren, S.C., et al.: Effect of pillow height on the biomechanics of the head-neck complex: investigation of the cranio-cervical pressure and cervical spine alignment. Peerj 4 (2016)
8. Wu, Z., Zhang, X., Li, S.: Treatment of 200 cases of cervical spondylosis with traction at different angles according to neck flexion. J. Zhejiang Univ. Tradit. Chin. Med. (01):90+93 (2007)
9. Chen, W.Y., Wang, H.H., Liang, F.F., et al.: Research progress of traction treatment of cervical spondylosis. Chin. J. Rehabil. Med. **31**(05), 599–601 (2016)

10. Dai, M., Nie, T., Xiong, J., et al.: Magnetic levitation joint: a new design of artificial joint. Chin. J. Orthop. Surg. **18**(12), 1053–1054 (2010)
11. Zhao, X., Lv, Y., Li, X., et al.: Design and application research of a magnetic levitation cervical spine traction device. In: China Association of Medical Equipment. Compilation of papers from China Medical Equipment Conference and 2020 Medical Equipment Exhibition. Department of Nursing, Faculty of Medicine, Xi'an Jiaotong University; Department of Orthopaedics, The First Affiliated Hospital of Xi'an Jiaotong University, vol. 5 (2020)

Yūgen Cloudstone Echo: Exploring Emotional Design Interaction Design in Sleep Facilitation

Tianxu Guo[1(✉)] and Mengting Zhang[2]

[1] Macau University of Science and Technology, Macau 999078, China
gtx13797937701@163.com
[2] Springer Heidelberg, Tiergartenstr. 17, 69121 Heidelberg, Germany
mtzhang@must.edu.mo

Abstract. Sleep plays a pivotal role in the preservation of human health. However, the prevalence of insomnia, attributable to multifaceted factors such as environmental disturbances, emotional distress, and cognitive hyperactivity, underscores a significant challenge to achieving restorative sleep. This research endeavors to mitigate primary insomnia through the development of an interactive smart speaker, christened the Yūgen Cloudstone Echo. This innovative device amalgamates principles of emotional design, emotional design, and interactive technologies to foster a harmonious and serene sleep environment. Drawing inspiration from the Chinese concept of yūgen, characterized by its embodiment of profound mystery and aesthetic beauty, and symbolized by the ethereal imagery of clouds and the enduring solidity of stones, this study delves into the symbiotic relationship between these elements to engender an ambiance conducive to restful slumber. By harnessing auditory stimuli, visual aesthetics, and intuitive interaction design, this research proposes a novel paradigm for addressing insomnia, accentuating the pivotal role of emotional resonance in the advancement of technology. This paper elucidates the mechanisms by which sound and light effects can facilitate sleep induction, elucidating the design principles underpinning the Yūgen Cloudstone Echo and its application of emotional design. Furthermore, it delineates the functionalities, interactive modalities, and underlying components of the device, notably leveraging Arduino platforms for implementation. Through an interdisciplinary lens that integrates insights from design theory, psychology, and cultural studies, this paper underscores the transformative potential of emotionally resonant interaction design in augmenting both sleep quality and overall well-being.

Keywords: Insomnia · Auditory Therapy · Light Therapy · Interaction Design · Emotional Design

1 Introduction

Insomnia involves prolonged sleep latency, maintenance difficulties, and poor-quality sleep, leading to cognitive decline, mood swings, and health risks such as cardiovascular diseases and depression [1–3]. Often linked to psychological factors, its increase among healthy individuals is noted [4, 5]. It's classified into primary and secondary types, with primary insomnia not resulting from other conditions [6].

C. Stephanidis et al. (Eds.): HCII 2024, CCIS 2118, pp. 342–349, 2024.
https://doi.org/10.1007/978-3-031-61963-2_34

Recent technological advancements in sleep monitoring, like wearable devices, have been complemented by research showing the benefits of auditory stimuli, such as white noise and ASMR sounds, in improving sleep. However, these technologies don't fully meet the needs of those with insomnia. This paper introduces a design approach focusing on varied auditory stimuli and the effect of light on sleep, aiming to provide a holistic solution for insomnia sufferers.

The proposed Yūgen Cloudstone Echo speaker incorporates Zen aesthetics and utilizes Arduino platforms, integrating white noises and ASMR sounds, along with adjustable lighting, to enhance sleep quality and user experience. The following sections will explore how these auditory and visual stimuli aid sleep, emphasizing practical implementation and user interaction.

2 Literature Review

2.1 Auditory Therapy

Auditory stimuli, traditionally avoided for sleep, have been reevaluated for their sleep-inducing potential, leading to products designed for this purpose [7]. Music therapy utilizes musical elements to influence mental states, reducing stress and anxiety, particularly in those with severe illnesses [8]. Types of sleep-promoting auditory stimuli include colored noises like white and pink noise, ASMR sounds from natural or human-made sources, and preferred music genres. These have been shown to shorten sleep onset time and enhance sleep quality, though variety remains limited. White noise offers a consistent background sound, while ASMR provides relaxing sensory experiences, evolving from simple to complex sounds. The effectiveness of these auditory stimuli extends to improving sleep efficiency and altering sleep architecture, indicating their broad impact on sleep patterns [7].

2.2 The Effect of Lighting on Insomnia

Environmental and lifestyle factors, especially lighting, significantly affect sleep quality by regulating circadian rhythms and neuroendocrine responses [9]. The ambiance of a room, influenced by color temperature and brightness of lighting, plays a crucial role in creating a relaxing atmosphere conducive to sleep [10, 11]. Studies have shown that cooler light temperatures are associated with poor sleep quality, while warm, dim lighting can enhance relaxation and sleep by promoting melatonin production [12, 13]. Given the contemporary trend against total darkness and its negative impact on sleep, this paper advocates for an environment with warm-colored, low-brightness lighting to improve sleep efficiency and mitigate insomnia.

2.3 Emotional Design

Emotional design aims to elicit specific responses in users, such as happiness or calm, influencing behavior and mood [14]. For example, the comforting signage at Umeda Hospital by Kenya Hara exemplifies how design can soothe and impact emotions.

Donald Norman's model [15] breaks emotional design into visceral (immediate reactions), behavioral (interaction between design and user behavior), and reflective (post-interaction contemplation) levels. This research emphasizes the visceral and behavioral aspects to improve functionality and influence insomniacs' mood through human-computer interaction, aiming for a balance between initial emotional responses and subsequent behavioral outcomes.

3 Design of Yūgen Cloudstone Echo

3.1 Emotional Design of Yūgen Cloudstone Echo

This design fuses Zen culture with emotional and visual elements, combining philosophical depth with aesthetic appeal. The speaker's stone-like form symbolizes stability, strength, and groundedness, echoing Zen principles and aiming to invoke a sense of permanence and focus in the present [16] Designed with durability and reliability in mind, its smooth, rounded shape promotes a serene environment, aligning with consumer desires for tranquility and safety in smart technology in Fig. 1.

Fig. 1. Stone shaped device with knitted surface and operator interface at the bottom

In contrast, the design's cloud motif symbolizes Zen principles of lightness, flexibility, and impermanence, reflecting life's transient nature. Incorporated into the cloud-shaped base of the stone speaker, this design element promotes adaptability and fluidity, essential in today's ever-evolving technology landscape, as depicted in Fig. 2.

The design's cloud base symbolizes buoyancy and comfort, encouraging a release of tension and promoting serenity, crucial for those with insomnia. The combination of stone and cloud represents Zen's themes of solidity versus ephemerality, aiming to foster balance. This approach extends beyond aesthetics to encourage philosophical reflection and enhance user experience through a blend of form, function, and Zen principles, inviting deeper engagement with the product.

3.2 Auditory Function of Yūgen Cloudstone Echo

STONE. The smart speaker improves sleep by offering various colored noises and ASMR sounds to reduce external disturbances and create a calming environment. It uses

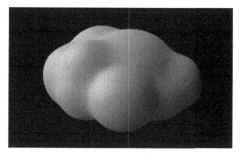

Fig. 2. Cloud shaped wireless charging device with soft silicone surface and memory material.

white, pink, and brown noise to mask disruptive sounds and provides ASMR audio to help users relax and ease into sleep.

Originating from 18th-century Europe, the music box, a time-honored and sophisticated automatic musical instrument, has undergone significant evolution. Traditionally encased in a refined metal or wooden exterior, it features a collection of preset metal teeth aligned with a rotating cylinder or disc. Operation is initiated by the user via turning a handle or pulling a string, causing the metal teeth to engage with cylinder protrusions in a precise order, resulting in melodious tunes. The music emitted by the box is distinctly charming, carrying a soft, ethereal quality that can evoke nostalgic sentiments and provide solace and relaxation. In this innovative design, the classical mechanics of the music box are seamlessly integrated into a sleep aid product, preserving the traditional knob mechanism for operation. This modern iteration allows users to start white noise playback by turning an "ear" in a counterclockwise direction, with the playback duration determined by the rotation's degree. The design thoughtfully incorporates a slow-releasing mechanism that emulates the music box's gradual cessation, ensuring that when playback concludes, the volume gently fades to silence, thus avoiding abrupt interruptions and fostering a smoother, more restful transition to sleep for the user, in Fig. 3.

Fig. 3. The operator interface is located at the bottom of the device and is a physical interface in the form of a carousel.

The product offers a feature that lets users record and personalize their sleep environment with natural sounds like forest rustling, ocean waves, or river flows. This customization enhances relaxation and promotes restful sleep by allowing users to integrate calming sounds from nature into their routine, fostering a deeper natural connection and creating an ideal setting for tranquility and rest.

To start recording, users press and hold the power button at the device's base for three seconds. This activates the device, indicated by the power button's illumination and LED lights within the upper section, shining through the mesh to signal recording initiation, as depicted in Fig. 4.

Fig. 4. Control buttons and backlit display.

CLOUD. The design focuses on user-product interaction to enhance user experience. By setting music and duration, users place STONE on a soft silicone base, which deforms to trigger warm, comforting LED lights, doubling as a night light to promote sleep, as shown in Fig. 5. The reversible deformation symbolizes the shift from daytime activity to nighttime rest, aligning with the natural process of falling asleep and creating a conducive environment for relaxation, mirrored in the contrasting designs of the hard STONE and the soft base.

Fig. 5. Emotional human-computer interaction experience.

In human-computer interaction, tactile feedback is crucial. When a user places the device on its charging base, the base's responsive design offers immediate physical feedback, validating device placement and beginning of charging. This interaction enhances the intuitive and satisfying user experience.

3.3 Light Therapy

Light significantly impacts the body's circadian rhythm and sleep cycles. The smart speaker, with its adjustable lighting, allows users to tailor brightness and color temperature to create an ideal sleep environment. Dimming lights and opting for warmer colors at night emulate natural darkness, promoting melatonin production and preparing the body for sleep. Furthermore, the speaker's base compresses to activate a warm LED glow, serving as both a night light and a charging indicator, thus providing visual comfort and convenience as shown in Fig. 6.

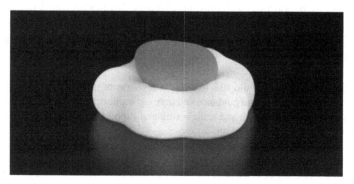

Fig. 6. After receiving the extrusion will emit low brightness warm light, the function is similar to the night light.

The smart speaker's design and features aim to reduce stress and create a peaceful sleep environment, blending Zen aesthetics with customizable settings to address individual sleep needs. This approach helps users tailor their surroundings for better sleep, effectively combating insomnia and enhancing sleep quality.

3.4 Interactive Components

STONE. The system employs an Electret Microphone Amplifier like MAX4466, connected to an Arduino, to record sounds, storing the data on an SD card. Sound playback is managed by the DFPlayer Mini MP3 module, which reads and outputs audio files through a speaker. A rotary encoder allows users to set playback duration, and a servo motor resets this encoder post-playback for convenience and system integrity.

CLOUD. The design features a deformable outer layer made from silicone or TPU, adapting shape under pressure. It utilizes a wireless charging module, compatible with Arduino, for power needs. A pressure sensor pad detects devices on the charging base, activating an Arduino-connected LED strip with warm LEDs. Brightness is modulated via PWM for soft lighting, and the system automatically turns off the LEDs when no device is detected, conserving energy and prolonging LED lifespan.

4 Conclusion

In conclusion, the Yūgen Cloudstone Echo presents an innovative solution to combat insomnia through a unique integration of auditory and light therapy grounded in emotional design principles. By combining the calming effects of white noise, ASMR sounds, and warm, dim lighting, this smart speaker aims to create a serene and conducive sleep environment. Drawing on Zen aesthetics, the device not only enhances the sleep quality of individuals but also offers an emotionally resonant experience that aligns with modern needs for relaxation and mental wellness. The integration of Arduino technology enables a customizable and interactive user experience, further advancing the potential of technology in addressing sleep-related issues. Ultimately, the Yūgen Cloudstone Echo exemplifies the transformative potential of combining traditional cultural elements with contemporary design and technology to address prevalent health challenges such as insomnia.

Acknowledgments. First, I would like to express my sincere gratitude to my supervisor, Ms. Mengting Zhang, for her profound guidance and untiring support. Her rigorous academic attitude, profound professional knowledge, and selfless care and support for students have enabled me to progress and grow on my research path.

Finally, I would like to thank my family for their support and understanding, they are a source of motivation for me to keep moving forward. I would like to thank all the people who have helped and supported me directly or indirectly, and together you have built every step of my academic career.

Disclosure of Interests.   The author has no competing interests to disclose regarding the content of this article.

References

1. Riemann, D., et al.: The hyperarousal model of insomnia: a review of the concept and its evidence. Sleep Med. Rev. **14**(1), 19–31 (2010)
2. Hertenstein, E., et al.: Insomnia as a predictor of mental disorders: a systematic review and meta-analysis. Sleep Med. Rev. **43**, 96–105 (2019)
3. Hertenstein, E., Benz, F., Schneider, C., Baglioni, C.: Insomnia—a risk factor for mental disorders. J. Sleep Res. e13930 (2023)
4. Kweon, Y.S., Shin, G.H.: Possibility of sleep induction using auditory stimulation based on mental states. In: 2022 10th International Winter Conference on Brain-Computer Interface (BCI), pp. 1–4. IEEE (2022)
5. Koffel, E.A., Koffel, J.B., Gehrman, P.R.: A meta-analysis of group cognitive behavioral therapy for insomnia. Sleep Med. Rev. **19**, 6–16 (2015)
6. Sateia, M.J.: International classification of sleep disorders. Chest **146**(5), 1387–1394 (2014)
7. Yoon, H., Baek, H.J.: External auditory stimulation as a non-pharmacological sleep aid. Sensors **22**(3), 1264 (2022)
8. Siddiqui, S., et al.: Artificial neural network (ann) enabled internet of things (IoT) architecture for music therapy. Electronics **9**(12), 2019 (2020)
9. Corbett, R.W., Middleton, B., Arendt, J.: An hour of bright white light in the early morning improves performance and advances sleep and circadian phase during the Antarctic winter. Neurosci. Lett. **525**(2), 146–151 (2012)
10. Custers, P.J., De Kort, Y.A.W., IJsselsteijn, W.A., De Kruiff, M.E.: Lighting in retail environments: atmosphere perception in the real world. Lighting Res. Technol. **42**(3), 331–343 (2010)
11. Schubert, E.F., Kim, J.K.: Solid-state light sources getting smart. Science **308**(5726), 1274–1278 (2005)

12. Hopkins, S., Lloyd Morgan, P., Schlangen, J.M.L., Williams, P., Skene, J.D., Middleton, B.: Blue-enriched lighting for older people living in care homes: effect on activity, actigraphic sleep, mood and alertness. Curr. Alzheimer Res. **14**(10), 1053−1062 (2017)
13. Obayashi, K., Saeki, K., Kurumatani, N.: Association between light exposure at night and insomnia in the general elderly population: the HEIJO-KYO cohort. Chronobiol. Int. **31**(9), 976–982 (2014)
14. Ho, A.G., Siu, K.W.M.G.: Emotion design, emotional design, emotionalize design: a review on their relationships from a new perspective. Des. J. **15**(1), 9–32 (2012)
15. Norman, D.A.: Emotional Design: Why We Love (or Hate) Everyday Things. Basic Books, New York (2004)
16. Suzuki, D.T.Q.: Zen and Japanese Culture (vol. 334). Princeton University Press (2019)

Digitally Controlled Light, Sound and Aroma Therapy

Guido Kempter[(⊠)] [iD], Walter Ritter[iD], Tobias Werner[iD], and Katrin Paldán[iD]

University of Applied Sciences Vorarlberg, Hochschulstraße 1, 6850 Dornbirn, Austria
guido.kempter@fhv.at

Abstract. Light, sound and aroma therapy are often used as complementary medical methods in the treatment of people with neuropsychiatric symptoms. However, there is a lack of systematization and individualization in the application. We present a solution that performs a coordinated light, sound and aroma therapy at the right time, for a suitable period of time, and with the required intensity as well as quality. In a field study, the solution was used for a total of 18 months with 130 elderly people suffering from dementia and 39 professional careers. The results show immediate effects of the interventions on physical activity, measured with motion sensors. Relaxation mode leads to calmer behavior and activation mode leads to more intense behavior. Long-term effects during medication treatment may be assumed in the neuropsychiatric symptoms. There are some methodological limitations in the interpretation, which typically result from field studies. We are able to demonstrate that a coordinated combination of light, sound and aroma therapy, tailored to a person's individual needs, is possible and can stimulate the expected behavior.

Keywords: Multi-sensorial Stimulation · Motion Activity · Neuropsychiatric Symptoms

1 Introduction

Light, sound and aroma therapy have long traditions and are based on many different mechanisms. One principle is that illumination, acoustics and scents in a room can have a direct psychological and biological influence on a person's mood. There is extensive literature on the details of which properties of these conditions promote which mood [1–3]. To put it simply, warm light, gentle sounds and soft scents have a calming effect, while cold light, lively sounds and fresh scents can stimulate people. Furthermore, this effect can be intensified by a mood transfer via people present in the room at the same time [4]. When one person becomes active or calms down, this mood can gradually spread to other people.

We looked at this approach in dementia care facilities. Traditionally, clients are exposed to sunlight, their favorite music is played for them and fragrance lamps are set up in order to use the therapeutic effect of light, sounds and scents [5]. However, these interventions are often not very systematic, but are applied depending on weather,

C. Stephanidis et al. (Eds.): HCII 2024, CCIS 2118, pp. 350–359, 2024.
https://doi.org/10.1007/978-3-031-61963-2_35

the presence of certain people or until the fragrance lamp is empty. In order to be able to implement multi-sensorial therapy plans precisely, we constructed a luminaire, an ultrasound player and a nebulizer that can be controlled digitally and can therefore generate illumination, sound and fragrance properties according to a required plan.

1.1 Hardware Description

The overall system consists of various modules that can be combined as required (see Fig. 1). The ultrasound module contains arbitrary sound files that are played on command. In our case, this was white noise with varying frequency, rhythm and volume (barely audible), overlaid with inaudible ultrasonic frequencies. The scent module contains two interchangeable atomizer bottles that spray dosed aerosols. In our case, these were essential oils of roses on the one hand and citrus fruits on the other. The light module generates direct and indirect lighting with a color temperature range of 2200 to 5000 K and a luminous flux of up to 7500 lm. A passive infrared sensor detects motion activity in up to four room sectors. Any interconnected wall switches and a web app are available as user interfaces. They can be used to initiate programmed sequences for the output devices, override them manually and activate an automated adjustment based on motion activity in the room. The controller also receives data from a wearable vital signs meter if it is put into operation. The controller uses the interface protocols provided by the input and output devices. In our case, this is a middleware stack for building automation, a wireless access point including routing and an OpenVPN client for remote management.

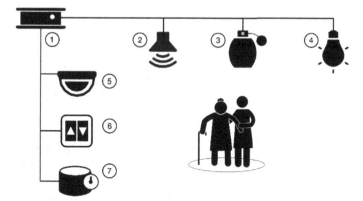

Fig. 1. Modules of the overall system for digitally controlled light, sound and aroma therapy. 1 WiFi controller, 2 Ultrasound module, 3 Scent module with two essences, 4 Light module with direct/indirect light color and intensity variation, 5 Passive Infrared (PIR) Sensor, 6 User Interface, 7 Wearable vital signs meter.

1.2 Software Description

The control concept is based on a simple principle: Multi-sensory activation in the case of hypoactivity and multi-sensory calming in the case of hyperactivity. The level of activity is either estimated by the care staff, who create a time program accordingly or control it manually, or determined by the PIR sensors. Figure 2 shows the measurement results of a PIR sensor for an entire day in the common room of a dementia care unit. The curves show the upper and lower limits of motion activity for this room. They are calculated as a confidence interval from the moving average of all previously recorded motion data sets. The vertical lines represent the current motion detector data for the selected day as an average value in a five-minute observation interval. If a currently measured motion is below the lower limit value three times in succession, the output devices in automatic mode give an activation impulse (flash symbol). The reverse is true if the upper limit value is exceeded (sleep symbol). As a stimulus lasts for twenty minutes (activation) or one hour (relaxation), the output devices no longer accept automatic triggering for these time intervals. However, the care staff can counteract this manually at any time via the user interface. The user experience with the overall system was successfully optimized with people from the target group population ($n = 139$ subjects) before it was deployed for the field test.

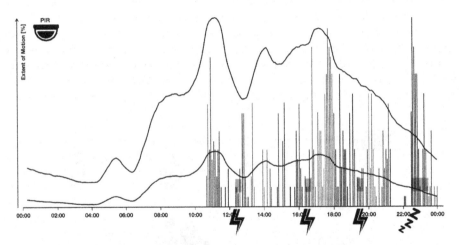

Fig. 2. Extent of motion in the common room of a dementia unit for one day, recorded with a passive infrared sensor (PIR). If the current extent of motion is below the lower limit value three times in succession, the output devices in automatic mode provide an activation intervention (flash symbol) and then remain passive for twenty minutes. If it is above the upper limit value three times in succession, the output devices in automatic mode give a relaxation intervention (sleep symbol) and then remain passive for one hour. Curves: Maximum and minimum limit determined on the basis of previous measurements. Vertical lines: Current extent of motion in the room (five-minute intervals).

1.3 Description of Therapy

Typical multi-sensorial stimulation includes modules for visual, acoustic, olfactory and vestibular stimulation [6]. The therapeutic goal is to create an optimally structured and stimulating environment that is adapted to the limited perceptual and cognitive abilities of clients suffering from severe dementia. A critical review of studies shows that the evidence for the therapeutic effect of multi-sensorial stimulation via light, sound and fragrances is generally weak [7]. In order to select the parameters for our stimulation, we used an experimental setting in advance to investigate the effect of different lighting situations, essential oil mixtures and sound variations in different combinations on a healthy population ($n = 2157$ subjects). Finally, the parameters shown in Table 1 were identified which showed the greatest effects in terms of psychological and physiological activation and relaxation.

Table 1. Selected parameters for the activation and relaxation intervention. The activation (flash symbol) lasted twenty minutes and the relaxation (sleep symbol) lasted one hour.

	Pitch rise: 200 cents	Aerosols: citrus essence	Indirect flux: 7000 lm
	Slope: 18dB/octave	Start level: 1200 ppb	Direct flux: 1500 lm
	Lowcut: 100 hertz	Final level: 600 ppb	Light color: 4000 k
	Pitch drop: 300 cents	Aerosols: rose essence	Indirect flux: 1000 lm
	Slope: 12 dB/octave	Start level: 1200 ppb	Direct flux: 220 lm
	Reverb: 4.2 seconds	Final level: 600 ppb	Light color: 2200 k

2 Evaluation

2.1 Methods

Use Case. Light, sound and aroma therapy are often used in the treatment of people with dementia as a complementary medical method [1–3]. In order to find out whether the therapeutic approach presented here has a positive effect in this area of application, it was evaluated in a field study with a cluster sampling over 18 months in five facilities for older people with dementia, one facility with assisted living for senior citizens and one private home. Overall 130 older people with dementia and 39 professional careers took part in the field study. A total of 3875 interventions were counted during the study period. It was assumed that a coordinated light, sound and aroma therapy at the right time, for a suitable period of time, and with the required intensity as well as quality helps to achieve the therapeutic goal.

Therapeutic Goal. Neurodegenerative and vascular forms of dementia are based on diseases of the brain that are considered to be steadily progressive and incurable. Dementia is defined by the decline and loss of cognitive function and daily living skills. In addition to cognitive symptoms, clients with dementia also exhibit a range of behavioral and psychological symptoms (e.g. delusions, hallucinations, agitation, depression, anxiety, euphoria, apathy, disinhibition, irritability, abnormal motor behavior, sleep disturbances, appetite and eating disorders). These are recorded using the Neuropsychiatric Inventory (NPI). The NPI is the most commonly used instrument to measure these symptoms in clinical studies of dementia [8]. Accordingly, we are aiming for a more positive change in the NPI total score using digitally controlled light, sound and aroma therapy in addition to medical treatment, i.e. a decrease in NPI score.

Behavioral Goal. As a behavioral measure for agitation and apathy, we use the extent of motion shown by the clients, which is recorded with commercial motion detectors. The sensors detect motion in predefined areas of interest using a one second sampling interval. A parameter for five-minute observation intervals was calculated for further data processing. The parameter "Extent of motion" expresses the proportion of measuring cycles in the five-minute observation interval in which motion was detected and is 1 respectively 100% if motion was detected continuously. The question is whether the multi-sensory relaxation leads to a reduction in behavioral activity and whether the multi-sensory activation leads to an increase in behavioral activity.

2.2 Results

Most activation interventions ($n = 2331$) were triggered between 7 and 9 a.m. ($n = 841$) and most relaxation interventions ($n = 1544$) were triggered between 7 and 9 p.m. ($n = 541$). As a reference, the data from motion sensors were analyzed in both time windows for those cases in which no intervention took place (no intervention, $n = 171$). In order to find out which stimulus combination achieves a desired effect, the following intervention types were considered separately: light intervention only, aroma intervention only, sound intervention only, combined sound and aroma intervention, combined light and aroma intervention and, finally, combined light, aroma and sound intervention.

Behavioral Effect. In a first step, the interventions that were intended to lead to relaxation or activation were considered separately, without making further distinctions between the intervention types. Figure 3 shows the progression of the extent of motion in different phases of the interventions, complemented by the cases without intervention. It is first of all noticeable that the interquartile range (IQR) of the measured values in all phases and interventions overlaps at the lower end of the measurement scale. In this respect, no large effects and only a low discriminatory power can be expected for the interventions. In general, there is a wide range of measurement data. Statistically significant effects in the desired direction, however, can be observed, if we compare the mean values before and after the interventions. With the related-samples Friedman's two-way analysis of variance, the significance of the decrease in the extent of motion with relaxation intervention can be confirmed ($p_r = 0.001$) and the increase in the extent of motion with activation intervention can be confirmed ($p_a < 0.001$). In the absence of interventions, no significant changes in the extent of motion were observed.

Another important finding of the analysis is that the initial condition for both interventions and the initial condition in which no intervention was triggered were different. The independent-samples Kruskal-Wallis test calculated a significant difference (p = 0.022) when comparing all three averaged measured values before the interventions, including before no intervention, in Fig. 3.

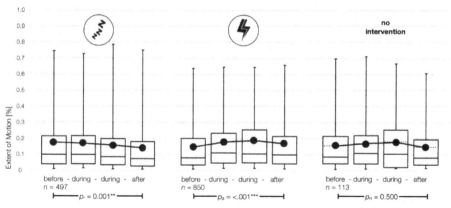

Fig. 3. Extent of motion in different phases of the interventions or in the absence of an intervention. The course of the mean values shows a significant decrease in the extent of motion with relaxation intervention ($p_r = 0.001$) and a significant increase in the extent of motion with activation intervention ($p_a < 0.001$). No significant changes in the extent of motion can be observed in the absence of interventions. Only those cases were considered here in which measurement data were available for all four phases of interventions.

Next, the effects of the different stimuli and stimulus combinations are of interest. Figure 4 shows the effects of the interventions designed to achieve relaxation. Once again, it can be seen that the IQR of the measured values for both intervention phases and all stimuli show overlaps at the lower end of the measurement scale.

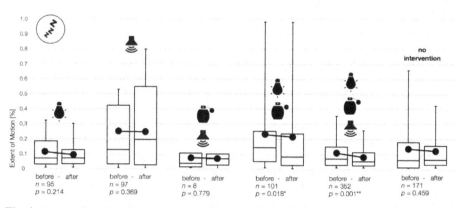

Fig. 4. Extent of motion before and after a relaxation intervention (light, sound, aroma, or combinations) and in the absence of an intervention. The course of the mean values shows a significant decrease in the extent of motion with combined light and aroma stimulus ($p = 0.018$) and a significant decrease in the extent of motion with combined light, aroma, and sound stimulus ($p = 0.001$). Only those cases were considered here in which measurement data were available for both phases of interventions.

The course of the mean values in Fig. 4 shows a significant decrease in the extent of motion with combined light and aroma stimulus ($p = 0.018$) and a significant decrease in the extent of motion with combined light, aroma, and sound stimulus ($p = 0.001$). The related-samples Wilcoxon signed rank test was used to test significance.

Finally, Fig. 5 shows the effects of the interventions designed to achieve activation. The IQR of the measured values for both phases and all stimuli are once more overlapping at the lower end of the measurement scale. The results of the related-samples Wilcoxon signed rank test show a statistical significance for the increase in the extent of motion with light stimulus ($p = 0.004$), aroma stimulus ($p < 0.001$), and sound stimulus ($p = 0.005$) but no significance for the stimulus combinations.

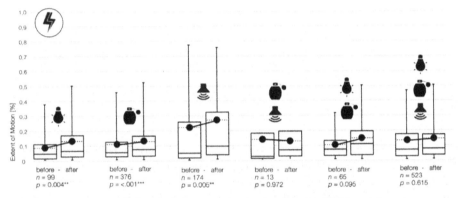

Fig. 5. Extent of motion before and after an activation intervention (light, sound, aroma, or combinations). The course of the mean values shows a significant increase in the extent of motion with light stimulus ($p = 0.004$), aroma stimulus ($p < 0.001$), and sound stimulus ($p = 0.005$).

Therapeutic Effect. The therapeutic effect was measured with the Neuropsychiatric Inventory (NPI). The NPI is the sum of several behavioral anomalies and ranges from zero to 144, whereby the higher the sum, the more frequently and strongly the anomalies were reported. Our NPI assessment was not carried out in all participating institutions. In the participating geriatric psychiatric clinic, it was carried out on admission to the clinic and before discharge from the clinic (with an interval of approximately 3 weeks). In one of the participating facilities for older people with dementia, it was carried out before the first intervention and before the end of the study (18 months later). The whole intervention group (IG) consists of 45 clients. In addition, we included a further 40 people suffering from dementia as a control group (CG) who were treated exclusively with medication, i.e. were not exposed to multi-sensory relaxation or multi-sensory activation. The NPI assessment was carried out with this group of people at the beginning and at the end of the study (18 months interval).

For the analysis, both subsamples (IG and CG) were divided into a group of subjects who showed an improvement or an unchanged overall score in the second neuropsychiatric assessment (NPI decrease) and another group of clients whose overall score increased compared to the first measurement (NPI increase). Figure 6 shows the distribution of these cases in a four-field table, which was subjected to a chi-square test. This test reveals a significant difference in the distribution of people with an NPI improvement between the intervention group and the control group (p = 0.031).

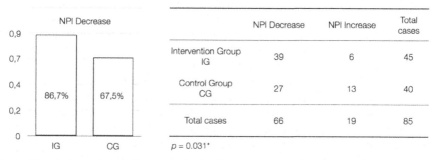

	NPI Decrease	NPI Increase	Total cases
Intervention Group IG	39	6	45
Control Group CG	27	13	40
Total cases	66	19	85

p = 0.031*

Fig. 6. The study participants' changes in the Neuropsychiatric Inventory (NPI) over an observation period from 3 weeks to 18 months. There is a significant difference in the distribution of people with an NPI increase and NPI decrease between the intervention group and the control group (*p* = 0.031).

The highest increase in the NPI score was observed in the control group, whose second measurement was carried out after 18 months (the entire subsample). This is not surprising, as dementia symptoms usually worsen during such a long period, despite medical treatment. It is therefore all the more surprising that this development did not emerge so clearly in the intervention group.

3 Discussion

Some people in the intervention group show no worsening of neuropsychiatric symptoms over a period of one and a half years, but rather an improvement. Whether this is caused by light, sound and/or aroma treatments cannot be fully clarified due to the methodological limitations of field tests. In any case, the effects of these treatments on the motion activity of patients indicate that they have a desirable effect. We do not exactly know for which and how many people in the room the lighting, acoustics and scents have a direct influence or whether the mood transfer between people had an effect. The latter includes the care staff in particular, who have a major influence on the behavior of the clients. This influence is again based on the daily structure, which is reflected in a regular increase in movement in the early morning and a decrease in the late evening. This moderating impact is particularly effective when the triggering of an intervention is only caused by a short time delay of behavioral activities.

For the interpretation of the results and the differences between the intervention and control groups, a detailed description of the two sub-samples would be helpful, for example with regard to the multimorbidity of the clients included, the severity of the illness or their age distribution. In this field study, less emphasis was placed on this because we opted for cluster sampling. We also do not have a precise protocol of the different situations in the course of a day on the dementia units. Perhaps there was more social contact in one of them due to higher public traffic or other situations that may have led to social activation. The very heterogeneous study groups and field test situations may be one reason for the weak effect.

When looking at the measurement results, the skewed distribution of the sensor data is noticeable, which has a main focus in the lower range of the measurement scale for all subgroups used for the statistical comparison. This distribution could be attributed to the fact that we did not exclude those cases in which the modules were triggered automatically but no person was present in the room. Furthermore, we cannot rule out the possibility that changes in the motion activity recorded by motion detectors were caused by people coming and going in the room. The wide range of the measurement data is again due to the very long period of the field test, during which many different situations could have arisen in the room (visits, empty rooms, etc.). This variety of situations must be taken into account in the further development of the control logic.

The sub-sample for the investigation of the combination of sound and aroma stimuli was ultimately very small, the sub-sample with aroma therapy alone for relaxation intervention is missing and the sub-sample that was exposed to a combination of light and aroma stimuli is missing completely. This has to do with the history of the technical development of the therapy modules, which took place in the course of the field study. The first prototype was the aroma module, which had at the beginning some data transmission problems. The main goal was a well-functioning combination of all three types of stimulus, which is why most of the data is available on this.

We have already gained a great deal of knowledge about the biological and psychological effects of light [9] and were able to use it in this study. But it was not easy to find the right sounds, as audible sounds are always linked to personal associations that do not always harmonize with the desired effects. We experimented with natural sounds, singing bowls, white noise and pure sine tones at different volumes, both in the audible frequency range and above (ultrasonic). An extensive repertoire of natural essential oils is also used in aroma therapy. In this study, we limited ourselves to citrus and rose essences. In addition, we focused on essences diffused in the room and on no other applications of aroma therapy, such as massage oils for body applications.

Furthermore, it seems apparent that the activation interventions result in significant activation with isolated stimuli, but not in combination. In contrast, the relaxation interventions do not show any significant effects with isolated stimuli, but do in combination. A study artefact cannot be ruled out, because the mechanism for producing the stimuli may have had a disruptive effect in some cases, e.g. if there were large differences in the initial values of the stimuli compared to the initial situation or noises when the stimuli were triggered. This may have led to increased movement activity, which is also intended in the case of activation. But if one trigger mechanism appears more dominant in stimulus combinations, the triggering of the other stimuli may go almost unnoticed. It is assumed that the latter can contribute more to relaxation.

Based on the results of this field study, we think that the development of the overall technical system introduced here provides a promising approach for light, sound and aroma therapy. However, the therapeutic effect for various clinical pictures beyond dementia still needs to be proven. It will be all the more important to carry out coordinated light, sound and aroma therapy at the right moment, for an appropriate period of time and with the required intensity and quality. Even if our system still has some potential for improvement, the experience gained from this one and a half year long field test shows that combining illumination, fragrances and acoustics in rooms is a possibly feasible way to lessen symptoms of neurogenerative diseases.

Acknowledgments. This project was co-financed by the European Commission and by public funding from Austria, Italy, and Switzerland. We would like to thank Bartenbach, University of Applied Sciences Ost, Apollis, Intefox, Griesfeld Retirement Home, Energy Management Team, Curaviva and Tyrolian Clinics for their cooperation.

Disclosure of Interests. The authors have no conflicts of interest. A positive ethics vote from the Medical University of Innsbruck (A) has been given.

References

1. Hjetland, G.J., Pallesen, S., Thun, E., Kolberg, E., Nordhus, I.H., Flo, E.: Light interventions and sleep, circadian, behavioral, and psychological disturbances in dementia: a systematic review of methods and outcomes. Sleep Med. Rev. **52** (2020)
2. Houben, M., Brankaert, R., Bakker, S., Kenning, G., Bongers, I., Eggen, B.: The role of everyday sounds in advanced dementia care. In: Proceedings of the 2020 CHI Conference on Human Factors in Computing Systems, pp. 1–14 (2020)
3. Li, B.S.Y., Chan, C.W.H., Li, M., Wong, I.K.Y., Yu, Y.H.U.: Effectiveness and safety of aromatherapy in managing behavioral and psychological symptoms of dementia. Dementia Geriatr. Cogn. Disord. Extra **11**(3), 273–297 (2022)
4. Ya-Hui Lien, B., Hsu, Y.C., Chen, Y.H., Chen, L.W.: The formation of positive group affective tone: a narrative practice. Small Group Res. **54**(2), 277–301 (2023)
5. Smith, B.C., D'Amico, M.: Sensory-based interventions for adults with dementia and Alzheimer's disease. Occup. Therapy Health Care **34**(3), 171–201 (2020)
6. Pinto, J.O., Dores, A.R., Geraldo, A., Peixoto, B., Barbosa, F.: Sensory stimulation programs in dementia: a systematic review of methods and effectiveness. Expert Rev. Neurother. **20**(12), 1229–1247 (2020)
7. Yang, H., Luo, Y., Hu, Q., Tian, X., Wen, H.: Benefits in Alzheimer's disease of sensory and multisensory stimulation. J. Alzheimers Dis. **82**(2), 463–484 (2021)
8. Cummings, J.: The neuropsychiatric inventory: development and applications. J. Geriatr. Psychiatry Neurol. **33**(2), 73–84 (2020)
9. Kempter, G., Ritter, W., Künz, A.: Guiding light for the mobility support of seniors. In: Ambient Assisted Living: 6th AAL-Kongress Berlin, 22–23 January, pp. 35–45, Springer (2013). https://doi.org/10.1007/978-3-642-37988-8_3

Evaluation of Stress Reduction Effects Using Physiological Indexes in Manga Reading

Souta Kurihara[✉], Chen Feng, and Midori Sugaya

Shibaura Institute of Technology, Tokyo, Japan
{ma23075,doly}@shibaura-it.ac.jp

Abstract. In recent years, the increasing stress within society has emerged as an issue, with many individuals reporting stress in their work and professional lives. Prolonged stress can lead to mental health disorder such as depression. This situation highlights the importance of finding ways to reduce stress. Among various options to reduce stress, manga has the advantage of its convenience and ease of reading anywhere, making it a beneficial option to reduce stress. The effects of manga on individuals include relaxation and cognitive transformation, as well as being effective in the care of psychosis. Although these effects have been investigated through descriptive questionnaires, research on the effects of manga in alleviating individuals' stress during the reading process remains lacking. On the other hand, it has been suggested that physiological indexes can be used to detect the stress of individuals by frequency analysis of heartbeat intervals. Therefore, the purpose of this study was to investigate the effect of reading manga on the reduction of stress felt by individuals by using physiological indexes. As a preliminary experiment to achieve this objective, we investigated the effect of reading manga on stress reduction using two manga. The results showed that LF/HF, a heart rate variability index, was reduced after reading manga than after resting after the stress-loading task, indicating that reading manga reduced stress.

Keywords: Stress Reduction Manga · LF/HF

1 Introduction

In recent years, the increasing stress within society has emerged as an issue, [1]. The Ministry of Health, Labour and Welfare of Japan conducted a survey that revealed many individuals experience stress in their work and professional lives [1]. Prolonged stress can lead to mental health disorder such as depression [1], and it is important to reduce stress by changing one's mood to relax at appropriate times. There are many options to reduce stress, such as going to the movies or hiking, however each requires travel and preparation costs. On the other hands, manga has the advantage of its convenience and ease of reading anywhere, making it a beneficial option to reduce stress [2]. Reading manga is easy and can be done anywhere. In addition, since manga is expressed with pictures and text, it can be read in a shorter time than a book with only text [3].

© The Author(s), under exclusive license to Springer Nature Switzerland AG 2024
C. Stephanidis et al. (Eds.): HCII 2024, CCIS 2118, pp. 360–367, 2024.
https://doi.org/10.1007/978-3-031-61963-2_36

There have been several studies on the effects of manga. Shiraishi et al. conducted an online survey of 95 university students using Google Forms to examine the effects of manga. The survey asked students whether or not they had read manga before, and for those who had read manga, whether or not they had experienced any positive effects from reading manga, and for those who had experienced positive effects, what kind of effects the reading had on them. The results suggest that reading manga can have the effect of relaxing and changing cognition [4].

Leon et al. found that the content of war manga and the treatment of trauma [5]. Specifically, they suggested that psychological graphic representations may be more effective than verbal therapy for psychological problems [5]. These studies have shown that reading manga relaxes individuals and has effects similar to those of therapy. However, these studies used questionnaires and other methods, and did not evaluate whether or not the reading of manga actually reduced stress. In studies investigating the positive effects of reading manga, open-ended questionnaires were used to investigate the positive effects, and it is possible that positive effects that are not remembered in the descriptions may be measured by physiological indexes as psychological effects, and that the positive effects obtained by reading manga may not be fully investigated.

In contrast, Yamaguchi et al. conducted a study to analyze stress using physiological indexes [6]. In this study, it was suggested that an index called LF/HF, which is obtained by measuring the heartbeat interval and analyzing the frequency, is a significant index in the study of stress. However, this method has not been applied to the effect of stress reduction during manga reading.

Therefore, the purpose of this study was to investigate the effect of reading manga on decreasing the stress that individuals are exposed to by using physiological indexes. To achieve this objective, we read manga after a task which applied stress-load and compared the changes in heart rate variability indices afterwards with those at rest. The reason for using the heart rate variability index is that the sympathetic nervous system becomes dominant among the autonomic nerves when a person is under stress.

2 Purpose/Proposal

In a study by Shiraishi et al. to investigate the positive effects of manga [4], the positive effects of manga on individuals while reading manga were investigated using a descriptive questionnaire. Since the descriptive questionnaires is rely on subjective opinion and are susceptible to the cognitive biases and memories of the subjects, and thus cannot measure changes in physiological responses, the positive effects of manga on individuals while reading manga were not sufficiently investigated. On the other hand, a study by Yamaguchi et al. suggests that physiological indexes can be used to detect stress felt by individuals [6]. Therefore, the purpose of this study was to investigate the effect of reading manga on stress reduction by using physiological indexes, and to confirm the effectiveness of this method through preliminary experiments.

3 Physiological Indexes

Based on the previous study by Yamaguchi et al., LF/HF is considered to reflect changes in sympathetic nervous activity [6]. Therefore, this study utilizes LF/HF, an index of heart rate variability, as a physiological measure of stress levels. LF is a fluctuating wave that appears in both sympathetically and parasympathetically predominant states and is based on a signal from blood changes with a cycle of approximately 10 s, called Mayer wave, while HF is a fluctuating wave with a cycle of approximately 3 to 4 s that appears when the parasympathetic nervous system is dominant, and is based on a signal from respiration. When a person is under stress, that is, when the sympathetic nervous system is dominant, the LF/HF value increases since LF appears and HF decreases. When a person is in a relaxed state, i.e., when the parasympathetic is dominance, the HF increases and the LF/HF value decreases, which relative to the stressed state.

4 Experiment

4.1 Purpose of the Experiment

This study conducts an experiment to explore the effect of manga reading on stress reduction. In the experiment, we applied a stress load to the participants using a stress load task, then analyzed and compared the reduction of stress from resting without reading manga, resting after reading battle manga, and resting after reading shojo manga (one type of Japanese comics targeted primarily at young female audiences, characterized by romantic plots, emotional depth, and visually expressive art styles), based on LF/HF, the heart rate variability index.

We selected one battle manga and shojo manga as the manga used because battle manga is more popular among male readers and shojo manga is more popular among female, and we thought that battle manga would be more effective in reducing stress than shojo manga when male read manga, and shojo manga would be more effective in reducing stress than battle manga when female read manga.

The reason for using LF/HF as a method of detecting stress is that LF/HF has been suggested to be significant in detecting stress in a study by Yamaguchi et al. [6].

The PASAT (Paced Auditory Serial Addition Test) was used as a stress test. The PASAT is a cognitive ability test in which participants are asked to listen to a series of numbers presented at a constant rate and then add those numbers continuously. Participants calculate the numbers as they hear them and add them up one after the other. In this study, we applied it as a stress-loading task.

4.2 Mental Procedures

Three males in their 20 s were used as participants in the experiment. The experimental procedure was as follows.

1. Questionnaire on participant's stress level
2. Sit in front of the display and wear a heart rate sensor
3. Resting for 5 min to stabilize the physiological index

4. Conduct a stress-loading task
5. 5 min of rest
6. Conduct the stress-loading task
7. Read the one selected manga
8. 5 min of rest
9. Post-questionnaire

(6), (7), and (8) were conducted twice in total, using different manga. Figure 1 illustrates the above description.

The manga used was selected from the manga existing in MANGA 109, whose genres were battle and romance, and whose publication date was the most recent [7, 8]. MANGA109 is a dataset consisting of 109 manga drawn by Japanese professional manga artists, compiled by the Aizawa, Yamazaki, and Matsui Laboratory of the Graduate School of Science and Engineering, The University of Tokyo, for use in academic research on media processing of Japanese manga.

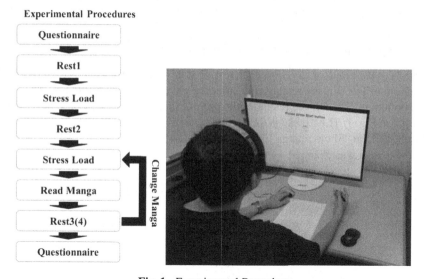

Fig. 1. Experimental Procedure

5 Result

5.1 Analysis by Time Series Graphs

Figure 2 shows the time-series graph of LF/HF from Rest 1 to Rest 4 for participants A.

In the graph in Fig. 2, LF/HF increases by 1.5 at load 1. This is thought to be due to the fact that 200 s of data is required to calculate LF/HF, and the effect of the stressful task appears shifted by 200 s. In this graph, the effects of the stress-loading task and reading the manga appeared 200 s after the time of the action, making it difficult to compare

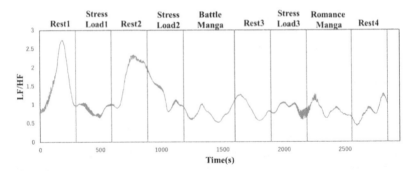

Fig. 2. Time-series graph of heart rate variability indices for participants A

the stress reduced by reading the manga with the stress reduced spontaneously by doing nothing. Therefore, in this study, we calculated and compared the mean value of LF/HF during each of the periods from rest 1 to 4, in which the effects of the stress-loading task and reading the cartoon appeared.

5.2 Comparison of Mean Value Between Each Rest

Figure 3 is a bar graph of LF/HF at each resting state for Subject A. The "resting state" at the bottom of Fig. 3 is the resting state after the pre-questionnaire in Fig. 1. The "Rest" at the bottom of Fig. 3 is the rest after the pre-questionnaire in Fig. 1, and the "Task" is the rest 2 in Fig. 1. The "Task" is the resting state in Fig. 1. The "Battle manga" is rest 3 in Fig. 1, and the "Shojo manga" is rest 4 in Fig. 1, which is rest after reading the manga after the manga was changed.

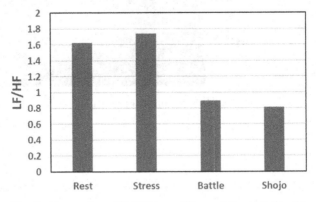

Fig. 3. Mean value of LF/HF in each interval for participant A

In Fig. 3, LF/HF increased by about 0.2 when compared between the rest and the loading task, and LF/HF decreased by about 1 for both the loading task and the battle and shojo manga. This indicates that the stress load task made Experiment Subject A feel stressed, and that reading manga tended to decrease his stress.

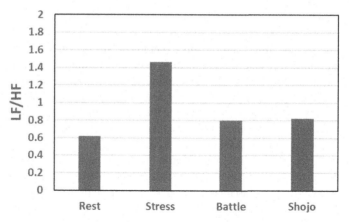

Fig. 4. Mean value of LF/HF in each interval for participant B

In Fig. 4, comparing the resting and loading tasks, we see that LF/HF increased by about 0.8, and decreased by 0.6 for both the loading task and the battle and shojo manga. This indicates that, like Subject A, Subject B felt stressed by the stress load task, and that reading manga tended to decrease her stress.

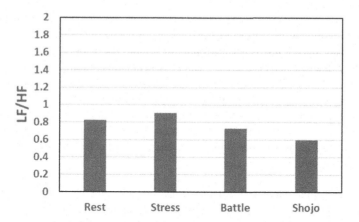

Fig. 5. Mean value of LF/HF in each interval for participant C

In Fig. 5, comparing the resting and loading tasks, we see that LF/HF increased by about 0.1, decreased by 0.2 for the loading task and the battle manga, and decreased by 0.3 for the loading task and the shojo manga. The results from participants A, B, and C showed that participant feel stress when they are subjected to a stressful task and that reading manga tends to reduce stress.

6   Discussion

During the PASAT test, three participants experienced stress. The test was designed as a stress-loading task. The one-second reading interval for numbers contributed to their stress. They had to concentrate on listening and adding numbers. This led to a strong stress. They feared missing numbers if they lost concentration even momentarily. The reason why the stress was reduced by reading the cartoon may be that the concentration and tension that were present during the stressful task changed to an attempt to understand the content of the cartoon, which may have eased the stress.

In this experiment, the participants read a battle manga and a shojo manga in succession, so there was a possibility that the stress reduction effect from reading the battle manga remained until the shojo manga was read. Therefore, it is possible that the effects of the shojo manga were not fully investigated, and it is necessary to consider the order in which the manga were read when redesigning the experiment.

7   Conclusion

In this study, we conducted a preliminary experiment to evaluate the stress reduction effect during manga reading. We compared HRV index LF/HF during rest and after reading manga following the stress-loading task. In the time-series graphs, about 200 s of data were required for the calculation of LF/HF, and the effect of the stress-loading task began to appear after a 200-s shift. Therefore, it was considered difficult to make comparisons using a time series graph, so comparisons were made by plotting the mean value of LF/HF between rest periods on a bar graph. The results showed that all three participants felt stressed by the stress-loading task, and that reading the manga decreased their stress. Also, LF/HF during each rest period was compared, however the transition to rest was delayed by the time spent reading the manga when the participants were reading the manga and when they were not reading the manga, and the natural decrease in stress during the time spent reading the manga was not considered. For this reason, we would like to make comparisons and redesign the experiment to take into account the time spent reading the manga.

Acknowledgments. The authors would like to thank Mr. Takeshi Hanada, Mr. Taiyo Nakashima, Mr. Kumpei Takasaki, and Mr. Yu Matsumoto of Coamix Inc. for their assistance in this research.

References

1. Ministry of Health, Labour and Welfare. https://www.mhlw.go.jp/content/11200000/000845 811.pdf. Accessed 26 Feb 2024
2. Andy Chilies: Reading can help reduce stress, according to U, The Argus. 30th March 2009. https://www.theargus.co.uk/news/4245076.reading-can-help-reduce-stress-acc ording-to-university-of-sussex-research/. Accessed 26 Feb 2024
3. Sato, K.: Effects of Comic Expression on Mangatrip Comprehension, Bulletin of the Faculty of Education, Ehime University. Section 1, Educational Sciences, vol. 43, no. 2, February 1997, pp. 85–95. https://ndlsearch.ndl.go.jp/books/R000000004-I4200580

4. Shiraishi, S.: A survey on reading manga and positive reading effects among undergraduates: from the perspective of prevention for depression, J. Sch. Reg. Des. Utsunomiya Univ. **12**, 1–12 (2023)
5. Leone, J.M.: Drawing invisible wounds: war manga and the treatment of trauma. J. Med. Humanit. **39**(3), 243–261 (2018)
6. Yamaguchi, K.: Influence of the mental stress on heart rate variability. Res. Bull. Fac. Humanit. Shigakukan Univ. **31**(1), 1–10 (2010)
7. Matumoto, Y., et al.: Building a manga dataset "MANGA 109" with annotations for multimedia applications. Multimedia Tools Appl. **76**(29), 21811—21838 (2017)
8. Aizawa, K., et al.: Sketch-based Manga Retrieval using MANGA 109 Dataset, pp. 8–18, 27 February 2020

Mental Health Management App Interface Design for Women Based on Emotional Equality

Yangkun Li[✉]

Xiamen University, Zhangzhou 363100, People's Republic of China
liyangkunamber111@163.com

Abstract. In today's world, the media's inappropriate portrayal of emotions leads many to resist and resent negative emotions, favoring only positive ones. However, emotions are inherently equal, with no intrinsic good or bad. Excessive suppression of negative emotions only worsens psychological states. In China, the increasing mental health issues among the population, especially the higher incidence of mental illnesses in women compared to men, underscore this problem. Yet, services catering to women's mental health are limited. This paper aims to assist women in recognizing and better accepting their emotional patterns, including negative emotions, to achieve psychological healing. The study first utilizes competitor analysis to examine the interface design styles of similar apps in the market to identify a design language that aligns with the app's purpose. Subsequently, it employs user research, including questionnaires, to delve into psychological healing within women-centric design contexts. Diverging from traditional "psychotherapy" apps, this paper concentrates on psychological healing within the framework of "emotional equality". The study introduces an app designed to aid women in better understanding and managing their emotions. Its primary contribution lies in the innovative integration of user emotions with plant care, transforming emotions into nutrients for plant growth. This approach aids users in acknowledging emotional equality and fosters better acceptance of their feelings. Additionally, leveraging users' desire to care for plants ensures the continuity of emotion recording, enabling more precise analysis of emotional patterns. Lastly, in response to the market's oversight of women's mental health services, the study proposes new methodologies and pathways for psychological healing.

Keywords: Emotional Equality · Psychological Healing · App Design · Women's Mental Health

1 Introduction

Nowadays, social media is putting more and more emphasis on keeping people optimistic and positive in all situations, while negative emotions such as sadness, anger, etc. are being labelled as unhealthy and are gradually being seen as taboo. People begin to feel guilty about the negative emotions they feel, and even think that the negative emotions they feel are emotions that shouldn't exist. In reality, there are no absolute good or bad emotional feelings, and in many cases bad emotions can have a positive effect on oneself.

Studies have shown that increased anger on one side of a negotiation can make it easier for the other side to give in to their demands, thus gaining a greater advantage [1]. Each emotion has its own existence and plays a different role in life [2]. Only by facing up to our own emotions and treating each emotion equally can we prevent psychological problems from arising. In the face of the gradual expansion of psychological problems in the world, such as horticultural therapy, music therapy, theatre therapy and other therapies combining elements of art have gradually entered the public's vision. In horticultural therapy, which is a multi-sensory approach, the visual senses play an important role. Studies have shown that looking at pictures of gardens or plants can be relaxing and rejuvenating. And among the activities of horticultural therapy, the process of planting seedlings, observing the growth of the plant and constantly reflecting on its status helps to distract the patient, thus reducing the level of anxiety and regulating the individual's mood [3].

The incidence of psychological problems in the Chinese population has been increasing in recent years, and the incidence of psychological disorders in women is particularly significant compared to men [4]. The pressure of women in the workplace is also increasing day by day [5], however, there are few services for women's mental health in the market, and the existing apps that provide mental health services also have many problems [6]. From the survey, only a few domestic mental health apps focus on the aspect of physical therapy, mainly focusing on the aspect of psychotherapy, including psychological counselling, psychological testing, community communication and other major sections. In terms of professionalism, psychotherapy is essentially a medical practice, and practitioners need to have professional qualities. However, there are many psychotherapists in the market, and the market access bar is low, and most of their qualifications are yet to be examined. In terms of service quality, the software for psychotherapy services available in the market is not segmented into customer types, resulting in the services provided are usually general and redundant, the app shows strong homogeneity in visual design and functionality, and the cumbersomeness of the service procedure further sets up barriers to the solution of psychological problems of the customer group.

Therefore, this paper will discuss the emotional design and interaction design for female customers. Through the development of a mental health service product, women will be able to face their own emotions, better accept and digest multiple emotions including negative emotions, and recognise the equality of emotions so as to achieve the purpose of psychological healing.

2   Method

2.1   Competitive Analysis

In this paper, we have selected a highly rated mood recording app (DAILY JOURNAL, MOODA) on the market for interface analysis.

In terms of functional design, these two apps are mainly divided into the functions of daily recording of emotions as well as emotion analysis. In Fig. 1 and Fig. 2, the emotion recording function, firstly, the emotion options with five colours with different expressions will appear, and the emotions are arranged from high to low. It enables users to clearly distinguish the emotion options through the visual feeling of different colours and clarify the boundary of each emotion, but the flaws of these two apps in this interface design are very similar, and the emoticons paired with each option have a more subjective expression, which makes the users inclined to the options, which is not conducive to the objective recording of one's own emotions, and is not sufficiently objective in terms of the expression of the equality of emotions. In the subsequent design of the app, the authors will make the design of the emoticons more objective, retain the colour differences in the presentation of emotional options, and improve the subjective tendency of the emoticons on the options.

Fig. 1. Screenshot of Daily Journal software in the emotion recording section

Fig. 2. Screenshot of MOODA software in the emotion recording section

Second, after identifying the basic areas of emotion, both apps moved to a more detailed recording process. In MOODA, a recording function shaped like a diary (See Fig. 3) appeared directly, aiming to enable users to record the current emotional state more accurately. However, in the absence of further guidance from the system, users were unable to accurately focus on the emotional development and changes in words, and in most cases, the content of the record was off-topic or could not be written, which greatly reduced the functionality of emotional recording. On the contrary, DAILY JOURNAL (See Fig. 4), after confirming the basic emotion thresholds, in order to assist the user to make a more detailed emotion division, it continues to provide potential choices to the user by offering options, and guides the user to perceive their own emotions step by step. After the selection is completed, the options selected above will appear as keywords at the top of the text field during the diary recording process. When users use text recording, it can effectively reduce the situation that users can't write the content or the content deviates from their own emotions. In the subsequent design of the app, the author will provide guidance for users to recognise their emotions, so that they can recognise their emotions more easily and accurately.

It is worth mentioning that both MOODA and DAILY JOURNAL have a feedback page for the user's completed recording of emotions. MOODA provides feedback based on the user's emotions of the day, with different interactions for different emotions (see Fig. 5). DAILY JOURNAL's feedback page is based on the number of days that the user has been using the app, and an interaction page similar to an award page appears. The purpose of the award-like interaction page is to encourage users to consistently record

 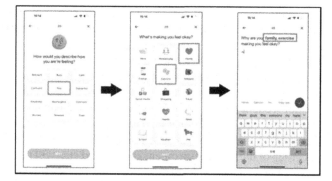

Fig. 3. Screenshot of **Fig. 4.** Operation flow of Daily Journal software in the transcription
MOODA software in section
the transcript section

their emotions using the app (see Fig. 6). Continuous recording of emotions is the basis
for recognising one's own emotional patterns and achieving psychological healing, and
only when one is familiar with one's own emotional changes over a period of time is
it possible to grasp one's own emotional patterns and thus better deal with emotional
problems. Therefore, app design should not only focus on the functional design of user
emotion collection, but also need to pay attention to how to let users continuously use
the app to record their own emotions, so as to facilitate the next step of the app to help
analyse the user's cognition of their own emotions in the way of data visualisation. Both
of these apps do not have in-depth design on the latitude of keeping users sticky. In
the subsequent design of the app, the authors will think about how to make users have
positive feedback on the continuous recording of emotions and reduce the inert response
to the daily emotion recording.

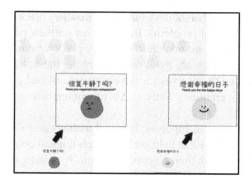 

Fig. 5. MOODA software gives different feedback for
different emotions of the user

Fig. 6. Daily Journal
software's incentive page for
users who have completed the
emotion logging

In summary, these two apps have their own strengths in sentiment collection and analysis, but they also appear to have similar colour choices and similar functional designs. Both apps do not refine the audience population, and under the generalised audience analysis, the service population of the two apps is highly overlapped, and there is a serious homogeneity in the interface performance. On the basis of the large audience population, the interaction of these two apps is also very basic and uniform. In the subsequent design, the concept of emotional equality will be integrated into the design, and the use of emotional guidance allows users to record their emotions in detail and accurately, and other aspects will be optimised. This paper establishes that the main target group of the service is women, and the next step will be based on the questionnaire survey of the audience to further pinpoint the needs of the users, refine the functional design, optimise the interaction method, and create the characteristics of the app.

2.2 Questionnaire

Based on the above analyses, the authors identified the target users as the female group and initiated a questionnaire called the Survey of Women's Mental and Emotional Management Needs to understand what kind of mental health management apps are needed by women. The main body of the questionnaire is divided into two parts. The first part mainly investigates the current emotional state of women, and the second part focuses on understanding the current needs of women for mental health management. The authors collected 87 valid questionnaires using the Questionnaire Star platform. The following results were obtained by analysing the questionnaires.

The First Part of the Survey. Overall, the age levels involved in the eighty-seven women who participated in the survey were 10–50 years old. Most of the women were 20–30 years old accounting for 45.98% of the total, and the number of women in the age bracket of 10–20 years old and 30–40 years old was about the same, with the former accounting for 27.59% of the total, and the latter accounting for 24.17% of the total.

In the first part of the survey, more than half of the women said that they often have bad moods and have faced some psychological problems. In the survey on their perception of emotions, the vast majority of women are unable to correctly perceive emotions as equal, with 94.25% believing that emotions are good or bad. Among them, 87.36% of women rejected bad emotions, blamed themselves for the emergence of bad emotions, and were unable to embrace their own emotions. Only 1.15% of women believe that bad emotions do not affect their lives.

At present, 35.63% of women choose to suppress their bad feelings and keep them inside. None of them chose to seek professional help such as psychological counselling. Nearly half of the women chose to deal with their negative emotions by talking to people around them (See Fig. 7).

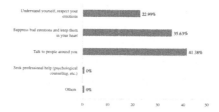

Fig. 7. Statistical chart on how women choose to deal with bad moods.

In conclusion, the first part of the survey shows that most women face serious emotional problems, are not able to accept their emotions equally and their methods of dealing with them are still very ineffective and unprofessional.

The Second Part of the Survey. Fewer than 40% of the women surveyed reported having used mental health apps (See Fig. 8). The vast majority of these women who had been exposed to mental health apps tended to use emotional healing mental health apps, with only 6.25% of women choosing to use psychotherapy apps (See Fig. 9).

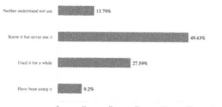

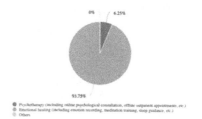

Fig. 8. Chart of survey on women's use of mental health apps

Fig. 9. Graphical representation of women's preferences for types of mental health apps

In a survey about the design of mental health apps, the vast majority of women preferred a low-saturation, breathable interface. In terms of functionality the majority wanted to enjoy the professionalism of the service with the addition of an interesting design for interaction. And in the segment of message notification, the vast majority of the group wanted a low-frequency reminder to enter the app on the lock screen page (See Fig. 10).

The second part of the questionnaire shows that the popularity of mental health apps is not high among women, and more people will choose to use emotional healing apps, but most of the users can't stick to one software. In terms of suggestions for improvement, low-saturated interface, interesting functional design, and low-frequency message reminders are favoured by the female clientele.

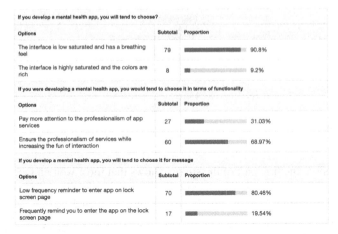

Fig. 10. Survey of women's design preferences for mental health apps.

2.3 Requirements Summary

See Fig. 11.

Functional Requirements	Visual Requirements	Emotional Requirements
1. Provide users with guidance on emotional recognition in the text recording section. 2. Combine professional knowledge of mental health to provide users with suggestions for adjusting their emotional state based on the results of data analysis. 3. Interesting functional design that can attract users to continue using it 4. Send low-frequency reminders to record emotional messages on the lock screen page	1. Keep the color differences of expression designs to represent different emotions 2. Remove the subjective expression of expression design 3. Low saturation and breathable interface design	1. Reduce laziness about daily recording of emotions 2. Need to accept all your emotions equally

Fig. 11. Summary table of women's needs.

3   Result

3.1   Design Concept

Design Style. Based on the analysis of the competitors and the research on the target audience, this design will adopt a user-centred linear design. Soft and breathable colours are used as the main tone of the app. In terms of design details, the design of emoticons that measure emotions in the app is more objective and guides users to record their emotions in a detailed way. Innovative introduction of plant culture to increase the fun and sustainability of the activity of women recording their emotions.

Brand Philosophy and Innovation Point Mind Map. The brand provides users with a simple and efficient service for recording and analysing their emotions. We will creatively combine the user's emotional content with plant care, generate the nutrients needed by plants by recording emotions, and ensure the continuity of the activity of recording emotions by taking advantage of the user's desire to take care of the plants, so as to further analyse the user's emotional patterns accurately. At the same time, it allows users to pay more attention to the emotional patterns projected on plants and better detect emotions.

We want to help users to be aware of their emotions in a sustainable way, on the one hand, by introducing a plant management section that allows users to project their emotions on the plants they care for, and to be aware of their own emotions by observing the state of the plants they cultivate. On the other hand, we are trying to digitise gardening therapy so that users can have a relaxing and enjoyable spiritual experience. We want to make the perception of emotions a part of the user's daily life. We are committed to making more people aware of the importance of mental health, so that everyone can live in a healthy mood.

This app categorises emotions into five types in the first stage, and each of these five different emotions corresponds to the nutrients needed for a plant to grow (see Fig. 12). As users record their emotions, the emotional plants they cultivate are able to grow. The first benefit of this system is that it helps users realise that emotions are no longer good or bad, but are as essential to the growth of a plant as any other ingredient. The second benefit is that it increases user stickiness. When a user stops recording his/her emotions, the plant he/she is cultivating will also stop growing, and this mapping attracts users to keep recording their emotions on a daily basis.

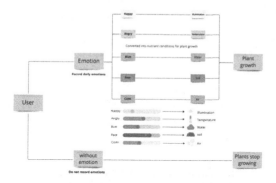

Fig. 12. Innovation point mind map.

Design Standard Colours. The primary colour of the app comes from the natural wood colour, which represents naturalness, relaxation, serenity and calmness. It fits the app's philosophy of gentleness, reliability and privacy, and as the brand's most important colour, it appears in most occasions (see Fig. 13).

The app's secondary color is representative colour groups of emotions. They also highlight the concept of symbiosis between the brand's emotions and plants. They represent both the emotions of people and the nutrients that plants need to grow. The balanced use of each colour reflects the brand's inclusiveness of emotions and conveys the idea of emotional equality.

Fig. 13. Color layout used in app design.

Plant Design. The following plant designs are based on Phalaenopsis, hydrangea, narcissus, lily of the valley, and fungi (see Fig. 14). Their plant characteristics were extracted respectively and redesigned. Colors that reflected emotions were applied to the plants, so that the plants and the user's emotions can visually symbiosis. The visual effects presented by plants are close to the plant forms in real life but do not exist in reality. This can not only bring users a realistic plant cultivation process similar to the real world, but also use the uniqueness of plants to attract users' interest in cultivation. It also provides the possibility of digitizing horticultural therapy.

Fig. 14. Plant design display.

Design that Embodies the Concept of Emotional Equality. The expressions in the emotion recording section of the apps included in the competitive product analysis all have subjective expressions. Subjectification mainly manifests itself in several aspects. First of all, in these expressions, the design with the nose, eyes, and mouth displayed gives people an anthropomorphic impression, making it easier for people to think of the human faces they face in reality. For people with high empathy, they will instinctively reject expressions such as anger and sadness, making it impossible to objectively view the emotions behind these expressions, leading users to the misunderstanding of emotional inequality. Such a design weakens the objectivity of users' evaluation of their own emotions in the emotion recording process. Secondly, the cartoonish images presented by these hand-drawn expressions further weaken the objectivity of emotional presentation and are not conducive to the transmission of the concept of emotional equality. The emotional evaluation expressions that appear in the original app lead users to the misunderstanding of emotional inequality. The visual impression is that bad emotions are bad and positive emotions are good, which is not conducive to the concept of user cognitive emotional equality (See Fig. 1, Fig. 2).

In this design, the expressions involved in the section where users evaluate their own emotions in the app were designed to be objective and anthropomorphic was removed (see Fig. 15). In terms of presentation, elements such as eyes and noses are removed; in terms of style, a linear design style is used to express different emotions concisely; in terms of color, no color will appear before the user selects an emotion, to the greatest extent visually This ensures the uniformity of expression design. The purpose is to get rid of users' subjective rejection reactions to bad emotions and to get rid of users' over-beautiful reactions to positive emotions. Allow users to effectively record their own emotions based on awareness of the concept of emotional equality.

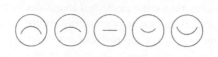

Fig. 15. Emoticon design expressing the concept of emotional equality in the app.

High-Fidelity Page Design Display. In terms of page design ideas, the design standard colors and logo variations are applied to each type of page to maintain the unity of page design and the accuracy of conveying concepts (Fig. 16).

Fig. 16. High-fidelity interface displays.

4 Conclusion

This paper takes the current state of women's mental health as the background, and discusses the psychological needs of young women as a group. The innovative psychological healing app operation mechanism helps women manage their own mental health condition, combines user's emotions with plant maintenance, so that any user's emotions can be transformed into nutrients needed for plant growth, helps users better accept emotions on the basis of the concept of cognitive equality of emotions from the content, increases the aesthetics and interest of the app from the form, and strengthens the user's motivation to record and manage their emotions. In the form, it increases the aesthetics and interest of the app, and enhances users' motivation to record and manage their emotions in order to conduct self-healing behaviour. Functionally, the positive feedback from users can enhance the app's close tracking of users' daily emotions, integrate information in a timely manner, and improve the accuracy of users' emotional feedback. In terms of market, it makes up for the neglected loopholes in the market for women's mental health services, and provides new possibilities for the development of the mental health market by applying new ways and paths of psychological healing.

The designs mentioned in this paper are conceptual designs based on thorough research and still lack in terms of market use. However, the combination of digital plants and psychological healing mentioned in this paper is still an innovative idea with great market potential. On the one hand, it will further expand the way of psychological healing and interest, and on the other hand, it will also allow horticultural therapy, which is a niche psychological treatment limited by location, to be more widely disseminated through digital means, thus maximising its effectiveness.

References

1. Tamir, M., Ford, B.Q.: When feeling bad is expected to be good: emotion regulation and outcome expectancies in social conflicts. Emotion **12**(4), 807 (2012)
2. Tice, D.M., Baumeister, R.F., Zhang, L.: The role of emotion in self-regulation: differing role of positive and negative emotions. Regul. Emot., 213–226 (2004)
3. Scott, T.L.: Horticultural Therapy, 1st edn. Springer, Australia (2017)
4. Wenzhen, Y.: Women's mental health in China: current situation, causes and countermeasures. Marx. Real. **5**, 166 (2010). (in Chinese)
5. Tingting, X., Yuxiu, Z., Cunhong, M.: Survey on pressure situation of professional women and causes analysis. Comput. Inf. Sci. **9**(2) (2016)
6. China's pan-mental Health Service industry White Paper 2022. https://djyanbao.com/report/detail?id=3486836&from=search_list&aiStatus=undefined%3Finvite_code%3DRf2i6n?invite_code=Rf2i6n. Accessed 13 Mar 2024

Workplace Stress Release with Nature Interaction

Win Kee Lim, Jennifer Gohumpu, and Mengru Xue(✉)

Ningbo Innovation Center, Zhejiang University, Ningbo, China
mengruxue@zju.edu.cn

Abstract. Workplace stress has been an issue which risen these years, yet scientific research on this particular topic is still holds a high position on the chart. Due to the heavy workload and long hours, it is crucial to take into consideration the employees' health and well-being for productivity and creativity. Researchers have explored spatial elements as interactive interfaces for stress release. However, the connection with nature and the potential design space needs further exploration. By using an interactive interface in a virtual natural setting, employees are able to have a deeper understanding of their stress tolerance, and be reminded of stress recovery sessions when they get stressed. The combination of nature interaction and stress recovery can serve as a starting point for better natural restorative outcomes with the involvement of nature.

Keywords: Workplace stress · Stress recovery · Nature interaction · Interaction interface

1 Introduction

In recent years, workplace stress has become a growing concern for employers and employees alike. Stress can lead to burnout, decreased productivity, and a variety of physical and mental health problems. Research shows that restorative environments are nature settings where individuals can experience positive changes in their emotional tone, physiological activity levels, behaviour, and cognitive functioning [1]. The benefits of nature exposure and restorative environments have been well-documented, leading to a growing interest in incorporating these elements into workplace design [2].

Despite growing interest in using nature interaction as a means of stress recovery in the workplace, there is still a lack of understanding regarding the efficacy of this approach. Additionally, little is known about the specific design elements and parameters that are necessary to achieve effective stress recovery outcomes. Therefore, there is a need for further research to identify the impact of nature interaction on stress recovery in the workplace and to inform the development of evidence-based strategies for integrating nature into work environments.

Over the past decade, there has been growing interest in the role of nature in promoting psychological and physiological recovery from stress, particularly in the workplace setting. Other studies have shown that exposure to natural light, views of nature or active engagement with nature can improve mood, reduce stress, and enhance cognitive function [2, 7, 9]. While the benefits of nature on stress recovery outcomes are well-established, there is still limited understanding of the specific design elements and parameters that are most effective in promoting these outcomes in the workplace context.

In this context, this article aims to design a human-interaction interface referring to the existing literature on the effectiveness of nature interaction in promoting workplace stress recovery. Through a comprehensive understanding of the effectiveness and practical applications of nature interaction as a means of promoting workplace stress recovery, this study aims to provide a comprehensive understanding of the effectiveness and practical applications of nature interaction as a means of promoting workplace stress recovery, and to inform the development of evidence-based strategies for integrating nature into work environments.

2   Design

2.1   Design Approach

A study by Kellert et al. [8] identified six design principles for promoting the human-nature connection. Similarly, Kaplan [3] proposed the concept of attention restoration theory (ART), which argues that exposure to natural environments can help to restore mental fatigue and improve cognitive functioning. Despite the potential benefits of nature interaction for workplace stress recovery, there may also be cultural factors and factors such as individuals' preferences, personality characteristics, and job demands, suggesting that tailored interventions may be necessary for different work environments and employee populations [4, 5].

Some of these challenges include cost considerations, limited space or access to natural environments, and concerns about maintenance and upkeep. Interface design is a critical component of research into workplace stress recovery with nature interaction. The interface design should be intuitive, user-friendly, and visually appealing to encourage participation and engagement from users.

2.2   Interface Design

Design Consideration. The research team should consider creating data visualization tools to help users interpret their results, which could aid in their overall feedback perception. Devices and screen sizes were not taken into account as the interface design is planned to be accessed through same model of devices. Finally, the interface design should undergo usability testing to ensure it is user-friendly and effective in promoting engagement and data accuracy. The success of a study on workplace stress recovery with nature interaction can depend on the quality of its interface design, and close attention should be paid to every aspect of its development. Additional features such as special interaction between the display and users also needing to be consider, namely the check-in time of users on the start-up display in Fig. 1.

Design Concept. The interactive interface is designed in visual display of nature setting, by portraying the growing of pot plant as shown in Fig. 1. The plant will grow and wilt

Fig. 1. The interface start-up display from a tablet.

according to the work stress accumulated from user through the data evaluation from wearable device connected between user and the interface. To point out the importance of stress recovery, the interface was designed in more intelligible and understandable way by illustrating the defoliation and flourishing as the stress healing process.

Design Detail. The interface will start-up by displaying a flower pot, eventually the plant will start to grow as the user commence to work, as shown in Fig. 2. By the increasing of work stress accumulated, the plant will eventually wilt to emphasize employees their stress tolerance. To enlighten the user about their stress level, the plant will be going through defoliation as a metaphor for one of the over-stress symptoms, hair loss. Employees will be reminded for some stress recovery session during working hour. While employees taking break with doing some breathing exercise, the plant will start flourishing, as to show the succession of stress recovery.

2.3 System Design

Design Phrase 1: Connection Plan. In order to design a minimalist and undemanding interface, the workflow and system connection are planned. Using wearable devices like PPG, the user's stress level will be measured and then transmitted to the Arduino, which acts as the central hub for the entire interface. As shown in Fig. 3, the Arduino established an interconnection between the hub and the interface display on TFT Screen.

Design Phrase 2: Stress Level. In the second phase, various stress level was taken into consideration for progression of plant growth and wilting as shown in Table 1. After that, Processing software will be used for running and executing codes by processing the data gathered to Arduino. Through some research [12], a shortlist of plant selection has been compiled as listed in Table 2. The display platform will provide these plants as option, and the user will need to choose their plants among according to their own preferences.

Design Phrase 3: User Setting. The interface is designed for personal use in workplace setting as illustrated in Fig. 4. Based on the Stress Recovery Theory (SRT), restorative environments have the ability to promote positive emotional states [2]. Thus, the primary

Fig. 2. The interface design draft using Boston fern for displayed plant growth under different emotional status.

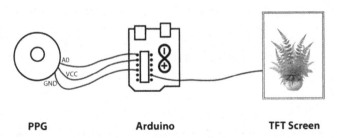

PPG   **Arduino**   **TFT Screen**

Fig. 3. System connection plan.

idea behind the interface design is to represent the growth of a potted plant in a natural setting using visual display. Additionally, the interface display will provide visual feedback when users are detected at high stress state, such as alerts and notifications for reminding users to prioritize and perform stress recovery more effectively.

2.4 Evaluation Plan

Developing a precise and methodical strategy for managing variables is essential for obtaining valid and accurate results in research. In this study, SDNN, a heart rate variability indicator, was measured using wearable technology. The working environment remain quiet and constant to minimize the impact of extraneous variables that may affect the results.

Table 1. Illustration of plant on display from each stress level, Boston fern is used for illustration of stress on the display.

Stress Level HRV (SDNN)	Low (SDNN>100)	Neutral (100>SDNN50)	High (50>SDNN>25)	Extreme (25>SDNN>0)
Plant on Display				

Table 2. Plant selection which have stress-relieving benefits.

Plant Selection	English Ivy	Snake plant	Golden Pot-hos	Boston fern	Spider plant
Benefits	Lower stress level	Reduce stress level	Alleviate stress	Alleviate stress	Reduce stress level

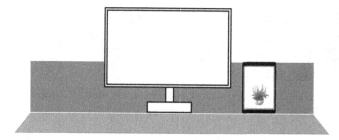

Fig. 4. User feedback study in workplace setting.

Data collection involved wearable sensors like PPG to observe the physiological impact on employees before and after implementation, and ascertain the extent of the relationship between workplace stress recovery and nature interaction. By analyzing the changes of heart rate variability (HRV) that verify stress level, it is proved that SDNN can serve as a key indicator of stress [10].

Combining quantitative and qualitative data will offer deeper and more comprehensive insights into how nature interaction aids workplace stress recovery. The outcomes of this research could significantly influence workplace policies and practices, underscoring the value of nature-based initiatives in enhancing employee health and productivity.

3   Method and Discussion

3.1   User Experiment

To test the efficiency of the stress-relieving interactive interface, 12 gender equal office workers (mean age = 27.5), were asked to carry out a block-stacking task using a total of 54 Jenga wooden [14] blocks for 6 min in an open office space as shown in Fig. 5. During the task, bell dinging and ticking sounds with a timer will be incorporated to increase the level of stress-inducing situations and create a sense of urgency for completing the task on 3 min and last 3 min [15, 16].

Through these pressure points, the researchers were able to assess the effectiveness of the stress-release interactive interface as a holistic solution for stress-relief towards enhance knowledge on stress tolerance. Pre-data reading through PPG will be performed to ensure the stability of data collection at the first 3 min. The anticipated time allocation for this activity is approximately 15 min, which includes additional time set aside to fill out the questionnaire.for collecting the feedback after the testimonial, taking in the awareness of participant's stress tolerance, applicability and rationality of the interface content.

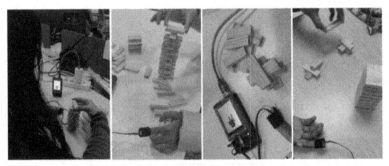

Fig. 5. Participants executing wooden block-staking task on dominant hand, while PPG sensor is wearing on non-dominant hand.

3.2   Results and Discussion

Throughout the 10-min Jenga stacking activity, participants interacted with the engaging interface. Based on the SDNN outcomes, the average SDNN level observed in participants while they were stacking the Jenga blocks was 47.8. Upon the collapse of the blocks, this average level rose to 52.4. The incorporation of sensory cues, such as the ringing of a bell and the ticking of a timer for time-sensitive tasks, introduced a sense of urgency that escalated participants' stress levels, resulted that the average stress level rose to a 31.5 SDNN level.

From the survey, the depiction of stress levels using the plant growth cycle piqued the interest of eight participants. More than 90% of them acknowledged that it heightened their awareness and understanding of stress and stress tolerance. Additionally, 83% of the participants viewed the interface as an all-encompassing and user-friendly approach to alleviating stress, with over 70% indicating they would keep using this interface in the future.

Apart from that, participants highlighted some limitations and obstacles encountered during the study in Table 3. They noted difficulties and discomfort in performing tasks one-handed, yet the display is somehow taking away their attention. Nearly 58% recommended transitioning the sensor to a wearable device to free up their hands, and eight participants suggested incorporating sound features into the interface to maintain focused attention.

Table 3. Feedback from the participants on limitations and suggestions through interview.

Limitations	Suggestions
• "Having the sensor taped around finger feel uncomfortable, the interface being displayed on a second screen seems disturbing me on performing the task." (P1) • "…challenging to pay attention to the plant, because it stays static for long period until stress changes are detected." (P3) • "I couldn't use my left hand." (P7) • "The interface is neglected due to too concentrated towards the task." (P8) • "…hard to stay focus on one at the same time." (P12)	• "…wear-on device with sound would be better to be remind for recovery session." (P1) • "…More responsiveness in the plant status, add animations that react to stress level in real time." (P4) • "Make artificial plant showing how you stress in real life would be better." (P5) • "…add some sound it and maybe make it a wearable device." (P7) • "It would be better if the device is not wearable, for example imply the system into chair in working space." (P8)

4   Conclusion and Future Direction

This study set out to design an interactive interface by connecting nature interaction and stress recovery under workplace setting, demonstrated the potent ability of sensory cues to escalate stress levels, ultimately enhancing participants' awareness and understanding of stress and stress tolerance. The overwhelming majority of participants appreciated the innovative approach to stress visualization through the plant growth cycle and found the interface comprehensive and accessible for stress relief.

However, the study also uncovered certain limitations and challenges, primarily concerning the practical aspects of interaction with the interface. The feedback captured concerns about the usability of the system, especially regarding the one-handed operation and the attention-diverting potential of the display. These insights offer a valuable direction for future revisions and enhancements, such as incorporating an immersive and realistic virtual nature environment for stress release.

Additionally, future studies may look into extending the use of the interface to other settings beyond the workplace and further assessing its impact on health and well-being. Considering its potential in public spaces and infrastructure could lead to societal benefits. By continuing the exploration of innovative and interdisciplinary methods will contribute to healthier, more supportive workplace environments. This study establishes a foundation for advancing stress-relief solutions, emphasizing the importance of user feedback and technological innovations for developing more effective and engaging stress management tools.

References

1. Kim, K.Y.: The association between working posture and worker's depression. Healthcare **10**(3), 477 (2022). Napoli, C. (ed.). https://doi.org/10.3390/healthcare10030477
2. Berto, R.: The role of nature in coping with psycho-physiological stress: a literature review on restorativeness. Behav. Sci. **4**(4), 394–409 (2021). Nasar, J.L. (ed.). https://doi.org/10.3390/bs4040394
3. Stephen, K.: The restorative benefits of nature: toward an integrative framework. J. Environ. Psychol. **1995**(16), 169–182 (1995). https://doi.org/10.1016/0272-4944(95)90001-2
4. Matilda, A., Peter, W.: Nature-assisted therapy: systematic review of controlled and observational studies. Scand. J. Public Health **41**(5), 442–455 (2011). https://doi.org/10.1177/1403494810396400
5. Bratman, G.N., Hamilton, J.P., Gross, J.J.: Nature experience reduces rumination and subgenual prefrontal cortex activation. Proc. Natl. Acad. Sci. **112**(28), 8567–8572 (2015). https://doi.org/10.1073/pnas.1510459112
6. Daniel, T.C.C., Hannah, L.H., Danielle, F.S., Richard, A.F., Kevin, J.G.: The rarity of direct experiences of nature in an urban population. Landsc. Urban Plan. **160**, 79–84 (2017). https://doi.org/10.1016/j.landurbplan.2016.12.006
7. Dan, B.: What makes nature-based interventions for mental health successful? BJPsych Int. **14**(4), 82–85 (2017). https://doi.org/10.1192/s205647400000206.3
8. Kellert, S.R., Heerwagen, J.H., Mador, M.L. (eds.): Biophilic Design: The Theory, Science, and Practice of Bringing Buildings to Life. Wiley, Hoboken (2008)
9. Lohr, V.I., Pearson-Mims, C.H.: Physical discomfort may be reduced in the presence of interior plants. HortScience **10**(1), 53–58 (2000). https://doi.org/10.21273/HORTTECH.10.1.53
10. Kim, H.G., Cheon, E.J., Bai, D.S., Lee, Y.H., Koo, B.H.: Stress and heart rate variability: a meta-analysis and review of the literature. Psychiatry Investig. **15**(3), 235–245 (2018)
11. Hedblom, M., et al.: Reduction of physiological stress by urban green space in a multisensory virtual experiment. Sci. Rep. **9**, 10113 (2019). https://doi.org/10.1038/s41598-019-46099-7
12. Wolverton, B.C.: How to grow Fresh Air: 50 Houseplants that Purify Your Home or Office. Penguin Books (1997)
13. Xue, M., Liang, R.H., Yu, B., Funk, M., Hu, J., Feijs, L.: AffectiveWall: designing collective stress-related physiological data visualization for reflection. IEEE Access **7**, 131289–131303 (2019)
14. Russoniello, C.V., O'Brien, K., Parks, J.M.: The effectiveness of casual video games in improving mood and decreasing stress. J. Cyberther. Rehabil. **2**(1), 53–66 (2009)
15. Naef, A.C., et al.: Investigating the role of auditory and visual sensory inputs for inducing relaxation during virtual reality stimulation. Sci. Rep. **12**, 17073 (2022). https://doi.org/10.1038/s41598-022-21575-9
16. Caviola, S., Carey, E., Mammarella, R.C., Szucs D.: Stress, time pressure, strategy selection and math anxiety in mathematics: a review of the literature. Front. Psychol. **8**(1488) (2017)

Activation of Motivations, Emotions, the Law of Force and Theories of Change in Sensitivity for Personality Testing

Sergey Lytaev$^{(\boxtimes)}$ (iD)

Saint Petersburg State Pediatric Medical University, Litovskaya 2, 194100 Saint Petersburg, Russia
physiology@gpmu.org

Abstract. This research was aimed to assess the severity of emotional and motivational processes during the perception of chess patterns of varying contrast and registration of visual evoked potentials (VEPs) with subsequent analysis of personal and cognitive processes on this basis. An increase in the intensity of the contrast of a reversible chess field, regardless of the emotional sphere is accompanied by an increase in the amplitude of the amplitude of the N_{150} wave in persons with a high degree of tension and reduced emotional stability was traced. For persons with a low degree of tension and high emotional stability in the occipital-parietal leads, an inverse relationship between the magnitude of contrast and amplitude N_{150} is noted. Comparison of behavioral investigation results with electrophysiological data enabled to find that the first variant of reaction was characterized by lower degree of visual images identification, under condition hampering their identification, irrespective of test objects modality.

Keywords: Visual Evoked Potentials · Change of Sensitivity · Emotions · Reversible Pattern · Personality Testing

1 Introduction

Over the course of 100 years a line of concepts has been formed that explain adaptive changes in the central nervous system under the influence of stimuli of varying intensity. Firstly, this is the theory of activation of motivation, which is known as the Yerkes – Dodson law, when the optimum of motivation is determined by the most productive work and is aimed at maximum effect. Thus, the dependence of effective work on the level of motivation itself was proven [1]. Chronologically, the next will be the law of force and, as its continuation, the law of transcendental protective inhibition [1]. These mechanisms include inhibition of reflex activity in neuropsychiatric patients to conserve energy resources [9, 13, 16, 20, 21, 25]. One of the most known neuroscience theories of personality is the reinforcement sensitivity theory (RST). In the study of reflex activity, the concept of the behavioral inhibition system (BIS) and the behavioral approach system (BAS) was proposed. In origin, RST is related to the kinesthetic psychological phenomenon of augmentation/reduction (A/R), which was developed in sensory physiology [2, 5, 7, 18, 22].

C. Stephanidis et al. (Eds.): HCII 2024, CCIS 2118, pp. 387–393, 2024.
https://doi.org/10.1007/978-3-031-61963-2_39

Specifically, BAS consists of four main processes. Two processes relate to early approach behavior (reward interest and goal persistence), and two processes relate to later approach behavior (reward reactivity and impulsivity). It was found that although later approach processes predicted greater attention to negative images, there were no similar associations for earlier approach processes [8–10, 23].

There is evidence that people with stronger BAS showed increased sensitivity to the positive emotions of happiness, while people with stronger BIS showed increased sensitivity to the emotions of anger, fear and disgust (as assessed by EEG alpha band power). Other results showed that people with stronger BAS showed increased sensitivity to negative images. The differences between the two studies may reflect differences in performance (alpha band power versus ERP) [3, 11, 12, 24].

The purpose of this study was to assess the severity of emotional and motivational processes during the perception of chess patterns of varying contrast and registration of visual evoked potentials (VEPs), with subsequent analysis of personal and cognitive processes on this basis.

2 Methods

The research of 52 healthy men (age 20–22 years) and 39 psychiatric patients (males: mean age 38.5, range 21–53) without active productive pathology was performed. VEPs using 19 monopolar sites system 10/20 with neuromapper were recorded. Stimulation was carried out with eyes open by presenting reversible patterns on the display screen, which are black and white chess squares. 3 series of stimuli differing in degree of contrast of checkerboard field elements – low, medium and high were used [16].

Cognitive research consisted in testing vision system by screen presenting images. The set of 32 complex geometrical fragments of the Perret's figures for testing short time visual memory, independent of language abilities was used. Line of the 9 images with incomplete set of signs, consisting of familiar objects was presented to examinees under conditions of time deficit (exposition of 4.0– 3000.0 ms) [16, 17].

An estimation of emotional activity was executed by two factors C (emotional stability) and Q4 (relaxation – tension) of Cattell's test.

3 Outcomes

According to the nature of the response to an increase in the chess contrast, patients and healthy subjects into two groups were divided. In the first variant (21 patients and 29 healthy subjects) a direct dependence of the amplitude of visual EPs on the level of pattern contrast was recorded. In the second variant (18 patients and 23 healthy subjects) an increase in the VEP amplitude was initially observed, but next with an increase in the contrast level, the amplitude of the evoked responses was reduced (Fig. 1 and Fig. 2).

Groups formed on the basis of the amplitude of evoked potentials in response to changes in the contrast of chess patterns were compared with the results of visual cognitive testing under deficit of time. It is characteristic that in general the level of image recognition, regardless of the character of the VEP response and the modality of the test objects, was higher in healthy subjects. A line of differences in psychopathology was recorded. In the second group, the identification of successive parts of Perrett's figures approached normal, while in the first group the number of correct answers was significantly lower (P < 0.05). Similar correlations between the studied groups also were observed when identifying images with an incomplete set of features (Fig. 3).

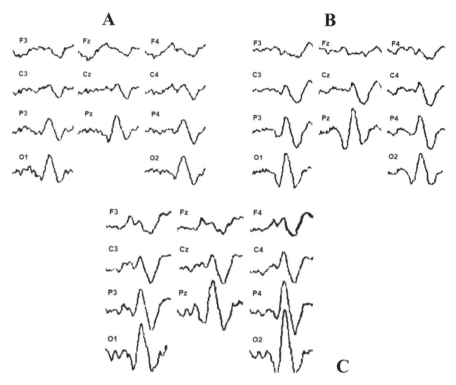

Fig. 1. VEPs distribution from reversal pattern stimulation of min (A), middle (B) and max (C) contrast for augmentation by 10/20 system (O2, O1, P4......F3).

Evaluation of profiles by factors C and Q4 allowed to characterize the individuals being tested. The values of the factor "relaxation – tension" were distributed in the range from 1 to 6 points. Parameters of emotional stability were recorded within the range of 5–9 points. To determine the relationship between the influence of a person's emotional state on the nature of the brain VEP, healthy subjects were divided into 2 groups. 31 subjects were in the category of people with high performance (4–6 points) and 21 subjects had low scores for this indicator (1–3 points). It should be noted that higher scores (4–6) on factors Q4 corresponded to lower scores on factor C (5–6). Conversely, low scores of tension (1–3) corresponded to high scores of emotional stability (7–9).

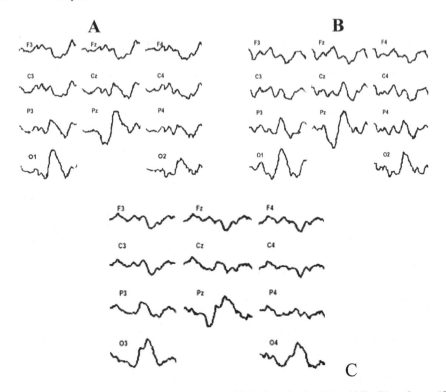

Fig. 2. VEPs distribution from reversal pattern stimulation of min (A), middle (B) and max (C) contrast for reducing by 10/20 system (O2, O1, P4......F3).

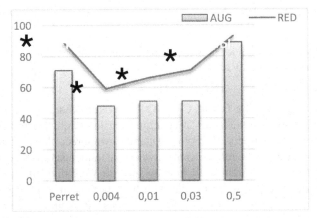

Fig. 3. The values of recognition (%) of Perret's figures and images with incomplete set of signs during short time presentation: 0.004, 0.01, 0.03 and 0.5 s. * – $P < 0.05$. Note. AUG – group of "augmentors", RED – group of "reducers".

4 Discussion

Often, when studying the mechanisms of processing sensory signals of varying intensities, excitation/inhibition processes in the central nervous system are used as justification [1, 10, 14, 19]. It is based on threshold theory, which assumes that the nature of the response depends on threshold sensitivity. The presence of low sensitivity, that is, an initially high threshold of absolute sensory sensitivity, increases the level of response to increasing intensity of the stimulator. On the contrary, a system with high sensitivity, that is, with a low absolute sensory threshold, runs a "program" that protects against "overload". Despite increasing stimulus intensity, a reduced evoked response is obtained. Accordingly, subjects in the first case are usually called "augmentators", and in the second – "reducers" [8, 16].

A visual, computerised ERP oddball paradigm measured participants' attention towards positive and negative emotion-based still images. Participants were exposed to two types of stimuli: one frequent stimulus (black and white checkerboard image) presented 76% of the time, and non-frequent target stimuli (oddball stimuli; road safety images) presented 24% of the time. On presentation of the non-frequent oddball stimuli, participants elicit an ERP response [12]. In accordance with RST, it was hypothesised that individuals with a stronger relative to a weaker BAS would elicit larger N100 and N200 mean amplitudes, reflecting greater earlier and later attention, respectively, towards the positive images. Since the FFFS (Fight-Flight-Freeze System) is sensitive to punishments, those with a stronger rather than a weaker FFFS were hypothesised to elicit larger N100 and N200 mean amplitudes on presentation of the negative images [6, 15, 22].

The neurophysiological basis of changes in sensitivity is explained by the author's line in different ways. In particular, the mechanism of switching the A/R phenomenon is sometimes associated with biochemical changes. The concentration of catecholamines, platelet monoamine oxidase, the level of endorphins, etc. may be important [10, 16]. A number of correlations between changes in bioelectrical activity (EEG, EP) and psychological testing data are of undoubted interest. According to some authors, the most informative for correlation with psychological information are frontal registration points [4, 8, 25]. Thus, in particular, factor Q4 (from the Cattell questionnaire) has a direct relationship with both components of the EP, which have a peak latency of about 150 ms and 300 ms. There are observations that, from the point of view of the holistic nature of nervous activity, the activation of the switching mechanism at low intensity of stimulation is more typical for extroverts [16].

The results of the present study are discussed in accordance with the concepts of activation of motivations, emotions, the law of force and the theory of change in sensitivity when testing personality psychology and visual perception under difficult conditions. The effectiveness of the functioning of specific mechanisms of sensory recognition - invariant evaluation of signals, short-term visual memory, spatial analysis and synthesis - is in the process of processing in connection with the electrophysiological features of the perception of structural images of varying contrast. It is assumed that a more pronounced response of the associative (frontal) cortex to a stimulator of medium intensity, which correlates with higher identification of images in the second group of patients with psychopathology, indicates a more synchronous operation of the cerebral hemispheres when processing significant information. The adaptive mechanism activated in the processing response to an increase in contrast, manifested by a decrease in the EP amplitude, probably indicates a decrease in the biological significance of this informative stimulator. In contrast, the absence of an adaptive switching mechanism is likely a reflection of more inert brain processes, as indicated by increased sensory image identification thresholds.

5   Conclusion

An increase in the intensity of the contrast of a reversible chess field, regardless of the emotional sphere is accompanied by an increase in the amplitude of the N_{70} VEP component. A similar relationship for the amplitude of the N_{150} wave in persons with a high degree of tension and reduced emotional stability was traced.

Images identification degree irrespective of VEPs response reaction character and test objects modality was higher with healthy examinees. However, among psychopathological groups under examination there some differences were observed. So, in the second group the identification of the Perret's figures consequent parts came near the normal one, whereas in the first group the number of correct answers was significantly lower ($P < 0.05$). Resembling correlations between groups under examination also in identifying images with incomplete set of signs were observed.

For persons with a low degree of tension and high emotional stability in the occipital-parietal leads, an inverse relationship between the magnitude of contrast and amplitude N_{150} is noted. At the same time, in the frontal areas, the switching mechanism of regulation is observed, which after the initial increase of the N150 amplitude is accompanied by its further decrease with increasing degree of contrast.

References

1. Belskaya, K.A., Lytaev, S.A.: Neuropsychological analysis of cognitive deficits in schizophrenia. Hum. Physiol. **48**, 37–45 (2022)
2. Bijttebier, P., Beck, I., Claes, L., Vandereycken, W.: Gray's reinforcement sensitivity theory as a framework for research on personality–psychopathology associations. Clin. Psychol. Rev. **29**(5), 421–430 (2009)
3. Choi, S.-O., Choi, J.-G., Yun, J.-Y.: A study of brain function characteristics of service members at high risk for accidents in the military. Brain Sci. **13**, 1157 (2023)
4. Corr, P.J., DeYoung, C.G., McNaughton, N.: Motivation and personality: a neuropsychological perspective. Soc. Pers. Psychol. Compass **7**, 158–175 (2013)
5. Corr, P.J.: Reinforcement sensitivity theory of personality questionnaires: structural survey with recommendations. Pers. Individ. Differ. **89**, 60–64 (2016)
6. Corr, P.J., McNaughton, N.: Neuroscience and approach/avoidance personality traits: a two stage (valuation–motivation) approach. Neurosci. Biobehav. Rev. **36**, 2339–2354 (2012)
7. De Pascalis, V.: Psychophysiological studies. In: The Reinforcement Sensitivity Theory of Personality, pp. 261–290. Cambridge University Press, Cambridge (2008)
8. De Pascalis, V., Fracasso, F., Corr, P.J.: Personality and augmenting/reducing (A/R) in auditory event-related potentials (ERPs) during emotional visual stimulation. Sci. Rep. **7**, 41588 (2017)
9. De Pascalis, V., Scacchia, P., Sommer, K., Checcucci, C.: Psychopathy traits and reinforcement sensitivity theory: prepulse inhibition and ERP responses. Biol. Psychol. **148**, 107771 (2019)

10. Gray, J., McNaughton, N.: The Neuropsychology of Anxiety: An Enquiry into the Functions of the Septo-Hippocampal System, 2nd edn. Oxford University Press, Oxford (2000)

11. Hensch, T., Herold, U., Diers, K., Armbruster, D., Brocke, B.: Reliability of intensity dependence of auditory-evoked potentials. Clin. Neurophysiol. **119**, 224–236 (2008)

12. Kaye, Sh.-A., White, M., Lewis, I.: Young females' attention towards road safety images: an ERP study of the revised reinforcement sensitivity theory. Traffic Injury Prev. **19**(2), 201–206 (2018)

13. Khil'ko, V.A., et al.: The topographic mapping of evoked bioelectrical activity and other methods for the functional neural visualization of the brain. Vestn. Ross. Akad. Med. Nauk **3**, 36–41 (1993)

14. Langer, K., Wolf, O.T., Jentsch, V.L.: Delayed effects of acute stress on cognitive emotion regulation. Psychoneuroendocrinology **125**, 105101 (2021)

15. Lever-van Milligen, B.A., Lamers, F., Smit, J.H., et al.: Physiological stress markers, mental health and objective physical function. J. Psychosom. Res. **133**, 109996 (2020)

16. Lytaev, S., Aleksandrov, M., Lytaev, M.: Estimation of emotional processes in regulation of the structural afferentation of varying contrast by means of visual evoked potentials. Adv. Intell. Syst. Comput. **953**, 288–298 (2020)

17. Lytaev, S., Vatamaniuk, I.: Physiological and medico-social research trends of the wave P_{300} and more late components of visual event-related potentials. Brain Sci. **11**, 125 (2021)

18. Lytaev, S.: Modern neurophysiological research of the human brain in clinic and psychophysiology. In: Rojas, I., Castillo-Secilla, D., Herrera, L.J., Pomares, H. (eds.) BIOMESIP 2021. LNCS, vol. 12940, pp. 231–241. Springer, Cham (2021). https://doi.org/10.1007/978-3-030-88163-4_21

19. Lytaev, S.: Long-latency event-related potentials (300–1000 ms) of the visual insight. Sensors **22**, 1323 (2022)

20. Lytaev, S.: Psychological and neurophysiological screening investigation of the collective and personal stress resilience. Behav. Sci. **13**, 258 (2023)

21. Lytaev, S.: Short time algorithms for screening examinations of the collective and personal stress resilience. In: Harris, D., Li, W.C. (eds.) HCII 2023. LNCS, vol. 14017, pp. 442–458. Springer, Cham (2023). https://doi.org/10.1007/978-3-031-35392-5_34

22. McNaughton, N., Corr, P.J.: The Neuropsychology of Fear and Anxiety: A Foundation for Reinforcement Sensitivity Theory. The Reinforcement Sensitivity Theory of Personality, pp. 44–94. Cambridge University Press, Cambridge (2008)

23. Noushad, S., Ahmed, S., Ansari, B., et al.: Physiological biomarkers of chronic stress: a systematic review. Int. J. Health Sci. **15**, 46 (2021)

24. O'Connor, D.B., Thayer, J.F., Vedhara, K.: Stress and health: a review of psychobiological processes. Annu. Rev. Psychol. **72**, 663–688 (2020)

25. Sylvers, P., Lilienfeld, S.O., LaPrairie, J.L.: Differences between trait fear and trait anxiety: implications for psychopathology. Clin. Psychol. Rev.. Psychol. Rev. **31**, 122–137 (2011)

An Examination of Why Smartphone Use Gradually Leads to Addiction

Jaehyun Park[✉]

Incheon National University, Incheon 22013, Republic of Korea
`jaehpark@inu.ac.kr`

Abstract. The rising concern of smartphone addiction highlights its neurobiological aspects, particularly focusing on the dopamine reward circuit, yet direct impacts on the brain are underexplored. Current research reveals a complex interplay of biological, psychological, and social factors, but there remains a notable gap in understanding the specific effects of smartphone use on neural processes. This paper emphasizes the need for a holistic approach, advocating for integrated research that spans biopsychosocial dimensions. Although providing concrete solutions is beyond its scope, the review encourages comprehensive studies aimed at bridging the gap between biological underpinnings and social consequences, thereby enriching our understanding and approaches to managing smartphone addiction within the larger addiction spectrum.

Keywords: Smartphone addiction · Dopamine reward loop

1 Introduction

It is evident that we have developed a dependency on our smartphones [1]. When the term 'addiction' is employed, it is presumed that the underlying concept is universally understood. However, significant controversy remains, indicating that the precise mechanisms are not yet fully elucidated. Nonetheless, from a phenomenological standpoint, despite being an antiquated notion, the following assertion retains its validity. Certain individuals use certain substances in certain ways, thought at certain times to be unacceptable by certain other individuals for reasons both certain and uncertain [2].

The prevailing traditional perspective on addiction posits that it originates from a multifaceted interplay of biopsychosocial factors [3]. Consider a scenario in which an individual becomes so addicted to smoking that cessation becomes unattainable. This individual might possess a genetic predisposition that renders him or her more susceptible to the challenges of quitting. Additionally, the inherent addictive properties of nicotine in cigarettes may contribute to the compulsion. Furthermore, personal or social circumstances may create environments that promote or sustain smoking behavior.

If we categorize the pervasive use of smartphones, or, more specifically, the activity of engaging in activities such as watching YouTube shorts or playing games, as an addiction, it necessitates a comprehensive explanation. Furthermore, the question arises as to whether this pattern of behavior can legitimately be classified as a disorder. To address these inquiries, it is imperative to review and analyze existing scholarly research.

C. Stephanidis et al. (Eds.): HCII 2024, CCIS 2118, pp. 394–398, 2024.
https://doi.org/10.1007/978-3-031-61963-2_40

2   Smartphone Use and Dopamine Reward Loop

Among the diverse theories elucidating the mechanisms underlying addiction, the dopamine reward circuit hypothesis has garnered substantial attention in recent research. Dopamine, synthesized within the midbrain, is transmitted along four primary pathways. Of these, the mesolimbic-mesocortical pathway, extending from the ventral tegmental area (VTA) to the limbic system, has been identified as significantly implicated in addictive behaviors [4]. Essentially, when dopamine is released in response to a specific stimulus, this engenders a subsequent desire for a similar stimulus. This phenomenon is referred to as a 'reward', and as the frequency of such rewards increases, there ensues a pursuit of cues associated with the anticipated reward. Consequently, dopamine release is triggered merely by the anticipation signaled by these cues, independent of the actual receipt of the reward.

Expanding this concept to encompass smartphone usage, particularly the aspect of notifications via vibration, it is plausible to assert that many individuals have experienced the pleasure of receiving positive messages, news, or content, at least once. Indeed, it is highly likely that such experiences have occurred multiple times. While it is conceivable that some vibratory alerts have resulted in insignificant outcomes, these are not of primary concern. The critical point is that enjoyable or gratifying memories contribute to the gradual construction of the dopamine reward circuit. Consequently, even in the absence of pleasant messages, the mere sensation of vibration can elicit dopamine release (See Fig. 1). This mechanism insidiously leads to our lives becoming progressively dominated by smartphones [5].

Recent research provides neurobiological evidence that addiction can manifest. While studies may not specifically target smartphone usage, research conducted on patients with internet addiction is relevant. Given that smartphones often serve as gateways to internet access, it is plausible to hypothesize that smartphone users may exhibit symptoms analogous to those observed in individuals with internet addiction. For instance, A significant decrease in dopamine D2 receptors was observed in patients suffering from internet addiction [6]. Similarly, abnormal functional activities was identified in brain regions associated with reward dependence in these individuals [7]. Moreover, structural changes were reported within the brain attributed to internet addiction [8]. It is particularly noteworthy that adolescents, whose prefrontal cortices are not fully developed, may experience detrimental structural changes due to addiction, potentially leading to various developmental issues [9].

3   Things not Covered in the Dopamine-Based Model for Smartphone

Since around 2010, there has been a notable surge in research focusing on dopamine and its relationship to addiction, thus highlighting a neurobiological perspective [5]. While many researchers underscore the undeniable impact of psychological and sociological factors, explanations from a biopsychosocial standpoint are sometimes perceived as less compelling. However, it is imperative not to disregard the psychosocial aspects. Given the prevalence of addiction to social networking services (SNS) and various applications

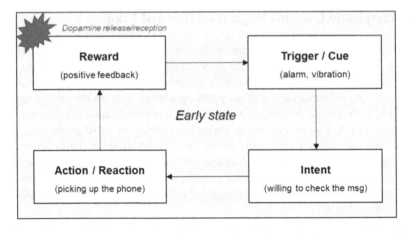

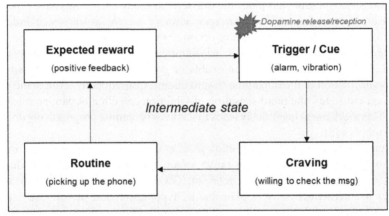

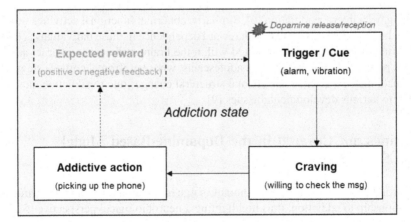

Fig. 1. Dopamine reward loops

facilitated by smartphones, there are undoubtedly viable social solutions that should be considered. For instance, efforts to mitigate polarized social atmospheres, though seemingly unrelated to smartphone addiction at first glance, may in fact hold subtle connections to it.

Research on dopamine has been actively conducted in the field of drug addiction, underpinned by the perception that addiction is a disease [10]. This is because addiction creates a problematic state, leads to withdrawal symptoms when attempting to quit, and involves intense cravings when abstained from. In the context of smartphone addiction, these questions are often not raised. Is smartphone addiction truly a disease? If so, then reducing or quitting usage becomes imperative, which may antagonize many internet services such as Facebook, Instagram, and TikTok. In severe cases, medication might be recommended. However, if it is not deemed a disease, then efforts to treat such levels of addiction might be deemed unnecessary. Despite alterations in brain structure due to addiction, some argue that it should not be classified as a disease, as this notion can lead to discrimination and other societal issues [11]. Additionally, addiction is viewed as immoral in some societies, and there is ongoing debate on whether the brain disease model can truly liberate addiction from moral judgments [12]. Presently, smartphone addiction is often regarded as mere gossip, but research is needed to determine whether it is a disease or an immoral act.

Addiction is a complex phenomenon. While the dopamine theory is widely accepted, it fails to explain certain aspects. For instance, while various drug addictions increase dopamine release, marijuana addiction appears to be less associated with the dopamine loop. This suggests that addiction can occur phenomenologically without being directly caused by dopamine [13]. Furthermore, research is being conducted on the impact of other factors like oxytocin, the autonomic nervous system, chronic stress, and orexin on addiction [5].

In addition, In reality, research directly investigating the impact of smartphone addiction on the brain has been relatively scarce. Extensive studies have been conducted on internet addiction, substance abuse, and food consumption disorders, and conclusions regarding smartphone addiction are often inferred based on findings from these related areas.

4   Conclusion

The current research on smartphone addiction primarily focuses on neurobiological mechanisms, such as the dopamine reward circuit, playing a crucial role in understanding the complex phenomena of addiction. However, there is a relative scarcity of studies directly investigating the impact of smartphone addiction on the brain. This lack highlights a significant gap in efforts to fully comprehend the complexities where biological, psychological, and social factors interact in addiction research. Therefore, studies on addiction, including smartphone addiction, require a multifaceted approach, suggesting that addiction should be addressed as a serious social and psychological issue, not merely as a moral failing.

Moreover, the concept of addiction remains contentious, especially in relation to smartphone usage, compounding the issue. There exists a continuing disparity between the perspective of addiction as a disease and its social perception, affecting treatment approaches, public policy, and societal attitudes toward addicts. To develop a deeper understanding and effective strategies for addressing smartphone addiction, comprehensive research encompassing the neurobiological, psychological, and social dimensions of addiction is needed. Such research could provide clearer and more practical solutions to the complex issues surrounding addiction.

References

1. Ratan, Z.A., Parrish, A.M., Zaman, S.B., Alotaibi, M.S., Hosseinzadeh, H.: Smartphone addiction and associated health outcomes in adult populations: a systematic review. Int. J. Environ. Res. Public Health **18**(22), 12257 (2021)
2. Burglass, M.E., Shaffer, H.J.: Diagnosis in the addictions I: conceptual problems. Addict. Behav. **3**, 19–34 (1984)
3. Griffiths, M.: A 'components' model of addiction within a biopsychosocial framework. J. Subst. Use **10**(4), 191–197 (2005)
4. Volkow, N.D., Wang, G.J., Fowler, J.S., Tomasi, D., Telang, F.: Addiction: beyond dopamine reward circuitry. Proc. Natl. Acad. Sci. U.S.A. **108**(37), 15037–15042 (2011)
5. Tereshchenko, S.Y.: Neurobiological risk factors for problematic social media use as a specific form of Internet addiction: a narrative review. World J. Psychiatry **13**(5), 160–173 (2023)
6. Kim, S.H., Baik, S.H., Park, C.S., Kim, S.J., Choi, S.W., Kim, S.E.: Reduced striatal dopamine D2 receptors in people with Internet addiction. NeuroReport **22**(8), 407–411 (2011)
7. Hong, S.B., et al.: Decreased functional brain connectivity in adolescents with internet addiction. PLoS ONE **8**(2), e57831 (2013)
8. Weinstein, A., Lejoyeux, M.: New developments on the neurobiological and pharmaco-genetic mechanisms underlying internet and videogame addiction. Am. J. Addict. **24**(2), 117–125 (2015)
9. He, J., Crews, F.T.: Neurogenesis decreases during brain maturation from adolescence to adulthood. Pharmacol. Biochem. Behav. **86**(2), 327–333 (2007)
10. Volkow, N.D., Koob, G.F., McLellan, A.T.: Neurobiologic advances from the brain disease model of addiction. N. Engl. J. Med. **374**(4), 363–371 (2016)
11. Heather, N., et al.: Challenging the brain disease model of addiction: European launch of the addiction theory network. Addict. Res. Theory **26**(4), 249–255 (2018)
12. Frank, L.E., Nagel, S.K.: Addiction and moralization: the role of the underlying model of addiction. Neuroethics **10**(1), 129–139 (2017)
13. Nutt, D.J., Lingford-Hughes, A., Erritzoe, D., Stokes, P.R.: The dopamine theory of addiction: 40 years of highs and lows. Nat. Rev. Neurosci. **16**(5), 305–312 (2015)

Impact of Technological Development on Human Cognitive Functioning

Carlos Ramos-Galarza[1]([✉]) [ID], Patricia García-Cruz[2] [ID], Jorge Cruz-Cárdenas[3] [ID], and Mónica Bolaños-Pasquel[1] [ID]

[1] Centro de Investigación en Mecatrónica y Sistemas Interactivos - MIST, Facultad de Psicología, Universidad Tecnológica Indoamérica, Quito, Ecuador
carlosramos@uti.edu.ec

[2] Facultad de Psicología, Pontificia Universidad Católica del Ecuador, Quito, Ecuador

[3] Research Center in Business, Society, and Technology, ESTec, School of Administrative and Economic Science, Universidad Tecnológica Indoamérica, Quito, Ecuador

Abstract. Human beings have several cognitive functions (memory, attention, language, perception, executive functions and others) that allow them to perform all their daily activities. In the context of the stimulation of human cognitive functions, classic activities based on tangible resources such as pencil and paper have been developed. In this context, there is an opportunity for technological development to make proposals to create games that stimulate human mental abilities. In this context, this article reports a quantitative systematic review of research about games to cognitive stimulation. Among the main results obtained, games that stimulate skills such as perception, attention, memory, executive functions, psychomotor skills and information processing speed were identified. The following are some of the results processed in this systematic review.

Keywords: cognitive rehabilitation · systematic review · serious games · neuropsychology · technology

1 Introduction

The process of cognitive rehabilitation helps many people with brain injury to improve their quality of life through the stimulation and rehabilitation of different affected areas of the brain [1]. This process consists of different techniques, strategies for the evaluation and intervention of the affected cognitive functions, because many people with brain damage present attentional deficit, memory disorders, impairment in executive functioning, difficulties in perceptual and visuoconstructive skills, as well as emotional alterations, changes in behavior and loss of social skills among many others that are related to the extent and location of the lesion [2]. For a long time, the ways to assess and cognitively rehabilitate patients have consisted of strategies and tools presented in paper and pencil, however, with the advancement of technology these strategies and tools have been innovating and adapting to the needs of more effective neuropsychological therapeutic processes [3, 4].

C. Stephanidis et al. (Eds.): HCII 2024, CCIS 2118, pp. 399–406, 2024.
https://doi.org/10.1007/978-3-031-61963-2_41

Neuropsychology is a science that has contributed to the knowledge we have about the way the brain works and the consequences of alterations in its functioning [4]. It is from this science that the term cognitive rehabilitation emerged; however, cognitive function rehabilitation already existed before, because the first rehabilitators were well-known neurologists who worked in Germany, Russia and England during the First and Second World War, such as Alexander Luria [5]. However, cognitive rehabilitation, also known as neuropsychological rehabilitation, did not have its beginnings in the First World War or later, thanks to the discovery in Luxor in 1862 of a document that addressed the treatment of people with brain damage 3,000 years ago [4].

According to the Spanish Federation of Brain Injury, there are more than 435,400 people with acquired brain injury in Spain [6]. Likewise, in the United States it is known that approximately 1.7 million people have a diagnosis of brain injury [7], which demonstrates the impact of these conditions on the population worldwide. The people who have benefited from neuropsychological rehabilitation are not only people with brain damage due to injury or after an illness, but also their families. It is recognized that loss of productivity and thus loss of opportunities significantly affect people with brain injury-related diagnoses and their families; however, cognitive rehabilitation can help to improve the quality of life of these individuals [8].

As we have seen, cognitive rehabilitation has helped many people over the years, which is why the constant innovation and adaptation of intervention and evaluation strategies has favored the accessibility and effectiveness of these treatments. By understanding technology in cognitive rehabilitation as those instruments that impact the performance and functional capacity of people with brain damage [9]. Due to all the brain structures and functions that can be affected with brain damage and the different approaches and models that help us to understand and explain these models, it is important to adapt the rehabilitation tools [10], which is why websites, cell phone applications, electronic devices, toys, games and the use of virtual reality have been created to make the procedures more attractive [11].

Many people with brain damage who are undergoing cognitive rehabilitation treatments face very high costs due to the care they require. According to a study in Spain the approximate total cost of a patient with cognitive impairment would be around 30,000 euros [8]. In view of the high costs and low accessibility to cognitive rehabilitation processes, it is necessary to carry out a systematic review of technological devices that favors the spread of new forms of evaluation and intervention for both children and adults and thus improve the accessibility and effectiveness of treatments.

2   Method

2.1   Research Design

In this research we worked on a systematic review of games based on technological developments that have been applied for psychological treatments with humans. The present research was carried out by means of a systematic review methodology of the collection of 24 academic articles [12–35].

3 Results

3.1 Types of Participants

Regarding the type of participants in the study, people with health problems, cognitive alterations and healthy participants were identified. Most studies established group comparison methodologies to identify the impact of technology on cognition. Figure 1 shows the percentage distribution of the type of population.

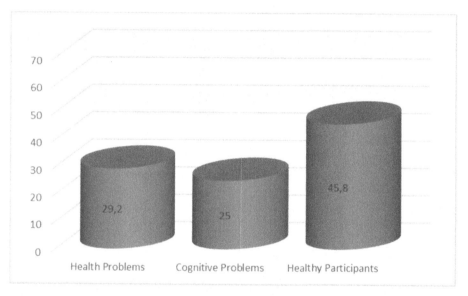

Fig. 1. Types of Participants

3.2 Types of Psychological Tests Applied

In the neuropsychological assessments carried out in the research, the impact of technology on cognitive and behavioral aspects was analyzed by applying tests and questionnaires. Figure 2 shows the percentage distribution of this result.

3.3 Cognitive Enhancement in Technological Interventions

In the studies analyzed, a maximum improvement of 24.44 points and a minimum of 1.34 points of cognition tests. This data was found when assessing scores before and after receiving a technological intervention to improve the cognitive status of the participants. Figure 3 shows the average pre- and post-test scores of technological interventions.

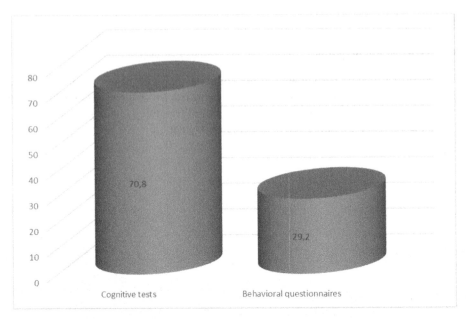

Fig. 2. Types of Psychological Tests Applied

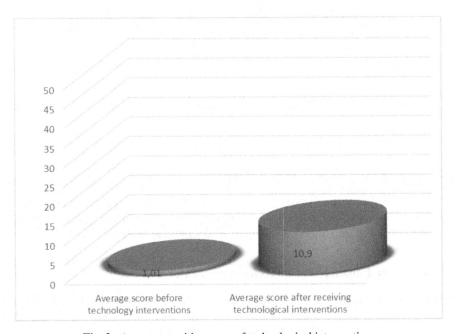

Fig. 3. Average cognitive score of technological interventions

3.4 Neuropsychological Skills Benefited by Technology

The impact of technology on cognitive skills is significant, since participants who benefit from this type of intervention improve their levels of perception, attention, memory, executive functions, psychomotor skills and information processing speed. Figure 4 shows the percentage organization of this result.

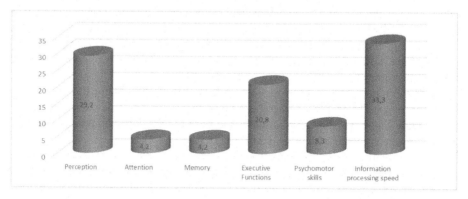

Fig. 4. Neuropsychological Skills Benefited by Technology

3.5 Technological Devices Developed

Different devices created for cognitive intervention processes were found in the studies analyzed. The main ones were electroencephalographic devices for brain stimulation, computerized platforms to assess brain functions, online cognitive assessment platforms, serious cognitive stimulation video games and portable electronic brain stimulation devices. Figure 5 shows the results found in this analysis.

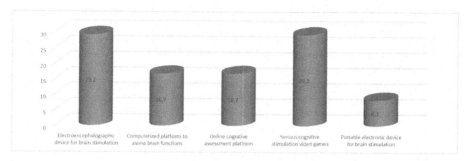

Fig. 5. Technological devices developed

4 Conclusions

In the research presented in this article, we have conducted an analysis of the research published in recent years on technological developments in favor of cognitive stimulation of human beings. We found studies that seek to improve skills such as attention, memory, perception, psychomotor skills and executive functions.

An interesting fact from the systematic review is the rate of cognitive improvement achieved with the use of technological devices, which is around an average of 10% improvement for patients with brain disorders. This finding is of vital importance, since this type of intervention becomes a useful tool for the clinician in neuropsychological rehabilitation, taking into account that it should not be the only option, but a valid resource that contributes to the patient's treatment [36].

An important contribution of this research lies in the benefit for the clinician in charge of the care of people with acquired brain damage, since the evidence described in this study highlights the contribution of the use of technology in favor of cognitive improvements in people with brain damage [37].

Future research arising from this work has to do with creating our own electronic device for human cognitive stimulation and analyzing its impact on the brain-damaged patients we serve in the clinical context. In addition, it is of interest to execute experimental studies with pre- and post-test evaluations as well as control and experimental groups that will allow us to determine the impact of technological developments on human cognition [38].

References

1. Ramos-Galarza, C., et al.: Fundamental concepts in the neuropsychological theory. Revista Ecuatoriana de Neurología **26**(1), 53–60 (2017). https://revecuatneurol.com/magazine_issue_article/conceptos-fundamentales-en-la-teoria-neuropsicologica-fundamental-concepts-neuropsychological-theory/
2. Ramos-Galarza, C., Benavides-Endara, P., Bolaños-Pasquel, M., Fonseca-Bautista, S., Ramos, D.: Scale of clinical observation to evaluate the third functional unit of the Luria theory: EOCL-1. Revista Ecuatoriana de Neurología **28**(2), 83–91 (2019). https://revecuatneurol.com/wp-content/uploads/2019/10/2631-2581-rneuro-28-02-00083.pdf
3. Martínez, E., Pérez, A., Crespo, M.: Theoretical, methodological and practical foundations of cognitive rehabilitation in adults with acquired brain damage. Revista Cubana de Medicina Física y Rehabilitación **13**(2) (2021)
4. Ramos-Galarza, C., Acosta-Rodas, M., Sánchez-Gordón, S., Calle-Jiménez, T.: Mobile technological Apps to improve frontal lobe functioning. Adv. Intell. Syst. Comput. **1201**, 89–93 (2021). https://doi.org/10.1007/978-3-030-51041-1_13
5. Rufo-Campos, M.: La neuropsicología: historian. Revista de neurología **43**(1), 57–58 (2006)
6. FEDACE: Federación Española de Daño Cerebral (2022). https://fedace.org/cifras_dano_cerebral
7. Georges, A., Das, J.M.: National Library of Medicine, 2 January 2023. https://www.ncbi.nlm.nih.gov/books/NBK459300/
8. Wilson, B.: Neuropsychological rehabilitation: state of the science. S. Afr. J. Psychol. **43**(3), 267–277 (2013). https://doi.org/10.1177/0081246313494156

9. Silva-Barragán, M., Ramos-Galarza, C.: Brain organization models: a neuropsychological journey. Revista Ecuatoriana de Neurología **29**(3), 74–83 (2020). https://doi.org/10.46997/revecuatneurol29300074

10. Ramos-Galarza, C., Arias-Flores, H., Cóndor-Herrera, O., Jadán-Guerrero, J.: Literacy toy for enhancement phonological awareness: a longitudinal study. In: Miesenberger, K., Manduchi, R., Covarrubias Rodriguez, M., Peňáz, P. (eds.) ICCHP 2020. LNCS, vol. 12377, pp. 371–377. Springer, Cham (2020). https://doi.org/10.1007/978-3-030-58805-2_44

11. Gaibor-Estévez, J., Ramos-Galarza, C.: Neuropsychological analysis of a case with anosognosia. Rev. Chil. Neuropsiquiatr. **58**(3), 294–299 (2020). https://doi.org/10.4067/S0717-922 72020000300294

12. Kozora, E., Zell, J.L., Baraghoshi, D., Smith, R.M., Strand, M.: Improved executive function in patients with systemic lupus erythematosus following interactive digital training. Lupus **31**(8) (2022)

13. Goulart, A.A., Lucatelli, A., Silveira, P.S.P., Siqueira, J.d.O., Pereira, V.F.A., Carmona, M.J.C., et al.: Comparison of digital games as a cognitive function assessment tool for current standardized neuropsychological tests. Braz. J. Anesthesiol. (Engl. Ed.) **72**(1) (2022)

14. Lucatelli, A., Goulart, A.A., Silveira, P.S.P., Siqueira, J.d.O., Carmona, M.J.C., et al.: Assessment of a digital game as a neuropsychological test for postoperative cognitive dysfunction. Braz. J. Anesthesiol. (Engl. Ed.) **72**(1) (2022)

15. Iliadou, P., Paliokas, I., Zygouris, S., Lazarou, E., Votis, K., Tzovaras, D., et al.: A comparison of traditional and serious game-based digital markers of cognition in older adults with mild cognitive impairment and healthy controls. J. Alzheimer's Dis. **79**(4) (2021)

16. Menascu, S., Aloni, R., Dolev, M., Magalashvili, D., Gutman, K., Dreyer-Alster, S., et al.: Targeted cognitive game training enhances cognitive performance in multiple sclerosis patients treated with interferon beta 1-a. J. NeuroEng. Rehabil. **18**(1) (2021)

17. Gómez-Tello, M.F., Rosetti, M.F., Galicia-Alvarado, M., Maya, C., Apiquian, R.: Neuropsychological screening with TOWI: performance in 6- to 12-year-old children. Appl. Neuropsychol. Child **11**(2) (2022)

18. Rosetti, M.F., Gómez-Tello, M.F., Maya, C., Apiquian, R.: Feasibility of TOWI as a cognitive training video game for children. Int. J. Child-Comput. Int. **25** (2020)

19. Van De Weijer, S.C.F., Duits, A.A., Bloem, B.R., De Vries, N.M., Kessels, R.P.C., Köhler, S., et al.: Feasibility of a cognitive training game in Parkinson's disease: the randomized Parkin'Play study. Eur. Neurol. **83**(4) (2020)

20. Pitteri, M., Dapor, C., Ziccardi, S., Guandalini, M., Meggiato, R., Calabrese, M.: Visual-attentional load unveils slowed processing speed in multiple sclerosis patients: a pilot study with a tablet-based videogame. Brain Sci. **10**(11) (2020)

21. Tong, T., Chignell, M., DeGuzman, C.A.: Using a serious game to measure executive functioning: Response inhibition ability. Appl. Neuropsychol. Adult **28**(6) (2021)

22. Benoit, J.J., Roudaia, E., Johnson, T., Love, T., Faubert, J.: The neuropsychological profile of professional action video game players. PeerJ **8** (2020)

23. Burdea, G.C., Grampurohit, N., Kim, N., Polistico, K., Kadaru, A., Pollack, S., et al.: Feasibility of integrative games and novel therapeutic game controller for telerehabilitation of individuals chronic post-stroke living in the community. Top. Stroke Rehabil. **27**(5) (2020)

24. Perrot, A., Maillot, P., Hartley, A.: Cognitive training game versus action videogame: effects on cognitive functions in older adults. Games Health J. **8**(1) (2019)

25. Pin, T.W., Butler, P.B.: The effect of interactive computer plays on balance and functional abilities in children with moderate cerebral palsy: a pilot randomized study. Clin. Rehabil. **33**(4) (2019)

26. Bove, R.M., Rush, G., Zhao, C., Rowles, W., Garcha, P., Morrissey, J., et al.: A videogame-based digital therapeutic to improve processing speed in people with multiple sclerosis: a feasibility study. Neurol. Therapy **8**(1) (2019)

27. Boivin, M.J., Sikorskii, A, Nakasujja, N., Ruiseñor-Escudero, H., Familiar-Lopez, I., Opoka, R.O., et al.: Evaluating immunopathogenic biomarkers during severe malaria illness as modifiers of the neuropsychologic benefits of computer cognitive games rehabilitation in Ugandan children. Pediatric Infect. Dis. J. **38**(8) (2019)

28. Nef, T., Chesham, A., Schütz, N., Botros, A.A., Vanbellingen, T., Burgunder, J.M., et al.: Development and evaluation of maze-like puzzle games to assess cognitive and motor function in aging and neurodegenerative diseases. Front. Aging Neurosc. **12**(87) (2020)

29. Faust, M.E., Multhaup, K.S., Ong, M.S., Demakis, G.J., Balz, K.G.: Exploring the specificity, synergy, and durability of auditory and visual computer gameplay transfer effects in healthy older adults. J. Gerontol. Ser. B Psychol. Sci. Soc. Sci. **75**(6) (2020)

30. Palaus, M., Viejo-Sobera, R., Redolar-Ripoll, D., Marrón, E.M.: Cognitive enhancement via neuromodulation and video games: synergistic effects? Front. Hum. Neurosci. **14**(235) (2020)

31. McCord, A., Cocks, B., Barreiros, A.R., Bizo, L.A.: Short video game play improves executive function in the oldest old living in residential care. Comput. Hum. Behav. **108**(106337) (2020)

32. Bellens, A., Roelant, E., Sabbe, B., Peeters, M., van Dam, P.A.: A video-game based cognitive training for breast cancer survivors with cognitive impairment: a prospective randomized pilot trial. Breast **53** (2020)

33. Song, H., Yi, D.J., Park, H.J.: Validation of a mobile game-based assessment of cognitive control among children and adolescents. PLoS ONE (2020)

34. Amjad, I., Toor, H., Niazi, I.K., Pervaiz, S., Jochumsen, M., Shafique, M., et al.: Xbox 360 kinect cognitive games improve slowness, complexity of EEG, and cognitive functions in subjects with mild cognitive impairment: a randomized control trial. Games Health J. **8**(2) (2019)

35. Jirayucharoensak, S., Israsena, P., Pan-Ngum, S., Hemrungrojn, S., Maes, M.: A game-based neurofeedback training system to enhance cognitive performance in healthy elderly subjects and in patients with amnestic mild cognitive impairment. Clin. Interv. Aging (2019)

36. Ramos-Galarza, C., Acosta-Rodas, P., Bolaños-Pasquel, M., Lepe-Martínez, N.: The role of executive functions in academic performance and behaviour of university students. J. Appl. Res. High. Educ. **12**(3), 444–455 (2020). https://doi.org/10.1108/JARHE-10-2018-0221

37. Ramos-Galarza, C., Jadán-Guerrero, J., Gómez-García, A.: Relationship between academic performance and the self-report of the executive performance of ecuadorian teenagers. Avances en Psicología Latinoamericana **36**(2), 405–417 (2018). https://doi.org/10.12804/revistas.urosario.edu.co/apl/a.5481

38. Cóndor-Herrera, O., Ramos-Galarza, C.: The impact of a technological intervention program on learning mathematical skills. Educ. Inf. Technol., 1–13 (2020). https://doi.org/10.1007/s10639-020-10308-y

Assessing Stress Reduction of Relaxation Gaming: Investigating the Interrelation of Gamification, Advertising Intrusion and Stress Responses in Master's Students

Catarina Santos Faria[1,2]([☒]) [ⓘ], Vanessa Cesário[1,2] [ⓘ],
Pedro Filipe Campos[1,3] [ⓘ], Muhammad Satar[4], and Teresa Alvadia[4]

[1] University of Madeira, Funchal, Portugal
catarina.santos.faria@gmail.com, vanessa.cesario@tecnico.ulisboa.pt
[2] ITI-LARSyS, IST, University of Lisbon, Lisbon, Portugal
[3] WowSystems, Funchal, Portugal
pcampos@staff.uma.pt
[4] Infinity Games, Odivelas, Portugal
{m,teresa}@infinitygames.io

Abstract. Mobile gamified interventions for reducing stress among students have been thoroughly evaluated by academia and the industry. However, there needs to be more knowledge as to whether the interference of advertisement - as a means to monetise such interventions - is feasible. This study investigates the impact of a gamified intervention by conducting a comparative stress analysis and examining the influence of advertising within a relaxation game, 'Energy' from Infinity Games, on stress levels among Master's students. The research design enables a comparative analysis involving fourteen students with a strong gamer profile divided into two groups. The study employed the Perceived Stress Scale for data collection and a questionnaire to assess user engagement, encompassing an initial and post-intervention assessment. The results did not conclusively support the influence of advertising interference on stress outcomes; our work discusses potential explanations for non-statistically significant results, including the sensitivity of stress measures, individual variability in stress responses, the influence of gaming experiences and the concept of psychological reactance, suggesting that participants might resist advertising interference, influencing stress outcomes.

Keywords: Gamification · Advertising interference · Stress reduction

1 Introduction

In the rapid landscape of technology, the academic discourse has increasingly focused on the impact of digital interventions on education and well-being, particularly on students [1,4]. Gamification, defined as integrating game elements into non-games, emerged as a promising tool for fostering engagement and motivation in educational settings [7]. Recognised for enhancing engagement and

C. Stephanidis et al. (Eds.): HCII 2024, CCIS 2118, pp. 407–415, 2024.
https://doi.org/10.1007/978-3-031-61963-2_42

supporting behavioural change [10], concerns persist about potential stress-inducing factors within gamified approaches as educational technologies evolve. Previous research highlights the importance of acknowledging the dual nature of gamification, emphasising its potential to evoke both positive and negative emotional responses [11,17]. At the same time, game elements can enhance motivation, competition, and task enjoyment, and they may also introduce stressors, particularly when tied to performance evaluation [9]. Zainuddin et al. suggest exploring the effects of gamified interventions across various areas to comprehend the broad applicability of gamification in different contexts [19]; Six et al. specify that understanding the impact of gamification on different psychological factors can guide the development of more targeted and effective interventions [15]. In the systematic overview by Van Berlo et al. [3], they found several studies that used multiple theories to explain the effectiveness of advertising in order to recognise its effects. However, more than half of the papers did not use any theories to grasp a better understanding of these same topics.

Among these previous studies, we believe relaxation games have emerged as effective for stress management and can be helpful for Master's students due to their confluence of academic rigour and personal commitments. Analysing their behaviour can provide a unique lens for examining the interplay between gamification, advertising intrusion and stress responses.

The 'Energy' mobile game is a relaxation-focused gamified approach that fosters well-being with gamification elements. Its free version includes advertisement intrusion that prompts critical questions about the consequences on stress levels. To better understand these dynamics, insights are drawn from diverse studies examining gamification and the impact of advertising intrusion [14,18].

Given the experimental nature of researching the impact of advertising interference within the 'Energy' game, this study addresses the following research question: "How does the inclusion of advertising interference in the 'Energy' contribute to variations in stress levels among Master's students, compared to a control group - without advertisement?" We hypothesise that students exposed to 'Energy' with advertisements will exhibit higher stress levels than the control group. We believe our results can indicate how the inclusion of advertising contributes to variations in stress levels within the targeted population. By conducting a comparative stress analysis before and after the intervention, the study aims to contribute to a comprehensive evaluation of the impact of advertising within the relaxation game.

2   Methods

2.1   Data Collection

Socio-demographic Questions: Our initial questions focused on the participant's age and gender.

Perceived Stress Scale (PSS): The assessment involved self-reported stress evaluation through a standardised stress assessment scale (Perceived Stress

Scale), the 10-item original version [5] and the Portuguese version [2], provided quantitative measurements of the participant's stress levels, allowing an evaluation of the intervention's effectiveness in reducing stress, where they could report their perceived stress related to specific stressors or life circumstances [6]. The scale is commonly evaluated among college students and workers, indicating its widespread use and acceptability [12]. Data on user engagement were collected through a questionnaire composed of 12 Likert-style questions ranging from 1 to 5.

Post-hoc Questions: To know the participants and engagement with the 'Energy' game, we conducted the following questions:

1. How would you rate your stress level on a scale of 1 to 10? (1 represents low, and 10 represents high)
2. On a scale of 1 to 5, please evaluate your experience with the game 'Energy'.
3. On a scale of 1 to 5, what was your level of optimism regarding the game's effectiveness in stress relief before using it?
4. To what extent did the game meet your expectations?
5. On average, how many minutes per day did you dedicate to the game 'Energy' over the last week?
6. On a scale of 1 to 5, rate the consistency of your daily usage.
7. On a scale of 1 to 5, evaluate your overall engagement with the game 'Energy', where 1 represents no engagement and 5 high engagement.
8. How effective do you consider the game for stress relief?
9. Evaluate the usefulness of specific game features for stress relief on a scale of 1 to 5.
10. On a scale of 1 to 10, rate the game 'Energy' impact on your stress levels at the end of the week.
11. On a scale of 1 to 5, did you notice any improvement in your mood or stress-coping abilities after using the game?
12. On a scale of 1 to 5, how likely are you to recommend this stress relief game to others?

2.2 Sample

The participants in this study were Master's students. The eligibility criteria included students who were currently enrolled in a master's program, had a strong gamer profile, and were willingly committing to engage with the designated game for one week on their smartphone. This study followed the ethical guidelines, emphasising participant confidentiality, voluntary participation, and rigorous data protection measures. Participants were provided with detailed information about the research and its objectives. They cooperatively signed a consent form agreement, affirming their understanding of the study's purpose, procedures, and voluntary participation. This ethical safeguard ensured transparency and respect for participants' autonomy that followed established ethical standards in research. Potential benefits for participants in this study included engaging in a gamified intervention designed to reduce stress levels, offering a pleasurable and immersive experience.

This study involved 14 university students (seven in each group), averaging 27 years old (SD = 4). Regarding gender, in group one five were female and two were male; in group two, three were female and four were male).

2.3 Experimental Procedure

Participants first provided informed consent and were provided with information about the study. After consented to participate, they began the study by filling out the questions on the PSS scale. These questions were used as a baseline. After this, participants were asked to play the 'Energy' game[1] (Fig. 1) on their mobile phones for one week at least once a day. At the end of the week with the 'Energy' game being played, participants were asked to complete the PSS scale and the post-hoc questions to know their user experience and engagement.

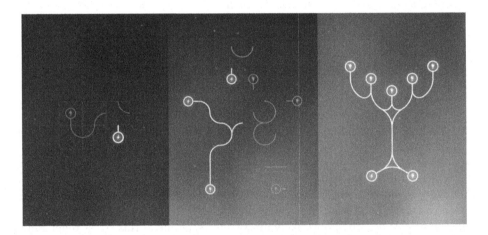

Fig. 1. Example of 'Energy' game levels

3 Results

3.1 Data Analysis

Data was analysed by using IBM Statistics SPSS version 29. The data was ordinal, and because of that, non-parametric tests were used. First, The Mann-Whitney U test was used for between-group comparisons in stress levels. Then, we used the Wilcoxon paired signed-rank test to analyse the differences in stress levels before and after each group's playing the 'Energy' game.

---

[1] 'Energy' game in Play store: https://play.google.com/store/apps/details?id=com.infinitygames.loopenergy&hl=en&gl=US&p.

  'Energy' game in Apple store: https://apps.apple.com/us/app/energy-anti-stress-loops/id1301967636.

3.2   Quantitative Data

The stress level (Table 1) between group one (Mdn = 22, IQR = 14) and group two (Mdn = 17, IQR = 12) before playing the game did not differ significantly, with U = 21, p = 0.653 (two-tailed test) with a small effect size of r = 0.1.

Comparing stress levels before and after playing the 'Energy' game for each group (Table 1), reported levels of stress from group one were statistically significant (p = 0.046 (two-tailed test), r = 0.5), as opposed to the ones reported from group two that were not statistically significant (p = 0.865 (two-tailed test), r = 0.05). Finally, when compared between groups after playing the 'Energy' game (Table 1), the level of stress of group one (Mdn = 18, IQR = 8) and group two (Mdn = 18, IQR = 11) did not differ significantly, with U = 21, p = 0.653 with small effect size of r = 0.1.

Table 1. Results of stress levels of the group one and group two

Variable	group one before and after exposure (p-value)	group two before and after exposure (p-value)	Between-group comparison before exposure (p-value)	Between-group comparison after exposure (p-value)
Stress levels	0.046	0.865	0.653	0.653

4   Discussion

Our study revealed non-statistically significant results in stress reduction. Stress is a multifaceted construct, and relying uniquely on self-reported measures might not capture subtle variations. The possible explanation for our non-significant findings revolves around the following several factors:

The sensitivity of our stress measures may not be sufficient to detect subtle variations induced by the gamified intervention. Individual variability in stress responses, influenced by personal coping mechanisms and gaming experiences, could have hidden statistically significant differences. Additionally, unaccounted variations, as academic stressors and individual differences within the Master's students, might have influenced the observed outcomes. The engagement level and immersion within the game, as influenced by design and interactive features, as reported by the systematic overview as important variables [3], could have reduced the impact of advertising interference on stress reduction. Participants may not have perceived advertisements as significantly intrusive; the advertisements could have been contextualised with the game, as referred to by [13]. Individual factors, including personality traits, coping mechanisms, prior gaming experience and the advertisement content and frequency, might not have notably affected stress levels.

Understanding the cognitive and emotional processes involved in individuals' responses to gamification and advertising interference can offer valuable insights for refining interventions and adjusting to specific needs [14]. Incorporating these variables into the research design can provide a more detailed exploration of individual differences in response to gamified interventions and advertising interference. The introduction of advertising interference, even within a relaxation-oriented game, could be perceived as an imposition on the immersive and stress-reducing nature of the gaming experience. This perceived intrusion might have triggered a psychological reactance response, where the participants consciously or subconsciously resisted the advertisements' influence, influencing their stress outcomes.

The concept of psychological reactance introduces a noteworthy dimension to our interpretation of the study results. Psychological reactance and its underlying mechanisms can be helpful in understanding the practical contexts in real-world scenarios [16]. Participants might have experienced psychological reactance, where participants could not have reacted contradictory to perceived attempts to limit their freedom or autonomy. Reactance theory suggests that individuals may resist perceived attempts to limit their freedom, potentially influencing stress outcomes. Edwards et al. indicate that the higher the cognitive intensity at the moment of the intrusion, the more likely the advertisement will be perceived as disruptive and intrusive in the game [8].

5   Study Limitations and Future Research

5.1   Stress Individual Responses

While our findings did not support an apparent influence of advertising interference on stress outcomes in relaxation games, it is crucial to acknowledge the complexity of individual responses to gamified interventions. The absence of statistical significance emphasises the need for further exploration and refinement of gamification strategies in stress management. Future research should continue exploring the long-term effects of gamification on stress reduction.

5.2   Engagement and Immersion

While the study targeted a specific academic population with a strong gamer profile, stressors related to academic workload or individual differences might contribute to the observed non-significant results. The engagement and immersion level within the game may be another critical factor. The game design appeal and interactive features could influence participants' experiences differently, mitigating the impact of advertising intrusion. The type, frequency, or content of advertisements may not have elicited a notable effect on participants' stress levels. Future research should optimize game design appeal, interactive features, and overall user experience, investigating how these components impact stress reduction outcomes and potentially mitigate the effects of advertising on stress levels.

5.3 Data

Our study had quantitative and qualitative data; however, in this paper, we only analise the quantitative data of PSS scale as we aimed to investigate the impact of advertisements on Master's students stress levels. However, future research could analyse the qualitative data to provide a richer understanding of their experiences since analysing qualitative data could provide a more comprehensive understanding, leading to the development of personalised and efficient gamified interventions.

5.4 Duration of the Study

Our one-week intervention duration may not have prevented sufficient time for measurable changes in stress levels. Stress reduction, particularly in response to gamified interventions, might require prolonged exposure for observable effects. The prolonged timeframe will enable a more comprehensive evaluation of the effectiveness and sustainability of gamification in mitigating stress among participants.

6   Conclusion

Despite the rigorous methodology and comprehensive analysis, the absence of statistical significance does not diminish the importance of our research. Instead, it highlights the need for further refinement and exploration. The findings may not support an evident influence of advertising interference within the 'Energy' on stress outcomes. However, it is crucial to consider potential contributing factors and limitations. We were unable to determine whether advertising had any influence on the stress levels of master's students. As a result, the effectiveness of utilising advertisements and their potential monetisation remains uncertain.

Acknowledgments. We are grateful to all the participants that provided their time for this study. We would like to express our sincere gratitude to Francisco Vasconcelos and Filipe Tomé for their support throughout the duration of this research project. Additionally, we extend our appreciation to Beatriz Peres for her assistance in analysing the data and support in this final manuscript.

This project has received funding from the Portuguese Recovery and Resilience Program (PRR), IAPMEI/ANI/FCT under Agenda C645022399-00000057 (eGames-Lab).

Disclosure of Interests. No potential conflict of interest was reported by the author(s).

References

1. Abadi, B.M.F., Samani, N.K., Akhlaghi, A., Najibi, S.: Pros and Cons of tomorrow's learning: a review of literature of gamification in education context. Med. Educ. Bull. **3**, 543–554 (2022)

2. Amaral, A., et al.: The perceived stress scale (PSS-10)- a Portuguese version, September 2014
3. van Berlo, Z.M.C., van Reijmersdal, E.A., Waiguny, M.K.J.: Twenty years of research on gamified advertising: a systematic overview of theories and variables. Int. J. Adv. **42**(1), 171–180 (2023). https://doi.org/10.1080/02650487.2022.2143098
4. Caponetto, I., Earp, J., Ott, M.: Gamification and education: a literature review (2014)
5. Cohen, S., Kamarck, T., Mermelstein, R.: A global measure of perceived stress. J. Health Soc. Behav. **24**(4), 385 (1983). https://doi.org/10.2307/2136404, http://www.jstor.org/stable/2136404?origin=crossref
6. Crosswell, A.D., Lockwood, K.G.: Best practices for stress measurement: How to measure psychological stress in health research. Health Psychol. Open **7**(2), 2055102920933072 (2020). https://doi.org/10.1177/2055102920933072, https://www.ncbi.nlm.nih.gov/pmc/articles/PMC7359652/
7. Deterding, S., Dixon, D., Khaled, R., Nacke, L.: From game design elements to gamefulness: defining "gamification". In: Proceedings of the 15th International Academic MindTrek Conference: Envisioning Future Media Environments, pp. 9–15. ACM, Tampere Finland, September 2011.https://doi.org/10.1145/2181037.2181040
8. Edwards, S.M., Li, H., Lee, J.H.: Forced exposure and psychological reactance: antecedents and consequences of the perceived intrusiveness of Pop-Up Ads. J. Adv. **31**(3), 83–95 (2002). https://doi.org/10.1080/00913367.2002.10673678
9. Hamari, J., Koivisto, J., Sarsa, H.: Does gamification work? – a literature review of empirical studies on gamification. In: 2014 47th Hawaii International Conference on System Sciences, pp. 3025–3034. IEEE, Waikoloa, HI, January 2014.https://doi.org/10.1109/HICSS.2014.377, http://ieeexplore.ieee.org/document/6758978/
10. Hoffmann, A., Christmann, C.A., Bleser, G.: Gamification in stress management apps: a critical app review. JMIR Serious Games **5**(2), e13 (2017). https://doi.org/10.2196/games.7216, http://games.jmir.org/2017/2/e13/
11. Hollis, C., et al.: Annual research review: digital health interventions for children and young people with mental health problems – a systematic and meta-review. J. Child Psychol. Psychiat. **58**(4), 474–503 (2017). https://doi.org/10.1111/jcpp.12663, https://onlinelibrary.wiley.com/doi/abs/10.1111/jcpp.12663
12. Lee, E.H.: Review of the psychometric evidence of the perceived stress scale. Asian Nurs. Res. **6**(4), 121–127 (2012). https://doi.org/10.1016/j.anr.2012.08.004, https://www.asian-nursingresearch.com/article/S1976-1317(12)00052-7/fulltext
13. Lewis, B., Porter, L.: In-game advertising effects: examining player perceptions of advertising schema congruity in a massively multiplayer online role-playing game. J. Interact. Adv. **10**(2), 46–60 (2010). https://doi.org/10.1080/15252019.2010.10722169
14. Mishra, S., Malhotra, G.: The gamification of in-game advertising: Examining the role of psychological ownership and advertisement intrusiveness. Int. J. Inf. Manage. **61**, 102245 (2021). https://doi.org/10.1016/j.ijinfomgt.2020.102245, https://linkinghub.elsevier.com/retrieve/pii/S0268401220314444
15. Six, S.G., Byrne, K.A., Tibbett, T.P., Pericot-Valverde, I.: Examining the effectiveness of gamification in mental health apps for depression: systematic review and meta-analysis. JMIR Mental Health **8**(11), e32199 (2021). https://doi.org/10.2196/32199

16. Steindl, C., Jonas, E., Sittenthaler, S., Traut-Mattausch, E., Greenberg, J.: Understanding Psychological Reactance. Zeitschrift Fur Psychologie **223**(4), 205–214 (2015). https://doi.org/10.1027/2151-2604/a000222, https://www.ncbi.nlm.nih.gov/pmc/articles/PMC4675534/

17. Tang, A.K.: A systematic literature review and analysis on mobile apps in m-commerce: Implications for future research. Electron. Commer. Res. App. **37**, 100885 (2019). https://doi.org/10.1016/j.elerap.2019.100885, https://linkinghub.elsevier.com/retrieve/pii/S1567422319300626

18. Terlutter, R., Capella, M.L.: The gamification of advertising: analysis and research directions of in-game advertising, advergames, and advertising in social network games. J. Adv. **42**(2–3), 95–112 (2013). https://doi.org/10.1080/00913367.2013.774610

19. Zainuddin, Z., Chu, S.K.W., Shujahat, M., Perera, C.J.: The impact of gamification on learning and instruction: a systematic review of empirical evidence. Educ. Res. Rev. **30**, 100326 (2020). https://doi.org/10.1016/j.edurev.2020.100326, https://www.sciencedirect.com/science/article/pii/S1747938X19301058

Research on the Design of an Application for Eliciting Childhood Memories in Emerging Adulthood Based on Nostalgic Psychology

Yibin Xu and Yan Zhuang[✉]

Harbin Engineering University, 145 Nantong Street, Nangang District, Harbin, People's Republic of China
zhuangyan@hrbeu.edu.cn

Abstract. Nostalgia among youth in Emerging adulthood is gradually becoming generalized. However, although nostalgia psychology has begun to receive attention in theoretical studies among youth groups in Emerging adulthood, there is still a relative lack of exploration of nostalgia psychology application and practice. Fewer studies focus on the nostalgia psychology of youth groups in Emerging adulthood and explore the practice at the interaction level to fulfill the nostalgia needs of youth in Emerging adulthood. Therefore, this paper explores the correlation between the characteristics of nostalgia at the psychological level and emotional design and designs an APP based on the nostalgia concept emotionally by carrying out interface and interaction design from the visceral, behavioral, and reflective levels of emotional design.

Keywords: Nostalgic Psychology · Emotional design · Emerging adulthood

1 Introduction

Nowadays, Nostalgia is regarded as an emotional experience of the self, i.e., a complex emotional state when thinking about the past [1, 2]. With the deepening of psychological research, scholars believe Nostalgia is a common experience for most people of different ages and cultural backgrounds. It is a universal and everyday human psychology that may be present in all stages of human life [2]. Nostalgia is not only present in old age but also in young age. Nostalgia is not only found in old age but also in young age.

Currently, there is a wave of nostalgia among young people on the Chinese Internet, which is manifested by the fact that young people nowadays pay great attention to news or videos related to animations, movies, and games from their childhood. They are eager to re-experience through these media the experiences that once made them laugh and moved them, and feel the warmth and happiness brought by those good times, thus re-immersing themselves in the emotional memories of the past. This nostalgic trend has become an essential element in the Internet culture of contemporary young people. This phenomenon is especially prominent among people aged 18–25 and is called "Emerging adulthood" [3].

© The Author(s), under exclusive license to Springer Nature Switzerland AG 2024
C. Stephanidis et al. (Eds.): HCII 2024, CCIS 2118, pp. 416–422, 2024.
https://doi.org/10.1007/978-3-031-61963-2_43

The concept of "adulthood" is a complex, multifaceted combination of social roles and responsibilities, and the transformation of a minor into an adult is an ongoing, dynamic process that takes place during the period that corresponds to Emerging adulthood [3, 4]. Young people seek their own independent lives in this period. Young people in this period begin to pursue their own separate lives, and their living environment and interpersonal relationships change, resulting in loneliness and helplessness. When such negative emotions arise, nostalgia becomes a psychological compensation mechanism for them [5]. More and more studies confirm that nostalgia can enhance positive self-evaluation and strengthen individuals' social ties. At the same time, nostalgia amplifies an individual's perception of social support, which counteracts loneliness and enhances a sense of belonging [6]. These effects are critical in helping young people transition from adolescence to adulthood.

However, at this stage, the research on the nostalgia psychology of Emerging adulthood youth mainly focuses on the concept, characteristics, functions, and influencing factors of nostalgia and lacks the exploration of nostalgia application and practice and the nostalgia needs of Emerging adulthood youth have not yet been satisfied under the existing conditions. Therefore, using the three levels of affective design as the research framework, this study designed a nostalgia concept-based emotional APP to provide a platform for Emerging adulthood youth to review and relive their childhood memories, thus enhancing their psychological health regarding self-identity, social support, and emotional regulation.

2 Background and Related Work

Routledge et al. [2] identified nostalgia as an essential resource for promoting mental health and well-being. Wildschut et al. (2006) [7] examined nostalgia's triggers and functional utility and determined that nostalgia enhances social bonds, increases positive self-evaluations, and generates positive affect. Nostalgia is common among youth in Emerging adulthood. Zhou et al.'s [8] study on a sample of Chinese college students confirmed that youth loneliness at this particular age is highly likely to trigger nostalgia, and Xu [9] analyzed a sample of college students from a college in Nanjing, China, and concluded that college students generally have a high tendency to be nostalgic. Based on this, nostalgia can also be regarded as a manifestation of the emotional needs of Emerging adulthood youth. Previous studies have affirmed that nostalgia is vital to human emotions [6, 7]. Liu et al. [10] analyzed the hierarchy of nostalgia demand and its triggering mechanism for Chinese cultural and creative products, summarized the hierarchy of nostalgia demand integration into the design, and integrated the nostalgia demand triggering factors into the design practice research. Studies have explored how to carry out the interaction design of APPs with emotional orientation. Qin et al. [11] studied the design method of social APPs that satisfy emotional needs from the perspective of emotional interaction design at the form, content, and behavioral levels.

However, although nostalgia has begun to receive attention in theoretical research among the youth group of emerging adulthood, more exploration of the application and practice of nostalgia in this subfield still needs to be done. In addition, although there have been some practices of using nostalgia psychology in product design, research in interaction design has yet to appear. Although there have been some studies on interaction at the level of emotional design, these studies have yet to be conducted in the specific field of nostalgia. At present, few studies focus on the nostalgia of the youth group of Emerging adulthood and explore the practice of nostalgia at the interaction level to meet the nostalgic needs of the youth of Emerging adulthood.

3   Theoretical Model and Design Strategy

3.1   The Association Between the Psychological Hierarchy of Nostalgia and Emotional Design

Contemporary research on the psychology of nostalgia suggests that nostalgia stems from an individual's negative perceptions and attempts to create an idealized spiritual home in a non-realistic world [12]. Cognitive, affective, and spatio-temporal aspects constitute the main characteristics of nostalgia psychology [13].

Donald Norman proposed three levels of Emotional Design: Visceral Level, Behavioral Level, and Reflective Level.

First, Cognitive aspect is closely related to the Visceral Level of Emotional Design. Cognitive focuses on the individual's perception of self and the world, while the Visceral Level focuses on the look and feel of the design. Users can be guided to perceive content related to their nostalgic experiences in the interface through well-designed visual elements and layouts, thus directly or indirectly triggering emotional resonance.

Secondly, the affective aspect is closely related to the Behavioral Level of emotional design. Emotionality focuses on the emotional changes experienced by individuals in the process of nostalgia, while the Behavioral Level focuses on the functionality and operability of the product. The user's emotional experience can be enhanced by designing a smooth interaction flow and an emotional feedback mechanism, such as conveying warmth and empathy when users interact with the platform.

Finally, the spatio-temporal aspect is closely linked to the Reflective Level of emotional design. Spatio-temporal aspect focuses on any state, time, place, event, etc. that can bring a sense of belonging to an individual, while Reflective Level focuses on the user's deeper reflection on the meaning and feeling of product usage. The emotional connection between users and products can be enhanced by providing warm and inspiring content and functions that guide users to deeply reflect on and experience nostalgic experiences at different times and places. The correlation between nostalgic psychological characteristics and emotional design is shown (see Fig. 1).

3.2   Interface and Interaction Design

This study adopts the three-tiered framework of emotional design as the foundation for page and interaction design.

At the Visceral Level, the visual style is characterized by vividness, liveliness, and charm, drawing upon the emotional resonance of individuals' most profound childhood memories. A vibrant color palette of warm yellow and caramel brown is utilized to cultivate an atmosphere brimming with vitality and dynamism. Additionally, childlike design

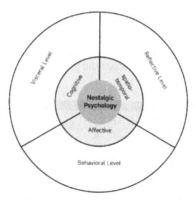

Fig. 1. Schematic illustration of the association between nostalgic psychological hierarchical properties and affective design

elements such as whimsical iconography, playful animations, and nostalgic references to classic childhood games and animations are incorporated. From a cognitive standpoint, this approach enables users to evoke their nostalgic identity, imbuing them with a sense of returning to the carefree world of childhood innocence and joy. As a result, users experience a pleasant emotional connection when interacting with the interface.

At the Behavioral Level, emphasis is placed on developing intuitive and personalized functional modules to accommodate users' diverse purposes and needs. A tailored user interface customization allows individuals to modify the content in their childhood memories library and manage the layout of related forums autonomously. Furthermore, the system generates recommendations for nostalgic content based on users' preferences and behavioral history. Through analysis of browsing records, likes, and favorites, the platform identifies users' interests and preferences, facilitating customized content recommendations to enhance user satisfaction and efficiency. Users are empowered to express their preferences and engage in sharing nostalgic memories with others, fostering emotional connections and social interactions. This contributes to the creation of an inclusive and harmonious emotional community, thereby realizing the construction of nostalgic values.

At the Reflective Level, a series of inspiring content recommendations and interaction mechanisms are designed to establish a collaborative platform for creators and audiences. This layer aims to encourage users to engage in deep thinking, experience, share, and create meaningful content with others. Firstly, personalized content recommendations and discussions based on users' browsing and interaction behaviors guide them to explore and contemplate nostalgic themes deeply. Through the provision of inspiring and guiding content, users' thinking and creativity are stimulated, promoting a profound understanding and experience of nostalgic topics. Secondly, a community interaction and co-creation mechanism enable users to share their nostalgic stories and memories, interact, and collaborate with fellow users in generating vibrant and meaningful content. By fostering an open and inclusive community environment, the platform cultivates a warm and supportive atmosphere, encouraging mutual assistance and collaboration among users. A diverse range of activities and topic discussions are provided to facilitate communication and sharing among users, fostering a sense of care and support. At the spatial and temporal level, the platform endeavors to shape a nostalgic space imbued with warmth and significance, forging new social bonds, fostering deep reflection, and enabling users to experience the perfection of nostalgic pursuits (Fig. 2).

Fig. 2. Part of the application page design

4   Discussions and Limitation

The practical exploration of this study focuses on the nostalgic psychology of the youth group of Emerging adulthood. It proposes a series of interaction design strategies to meet their nostalgic needs. Colorful visual styles, personalized functional modules, and warm and loving interaction mechanisms are adopted to give users a pleasant emotional experience when interacting with the platform and enhance user satisfaction and loyalty. The design of the visceral, behavioral, and reflective levels promote the cognitive construction of users about nostalgic identity, nostalgic value, and nostalgic object. It constructs alternative values and social connections based on nostalgia so as to bring users a sense of belonging, existence, and happiness.

However, we also face some challenges and limitations. The cases in this study are mainly Chinese college students. Due to the lack of comparative studies with youth in cultural contexts, it is difficult to accurately assess whether the characteristics and needs of Emerging adulthood youth in different countries or regions are similar in terms of nostalgia; the nostalgia elements chosen in the design are mainly based on the style of animation and gaming elements of the Post-00 generation in China, which may lead to the applicability of the results of the study in other cultural contexts. Despite the limitations of this study, the concepts and principles of emotional design based on nostalgia are universal. They can be used as a reference for research on the application of nostalgia.

5 Summary

This study aims to explore the psychological practices of nostalgia at the interaction level among the youth group of Emerging adulthood. Through research related to nostalgia psychology, the design was cut from three levels: the visceral level, behavioral level, and reflective level. Through emotional and nostalgic design elements, the aim is to create a warm and enjoyable user experience, evoking users' fond memories and establishing emotional connections. It provides practical guidance and inspiration for APP designers.

References

1. Xue, J., Huang, X.: The psychological research of Nostalgia (2011). https://doi.org/10.3724/SP.J.1042.2011.00608
2. Routledge, C., Wildschut, T., Sedikides, C., Juhl, J.: Nostalgia as a resource for psychological health and well-being. Soc. Pers. Psychol. Compass, 808–818 (2013). https://doi.org/10.1111/spc3.12070
3. Arnett, J.J.: Are college student's adults? Their conceptions of the transition to adulthood. J. Adult Dev. **1**, 213–224 (1994). https://doi.org/10.1007/bf02277582
4. Hartmann, D., Swartz, T.T.: The new adulthood? The transition to adulthood from the perspective of transitioning young adults. Adv. Life Course Res. **11**, 253–286 (2006). https://doi.org/10.1016/s1040-2608(06)11010-2
5. Wang, Y., Wildschut, T., Sedikides, C., Wu, M., Cai, H.: Trajectory of Nostalgia in emerging adulthood. Pers. Soc. Psychol. Bull. **50**, 629–644 (2024). https://doi.org/10.1177/0146167222 1143241
6. Sedikides, C., Wildschut, T., Arndt, J., Routledge, C.: Nostalgia. Curr. Dir. Psychol. Sci. **17**, 304–307 (2008). https://doi.org/10.1111/j.1467-8721.2008.00595.x
7. Wildschut, T., Sedikides, C., Arndt, J., Routledge, C.: Nostalgia: content, triggers, functions. J. Pers. Soc. Psychol., 975–993 (2006). https://doi.org/10.1037/0022-3514.91.5.975
8. Zhou, X., Sedikides, C., Wildschut, T., Gao, D.-G.: Counteracting loneliness. Psychol. Sci. **19**, 1023–1029 (2008). https://doi.org/10.1111/j.1467-9280.2008.02194.x
9. Xu, X.: Nostalgia and behavior, self-consistency of college students. Chin. J. Health Psychol. **22**(5), 687–689 (2014). https://doi.org/10.13342/j.cnki.cjhp.2014.05.020

10. Liu, W., Wang, Z., Jia, Y.: Emotional design of cultural and creative products derived from Chinese ancient books based on the perspective of Nostalgia needs. Packag. Eng. (02), 374–384 (2024). https://doi.org/10.19554/j.cnki.1001-3563.2024.02.041

11. Qin, J., Xu, S.: The affective interaction design in mobile social applications based on strong and weak ties. Packag. Eng. **14**, 80–84 (2017). https://doi.org/10.19554/j.cnki.1001-3563.2017.14.019

12. van Dijke, M., Wildschut, T., Leunissen, J.M., Sedikides, C.: Nostalgia buffers the negative impact of low procedural justice on cooperation. Organ. Behav. Hum. Decis. Process. **127**, 15–29 (2015). https://doi.org/10.1016/j.obhdp.2014.11.005

13. Qi, T., Zhu, Y.: Emotion, cognition, and identity: a figurative reconstruction of Nostalgia. J. Anhui Univ. (Philos. Soc. Sci. Ed.) **03**, 60–70 (2019). https://doi.org/10.13796/j.cnki.1001-5019.2019.03.008

Interactive Dream Analysis Devices in Artistic Design: A Multi-dimensional Exploration of Human Emotions and Needs

Qishan Ye, Jie Ling(✉), and Weilin Su

Zhongkai University of Agriculture and Engineering, Guangzhou 510220, Guangdong, China
47219382@qq.com

Abstract. This study explores how interactive dream analysis devices bridge psychological understanding and creative expression in art and design. Freud's theory that dreams reflect the subconscious has long influenced psychology and art, but modern technology offers innovative ways to interpret dreams. By analyzing the use of these devices, the research uncovers their potential in expressing human emotions and needs, providing new perspectives for art and design. Findings reveal widespread interest in dream analysis and diverse preferences in interacting with the devices, facilitating personal and emotional exploration. The study suggests applying technology-enhanced dream analysis to foster insight and emotional relief in art and design. Future research directions include personalized experiences, cross-cultural studies, technological optimization, mental health applications, and long-term impact studies.

Keywords: Dream Analysis · Interactive Installation · Artistic Design · Human Emotions · User Experience

1 Introduction

1.1 Research Objectives and Significance

In contemporary society, dreams are not just products of sleep but reflections of deep psychological states, imbued with mysteries and undiscovered insights. Freud's seminal work, "The Interpretation of Dreams," introduced dreams as manifestations of the human subconscious, profoundly impacting behavior and psychological well-being. However, significant disparities persist between modern science and the arts in interpreting and utilizing dreams. In the realm of art design, interpretations of dreams tend to be subjective and diverse. Hence, this study aims to explore how dreams are interpreted and applied in art design, examining their influence on understanding human emotions and needs [1].

With the advent of interactive technology, artists and designers have ventured into novel avenues to capture and express dreams. Interactive dream analysis devices have emerged as tools not only for users to explore their dreams but also to delve deeper into their meanings and emotional dimensions. However, despite their potential, designing

C. Stephanidis et al. (Eds.): HCII 2024, CCIS 2118, pp. 423–432, 2024.
https://doi.org/10.1007/978-3-031-61963-2_44

such devices poses challenges in striking a balance between technology and art while ensuring alignment with users' needs and emotions.

Therefore, this study delves into the design and application of interactive dream analysis devices, scrutinizing how they analyze human dreams and how this analysis impacts emotions and needs. By bridging art design and psychoanalysis, the study aims to enrich understanding of dreams through technology and examine how this understanding informs artistic creation and design strategies.

The research aspires to offer fresh perspectives and tools for the art design field, fostering understanding of dreams and exploring the role of interactive technology in personal emotions and creative expression. Moreover, the study seeks to uncover how these devices serve as multidimensional tools for exploring and addressing human emotions and needs, thereby charting new avenues for future art design and psychological research.

2   Literature Review

2.1   Psychological Foundations of Dreams

In psychology, dreams serve as a conduit between the conscious ego and the subconscious. Freud posited that dreams manifest subconscious desires, releasing repressed emotions and memories. Dream content often originates from daily minutiae, recent experiences, childhood memories, or external stimuli, reflecting real-life experiences through subconscious processing.

While the idea of dreams foretelling the future is debated, they offer insight into past experiences and current emotional states, encapsulating fears, expectations, and desires. This inherent nature of dreams finds artistic expression, where artists transform subconscious activities into visually compelling works, adding depth and empathy to their creations. Dreams, with their mix of reality and fantasy, fuel artistic imagination and emotional exploration.

Thus, dreams hold significance in both psychology and art, revealing individual psychological states and enriching artistic expression. By integrating dreams into artistic creation, artists delve into complex human emotions and experiences, offering audiences a unique lens to understand themselves and the world.

2.2   Dreams and Artistic Creation

Dreams have historically inspired artistic endeavors, shaping immersive public art experiences today. Three-dimensional installations, influenced by dream analysis, reveal inner landscapes and manifest dream imagery in tangible forms, fostering emotional resonance and prompting reflection, enhancing interaction with the environment.

"Inception" showcases dreams' impact on contemporary culture and art, blending Freudian theory and surrealist aesthetics into a visually captivating narrative. Through innovative visual techniques, the film delves into the complexities of reality, dreams, and the subconscious, illustrating film's power in depicting the intricacies of the dream realm [2].

Dream-themed illustration design offers novel avenues for brand promotion, using formal elements and artistic expression to convey abstract concepts and engage diverse audiences emotionally. Salvador Dalí's surrealist art further highlights dreams' influence on artistic expression, inviting viewers into a surreal world rich with symbolism and meaning, merging chaos and rationality to redefine art.

Historical insights from artists like Bertolucci and Brighton underscore Freud's pivotal role in inspiring artistic innovation, unlocking the depths of the human psyche through his exploration of the subconscious. Freud's work, "Da Vinci's Recollections of Childhood," underscores the intrinsic link between artistic thought and the subconscious, integrating artists into the realm of psychoanalytic inquiry [3].

In conclusion, the fusion of dreams and artistic creation provides profound insights into individual psychology and societal culture. Dream-inspired installations deepen our understanding of contemporary public art, offering artists boundless inspiration and expression. By prompting reflection on internal and external realms, these art experiences enrich our cultural landscape and collective consciousness.

2.3 Application of Interactive Dream Analyzing Device

Interactive dream analysis installations enable direct audience participation, seamlessly merging dream content with interactive forms. This immersive experience triggers multi-sensory responses, blurring the boundaries between dream and reality. By applying this technology in art creation, geographical and spatial limitations are overcome, bringing individuals closer to their inner selves and offering new avenues for artistic expression and humanistic reflection.

This paper delves into the application of interactive dream analysis devices in creating interactive experiences across time and space dimensions. Focusing on the participant's experience, it explores how interactive experiences unfold in physical mediums, optimizing time and space factors for enhanced immersion. Deep participation and immersion are realized through interventions based on real user emotions, facilitated by the Dream Measurement Instrument (Fig. 1).

Fig. 1. Graffiti Nature –Beating Cave, Red List. Source: https://art.team-lab.cn/w/graffiti_nature_beating_cave/

Team Lab, a Japan-based creative technology company, exemplifies this approach through its innovative art projects. Utilizing digital technology, projection mapping, and virtual reality, Team Lab creates immersive experiences that blend art, creativity, and technology. Their work, such as "Graffiti Nature - Beating Cave," showcases stunning visual effects and interactive elements, attracting global audiences and redefining the boundaries of art and technology [4].

2.4 Challenges and Opportunities of Dream Analysis

Although dream analysis provides a window into the psyche of an individual, it still faces many challenges in practical application, including how to accurately interpret the symbolism of dreams and how to incorporate these analyses into art and design practice. In addition, the subjective and polysemous nature of dreams makes any attempt to standardize and systematize them fraught with complexity and controversy. However, it also provides unique opportunities for artists, designers, and psychologists to explore new frontiers and possibilities of dreaming through interdisciplinary collaborations.

In summary, the study of dreams in psychology and art and design has demonstrated their potential as an important tool for understanding the human psyche and emotional world. By continuing to explore the multidimensional nature of dreams and applying interactive technologies to enhance the dream experience, we can expect to see more innovation and deeper understanding in art and design practice in the future [5].

3 Research Design

3.1 Perceptualized Image Representation

The aim of this study is to provide insight into how dreams are expressed through interactive art and design installations and their impact on users' emotions and perceptions. To this end, a multi-method research design was employed, combining quantitative and qualitative analysis to ensure a comprehensive understanding of the use of dreams in art and design and their impact on individuals (Fig. 2).

Fig. 2.   Experimental image display

3.2   Interactive Device Prototype Performance

The core of this research is the development of a prototype interactive dream analysis device. The device allows users to input their dream descriptions via touchscreen technology and convert these descriptions into interactive visual and sound images. The device supports multi-touch technology and is able to track every movement and pressure change of the user as a way to simulate different dream scenarios. We also designed an image conversion algorithm to convert the text entered by the user into corresponding visual images, and simulate the fluidity and variability of the dream world through dynamic effects such as color gradients, blurring, and abstract graphic changes [6] (Figs. 3 and 4).

Fig. 3. User Touchpad Drawing

Fig. 4. Projection Screen Display (left), Projection Interactive Display (middle), Venue Display (right)

3.3   Image Representation of Dreaming

We further explored how the user's dreams can be visualized as images through an interactive device, and in particular, how the individual's dream characteristics and emotional states can be transformed into visualization elements. We categorized and analyzed dream contents and classified them into different types, such as wish fulfillment, anxiety, or desire expression, each equipped with specific visual and sound identifiers. Users can explore different dream types through an interactive interface and interact with their dreams through drawing, touch and sound feedback to facilitate understanding and emotional release of their personal dreams (Fig. 5).

Fig. 5. Interactive Image Drawing and Interactive Experiment Demonstration

3.4 User Experience and Feedback Collection

In order to gain a deeper understanding of the impact that the interactive dream analysis device has on users, this study will introduce a series of comprehensive user experience and feedback collection methods. A refined questionnaire will be constructed through the Questionnaire Star website, and the questionnaire will be distributed and counted using the Questionnaire Star website for the tested population questionnaires, in order to reduce the error rate of manually entered questionnaires.

3.5 Data Analysis Methods

This study uses quantitative questionnaire data to investigate users, such as user questionnaire scores, and will apply statistical analysis methods, including descriptive statistics, to determine patterns and relationships in the data.

3.6 Ethical Considerations

Given that this study explores the dream experiences and emotional states of individuals, adherence to ethical guidelines is essential. The study will ensure that all participants have a clear understanding of the purpose of the study, the process and the voluntary nature of their participation, and that their explicit consent is obtained. Strict data confidentiality measures will also be taken to ensure the security of personal information. Detailed strategies will also be developed in the study to appropriately handle sensitive information provided by the participants and to ensure that the welfare and privacy of the participants are protected throughout the study.

4 Research Results and Analysis

4.1 Main Findings

The purpose of this report is to analyze the results of the dream experience questionnaire survey, and to provide reference for the design and optimization of the dream analysis device through data presentation and interpretation. Overview of the survey results, a total of 109 valid questionnaires were collected, involving respondents of different genders and age groups. Through the questionnaires, we understand the respondents' views and needs in terms of dream experience, dream analysis, and interactive dream devices.

Prevalence of dream experience: 63.3% of the respondents said they often dream, showing the prevalence of dream experience.

Awareness of dream analysis: 77.98% of the respondents have tried to analyze their dreams, showing that people think about understanding dreams (Fig. 6).

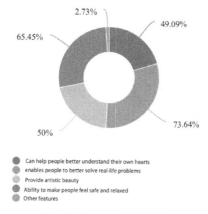

Fig. 6. Data analysis charts

Interaction preference: In interactive dream experiences, 59.63% of respondents preferred to immerse themselves in the experience alone, while 40.37% preferred to communicate with other users.

Benefits of dream analysis: 85.32% of respondents believe that dream analysis helps them to understand their own heart, showing the psychological value of dream analysis.

Demand for device features: Respondents generally believe that dream analysis stereoscopic devices should have features that help to understand the inner self, solve real-world problems, provide artistic aesthetics, and make people feel safe and relaxed.

Stress and dreams: 44.95% of the respondents often feel stress, which may be related to dream experience and content.

Interaction Mode Requirements: In terms of interaction mode, touch screen, gesture recognition and voice recognition are the more important interaction modes according to the respondents (Fig. 7).

Dream scenes and contents: Most of the dreams were related to daily life, while a considerable number of dreams involved future imagination. In terms of drawing content, respondents preferred realistic scenes (Fig. 8).

Favorite Interaction Scenarios: projection screen displays, projection interactive displays, and arena interactive displays were all equally popular.

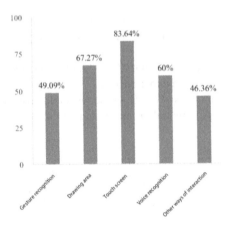

Fig. 7. Data analysis charts

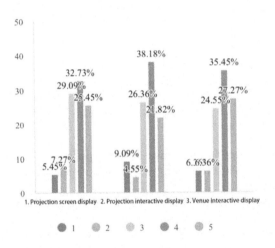

Fig. 8. Data analysis charts

4.2 Guiding Suggestions

Emphasis on inner exploration: the design of the device should pay attention to helping users understand their inner self, which can be realized by providing in-depth dream analysis functions.

Multiple interaction methods: Combine multiple interaction methods such as touch screen, gesture recognition and voice recognition to meet the needs and preferences of different users.

Daily life and future imagination: The design of the device content should incorporate daily life scenarios and future imagination elements to attract a wider range of user groups.

Optimization of display methods: Considering the popularity of different interactive scenes, it is recommended to further optimize the effect and experience of projection screen display, projection interactive display and venue interactive display. For example, we can increase the immersion of the interaction and improve user engagement.

With these suggestions, we can provide users with a dream experience that is more relevant to their needs and allow them to explore their inner world in the installation.

4.3 User Experience Depth Analysis

This study further explored the depth of user experience when interacting with the interactive dream analysis device. By meticulously analyzing user feedback, we found that participants generally reported enhanced self-awareness and emotional release. For example, a portion of respondents described the mental relaxation and emotional stability they felt after experiencing through the device, emphasizing the potential value of the device in promoting mental health.

4.4 Design Improvements and User Feedback

Based on user feedback, we identified several key design improvements. Respondents suggested adding more personalization options, such as customization and saving functions for personal dream content, to enhance the personalization and continuity of the user experience. In addition, users suggested specific improvements to the device's interface design and interaction logic, such as simplifying the operation process and adding more intuitive user guidelines.

4.5 Social and Cultural Impact Considerations

The study found that the cultural and social significance of dream experience and analysis cannot be ignored. User feedback suggests that users from different cultural backgrounds may have different interpretations and expectations of dreams. Therefore, the design and implementation of a dream analysis device needs to take this diversity into account to ensure that the device is able to provide a meaningful experience across cultures.

4.6 Results-Based Directions for Future Research

Although this study provided valuable insights, it also revealed areas for further exploration. For example, the study suggests that future work could delve more deeply into how psychological stress can be addressed and reduced through dream analysis devices. Additionally, the study should consider the development of more advanced data analysis tools to more accurately interpret dream data recorded by users through the device.

5 Conclusion and Outlook

5.1 Conclusion

This study, analyzing 109 valid questionnaires, sheds light on users' experiences and preferences with interactive dream analysis devices. Findings indicate widespread engagement with dream analysis, emphasizing the need for personalized device design. Users value the psychological benefits of dream analysis and express clear preferences for interaction methods and scenarios.

5.2 Outlook

Future directions include enhancing personalization, exploring cross-cultural differences, optimizing technical aspects, investigating mental health applications, and conducting long-term impact studies. This study marks the beginning of understanding and designing dream analysis tools, with potential for technological and design advancements.

Acknowledgments. This study was funded by several esteemed institutions and projects: The Guangdong Provincial First-Class Offline Course "Design Composition", and The 2023 school-level new agricultural science teaching research and reform practice project is an in-depth practice of information technology and "Design Composition" education and teaching under the concept of "Tolerating Mistakes and Seeking Beauty, Integrating Skills to Have Beauty, and Honoring Schools to Promote Beauty". Their generous support greatly facilitated the research.

Disclosure of Interests. The authors have no competing interests to declare that are relevant to the content of this article.

References

1. Zhao, J.: The aesthetic value of dreamlike art in film and television creation. Popul. Lit. Art (10), 124–125 (2021)
2. Li, K.: Advanced graphic design interpretation behind the stereoscopic images of dreams in the movie inception. Movie Rev. (19), 110–112 (2016). https://doi.org/10.16583/j.cnki.52-1014/j.2016.19.037
3. Yuan, H.: Surreal "dreams"-the influence of psychoanalysis on Dalf's art. Beauty Age (11), 73–74 (2021). (in Chinese). https://doi.org/10.16129/j.cnki.mysdz.2021.11.035
4. Li, T.C.: Spatial and temporal analysis of digital audiovisual art in the whole world: the case of TeamLab. Art Work (03), 100–103 (2022)
5. Teamlab digital art exhibition. Decoration (07), 10 (2016)
6. Malinowski, J.E., et al.: Predicting the affective tone of everyday dreams: a prospective study of state and trait variables. Sci. Rep. **9**(1) (2019). https://doi.org/10.1038/s41598-019-50859-w

Correction to: Designing 3D Avatar Influencer for Live Streaming Interactions

Alvaro Lourenço , Everton Aleixo, Matheus Nogueira , Raphael Moraes ,
Beatriz Dutra, Gabriele Penalber, and Mauro Teófilo

Correction to:
Chapter 5 in: C. Stephanidis et al. (Eds.): *HCI International 2024*
Posters, **CCIS 2118,**
https://doi.org/10.1007/978-3-031-61963-2_5

The original version of the book was inadvertently published with an incorrect address of the Institutional affiliations of the Authors in Chapter 5. This has been corrected.

The updated version of this chapter can be found at
https://doi.org/10.1007/978-3-031-61963-2_5

Author Index

Printed in the United States
by Baker & Taylor Publisher Services